AND THE REST IS COOKERY; A MANUAL FOR THE CARE AND KEEPING OF HISTORIANS

by
Sara A. Robinson, Afton Cochran,
Merry Schepers,
Barb Ruddle, and Sara McKenna

Illustrations by
Rachel Garstang Penman

Foreword by
Jodi Taylor
author of the best selling series
"The Chronicles of St Mary's"

And The Rest Is Cookery; A Manual For the Care and Keeping of Historians

Published with the help of Rushford Limited.

First Edition: 2021
© 2021 All Rights Reserved

Based on the Chronicles of St Mary's Book series by Jodi Taylor
For more information about the series visit:
https://joditaylor.online/

All profits from the sales of this book will be donated to a Children's Cancer Charity.

No part of this publication may be reproduced, stored in a retrieval system, or transmitted in any form or by any means without prior written approval of the publisher, nor be otherwise circulated in any form of binding or cover other than that in which it is published and without a similar condition being imposed upon the purchaser.

St Mary's is a fictional institute which sprang from the imagination of the author, Jodi Taylor.
Its mission is to record and document historical events in contemporary time, or in other words, time travel
(but don't call it that to them!).
This cookbook is based on the wonderful, madcap world she created.

Books From
The Chronicles of St Mary's Series
By
Jodi Taylor
Just One Damn Thing After Another
A Symphony of Echoes
A Second Chance
A Trail Through Time
No Time Like the Past
What Could Possibly Go Wrong?
Lies, Damn Lies and History
And The Rest is History
An Argumentation of Historians
And Now For Something Completely Different
Hope For The Best
Plan For The Worst
Another Time Another Place

Short Story Anthologies:
The Long and The Short of It
Long Story Short

For more information about this series and others by Jodi Taylor visit:
https://joditaylor.online/

Foreword:

My family – they're not bright. Even single syllable words have to be chopped up into their component parts for them – fell about laughing when they heard I'd been asked to write a foreword for a cookery book.

How to poison people in three easy stages – yes.

How to induce mass vomiting – yes.

How to prepare delicious and nutritious meals without injury – no.

Like many families, we get together for Christmas lunch, each bringing a little something to the feast. My brother does his killer roast potatoes and pigs in blankets. Mum brings dessert. Others do the vegetables or the starter. I'm allowed to bring the cheese. With all its wrappings intact to show I haven't meddled with it in any way. So my contribution is cheese. Which is fine if we all want to go time travelling in a tea pot afterwards but a less than exciting culinary challenge which is why I'm so excited over this cookbook.

Anyway, back to the family.

'Are you allowed to do that?' they enquired. 'Kill people with cooking, I mean. Or does the fact its for charity make everything all right?'

I ignored them but honesty compels me to admit I don't have very much to contribute to the cookery world. And then I had a thought. Of course! I can do soup.

There's my much-maligned Cauliflower and Mushroom soup – which, to be fair, isn't quite as delicious as it sounds. There's my Every Vegetable Found in the Fridge on Friday Soup – which can be quite dangerous if you don't know what you're doing. Obviously, I don't. I've spent several weekends in the bathroom with a good book to take my mind off things.

And then I remembered my *piece de resistance* – my Leek and Potato Soup from which, on a good day, people have been known to survive.

So – here's my recipe. And, at the insistence of my family who feel all you poor people should be given the opportunity to choose life instead – here's the obligatory word of warning.

This is not the charming, country-kitchen, matching-crockery, sprinkled with chopped parsley, and enjoyed with a glass of cool white wine soup. In this recipe, I tell it how it really is. This is Real Soup. Not for the faint-hearted. You take your life in your hands with this one.

So, ignoring family and Hazel, my agent – 'For God's sake, Taylor, is it not bad enough you kill off your characters all the time – leave your readers alone,' – here's my sad contribution to this lovely cookbook.

- Jodi Taylor (Autumn 2021)

Jodi's Take Your Life in Your Hands Leek and Potato Soup

Ingredients

Potatoes
Leeks
A bit of bacon found at the back of the fridge. It'll be fine.
Salt
Pepper
Anything else you fancy.
Primula cheese spread. Am I allowed to say Primula? Cheese spread, anyway.

Method

Chop and dice potatoes.
Staunch bleeding and apply plasters.
Fry potatoes until mildly golden. That's the potatoes – not you.
Do not wander off and do something else while waiting.
Add chopped bacon. Ditto with the wandering.
Chop the leeks and add to bacon and potatoes.
Curse and find a bigger saucepan.
Fry leeks and potatoes and bacon together until soft/golden/not on fire/whatever.
Add salt, pepper and any other seasonings that take your fancy. Not vanilla.
Do not add kale.
Cover with some stock or water. Not gin.
Use remainder of water to make a nice cup of tea.
Bring soup to the boil-ish.
Turn down heat. If you've done it properly it will simmer. If you haven't it will fester. Good luck.
Remember to cover saucepan with the lid unless you want to take your clothes off and enjoy a relaxing leek and potato flavoured sauna.
Remember to turn off the heat before the saucepan boils dry. Should this actually occur, bury saucepan, open windows and deny all knowledge.
When you think it's simmered sufficiently – remove from heat.
It is now safe to wander off and do something else. Take your tea with you. You know what you're like.
An unspecified amount of time later, hunt through the kitchen for your stick blender.
Assemble stick blender.
Reassemble stick blender.
Zhush contents of saucepan according to taste.
Wipe down splashback. And cooker.
And floor. And self.
Remain calm. Lumps in soup are a Good Thing. Nutritious.
Taste. Gag.
Add more seasoning.
Feel more optimistic.
Spoon into bowl. Stir in large dollop of Primula cream cheese according to taste.
Find bread.
Assemble tray. Soup, spoon, bread and top-up tube of Primula.
Take two sips. Tip soup down sink.
Take taste away with Hotel Chocolat product of your choice.
Open packet of leek and potato Cup a Soup.
Kids – do not try this at home. Probably best if you don't let any adults try it, either.

Table of Contents

Chapter One:
Notes For the New Kitchen Recruit
Gentle Welcome from the Boss	2
Store Cupboard Essentials	3
Notes on Food Names	4 to 5
General Cooking Terms	6 to 7
General Equipment Guide	8 to 12
Measurements and Conversions	15 to 16

Chapter Two:
The Most Important Food Group; Tea
How To Make the Perfect Cup of Tea	17 to 20

Chapter Three:
The History Department; "What are they eating now?" or Historical Foods for the Modern Palate

Ancient Barley and Wheat Loaf	22
Missiiiagan Pakwenigan/ Algonquin Sunflower Bannock	25
Paganens/ Algonquin Nut Soup	25
Msickquatash/ Succotash	26
Aliter Pullus/ (Another Chicken) Roman Honey Chicken	27
Isichia Omentata/ Roman Burgers	28
Minutal et Mala/ Roman Pork and Apple Stew	29
Mac and Cheese	30 to 31
A Tarte for Ember Day/ Onion Tart	32
Pea Soup	34
Bread Sauce	35
Jamaican Goat Curry with Caribbean Rice and Beans	37
Hoe Cakes	38
Crumpets	39
Victoria Sponge	40 to 41
Seed Cake, Victoria Sponge	
Carrot Fritters	42
Upside Down Cakes	44 to 46
Honey Cake, Pear and Ginger Skillet Cake, Pineapple Upside Down Cake	
Tarta de Santiago	47
Loaf in the Time of Cable Street	49
Lemon Ketchup	50
Cheese Toasty/ Grilled Cheese	52
Shooter Sandwich	53
Cowboy Stew	54
Nettle Soup	54

Chapter Four:
Kitchen Department; Feeding the Ever Hungry Horde or Comfort Foods

Breakfast at St Mary's — 56 to 61
Perfect Porridge, Cooked Breakfast, Potato Scones, Bacon Butty, Overnight Oats, Muffins, Pancakes

Soup and Sandwiches — 62 to 71
Soups: Slow Cooker Ham and Lentil Soup, Mud Soup, Creamy Vegetable Soup, Cullen Skink, Tortellini Sausage Soup with Spinach, Mushroom Stew, White Bean and Orzo Soup, Brown Stock or Bone Broth, Cool as a Cucumber Soup, Leek and Potato Soup, Chunky Chicken and Noodles
Sandwiches: Brioche Rolls, Cheese Puffs, Polenta Muffins, Sweet Potato Cheddar Scones, Cheese and Caramelized Onion Scones, Sandwich Fillings, Po' Boy

Swiss Beef and Chorizo Orzotto	72
Sausage Pasta and Chicken and Rice Dish	73
Just One Damn Casserole After Another	75
Fish Pie	76
Chicken and Vegetable Pie	78
Beef Stroganoff	81
Spicy Lamb Meatballs	82
Lancashire Hotpot	84
Big Murdoch Pie and Sausage and Bean Casserole	85
Nidi di Rondine	87
Toad in the Hole	88
Sunday Roast and sides	89 to 92

Chapter Five:
Security Department; Our Worldly Lovable Scamps or World Foods

Thai Corn Fritters	94
Sri Lankan Dhal and Bombay Aloo/ Bombay Potatoes	96
Cashew Chicken	97
Salt and Pepper Prawns and Curry Udon	99
Lahmacun/ Turkish Pizza	101
Tabbouleh and Jollof Rice	102
Bobotie and Geelrys	103
Mafe Stew	104
Shakshuka	106
Greek Fish Stew and Horiatiki/ Greek Village Salad	108
Pollo Alla Caccitore	109
Mediterranean Baked Cod	109
Carbonnade Flamande	110
Soupe à l'Oignon de ma Mère/ My Mothers Onion Soup and Croque Monsieur	112
Chicken and Mushroom Fricassee and Tartiflette	114
Red Onion Tarte Tatin	115
Hope for the Best, Plan for the Wurst	116
Borscht	118
Verlorene Eier in Kräutersoße/ Lost Eggs in a Herb Sauce and Peppercorn– Pothast	120
Hungarian Goulash	121
Pastel de Choclo	123
Slow Cooked Pork Carnitas	125
Guacamole	127
Canja and Ensalada de Portos con Cebolla/ Chilean Bean and Onion Salad	128

Chapter Six:
The Medical Department; Vegetarian and Vegan Foods with Vegetables. Seriously, did we mention the vegetables?

Vegan Sweet and Sour Cauliflower and **Vegetarian Wellington**	131
Vegan Burrito	132
Mujadara/ Middle Eastern Lentils, Rice and Onions	133
Sweet and Sour Lentils and **Leek and Cheese Pie**	134
Tossed Cauliflower with a Mustard Vinaigrette	136
Lentil and Vegetable Pie	137
Saag Paneer	139
Syracuse Salt Potatoes and **Lemon Orzo with Asparagus**	140
Caesars Tossed Greens	141
Vegan Mexican Style Bean and Lentil Stew	142
Roasted Vegetables	144
Roasted Vegetable Soup, Mushroom and Roasted Squash Risotto	
Red Lentil and Mango Dahl and **Vegetarian Lasagne**	145
Vegetable Stock or Broth and **Vegetarian Shepherds Pie**	146
The Great St. Mary's Salad and **Oven Chips** and **Jacket Potatoes**	147
Steamed Vegetables	148 to 149
Vegan Gluten Free Vanilla Cake	150

Chapter Seven:
Administration or What Really Keeps St. Mary's Going: Cakes, Biscuits, Tarts and Afternoon Tea

Mrs. Partridge's Afternoon Tea	152 to 155
Victoria Sponge, Tea Sandwiches, Blini Pancakes,	
Lemon Posset, Never-Fail Scones	
Whipped Shortbread	157
Millionaire's Shortbread and **Flavoured Shortbread**	158
Jam Tarts with Matthew	159
Knock! Knock! Guess Again Biscuits	159
Chocolate Chip Cookies	160
Oatmeal Chocolate Chip Cookies, Triple Chocolate Chip Cookies	
Crazy Brownies For the Professor	163
Oat Biscuits for Dr Dowson	163
Dr Stone's Rich Hot Cocoa Prescription	165
Quick Hot Cocoa, Spiced Hot Cocoa Biscuits	
More Tea Time Treats	166 to 167
Mad Madeleines, Tea Loaf, Spiced Lemon Ginger Biscuits	
Chocolate Cake	168 to 169
Pour L'Amour du Chocolat, Easy as Cake, Not Exactly 'Healthy' Cocoa Cake,	
Incredible Chocolate Orange	
Drizzle Cake	171
Lemon, Ginger and Chocolate Cakes	
Mars Bar Squares and **Peanut Butter Squares**	172
Bath Buns	174
TaDa Doughnuts and **TaDa Doughnut Pudding**	175
New High Energy Biscuits	177
Mrs Shaw's Chocolate Biscuits	178
Bourbon Biscuits for Good Boys and Girls	
Chocolate Forked Biscuits For Those Difficult Days	

Chapter Eight: Drinks at The Blue Swan

A Few for After Hours — 180
Can You Do the Dodo?, Is That a Woolly Mammoth on the Trolley?, Dr. B's Beloved Bentley, Rocket Fuel, Swan Attack, What the Hell?, The Rose of Windsor, Where's Pinky?, Eternal Youth, The Stuart Queen

More From the Bar — 181
Sneaky Peterson, Thor's Chicken, The Flash, Jump Start, Hope for the Best Margarita, We Really Need A Holiday Martini, Red, White or Rosé Wine

A Few More from the Bar — 182
Bashford's Stick Blender, Moon Over Stonehenge, Technical Breakfast Shot, The Chocolate Association, Bloody Bollocking Hell, The Nine Day Queen, Two Beer Mats and Half a Lime

Historical Drinks — 183
Water, Lemonade

More From the Bar, Because We Are Not Alcoholics — 184
Shirley Temple, Roy Rogers, Bashford Brakes, Almost Instant Lemonade, Blushing Sykes, Refreshing Knots, Hot Chocolate Milano, Winter Warmer

Drinks From the Bar When We Have a Jump the Next Day — 185
Hair of the Dog That Bit You, The Yeti's Milk, Orange you Glad to See Me?, Bombs Away!, Sock it to me!, The Black Point/ Rock Your Universe

Fresh Raspberry Kir — 185
Elderflower Cordial — 186
Raspberry Lemonade Cordial — 186
Rhubarb Cordial — 186

Chapter Nine: Those nutters in R&D; Experimental Recipes

Vanilla Extract and **Candied Citrus Peel** — 188
Cake Flour and **Self Raising Flour** — 188 to 189
Caster Sugar and **Golden Syrup** — 189
Icing Sugar and **Buttercream** and **Icing** — 190 to 191
Salted Caramel — 191
Quick and Easy Breads and what you can make from them — 192 to 193
Dinner Rolls, Iced Fingers, Chelsea Buns, Cinnamon Rolls, Pesto Whirls and Gorgeous Bread

Spice Mixes — 194 to 197
Pumpkin Pie Spice, Apple Pie Spice, Mixed Spice, Soup Spice, Italian Seasoning, Creole Spice, Cajun Spice, Sazon Spice, Caribbean Curry Seasoning, Markham's Season All, Onion Seasoning, Poultry Seasoning, Mild Curry Powder, Mexican Spice Blends, Better Than Spice

Vegetable Bouillon Powder — 197
Oven Dried Tomatoes — 198
Sauces — 198 to 200
Worcestershire Sauce, Stone Ground Mustard, Brown Sauce, Piccalilli, Mushroom Ketchup

Jam Sugar — 201
Jams and Chutney — 201 to 202
Red Chilli Jam, Vanilla Rhubarb Jam, Marmalade, Lemon Curd, Apple and Cranberry Chutney

Pesto Sauce and **Cornflour Slurry** — 203
Italian Sausage and **Sour Cream** — 204
Cabbage Bomb — 204

Dedication and Thank You — 206 to 207

Index — 208 to 211

Gluten Free Index — 212 to 213

The Institute of Historical Research

St. Mary's Priory Rushford

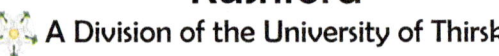
A Division of the University of Thirsk

Welcome, as you have survived and passed 'the interview' it is now our great pleasure to welcome you into the St Mary's family. Please refer to your 'All Staff' materials for further explanation and the completed forms which must be returned to Mrs Partridge within the first 48 hours. Also, there will be an exam so please familiarize yourself with the terms and equipment portion of this book.

St Mary's may look innocent, but behind a seemingly innocuous façade, our institute carries out highly skilled research into historical events. We do not, under any circumstances, call it Time Travel. This is a common misconception. Rather, we investigate major historical events in contemporary time. You can find out more about the Chronicles of St Mary's book series by best-selling author Jodi Taylor at https://joditaylor.online/ .

Jodi first bought St Mary's to life in 2013 with "Just One Damned Thing After Another", the first in the Chronicles of St Mary's series, and introduced us to her madcap, deeply flawed and truly loveable crew of Historians, backed up by departments of tetchy Techies, mad Medics, wily Wardrobe specialists and Research and Development… well, lunatics. The books rapidly became enormously popular and gained a loyal and slightly odd group of followers.

A fans group was formed to talk about the books and interact with Jodi herself - but then something extraordinary happened. A wildly diverse and truly international group of people discovered that we liked each other as, real people! Our Founding Member, Marietta Winfrey, was inspired to go one step further. In 2018, she set up a new group - Virtual St Mary's by the Disaster Magnets. Here we could 'live' together in the virtual world, choose a department to be part of, discuss exciting events in history, and let our imaginations run riot. This virtual world would go on developing various departments needed to keep an institution of this type running. Our department in the kitchen is an integral part of St Mary's both in the books and in our virtual world; with St Mary's, the Kitchen Staff Room becoming our virtual base of operation.

We are a group of professional chefs and cooks, farmers and enthusiastic amateurs, who share their recipes, ideas and disasters! We have hosted a virtual feasts for our intrepid Historians. Then, Afton Cochran had an idea – a COOKBOOK! We started sharing, testing, tasting and just one thing led to another…

All the recipes are tested and suitable for all levels of cooks, from learner to professional. We have everything to satisfy the hungriest of Not-Time-Traveler, from basic evening meals, elegant high teas fit for Mrs Partridge, hearty breakfasts, soups, stews, cakes, sweets, pickles, sauces, and pies. We hope you enjoy this book and are inspired to join us in our love of not only food, but also of all things St Mary's.

We proudly present the St Mary's Cookbook!

All proceeds from this book will go to a wonderful cancer charity that is close to our hearts. We are following in the footsteps of Jodi Taylor again, who already supports this and other charities. Our work and donations will help to fund the charities outstanding work.

Notes for Kitchen Trainees:

Welcome!
We are glad you are here! You have just taken the first step in becoming part of a great family. We work hard and have so much fun.

Store Cupboard Essentials:

There are certain essentials every cook should always have in their cupboard. We have tried to stay away from brand names because brands are not universal throughout the world. Although we all have our favourite brands, we can agree that there are some things that you just do not skimp on. This can be because they add so much flavour or are a vital part of the chemical reactions that make a recipe successful.

Use the best you can afford:
- Sea Salt
- Stock Cubes
- Olive Oil
- Chocolate Chips
- Marmite/ Vegemite
- Worcestershire Sauce
- English Mustard Powder
- Tomato Ketchup
- Vanilla Extract or Paste

Use the cheapest you can find:
- Pure Lemon Juice
- Plain and Self Raising Flour
- French or Brown Mustard
- Dijon Mustard
- Couscous
- Tinned/ Canned Chopped Tomatoes
- Tomato Puree
- Porridge Oats (Jumbo only!)
- Tinned/ Canned Fruit
- Caster/ Granulated Sugar

Use a mid-price range product
- Dried Mixed Mushrooms
- Rices (pudding/ risotto etc)
- Tinned/ Canned Plum Tomatoes
- Strawberry Jam
- Muscovado/ Brown Sugar
- Jarred Bolognese Sauce
- Baking Powder
- Bicarbonate Soda/ Baking Soda

Fridge Products:
- Whipping Cream or Double Cream
- Salted Butter
- Olive Oil Spread
- Unsalted Butter
- Semi Skimmed or 2% Milk
- Mayonnaise

Notes on Terms and Food Names Used:

There are some things that are universal between countries but there are also slight variations that we thought we would highlight. Dr Dowson and the library team has been helping with this research. Many hard to find ingredients are explained and have recipes in the R&D Section.

Food Names:

- **Aubergine** is the same vegetable as an **Eggplant**.
- **Courgettes** are the same vegetable as a **Zucchini.**
- **Spring Onions** are the same as **Scallions, Green Onions** or **Salad Onions**.
- In the U.K. we generally buy things in a **Tin**, and in the U.S. they buy the same things in a **Can**
- **Plain Flour** is the same as **All Purpose Flour**.
- **Strong Flour** is the same as **Bread Flour**.
- **Corn Flour** is the same as **Corn Starch**.
- There are some differences with **Self-raising Flour** outside the U.K. The U.K. doesn't add salt to the mix. *
- **Bicarbonate of Soda** is the same as **Baking Soda**.
- **Rape Seed Oil** is the same as **Canola Oil**.
- **Golden Syrup** is one product that we do not know a direct equivalent. The closest product that we know of is **Corn Syrup**, but honey would also be a good substitution. *
- **Caster Sugar** is a white granular cane sugar sometimes referred to as castor sugar or **Super Fine** sugar in the U.S. Granulated sugar found in the U.S. has a larger crystal. *
- **Icing Sugar** is the same as **Powdered Sugar** or **Confectioner's Sugar**.
- **Demerara Sugar** and **Turbinado Sugar** are a cane sugar with a large grain and light amber colour. These are sometimes sold as raw sugars as they are less processed then caster sugar.
- **Muscovado Sugar** is a brown cane sugar that usually comes in two choices of light or dark. There is a difference in the manufacturing process between Muscovado and **Brown Sugar**. Muscovado sugar is less refined and retains more of the molasses, whereas brown sugar is white sugar with molasses added back to make it brown. These are interchangeable in the recipes.
- **Jam Sugar** is white granulated sugar with dry pectin, there is not a direct exchange in the U.S. *
- There are many terms used for **Home Preserving** jams or foods in glass jars and bottles. These include **Canning, Preserving, and Bottling**.
- All preserved fruit spreads are called **Jam** in the U.K., whereas in the U.S. these are generally separated in-to jams that have pieces of fruit in the mix and jellies that are made mainly from fruit juices. Jellies are known, a little, in the U.K. but tend to be home made.
- **Jellies** in the U.K. generally refer to a set gelatine dessert that most people in the U.S. call by the company name of Jell-O.
- **Treacle** or Black Treacle is a sticky syrup left over after the cane sugar is boiled to produce sugar in the extraction process. Closest to this is **Molasses** or backstrap molasses in the U.S.
- **Stem ginger** is a candied ginger that is presented jarred with a thick and fiery syrup, but the closest substitute would be crystalized ginger or candied ginger.
- **Digestive Biscuits** are excellent ways to get more biscuits into your diet but the closest name outside the U.K. is a **Graham Cracker**.
- **Double Cream** is the same as **Heavy** or **Whipping Cream**.
- **Tagliatelle** and **Fettuccine** refer to the same Pasta.

-**Kitchen Roll** are the absorbent towels made of paper that generally are sold in a roll in the U.K., in the U.S., they are known as **Paper Towels**.
-**Mince** is a cutting technique that is generally used as a synonym for the well ground meat used to make sausages and hamburgers, in the U.S. it is culturally known as **Ground Meat**, or **Burger**.
-**Hob** is a U.K. term for the **stove top** or **burners** that are used to cook food.
-**Bell Peppers** are a sweeter pepper and come in many colours, but some people know them as **Capsicums**.
-**Coriander** is an herb plant that is used both for its leaf and its seed. When referencing ground coriander it is in regards to the ground seed. Coriander leaf or **Cilantro** as it is sometimes known is used both in fresh and in dried form.
-**Bacon** is served in rashers or slices. In the U.K. they refer to the thin pork belly style of bacon with marbled fat as streaky bacon, which is just called bacon in the U.S. The wider back bacon that is referred to in the U.K. as bacon the closest equivalent in the U.S. would be Canadian Bacon. Bacon can be either smoked or unsmoked.
-**Lardons** are small cubes of streaky bacon, and are usually on the fatty side.
-**Mangetout** are young tender pea pods. Good alternatives for this are thin green beans cut to short lengths of sugar snap peas.

Any item marked at the end with a * will have a corresponding recipe
in the R&D Section at the back of the book.

Cooking Terms:

-Bain-Marie: A bain-marie or double boiler is a gently steaming, but not boiling, pan of water on the stove with a heat proof bowl fitted on top of the pan. The bowl must not touch the water in the pan.

-Bake Blind: To blind bake a pastry is a process in which the unfilled raw docked pastry is cooked using a lining and pie weights. Pie weights are special ceramic beads available at most cooking shops, but you can also use dry beans or dry rice as a weight. Blind baking can be used for tarts and pies that do not need to be baked such as chocolate pudding, or in filled baked pies such as treacle tarts.

-Beat: To beat means to vigorously stir the mix adding air into the mixture. This is usually done with an electric mixer or a stand mixer but can be a good workout and done by hand.

-Blanche: Blanching is a cooking technique in which vegetables or fruits are scalded in boiling water for a very brief time and then plunged into icy water to shock the vegetables and to quickly stop the cooking process.

-Chiffonade: Chiffonade is a French cooking term meaning to thinly slice. To do this you must de-stem the leafy greens and stack them vertically. Once the greens have been stacked, roll them tightly. Using a sharp knife, cut the roll thinly with the knife angled to the perpendicular, giving long thin ribbony pieces. This is usually used with basil, spinach, swiss chard or cabbage and can be done for omelettes or crepes. It is not good for anything that doesn't have a smooth edge such as parsley.

-Crimp: This is the process of pressing together pastry such as to seal a top and bottom crust in a fluted or decorative manner.

-Cube: To use a knife to chop food into small even cubes.

-Cream: To cream together usually means, in baking terms to smash the (room temperature) butter and sugar together with a wooden spoon until they make a paste and there are no little bits that are just butter or just sugar.

-Curdle: This is a chemical reaction that results in the breaking of an emulsion or colloid such as when a hollandaise sauce is heated for too long. It can be a lactic acid reaction such as the curdling of milk when it sours. It is also a highly desirable function in making cheese and tofu.

-Docking: Docking is used in pastry and shortbread preparation to ensure that there are no bubbles or rise in the dough as it cooks. Most cooks stab the dough with a fork, perforating the dough all over the area that is to be baked.

-Dice: To use a knife to chop food into very small even pieces.

-Double Boiler: A double boiler or bain-marie is a gently steaming, but not boiling, pan of water on the stove with a heat proof bowl fitted on top of the pan. The bowl must not touch the water in the pan.

-Dress: No, this has nothing to do with the Wardrobe Department! To dress means to coat foods in a sauce such as salads.

-Dust: To coat very lightly with a powdery ingredient such as flour or coco powder.

-Egg Wash: An egg wash is a beaten egg, sometimes with a little water or milk in the mixture, that is used to brush the surface of pastry, breads and certain baked goods before they are baked. Egg washes are also used as a step in the breading process of foods to provide a substrate for the breading to stick to.

-Emulsion: There are two different forms of emulsion in cooking; fat dispersed in water and water that has been dispersed into fat. Fat into water includes such things as mayonnaise and hollandaise sauce. Water into fat emulsions take the form of such things as salad vinaigrettes.

-Essence: This refers to an aromatic extract that is concentrated. These can come from plants or synthetic sources.

-Extract: This means any substance made from extracting part of the plant, such as a nut or spice using alcohol. Almond extract and Vanilla extract are two very popular flavours.

-Fillet: To cut the bones from a piece of meat, poultry, or fish.

-Firm Peaks: Refers to beating cream or egg whites. Firm or stiff peaks stand straight up when the beater is lifted from the mixture.

-Fold: To combine light ingredients, such as whipped cream or beaten egg whites with a heavier ingredient. Working the mixture gently use an over and under motion so as to not deflate the eggs or cream.

-Ganache: A very basic ganache is made from heating 1-part cream or double cream and melting 2-parts of chocolate in the cream. (So 100g Cream with 200g Chocolate). Using this or other ganache recipes as a topping for cakes and cookies is a better option then using straight tempered chocolate.

-Vegan Ganache: Ganache can easily be made vegan with a straight swap using coconut cream and vegan chocolate.

-Julienne: Cutting vegetables into long, thin strips. These strips measure about ¼inch/ 0.6cm thick and 1inch/ 2.5cm long.

-Knead: The process of mixing dough with hands or a mixer to build gluten and combine ingredients.

-Lukewarm: This generally refers to liquid that is mildly warm to the touch and good for blooming yeast or adding to different mixtures.

-**Medium Peaks:** Refers to beating cream or egg whites. Medium peaks hold their shape pretty well when the beater is lifted out of the mixture, but the tip will curl instead of remaining straight.
-**Onion Cloute:** An onion cloute is a traditional French Culinary technique where chefs stud an onion with many cloves.
-**Onion Pique:** An onion pique is a traditional French culinary technique where chefs attach one or more bay leaves to an onion with whole cloves. See illustration on page 30.
-**Poach:** To gently cook something in liquid over a very low heat, with the liquid barely simmering and just covering the ingredient. Different to braising or stewing as the poaching liquid is not always part of the dish.
-**Purée:** To mash or grind food until completely smooth.
-**Rasher:** This refers to a slice of bacon.
-**Reduction:** This is a technique used to intensify flavour and thicken cooking liquid by bringing it to a rapid boil to reduce the water in the mixture by letting it escape as steam from the pan.
-**Roast:** Like baking but concerns meat, poultry and some vegetables which are cooked in the oven using dry heat.
-**Roux**: The beginning for many sauces with oil and flour being cooked together as a thickener for the sauce.
-**Rub in:** This is a technique where flour is rubbed into a fat such as butter for making pastry, crumbles, and scones. This process is important because it blocks water from being absorbed by the flour so less gluten is formed for flaky crusts. Also called cutting in.
-**Sauté:** To cook small pieces of food over a medium-high heat with oil in a pan, usually to brown food.
-**Scald:** To heat liquid almost to a boil until bubbles begin forming just around the edge.
-**Simmer:** Bring a pot to a boil, then reduce the heat until there are no bubbles in the water.
-**Steep**: To soak a dry ingredient in a liquid just under the boiling point to extract the flavour, such as tea.
-**Stew:** To cook covered over low heat for a long time.
-**Soft Peaks**: Refers to beating cream or egg whites. Soft peaks barely hold their shape when a beater is lifted.
-**Stiff Peaks:** Refers to beating cream or egg whites. Stiff or Firm peaks stand straight when the beater is lifted from the mixture with no curling.
-**Temper Chocolate:** Tempering or melting chocolate should be done over a double boiler or in very small increments in a microwave. Melt two thirds of your chocolate in this manner and then removing it from the heat, add the last third of the chocolate to the melted chocolate, stirring constantly until the chocolate has completely melted.

    If you overheat the chocolate, it can seize and become dry and chunky.
    There is no saving it. Start again.

-**Whip:** To beat ingredients together with a whisk or fork to create volume and increase air content.
-**Whisk:** To beat ingredients together with a whisk or fork.
-**Zest:** To zest something usually refers to a citrus fruit like an orange or a lemon that is unwaxed. Remove the outermost part of the skin and leave behind the white part just under the surface. This is then very finely cut into the smallest pieces possible. The reason the white under skin is left behind is that it generally can cause a bitter taste.

General Equipment Guide

For goodness sake don't let Angus or Vortigern anywhere near this stuff or the village Health and Safety Officer will be after us again! And heaven forbid, don't let R&D run off with the good cups or china! Mrs Partridge hasn't forgiven us for the last time.

To make amazing food you don't need all the latest gadgets, or huge amounts of equipment. There are some basic things that come in handy when in the kitchen. Look at these as an investment in your future that hopefully will last you many years.

A good rule of thumb is to buy the best that you can afford, but don't be afraid of shopping at car boot sales, garage sales, second-hand shops or charity shops. These places can be a treasure trove for good equipment for the kitchen. You might also look at restaurant supply companies online or in the real world.

Knives:

First, don't let anyone from the History Department use a knife unsupervised!
Maybe, just don't let them use a knife at all.

Knives are an investment and you will need to find one that feels right in your hand. Everyone is different and there is an amazing array of different handles on knives. The size is also important because you don't want something that you feel is unruly or too heavy to use properly.
Must Haves:

* * Chef's Knife: This is generally the workhorse in the kitchen and will cut everything from veggies and meats to finished pies.
* * Serrated or Bread Knife: This is for a lot more than just bread.
* * Paring or Peeling Knife: This is for those small jobs that your chef's knife is just too big for.
* * A Sharpening Stone: Don't be fooled by gadgets, nothing beats a good stone. There are a lot of videos online if you are unsure about using a stone.
* * A Good Steel: This will work in combination with your sharpening stone and will give a quick update on the edge of your knife but you need both a stone and steel to keep your knives in good working order.

Cutting Boards:

These are generally available at most stores but be forewarned that you need to get the largest that will safely fit on your counter space and the largest one that your budget will allow. This will also protect your knives and counter surfaces. A variety of wood and plastic boards are best when buying cutting boards, because they can be used as platters for serving guests or as cutting boards in the kitchen. The small cutting boards are cute and very economical, but there is nothing more frustrating or dangerous to work on as an overcrowded board that is sliding all over the place. Avoid the pretty glass cutting boards as the surface is too hard and will flatten the edge of your knife.

Health and Safety Tip:

To fix your cutting board in place wet a paper towel or very thin rag and wring as much water out of it as possible. Place the rag on your work surface and flatten completely so that there are no wrinkles or folds. Place your cutting board on top of the rag and test it to make sure it is stable and unlikely to move across the counter area. Then you are ready to work.

A Vegetable Peeler or Speed Peeler:

Not exactly a knife but they are marvellous at cutting things including fingers! These are for removing peel from such things as potatoes and carrots. They can also be used to make candied orange peel, shave off curls of chocolate over desserts or curls of parmesan cheese over pasta.

Pots and Pans:

General Pots and Pans:

There are a lot of pots and pans available. If you want your pots and pans to last, look for stainless steel that does not have a non-stick surface, ideally with a copper bottom. Copper bottoms are great for even heating of the pan, and stainless steel is durable and will last 30 years or more making them a good investment.

Non-stick surfaces are not particularly durable. Frequent use, washing in a dishwasher and using the wrong utensils on the non-stick surface can break down the surface quickly. This makes the non-stick surface uneconomical because it necessitates buying new pots and pans on a frequent basis.

Fully Copper Pans are amazing to look at, very expensive to buy, but they are not worth having. This is because copper is a reactive metal and will react to both acidic and alkaline foods giving the whole dish a metallic taste that is unpleasant. Frequent use of fully copper pans can be toxic.

Saucepans:

The size of your saucepans will depend on the size of the group of people you normally feed. For a kitchen, you will need first a small saucepan that can accommodate sauces and reductions. A medium sized pan that can accommodate rice, veggies and boxed mac and cheese. Lastly, a third saucepan that is slightly larger than the rest that can accommodate mashed potatoes, soups and pasta. To finish the set, if you are inclined, a very large pot can come in handy when creating food for a crowd at Christmas as well as useful for bottling, canning or preserving.

Accessories for the saucepans that we would recommend, a steamer basket and a well-fitting lid for each pot.

Frying Pans or Skillets:

We would recommend a heavy copper-bottomed stainless steel and/or a cast iron frying pan. These are available in a variety of sizes and finishes. The handles should be from the same material as the pan, and the weight of the handle should not pull the pan up when empty. With the handle being the same material the entire pan can go from the stove top/hob straight into the oven.

These pans are excellent for browning meatballs, frying potatoes, creating omelettes, frying eggs, searing meats, sautéing fish and can handle the higher heat needed for steaks. They can also be used for giant Yorkshire puddings and for baked puff pancakes.

For cast iron there are two different choices enamelled or seasoned. Both finishes have many good qualities, but neither should be cleaned in the dishwasher. It is generally a personal preference or financial considerations that make the determination between the two types.

Roasting Pans/Tins:

Two large enamelled roasting tins are a must for our kitchens. These are amazingly hard wearing and easy to clean. These can handle veggies, roasts, chicken and potatoes to name a few! We can also recommend a Yorkshire pudding pan/tin.

Mixing Bowls

Mixing Bowls are a general workhorse in the kitchen. They can be used for mixing a variety of things, holding bread that is rising, marinating meats/veggies or serving as a snacking device with popcorn.

Mixing bowls come in a variety of materials, colours and sizes. For materials, we would recommend stainless steel, glass and pottery but we do not recommend plastic as these can stain and take on flavours that will not be nice or hygienic. It is important to have two different material types of bowls in your kitchen. This is because a glass or pottery bowl is ideal for melting chocolate over a double boiler or in a microwave and a stainless-steel bowl is ideal to chill for making whipped creams and meringues. Colours of your bowls are a personal preference. Sizes of bowls are dependent on the crowd that you usually cook for, but we recommend at least four bowls of various sizes.

Baking Pans and Tins

General Cakes, Pies and Baking Pans/Tins:
There are a lot of different styles out there. A good mid-range pan will last you many years if you take care of it. We usually line the tins with parchment or baking paper and oil and flour them as needed. This allows the food to release from the pan/tin easily and simplifies washing.

We do not recommend non-stick surfaces here either. A properly treated pan/tin will last many years longer than one with a non-stick surface, even if it is treated well. We can recommend ceramic or enamel lined dishes as they are great at conducting heat and getting an even bake.

We do not recommend full silicone pans or dishes. These have neat designs and can be fun, but they are usually not as good as regular pans in getting a good, even bake. A silicone madeleine pan will never get the correct dome as an enamel madeleine pan will get. Although, silicone sheets are very handy when used with a rimmed baking sheet.

Cake Pans/Tins:
A variety of sizes are best here as well. We can recommend two loaf pans that can hold cakes, sweet breads, yeast breads and small recipes of cinnamon rolls. A square cake pan/tin that is excellent for brownies and small tray bakes, as well as a slightly larger rectangle cake pan/tin that is used for slab cakes, lasagne, tray bakes and many others. Round cake tins are nice, but they are not a necessity especially if you are just starting.

Sheet Pans or Cookie Sheets:
Rimmed and un-rimmed style of baking trays are both very useful. We can also recommend that you have silicone sheets and baking paper to use with these pans. There is some difference between the two. If you are creating a New York style chocolate chip cookie, the sheet is preheated in the oven for 5 minutes before the dough is put on it to then continue baking. A rimmed sheet with a silicone mat will not bake correctly. The rim will block some of the heat from the oven and the silicone mat will cool too quickly to take advantage of the preheated pan, resulting in a very uneven bake and not structurally sound cookie. If you are creating a normal chewy chocolate chip cookie then a rimmed sheet with a silicone mat will work well.

Bread Pans/Tins or Loaf Pans/Tins:
Bread pans are wonderful for a variety of purposes. These can be used for yeast breads, sweet breads or cakes and specialty breads, but they can also be used for small batch cinnamon rolls, meatloaf, donner meat, or even freeze them when making ice cream. We recommend having at least two of these in your kitchen.

Stoneware, Pyrex or Ceramic Pans:
These can be amazing to cook with because they can conduct heat at greater temperatures. They can make amazing roasted meats and vegetables as well as be used for yeast breads. Best yet, they are dishwasher approved! Additionally, many companies make well fitted lids for these dishes making them ideal for baking, freezing and storing foods.

Utensils or things to stir and flip

General Utensils:
Here again, work within your budget. Buy things that will last so that you are not having to replace them often. For utensils, it is optimum to get a variety of sizes and something that feels good in your hands and is not going to be unwieldy or is not so small so that you are expending too much energy for little result. Utensils should be made of a variety of materials such as metal, wood and plastic.

Spatula/ Fish Slice/ Pancake Turner/ Pallet Knife:
These utensils are kind of self explanatory, they flip things over. It is important to have both a silicone-covered surface one to protect the enamel on a pan and a plain stainless-steel variety to allow for a good scraping of the bottom of a cast iron frying pan to make a roux, or for slipping under a delicate biscuit/cookie.

Pastry Brush:
These come in traditional brushes or silicone varieties and it is down to personal preference which you use. Many cooks have moved to the silicone variety because they are easy to clean and can even be put through the dishwasher. Very useful for brushing meats and veg. Traditional brush do get a better brush over items such as breads and pastries but they are finicky to wash and take some care.

Long Handled Spoon or Jam Spoon:
This is a hard worker in the kitchen. We recommend at least two stainless-steel spoons and two wooden spoons. These spoons come in many different designs and you need to look for a spoon that is long enough that it will not disappear into the pot or bowl you are using and the handle is comfortable in your hand. Be aware though that the metal spoons can conduct heat and should never be left in the pot when it is not being actively stirred. Wooden spoons should have a larger handle and be comfortable in your hand.

Long Handled Slotted Spoon:
This is really the same as the long-handled spoon only there are holes in the scoop of the spoon to allow liquid to drain through without losing the object you were trying to spoon up.

Whisk:
These generally come as a traditional stainless steel whisk or one that has a silicone coating. We would recommend at least one larger whisk. Smaller whisks are cute and come in many colours but most of these take more energy output for less effect or mixing in the bowl.

Silicone Spatula or Bowl Scraper:
These are ideal for folding in whipped egg whites or getting the last little bit out of a bowl.

Bench Scraper:
This is a tool you might not know you need. A good metal bench scraper can be used for a lot of different purposes from segmenting doughs to mixing breads or pasta, a handy shovel for scooping up cut veggies or as a scraper to get dried dough off your board when cleaning up. A plastic one can also be useful for these purposes, but it is also a little more flexible for using in a bowl or tray.

Additional Kit that is fun but not necessary to start:

Deep Fat Fryer:
This is one that you don't need to spend a fortune on but should have two very clear safety features of a temperature gauge that is easy to read and a large basket to accommodate what you are frying.

The Security Department wants us to add that they can't do their job without proper chips, so they would find this a necessity to get without delay.

Wire Skimmer or Kitchen Spider Utensil:
This is an amazing basket type utensil that is a great help when frying anything in oil. You can use a slotted spoon for this but a wire skimmer has a larger capacity and not as much room for oil to be transferred with the piece of fried food.

Stand Mixer/Hand Mixer:
A stand mixer such as a Kenwood or KitchenAid are considered a gold standard in cooking equipment and can be used for a variety of kitchen adventures with the plentiful amount of add-on functions that can be bought for additional cost. A handheld electric mixer is a more economical option. Handheld mixers are able to do what most stand mixers can do but they will take a little extra time. To make good food you do not have to have a mixer of any type. They will save you time and energy though. Kneading bread dough or whipping egg white can be done by hand but it takes more time and personal energy to achieve the same results.

Slow Cooker:
These are a great fuss-free way to have a hands-off approach to cooking. Anything made in the slow cooker can also be done on a stove top or in an oven, but this method will take a lot more of your time to complete the recipe. If you do choose to buy one, make sure that the inner cooking pan is removable for easy cleaning and that there are at least three temperature settings.

Temperature Probe For Meats and Baking:
These are great for ensuring the meat you are cooking has reached safe temperatures. These are also wonderful for candy making and for baking breads.

Electric Kettle and/or Coffee Machine:
These are great for rapid drinks! Tea and Coffee is always on hand at St Mary's to keep everyone going. In purchasing these think of the environment and the extra waste that they can create and purchase wisely.

Conversions and Measurements

Dr Bairstow had us work with the Technical Department on all the measurements in this book. He was not pleased with some of the original measurements of '3 mugs well-filled' or 'pour it in until it looks about right'. So, we have worked tirelessly and have tried to make all the measurements in this book accessible to everyone with the first being US cups and teaspoons, the second being imperial and the third measurement being metric.

Keep in mind that:

1 cup of flour is equal to 16 tablespoons or about 150g of flour.

1 cup of caster sugar is equal to 16 tablespoons or about 200g of caster sugar.

1 cup of brown/muscovado sugar is equal to 16 tablespoons or about 220g of muscovado sugar.

1 tablespoon is equal to 15ml or 0.6floz.

1 teaspoon is equal to 5ml or 0.2floz.

1 Tablespoon is equal to 25g (1oz) of syrup, jam, honey

2 Tablespoons is equal to 25g (1oz) of butter, sugar

3 Tablespoons is equal to 25g (1oz) of cornflour/corn-starch, cocoa, custard powder, flour

4 Tablespoons is equal to 25g (1oz) of grated cheese, porridge oats

Some of the basic conversions are:

28g = 1oz	15ml = 0.5fl.oz
57g = 2oz	30 ml = 1fl.oz
85g = 3oz	74 ml = 2.5fl.oz
114g = 4oz	118 ml = 4fl.oz
255g = 9oz	266 ml = 9fl.oz

Temperatures

Temperatures are also given so that they will be accessible to all with the first being Fahrenheit, the second being Celsius, and the third being for Gas Mark, which is used by some gas ovens.

300°F	150°C	Gas Mark 2
325°F	165°C	Gas Mark 3
350°F	177°C	Gas Mark 4
375°F	190°C	Gas Mark 5
400°F	200°C	Gas Mark 6
425°F	220°C	Gas Mark 7
450°F	230°C	Gas Mark 8
475°F	245°C	Gas Mark 9

One Last Word Before Beginning

Dr Bairstow has asked us to write this.

In a kitchen, safety is paramount. This means that you need to store things correctly and do your best to keep the kitchen and kit clean and in working order.

Accidents in the kitchen are never a laughing matter.

This also means that you should read the recipes through entirely and then gather all ingredients. Then, because some recipes move quickly, it is a good idea to have all ingredients weighed, measured and prepared <u>before</u> you begin.

Most of all have good safe fun and make loads of yummy food.

Chapter Two:
The Most Important Thing To Make Correctly:
Tea

The Very Controversial Great British Cuppa
China out, Kettle Boiled and Pinkies Up
This is not for the faint hearted!
Which do you use?

   OR

HOW TO MAKE THE PERFECT ENGLISH CUPPA

1. Switch on the Kettle

Or put a kettle on the Aga

DO NOT put the plastic kettle on the Aga...

2. Prepare the Cup, MUST be china!

Matching saucer ..ALWAYS!

No not a Mug!!

3. From a milk jug

Pour in the milk FIRST

NO! Not straight from the pint bottle....

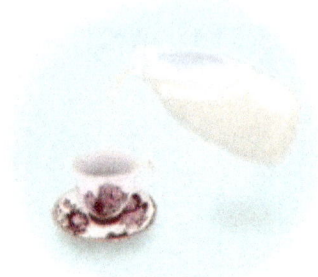

4. Pour hot water in the tea pot to warm it

Rinse and fill with hot water, then add tea leaves

Leave to steep for 2 minutes

HOW TO MAKE THE PERFECT ENGLISH CUPPA

19

5. Take a tea strainer, place in cup and pour

6. Stir vigorously in an anti-clockwise direction

1. **For our more Modern Drinkers**... Boil Water

4. Take a tea strainer, place in cup and pour

Use sugar lumps - not granulated, we do have standards...

Slide 2 fingers through handle and extend pinky finger out

2. Add tea leaves...Earl Grey of course....

5. Take a fresh lemon and chop into slices

Using silver tongs add 1 lump or 2....

Failure to do this may cause the universe to collapse and society as we know it....

3. NO! Do not add milk!!

6. Pinky finger in the air... optional

HOW TO MAKE THE PERFECT ENGLISH CUPPA

For the rest of the uncultured rabble at St Mary's......

1. Mug

2. Teabag

3. Water onto teabag

4. Add milk, leave teabag in for a bit...how long? Who cares!

Feet up, job done. Enjoy!!

Chapter Three:
The History Department
or What Are They Eating Now?
Historical Foods For
The Modern Palate

Recipes:

Ancient Barley and Wheat Loaf	22
Missiiiagan Pakwenigan/ Algonquin Sunflower Bannock	23
Paganens/ Algonquin Nut Soup	25
Msickquatash/ Succotash	26
Aliter Pullus/ (Another Chicken) Roman Honey Chicken	27
Isichia Omentata/ Roman Burgers	28
Minutal et Mala/ Roman Pork and Apple Stew	29
Mac and Cheese	30 to 31
A Tarte for Ember Day/ Onion Tart	32
Pea Soup	34
Bread Sauce	35
Jamaican Goat Curry with Caribbean Rice and Beans	37
Hoe Cakes	38
Crumpets	39
Victoria Sponge	40 to 41
Seed Cake, Victoria Sponge	
Carrot Fritters	42
Upside Down Cakes	44 to 46
Honey Cake, Pear and Ginger Skillet Cake, Pineapple Upside Down Cake	
Tarta de Santiago	47
Loaf in the Time of Cable Street	49
Lemon Ketchup	50
Cheese Toasty/ Grilled Cheese	52
Shooter Sandwich	53
Cowboy Stew	54
Nettle Soup	55

ANCIENT BARLEY AND WHEAT LOAF

This chewy, dense loaf is like bread found throughout the ancient world. Bread like this was widely eaten; from Egypt to Sumeria, from Greece to Pompeii. It has been strengthening jaws and loosening teeth for millennia! For a more authentic loaf, substitute the yeast with sourdough starter, and use spelt or einkorn whole meal. For a more modern take, use yeast, and substitute out half of the whole wheat flour with strong bread flour. You can make either a flat-ish loaf (why flat loaves? They stacked easily on the counters at the ancient bakeries) or a rounded one, but they will both be equally dense, chewy, and deliciously nutty tasting.

Ingredients:
1 cup/ 4.2oz/ 120g Whole Meal Flour
½ cup/ 2.1oz/ 60g Barley Flour
1 teaspoon/ 0.24oz/ 7g Dry Instant Yeast
½ teaspoon/ 0.1oz/ 3g Sea Salt
¾ to 1 cup/ 6 to 8fl.oz/ 180 to 250ml Warm Water, non-chlorinated
Neutral Oil

In a mixing bowl, combine yeast, ¼cup/ 60ml water, and ¼cup/30g whole meal flour. Stir and set aside for 20 minutes until the yeast is bubbling vigorously. Add the rest of the wheat flour and water. Stir, then add barley flour. Begin with the lower measure of water and add more as needed. This dough will be very sticky. If you have a stand mixer with a dough hook, it is recommended that you use it.

With a stand mixer: knead the dough at medium speed, scraping down the sides, until a ball is formed. Knead by machine for 15 minutes. By hand: keep a bowl of water nearby. Moisten hands and knead the dough for 15 minutes. Moistens hands only as needed. The dough is very sticky. Using flour instead will result in a very dry loaf. After kneading, add enough oil to the bowl to coat the dough ball enough so that it does not stick during the rise. Roll the dough ball in the oil, making sure to cover it completely.

Cover with a clean, dry cloth. Place in a warm, draft-free place to rise (I place the bowl in a cold oven, then turn on the oven light, which provides just enough heat for a good rise. Warn your familial Disaster Magnets, so no one starts the whole thing on fire inadvertently). Set a timer for 3 hours. Yes, a 3 hour rise. This will develop the gluten in the bread and allow the dough to become smooth and elastic. This will be your only knead and rise on this loaf.

At the end of the rise, gently lift the ball of dough from the bowl. Fold it over on itself as gently as possible. For a flat roll, carefully press into a thick disc; for a rounded loaf, tuck the ends under the dough, gently shaping into a ball or boule. Place on a sheet of parchment paper. Dust with flour and use a sharp knife to score the surface. This helps release steam and allows the dough to rise without splitting the loaf. Try scoring the top of a flat loaf with 4 cuts from side to side, like slices, to simulate the Roman pannus quadraticus.

Place a shallow pan on the lowest rack. Fill with boiling water prior to preheating the oven. The water will help give the bread a crackly crust. Heat the oven to 425°F/ 220°C/ Gas Mark 7. When preheated, place a cooking sheet in the oven and heat for another 10 minutes.

When the oven reaches temperature, pull the rack out slightly with the flat cooking sheet. Holding the parchment paper taut, lift the loaf and transfer to the cooking sheet. Shut the oven, and bake for 45 minutes.

Remove to a rack and cool. This bread is very dense and filling; a small slice goes a long way. It has a wonderfully nutty flavor.
Small loaf, serves 4.

If you can't find barley flour, grind flaked barley in a blender, pulsing until it achieves the texture of coarse flour.

Photo and Contribution By: Merry Schepers

Missiiiagan Pakwenigan
Algonquin Sunflower Bannock

This is a recipe originally made by the native peoples of what is now known as New England, most likely the Algonquin. This recipe recreates it using entirely Precolonial ingredients. These would have most likely been wrapped in leaves or husks and placed in hot coals to cook, but this recipe calls for frying for easier cooking.

Ingredients:
- 17oz/ 500g Shelled Unsalted Sunflower kernels or seed hearts
- 2 ¾ cups/ 22.8fl.oz/ 625ml Water
- 2 teaspoons/ 0.17oz/ 5g Salt
- 4 to 6 Tablespoons/ 1.4 to 2.1oz/ 40 to 60g Cornmeal/ Polenta
- Corn or Sunflower Oil, for frying
- 2 to 3 Stalks of Wild Garlic, finely chopped, or 2 Tablespoons Chives, snipped finely (optional)

Place the sunflower seeds, water and salt into a pot. Cover, bring to the boil and then turn the heat down so it barely simmers. Simmer the seeds until they are soft and the water is mostly absorbed. Using a stick blender or masher, mash the seeds well until it forms a wet paste, leaving some whole seeds in for texture. Add the wild garlic or chives if desired and mix well. Add the cornmeal, one tablespoon at a time until the mixture has thickened and does not stick to your hands when handling. Mix well with your hands, disposable gloves are recommended here, and divide into 3oz/ 85g portions. Roll into balls and flatten into pancakes about 1cm thick. Heat up enough oil in a frying pan, or use a deep fryer set to 350°F/ 180°C. Fry the bannocks until they are golden brown and are cooked through and reach an internal temperature of 167°F/ 75°C. Drain well on a plate lined with kitchen roll.

Allow to cool slightly before eating.

Paganens
Algonquin Nut Soup

Ingredients:
- 16oz/ 500g Whole Blanched Hazelnuts/ Filberts (See note)
- 8 Stems of Wild Garlic/ Ramps or 1 Shallot and 1 Clove Garlic
- 5.5oz/ 160g Watercress, Not Salad Cress, Rocket (Arugula), or Spinach
- 2 Tablespoons/ 1fl.oz/ 30ml Hazelnut or other Vegetable Oil
- 6 ½ cups/ 1.5L Vegetable Stock or Water
- Salt and Pepper to taste

Note: Make sure that you use blanched hazelnuts, not raw ones with the dark brown skins on them. If you only have raw hazelnuts, heat the oven to 180C/160 fan/350F. Place the hazelnuts on a baking sheet in one layer. Bake for about 15 minutes. Do not allow them to burn. Remove from the oven and set aside to cool. When cool, rub the skins off using a towel. Then use as directed in the recipe above.

In a dry frying pan, over a medium heat, carefully toast the hazelnuts. Do not allow them to burn. Set aside on a plate to cool. When cool, roughly chop. Set aside, reserving some for garnish.

Rinse the wild garlic (ramps) and pat dry. Trim the roots from the wild garlic and remove any woody stems and flowers. Thinly slice and set aside.

Or: peel and thinly slice the shallot, and peel, crush, and finely mince the garlic. Set aside.

Rinse and drain the watercress (or rocket or spinach). Remove the woody stems and chop up coarsely. Save a few leaves for garnish. Heat the oil in a large saucepan over a medium heat. Add the wild garlic (or shallot and garlic) and watercress and a bit of salt and gently fry for a few minutes allowing them to wilt. Stir continuously. Add the stock and chopped hazelnuts. Increase the heat and bring to the boil. Turn the heat down to low and allow to simmer. Cook until the nuts are soft. Add more water or stock, if needed.

When the nuts are soft and the flavours developed, remove from the heat. Using a stick blender, purée the soup until smooth, or working in batches, blend the soup in a blender. When the soup is blended, return to the heat, adjust the seasoning and add more stock if needed or desired to reach preferred consistency. Heat through and then ladle into bowls and garnish with the remaining hazelnuts and watercress.

Contribution and Photo By: Afton Cochran

MSICKQUATASH
SUCCOTASH

This dish comes from the Narragansett (Algonquin) word meaning "broken corn". It would have originally been made with corn, beans, and squash. In summer, it would have been made with fresh sweet corn, shelling beans, and summer squash. In winter, it would be made with dried corn, dried beans, and pumpkin. Dried or fresh meat or fish could also have been added. This dish is popular all-over North America, with regional ingredients used as an addition.

Ingredients:
2 Tablespoons/ 1fl.oz/ 30ml Olive or Vegetable Oil
2 teaspoons/ 0.35oz/ 10g Butter
1 Small Red Onion, finely diced
1 Red Pepper, diced
1 Jalapeño, seeded and diced
4 Cloves Garlic, crushed and minced
½ teaspoon/ 0.03oz/ 1g Cayenne Powder
1 teaspoon/ 0.07oz/ 2g Cumin
2 Tomatoes, seeded and diced
3 Courgette/ Zucchini, Patty Pan Squash, Yellow Summer Squash, or a mixture of each, cut into cubes
6oz/ 170g Green Beans, cut into ½ inch/ 1cm pieces
¼ cup/ 1.6fl.oz/ 50ml Water
3 Ears Sweet Corn on the Cob
9oz/ 250g Butter beans/ Lima beans fresh, tinned or frozen and defrosted (see note)
2 Spring Onions, sliced or 3 stalks Wild Garlic (ramps), sliced
Salt and Pepper to taste.
Other optional ingredients: sliced okra, bacon lardons, shredded smoked ham hock, or diced carrots.

Grill the corn cobs under the oven grill or on a BBQ grill until the kernels have a nice char all over. Set aside to cool, and then carefully cut the kernels off the cob. Set aside. Heat the oil and butter in a skillet over a medium heat. Add the onion, and a little salt and fry until the onion is soft and translucent. Add the red pepper, jalapeño, garlic and cook for a further 3 to 4 minutes or until the pepper starts to soften. Add the tomato, cumin, cayenne, and a little salt and pepper and mix well. Add the courgette (or your choice of squash), green beans, and water. Cook until the courgette begins to soften. Add in the corn kernels, beans and heat through. Adjust the seasoning to your liking and stir in the spring onions or ramps.

Note: if using frozen Butter/ Lima beans, defrost thoroughly before use. If using tinned, drain and rinse and drain again. If using fresh, remove from the pods, add to a pot, boil with a bit of salt for one hour or until tender. Drain and use.
Serves 8

Adapted from: Chef John   Contribution By: Afton Cochran

Aliter Pullus
(Another Chicken) Roman Honey Chicken

Most of what we know about Roman food comes from a book "On The Subject Of Cooking" which is commonly attributed to an otherwise unknown writer called Caelius Apicius. The text mainly contains ingredients only used by the wealthy but offer a lot of opportunity for redacting recipes. The Romans loved their sweet and sour and many of the ingredients they favoured are still available to us today - honey, figs, dates, caraway, dill, thyme and cumin would all have featured. Some are harder to come by, such as garum, a flavouring made from fermented fish. The closest we have to this today is probably Thai fish sauce, or nam pla. This gives a salty flavour to dishes and was used in place of salt in De Rerum Coquinaria; only three recipes contain actual salt. Sadly, one of their very favourite ingredients was a herb called silphium which was very hard to come by, and only grew in Cyrenica on the coast of modern-day Libya. Legend says it was a gift from the god Apollo, and was used as a flavour in food, a perfume and an aphrodisiac. They loved this herb so much it featured on coins, and the fruit of the plant was vaguely heart-shaped and is possibly where we get the love heart image from today. It's unclear how this herb went extinct, but possibly it was over-farmed or there was a change in the soil or climate that made it unable to thrive there.

Meat-wise, the rich Romans loved their birds; flamingos, songbirds and other exotic birds were prized. Our local supplier only laughed when Professor Rapson tried to order flamingo, so we have settled for chicken.

Honey Chicken

Ingredients:

2 medium/ 10oz/ 300g Chicken Breasts, diced
1 Tablespoon/ 0.5fl.oz/ 15ml Olive Oil
2 Tablespoons/ 0.7oz/ 20g of Dried Raisins
½ teaspoon/ 0.03oz/ 1g Caraway Seeds
½ teaspoon/ 0.03oz/ 1g Cumin Seeds
½ teaspoon/ 0.03oz/ 1g Ground Nutmeg
4 Cloves Garlic, minced
3 Tablespoons/ 1.5fl.oz/ 45ml Good Quality Honey
½ teaspoon/ 0.06fl.oz/ 2ml Garum, or Thai Fish Sauce

Lightly toast the spices in a hot, dry pan to release their aromas. Grind them into a fine powder and set aside. Add a little oil and chicken to the pan and cook until golden brown. Stir in the ground spices, reduce the heat and add in the garlic and raisins. Stir to keep the garlic from burning.

Add the honey and mix through. Add the fish sauce - taste at this point and if you think it is still too sweet, add a couple more drops of fish sauce. Be careful a little garum goes a long way.

If the mixture is too dry add 4 tablespoons/ 2fl.oz/ 60ml of boiling water to loosen it up. This is optional, but you do not want the pan to go dry and start burning everything.

Serve with flat breads, salad greens and maybe a little mustard. Lean back and relax like a Roman.

Serves 2

Contribution By: Gina Burnside

Isichia Omentata
Roman Burgers

Roman food was as complex as the many different cultures that were brought under the control of the empire. Romans are known to have had lavish feasts for the wealthy, that included door mice and swan on the menu. The Kitchen Staff is all for historically accurate foods but refuses point blank to engage with the St. Mary's swans, even with the inducement of hazardous duty pay. Plus, we are interested in more than just what the rich ate. Rome was the original city, with noise, pollution, people and street food. Food was served from vendors, or snack bars called thermopolii and from street hawkers with trays almost everywhere, with food served hot and quick. This was the original fast food for people on the move so everything could be eaten on the go but it also could be taken home for convenience.

This Roman version of a burger, found in the Apicius cookbook, was a minced meat patty flavoured with nuts, spices and garum (fish sauce) that could be made quickly and taken away on a flat bread plate for a satisfying meal on the run. Depending on which part of the empire one inhabited, the meat, nuts and spices would be those that were locally available and affordable.

Ingredients:
- 16oz/ 500g Minced Beef, Pork, Lamb, or Any Combination
- 1 Clove Garlic, finely minced
- 1 Shallot, finely minced
- 1 Tablespoon/ 0.5fl.oz/ 15ml Wine or Balsamic Vinegar
- 4 Tablespoons/ 2.1oz/ 60 g Almonds, Pine nuts or Hazelnuts, hulled and coarsely chopped
- ½ teaspoon/ 0.01oz/ >1g Lovage, dried or Celery Seed
- 1 teaspoon/ 0.07oz/ 2g Ground Coriander or Ground Cumin
- 3 to 4 Juniper Berries, crushed
- 1 Tablespoon/ 0.5fl.oz/ 15ml Garum, which is a Roman fish sauce, but any good fish sauce will do. For those with a fish allergy 2 tsp/ 12g of salt can be substituted but will not lend the complexity of flavour.

Add all ingredients together in a bowl and mix until they are all thoroughly incorporated. Shape into patties. Place on a hot skillet or grill. Cook until well-browned on both sides and the nut meats are toasted brown but not burnt. Serve hot on buns, pita, flatbread, or just by themselves.

A bit of *mustum ardens* – mustard – would be an appropriate and tasty addition.

Enjoy, and walk around like you own the place for that full Roman experience.

Serves 4

Contribution By: Merry Schepers

MINUTAL ET MALA
ROMAN PORK AND APPLE STEW

Ancient civilizations had leftovers too. It is truly an age-old problem. The Romans loved pork and the leftovers were incorporated into a tasty pork and fruit stew. While this one is made with apples, do not be afraid to try some other combinations. Dried fruit was a staple in many Roman kitchens, so try this rich, complex stew with dried apricots or figs. Omit the honey in these recipes, as the dried fruits are sweet enough, and add another 20 minutes to the cooking time.

Ingredients:
- 16oz/ 455g Pork Shoulder or Loin Roast, Cooked, so leftovers are best
- 2oz/ 57g Bulk Pork Sausage, cooked
- 2 Tablespoons/ 1fl.oz/ 30ml Olive Oil
- 1½ Tablespoons/ 0.7fl.oz/ 22ml Garam or Fish Sauce
- 1 Apple, peeled, cored, and sliced thinly
- 2 Shallots or 1 Small Onion, slivered
- 1 Clove Garlic, minced
- 1 cup/ 8fl.oz/ 250ml Dry Wine, white or red
- 1 cup/ 8fl.oz/ 250ml Broth or Stock
- 2 Tablespoons/ 1fl.oz/ 30ml Balsamic Vinegar or Pomegranate Molasses
- ½ teaspoon/ 0.03oz/ 1g Ground Cumin
- ½ teaspoon/ 0.03oz/ 1g Ground Coriander
- ½ teaspoon/ 0.01oz/ >1g Dried Dill
- ½ teaspoon/ 0.03oz/ 1g Ground Black Pepper
- 1 Tablespoon/ 0.5fl.oz/ 15ml Honey

Heat oil over medium-high heat and add cooked meats, sauté the meats until heated through. Add fish sauce and stir. Add onions and garlic, lower heat to medium, and cook till the onions just start to turn clear, about 5 minutes.

Add coriander, cumin, dill and pepper. Stir in and cook till the spices become fragrant, about 1 to 2 minutes. Add wine and balsamic vinegar or pomegranate molasses, stirring well to incorporate. Add honey, broth and apples, stirring to combine. Turn the heat back up to medium high and bring the mixture to a boil, then reduce the heat to medium low. Simmer the mixture for about 30 minutes. If you want a thicker stew, remove the solids, and reduce the liquid by raising the temperature and boiling down by a quarter of the volume. Return solids to the liquid, heat another 5 minutes.

Serve with pearl barley, farro, or rice.

Serves 4 to 6

Contribution By: Merry Schepers

Mac and Cheese

Mac and Cheese or cheese with noodles predates the cute little elbow macaroni noodle shapes that became so popular in the mid twentieth century.

Mac and Cheese—England 1390

Yes, it is true! The English were actually the first to publish the fresh noodle and cheese dish, and it predated anything from Italy by about 80 years. Before any of the historians faint, all of these recipes could have been based on Roman dishes. The tag "alla romana" or Roman Style figures into many of these later Italian Works.

This Mac and Cheese recipe is found in the English cookbook
The Forme of Cury compiled in 1390.

Makerouns

Take and make a thynne foyle of dowh, and kerue it on pieces, and cast hym on boiling water & seep it wele. Take cheese and grate it, and butter imelte, cast bynethen and abouven as losyns; and serue forth.

Macharoni Romaneschi, from Naples in 1465 and attributed to Maesto Martino, calls for thick noodles cut into strings then boiled in broth, or water if it was a fasting day, with butter, sweet spices and cheese.

Maccaroni Alla Romanesca—Bartolomeo Scappi—1570

Scappi was a bit of a genius in the kitchens. He used crustless white bread soaked in milk and egg yolks in the creation of his pasta, giving it a much richer taste. This was a bit daring considering the time period and the need to be able to fast on holy days, which didn't include milk or eggs. Scappi's masterpiece was layers of long rounded noodles with layers cheese, sugar and spices with additional knobs of butter.

To Dress Macaroni —1769

Elizabeth Raffald's book in the mid- eighteenth century, put yet another spin on the dish with the addition of cream, and notes for serving the dish.

The Experienced English Housekeeper, compiled in 1769.

To dress Macaroni with Permasent Cheese

Boil four Ounces of Macaroni 'til it be quite tender and lay it on a sieve to drain, then put it in a Toffing Pan, with about a Gill of good cream, a lump of butter rolled in flour, boil for five Minutes, pour it on a Plate, lay all over it Permafent Cheese toasted; send it to the table on a Water Plate, for it soon goes cold.

Mac and Cheese

Thomas Jefferson, popularizing Mac and Cheese

Thomas Jefferson was wrongly attributed with the creation of mac and cheese for years. He was a huge fan of the dish but it is thought that he came across it while in Europe. It is noted as being served several times while he was President of the United States, including the 1802 state dinner.

The Rise of Modern Mac and Cheese

Kraft Foods introduced the boxed macaroni and cheese in 1937 to the United States. These popular little boxes sold for 19 cents and the company sold over 8 million boxes in its first year even though the country was grappling with the Great Depression.

Mac and Cheese

Ingredients:
14oz/ 400g Dry Elbow Macaroni Pasta
¼ cup/ 1.8oz/ 50g Butter
4 Whole Cloves
2 cups/ 17fl.oz/ 500ml Whole Milk
1 cup/ 7oz/ 200g Mature Cheddar Cheese, grated
1/3 cup/ 1.8oz/ 50g Plain Flour
½ Onion, peeled
2 Bay Leaves
1 teaspoon/ 0.1oz/ 3g Dry Mustard Powder
½ cup/ 2oz/ 50g Parmesan Cheese, finely grated

Attach the bay leaves to the onion with the cloves, to make a pique. Place in a small saucepan with the milk and heat through until it begins to simmer, but do not it let boil. Remove from the heat and set it aside to allow the flavours of the onion pique to infuse into the milk. Strain the milk into a jug and discard the pique. Set aside. Cook the macaroni in salty water to al dente, reserving a cup of the pasta cooking liquid. Drain well and set aside. Heat your grill/ broiler to hot. In a saucepan, melt the butter until it begins to foam. Turn the heat down to low, add the flour and a bit of salt and pepper and mix well. Cook it for 2-3 minutes, to cook out the floury taste. Slowly add the milk, a bit at a time, mixing well so it does not become lumpy. When it is smooth and all the milk has been incorporated, allow it to cook for a further few minutes, stirring well, so it does not stick to the pan. Add 2/3 of the mature cheddar to the white sauce. Stir well and allow it to fully melt. Mix with the macaroni. If it is too thick, add a bit of the pasta water to allow it mix smoothly. Pour into a suitably sized dish that is oven safe. Sprinkle the remaining cheddar and Parmesan and place under the grill until the cheese is melted and the pasta is piping hot.

Buffalo Mac and Cheese

Add ½ cup/ 4fl.oz/ 128ml Buffalo Wing Sauce to the béchamel sauce just before adding the cheese.
Add 16oz/ 500g shredded cooked chicken and 2 stalks celery, finely diced to the cheese sauce along with the macaroni. Pour into a greased casserole dish. Top with crumbled blue cheese and a bit more Buffalo Wing Sauce. Then finish off as per the instructions.

Jalapeño Popper Mac and Cheese

Use half shredded Monterey Jack cheese and half mature Cheddar cheese. Omit the Parmesan.
Add ½ cup/ 2oz/ 60g cream cheese and 1 teaspoon/ 0.1oz/ 3g garlic granules to the béchamel before adding 2/3 of the other cheeses.
When combining the sauce and macaroni, stir in: 250g (9oz) smoked bacon lardons that have been cooked until crispy, 2 Jalapeños that have been seeded and finely minced. Mix well, pour into a greased lined casserole and cover in remaining cheese, and ¾ cup/ 3oz/ 90g Panko breadcrumbs. Bake at 350 °F/ 180 °C (160°C fan)/ Gas Mark 4 for 15 minutes or until the panko is golden brown and the macaroni and cheese reaches 168°F/ 75°C internally. Garnish with sliced Jalapeños, if desired.

Serves 6

Contribution By: Afton Cochran

A Tarte for Ymbre or Ember Day

Ember Days date back to the 5th century C.E. and are mentioned by Pope St. Leo the Great. These are days that happen four times a year corresponding with saints' days and seasons, for the devout to give thanks. During these times one full main meal with meat and two partial meals without meat were allowed each day. Filling meat free dishes such Egg and Onion Tarts date back to medieval times being found in the English cookbook The Forme of Cury compiled in 1390.

TART IN YMBRE

Take and parboile Oynouns presse out þe water & hewe hem smale. take brede & bray it in a morter. and temper it up with Ayren. do þerto butter, safroun and salt. & raisouns corauns. & a litel sugur with powdour douce. and bake it in a trape. & serue it forth.

Onion Tarts are filling and guaranteed to keep historians going through the most difficult jumps.

Onion Tart

Ingredients:

Crust:

1 cup + 2 Tablespoons/4 oz./113g of Wholemeal or Spelt Flour

1/4 teaspoon/4g of Salt

6 Tablespoons/3oz/ 85g of Butter, cold and cut into small bits

3 Tablespoons/1.5 fl oz/44mL of Ice Water

Filling:

1 ½ pounds/680g of White or Yellow Onions (about 3 medium sized)

2 slices of Bacon (optional), cut into small pieces

1 teaspoon/3g of Fresh Thyme Leaves or 2 pinches of Dried Thyme

Salt and Pepper to taste

3 Eggs

½ cup/4.2 fl. oz./118ml Double Cream or Creme Fraiche

½ cup/4.2 fl. oz./118ml Milk

1 cup/4 oz./113g Gouda or Gruyère Cheese, grated

Tart pan with removable bottom or Springform pan.

Filling:
Peel and finely dice the onions.
Fry bacon if using and drain and cool. Drain off grease and add butter to the skillet. When the butter has melted, add onions, herbs 3/4 teaspoon of salt. Cook on medium heat for about 25 minutes, till the onions have developed a golden colour. Add pepper and then set aside to cool.
Whisk eggs, milk and cream together. Stir in the cool, cooked onions, bacon and the cheese.

Crust:
Put flour and salt into a stand mixer. Use the paddle attachment and add butter to the dry ingredients with the mixer running at low speed. Butter should be in small, pea-sized pieces and incorporated throughout the flour. This can be done in a standard bowl using a pastry cutter or fork to incorporate the butter into the flour.
Slowly add in the ice water until the dough looks just damp and clumpy.
Form the dough in a disc or rectangle, based on the shape of your pan and refrigerate.

Heat oven to 400°F/200°C/Gas Mark 6
Roll dough out to fit into and up the sides of your pan. For the crust you can do a fancy crimped edge, but you can also leave the edge a bit uneven and rustic. Set the pan with crust onto a baking sheet.
When the oven has reached heat, pour the egg and onion mixture into the crust, put into the oven and bake until the surface becomes golden and lightly brown, about 45 to 50 minutes.
Remove from oven and cool to just warm, remove the tart from the pan and serve.

Photo By: Afton Cochran   Contribution By: Merry Schepers

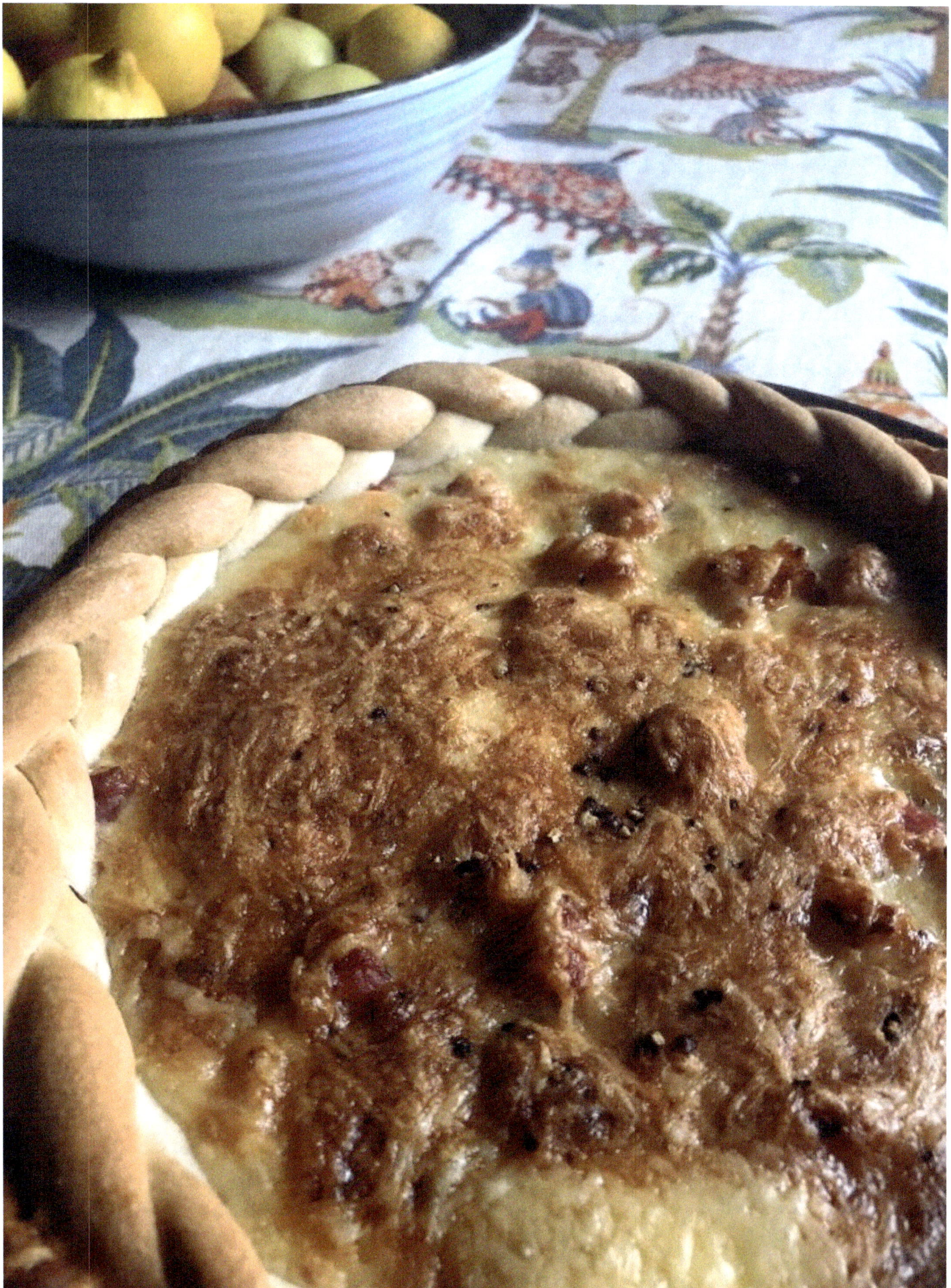

Pea Soup

This soup is amazingly popular at the Falconburg Arms. The warm thick soup can be made with or without meat, and is wonderful on a rainy day. Markham is very lucky that the popularity of the soup didn't change after he loudly proclaimed, …"it looks like baby sick up!"
Even though it isn't the prettiest dish, the soup has been popular for ages.

We have found that there is so much more to the history of pea soup then a nursery rhyme:
Peas Porridge hot, Peas Porridge cold * Peas Porridge in the pot, Nine days old
Some like it hot, Some like it cold * Some like it in the pot, Nine days old

Pottage or a thick soup or stew was a staple in the medieval diet. It was eaten by everyone from kings to peasants and had endless combinations.
For peasants it was usually what ever they had on hand including vegetables, herbs, a little meat or bone to add flavour and nutrients and might be thickened with barely or breadcrumbs.
The soup could also be made without meat so it was easy to serve on the sabbath or during Lent. Pottage was also very versatile with some recipes cooking very quickly and some would last for days simmering over the fire.

The Forme of Cury from England 1390, had several pottage recipes but none were specifically pea pottage, but rather relied heavily on leeks and cabbage.

In 'Ein new Kochbuch' by Rumpolt Marx that was published in 1581, contains a simple recipe for Pea Soup that includes peas with onions. This recipe was probably very well known and one of the many soups that had not changed for hundreds of years.
Erbeßsuppen
Erbeßsuppen mit klein gehackten Zwiebeln die geschweißt seyn pfeffers vnd gelbs so ist es auch gut

Chef Francatelli, chef to Queen Victoria, in 1861 outlined in his cookbook many soups for the working poor. Pea Soup was one of these recipes:

Cut up two and a-half pounds of pickled pork, or some pork cuttings, or else the same quantity of scrag end of mutton, or leg of beef, and put any one of these kinds of meat into a pot with a gallon of water, three pints is split or dried peas, preciously soaked in cold water over-night, two carrots, four onions, and ahead of celery, all chopped small; season with pepper, butt no salt, as the pork, if pork is used, will season the soup sufficiently; set the whole to boil very gently for at least three hours, taking care to skim it occasionally, and do not forget that the peas, etc., must be stirred from the bottom of the pot now and then; from three to four hours' gentle boiling will suffice to cook a good mess of this most excellent and satisfying soup. If fresh meat is used for this purpose, salt must be added to season it. Dried mint may be strewn over the soup when eaten.

Ham and Pea Soup

Ingredients:
2 Tablespoons/ 1fl.oz/ 30ml Butter
1 Onion, diced
1 Garlic Clove, minced
1 Large Potato, peeled and diced
4fl.oz/ 34fl.oz/ 1 litre Vegetable or Ham Stock
17.6oz/ 500g Peas, thawed if frozen
10.5oz/ 300g Ham, cooked, thickly diced, and trimmed
½ teaspoon/ 0.02oz/ >1g Dried Mint (optional)
Salt and Pepper to taste

In a large saucepan melt the butter and add the onion and potatoes. Sauté until the onions are almost translucent and the potatoes are softened. Pour in the stock, mint and peas as well as the salt and pepper. Simmer until softened, about 5 to 8 minutes. Remove from the heat and using an immersion blender blend the contents until smooth. Stir in most of the ham reserving some for garnish.
Serve with a crusty bread.

Serves 4

Contribution By: Sara Robinson

Bread Sauce

Bread Sauce is a great tradition in the U.K. Love it or hate it, most people in the UK are well aware of this contentious sauce. Bread Sauce can be found on the table for Sunday roast turkey or chicken, or at Christmas gatherings.

The history of bread sauce is a much longer story!

A Bread Sauce recipe was found in the English cookbook

The Forme of Cury compiled in 1390.

Galentyne

Take crustes of brede & grynde hem smale; do perto poudour of galyngale, of canel, of gynger, and salt it; temper hyt with vyneger & drawe it vp porow a straynour & messe hit forth.

Bread sauce was served with rabbit in the court of Henry VII according to the Good Huswifes Handmade for the Kitchen in 1594, and were a common type of sauce throughout the medieval period with the bread acting as a thickening agent.

Charles Esmé Francatelli, head cook to Her Gracious Majesty Queen Victoria further refined the bread sauce recipe in his 1861 publication.

Bread Sauce for Roast Fowl

Chop a small onion, or a shallot fine, and boil it in a pint of milk for five minutes; then add about ten ounces of crumb of bread, a bit of butter, pepper and salt to season; stir the whole on the fire for ten minutes and eat this bread sauce with roast fowl or turkey.

Bread Sauce

Ingredients:
1 Onion, peeled and whole
15 to 20 Whole Cloves (optional)
Bay Leaves
8 to 10 Black Peppercorns
2 1/3 cups plus 1 Tablespoon/ 19.2fl.oz/ 570ml (1 pint) Whole Milk, preferably Jersey or Guernsey milk, which has a higher fat content
3 ½ Tablespoons/ 1.7oz/ 50g Butter
2 Tablespoons/ 1fl.oz/ 30ml Double Cream
Pinch Nutmeg, freshly ground
Salt, to taste
¾ cup/ 3.8oz/ 110g Breadcrumbs, made from stale white bread

Peel your onion but keep it whole. Using the cloves, attach the bay leaves to cover the onion. This is called a cloute. In a saucepan, add the milk, the cloute, and the peppercorns and bring to the boil. Boil for about 15 minutes. Remove from the heat, cover, and set aside in a warm place to allow the flavours to meld into the milk, at least two hours, or more if you want a stronger flavour. When you are ready to finish your bread sauce, strain the milk, and discard the solids. Bring the milk back to a light simmer, add the breadcrumbs and half the butter and turn the heat down to the lowest possible setting. Stir occasionally. This will allow the breadcrumbs to swell up and thicken the sauce, about 15 minutes. Keep warm until ready to serve. When ready to serve, add in the remainder of the butter, the double cream, check the seasoning, and garnish with freshly grated nutmeg.
Serves 6-8

Discarding the bread crusts will make for a lighter coloured sauce.

Contribution By: Afton Cochran

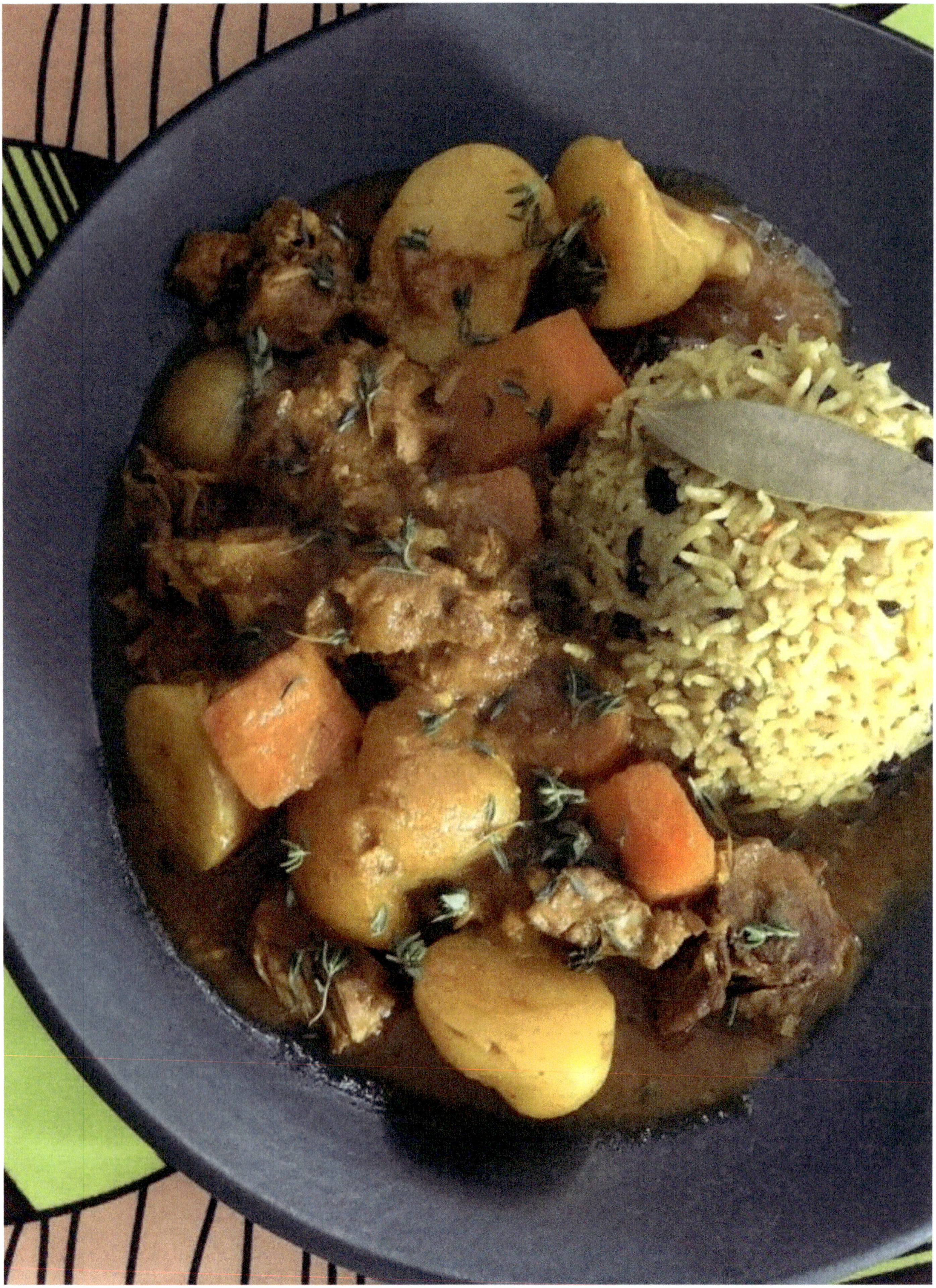

Jamaican Goat Curry

The Island of Jamaica has had so many traditions that are a part of the island's food heritage. African slaves were forced into working plantations and were known to be on the island from 1514 when it was under Spanish rule. The British East India company is credited with introducing curry to the island the 19th century. Jamaicans took all of these ideas and made something better and uniquely their own.
Jamaican Goat Curry is very popular around the world.

Ingredients:
- 2.2pounds/ 2kg Goat, Lamb, or Mutton
- ¼ cup/ 2fl.oz/ 60ml Vegetable Oil
- 3 to 4 Cloves Garlic, crushed and minced
- 1 Tablespoon Fresh Ginger, minced
- 1 Large Onion, thinly sliced
- 5 Tablespoons/ 1.12oz/ 32g Caribbean Curry Powder (recipe in R&D)
- 1 teaspoon/ 0.07oz/ 2g White Pepper
- 2 teaspoons/ 0.14oz/ 4g Ground Turmeric
- 2 Tablespoons/ 0.17oz/ 5g Fresh Thyme Leaves
- 3 Spring Onions, sliced
- 2.2pounds/ 1kg Baby Potatoes, halved
- 4 Large Carrots, chopped
- 2 Tablespoons/ 1fl.oz/ 30ml Tomato Purée/ Paste
- 1 Scotch Bonnet Pepper (or chilli pepper of your choice)
- 2 Tablespoons/ 0.5oz/ 15g Chicken Bouillon Powder
- Salt and Pepper, to taste

Season the goat, or lamb well with salt and pepper. Heat oil in a large pan over a high heat. Sear the meat off in batches, making sure you do not overcrowd the pan, until each piece is nicely browned all over. Remove to a plate with a slotted spoon. Repeat until all the meat has been browned.

Turn the heat down slightly and add the onions and cook until soft and translucent, scraping up any brown bits off the bottom of the pan. Add the garlic, thyme, tomato purée, green onions, curry powder and whole scotch bonnet and stir for a minute more. Add the goat back in, along with any juices and stir once more.

Add enough water to cover the meat. Give it a good stir, again making sure you scrape up any bits that may have stuck on the bottom. Cover. Bring to the boil, then reduce to a simmer and simmer for 2 hours, or until the lamb is tender, adding more water in should you feel it needs it. Add in the potatoes and carrots and cook them until they are soft, but still retain their shape. Check seasoning and serve with Caribbean Rice and Beans.

Should you wish a thicker sauce, you can thicken with a cornflour slurry.

Note: there are a lot of bones in goat meat and the flavour is quite strong.

Caribbean Rice and Beans

Ingredients:
- ¼ cup/ 2fl.oz/ 60ml Vegetable Oil
- 3 Garlic Cloves, crushed and minced
- ½ Onion, minced
- 2 teaspoon/ 0.14oz/ 4g Creole Spice Blend (recipe in R&D)
- 2 cups/ 14oz/ 400g Long Grain Rice
- Sprig of Fresh Thyme
- 1¾ cup/ 14oz/ 400ml Full Fat Coconut Milk
- 2 cups/ 14fl.oz/ 400ml Chicken Stock, heated through
- 1- 14oz/ 400g Tin Black Beans, or Red Kidney Beans, drained and rinsed
- Bay Leaf
- Scotch Bonnet or Habanero, or milder chilli pepper, if you want less heat
- 1 teaspoon/ 0.07oz/ 2g Paprika
- 1 teaspoon/ 0.07oz/ 2g Ground Turmeric
- Salt and Pepper, to taste
- 2 cups/ 14fl.oz/ 400ml Chicken Stock, heated through
- 2 teaspoon/ 0.17oz/ 5g Chicken Bouillon Powder

Rinse the rice well, until the water runs clear. Drain well and set aside.

In a jug, add the coconut milk, hot chicken stock, chicken bouillon, creole spice, turmeric, and paprika. Mix well. Set aside.

In a skillet or a pot, heat the oil over a medium heat. Add the onion and fry gently until soft and translucent. Add the garlic, thyme, whole scotch bonnet and sauté for another minute. Do not allow these to go brown. Add the rice and beans and mix well. Carefully pour the coconut milk/stock mixture into the rice and beans. It will splash, so be careful. Add the bay leaf, and a bit of salt and pepper, if desired. Place the lid on the pot, turn the heat down to a gentle simmer and allow the rice to cook until all the liquid has been absorbed, about 20 minutes. Keep the heat low and check on it from time to time so it doesn't burn. Remove from the heat, leave the lid on and let it continue to sit for 15 minutes. Fluff with a fork and serve alongside the Goat Curry or add meat of your choice.

To make vegan, change chicken stock for vegetable stock, and chicken bouillon powder for vegetable bouillon powder.

Photo and Contribution By: Afton Cochran

Hoe Cakes

Regardless of the stares from the Security Section, the Hoe Cake has nothing to do with women of the night, back-breaking work of using a garden implement to hoe weeds, or indeed anything to do with tilling a field at all.
Hoe Cakes, or Johnny Cakes are sometimes called Indian Hoecakes in older cookbooks. This origin of the Hoe Cake story is well founded, and it is believed that the Cherokee, Chickasaw, Choctaw, or Creek Native American Tribes taught early European settlers the method of preparation for the corn cakes. This is probably where the term 'hoe' in the name comes from. The word hoe, dates to the 1600's in England and is a word that is not used any longer. Instead of hoe we now use the word griddle exclusively to describe the same thing.

Hoecakes are like and unlike a pancake, but well worth trying.
It is said that George Washington loved the little griddle cakes as a breakfast served with butter and honey. Originally the batter would not have included baking powder, but some older recipes included eggs and yeast as a way of creating lift and bubbles.

Hoe Cake
Scald 1 pint is milk and put to 3 pints of Indian meal, and half pint of flower — bake before the fire. Or scald with milk two thirds of the Indian meal, or wet two thirds with boiling water, add salt, molasses and shortening, work up with cold water pretty stiff and bake as above.
- A Facsimile of "American Cookery", by Amelia Simmons, 1796.

Ingredients:
1 cup/ 5.6oz/ 160g Small Milled Polenta or Cornmeal
1 cup/ 4.2oz/ 120g Plain Flour, or GF Plain Flour
1½ Tablespoons/ 0.76oz/ 22g Baking Powder
1 Tablespoon/ 0.45oz/ 13g Brown Sugar
¾ teaspoon/ 0.14oz/ 4g Salt
3 Eggs
1¼ cups/ 10fl.oz/ 296ml Milk, plant-based milks work well
2 Tablespoons/ 1flo.oz/ 30ml Lemon Juice
4 Tablespoons/ 2fl.oz/ 60ml Neutral Oil, or Butter, for frying

Whisk together the dry ingredients polenta, flour, baking powder, sugar and salt. Add in the eggs, milk and lemon juice stir gently until just combined.
To cook the griddle cakes, preheat a frying pan or griddle over medium heat. Oil generously and ladle spoonsful onto the oiled surface. Working with just a few at a time wait until the batter starts to bubble and brown at the edges, usually 2 to 3 minutes. Carefully turn the cakes over with a spatula and cook an additional 1 to 2 minutes. Repeat with the rest of the batter until all the hoecakes have been cooked.
Serve sweet with lots of butter, and your choice of Maple Syrup, Honey or Treacle.
Serve savoury with crisp bacon, jalapenos, and grated Cheddar cheese.

Contribution By: Sara Robinson

CRUMPETS

The earliest known 'Crompid cake' which described a cake or loaf of crusted cake, that John Wycliffe a theologian in Yorkshire, translated from Latin in the Old Testament in 1382. These were flatter cakes that would have resembled crepes or pancakes with no resemblance to the modern crumpet.
It was not until the Victorian era that those crumpets began to take their more modern appearance. This is due to the invention of Baking Powder in 1843, as well as the introduction of crumpet rings. Baking Powder gave lift to the batter and the rings allowed for a taller cake.
There is one final difference, crumpets that are not cooked in a ring are called Pikelets. Pikelets are tasty and just more free form in appearance.

Ingredients:
1 cup/ 5.3oz/ 150g Plain Flour
¾ cup plus 1½ Tablespoons/ 6.7fl.oz/ 200ml Water, room temperature
½ teaspoon/ 0.1oz/ 3g Salt
1 teaspoon/ 0.14oz/ 4g Sugar
1 teaspoon/ 0.14oz/ 4g Baking Powder
1 teaspoon/ 0.1oz/ 3g Dry Yeast

To make the batter:
In a small bowl bloom the yeast with a few spoonful of water. In a large bowl whisk together flour, water, and salt. If you do not use an electric mixer, keep whisking vigorously for at least 5 minutes. Tell yourself it is a good thing and you are building muscle that even the security section will be jealous of.
Add the sugar, the bloomed yeast and baking powder to the flour mixture. Keep mixing! Build those muscles! Keep going until the mixture is well combined.
Cover the mixture and place in a warm place to rise, at least 15 minutes. It will expand a lot!

To bake the crumpets:
Place a metal biscuit cutter, a crumpet ring, or egg ring (any shape will work!) into the centre of a frying pan. Preheat the ring and frying pan over medium heat. Using a large ice cream scoop or regular ladle, the battle ladle is too large for this job, fill the ring with about 60g or about 2/3 full.
The tell-tail bubbles will start to form; after about 4 minutes carefully lift the ring from the crumpet. If the top is still a bit squidgy turn it over and cook for a few seconds.
Don't give up, the first one is not always the prettiest.
Cool the crumpets, you really don't want to burn your tongue.
Repeat as above until you have used all the batter.
Toast and enjoy with butter, jam or topping of choice.

Makes 6 crumpets

Adapted from: Warburtons   Contribution By: Sara Robinson

Victoria Sponge

These amazing cakes that take equal parts eggs, flour and sugar are part of the teatime traditions that took England by storm in the 1800's. The cakes are a lot older than that with the first references in England dating to 1615, in the book *The English Huswife*. Following the cake further to Spain where it dates to the mid-renaissance era or maybe even older! There have been some changes to the recipe and the addition of baking powder, after it's invention in 1843, gave the cake more of a rise and a more consistent crumb. After baking, the cakes were sandwiched with Scottish raspberry jam, the queen's favourite, and dusted with icing sugar.

There is some academic debate over how the Victoria Sponge was included into the emerging teatime tradition. The original tea time inclusion was for fruit cake and seed cakes to be served with tea. This is great because both cakes are dense and can be stored easily. The bad thing is that people at the time thought these were not good or could be harmful for children. The light sponge of the Victoria Sponge may have been put together for the safety of the young princess and served to her at teatime. It wasn't until much later that the cake started to be served at the adult tea table.

Seed Cake

Ingredients:
¾ cup/ 6.1oz/ 175g Unsalted Butter, softened
¾ cup/ 6.1oz/ 175g Caster Sugar
3 Large Eggs, beaten
3 teaspoons/ 0.24oz/ 7g Caraway Seeds
1½ cups/ 8oz/ 225g Plain Flour
1 teaspoon/ 0.14oz/ 4g Baking Powder
Pinch Salt
1 Tablespoon/ 0.24oz/ 7g Ground Almonds
1 Tablespoon/ 0.5fl.oz/ 15ml Milk
1 teaspoon/ 0.07oz/ 2g Orange zest, optional
1 teaspoon/ 0.07oz/ 2g Dried Lavender Flowers, optional

Preheat the oven to 350 °F/ 180 °C (160°C fan)/ Gas Mark 4
Butter and line a 2-pound or large loaf tin with baking paper.

Place butter, sugar and eggs in a medium sized mixing bowl. Using a hand mixer or large spoon, cream together the ingredients until well combined and a pale yellow in colour.

In a separate bowl add the flour, salt, caraway seeds, baking powder, and zest and flowers if using. Whisk the ingredients together until well combined.

Add the dry ingredients to the wet ingredients and add the milk. Mix everything together and to combine the batter.

Smooth the top of the batter and place in the preheated oven for 50 to 55 minutes. The cake should bounce back easily when poked and a skewer placed in the middle should come out clean.

Allow to cool completely before removing from the tin.

Cut into thick slices to serve.
Store in an airtight container

Adapted from: English Heritage   Contribution By: Sara Robinson

Victoria Sponge

Queen Victoria was renowned for having a 'sweet-tooth' and kept the kitchens quite busy to satisfy her and others appetite for the fashionable sweets and cakes. The kitchens at Windsor Castle were busy all year round. No matter where the court was centred the kitchen would send cakes and sweets four times a week!

The royal children were taught to cook and bake at the Swiss Cottage or Osborne House among other adult skills that Prince Albert believed would help them to become great leaders. Queen Victoria's journal contains several references to taking tea at the Swiss Cottage, with the nine children's cooking being relished and consumed.
The journal doesn't always go into detail about what was eaten, but Victoria Sponge and Battenburg were most likely there.

Victoria Sponge

Ingredients:
14 Tablespoons/ 7oz/ 200g Unsalted Butter, softened
¾ cup/ 7oz/ 200g Caster Sugar
½ teaspoon/ 0.08fl.oz/ 2ml Vanilla Paste
4 Eggs, beaten
1½ cups/ 7oz/ 200g Self Raising Flour
1 teaspoon/ 0.17oz/ 5g Baking Powder
2 Tablespoon/ 1fl.oz/ 30ml Whole Milk
Butter, to grease the tins
7 Tablespoons/ 3.5oz/ 100g Unsalted Butter
1 cup/ 7oz/ 200g Icing Sugar, sifted
2 Tablespoons/ 1fl.oz/ 30ml Double Cream
½ teaspoon/ 0.08fl.oz/ 2ml Vanilla Paste
1 cup/ 12oz/ 340g Good Quality Scottish Raspberry Jam (strawberry will also work)
Icing sugar for dusting.

Preheat oven to 375 °F/ 190 °C (170°C fan)/ Gas Mark 5

Grease two 8 inch/ 20cm round sandwich/ cake tins and line the bases with parchment paper. In a large bowl, preferably using a stand mixer, beat the cream and sugar together until light and fluffy and almost doubled in size, scraping down the sides of the bowl occasionally. Add the beaten eggs, milk, and vanilla and mix well, again scraping the sides of the bowl. Sift the remaining ingredients in, and mix well, scraping the sides of the bowl, until you have a smooth batter. Divide the batter evenly between the two tins and smooth the batter with a spatula.

Bake for 20 to 35 minutes. Do not open the door to the oven during this time. The cakes will be done when they are a golden-brown colour and coming away from the edge of the tins. They should be springy to the touch. Remove from the oven and set aside to cool for 5 minutes in the tins. Run a knife or palette knife around the inside edge of the tins, and carefully remove the cakes to a cooling rack to cool completely.
In a clean mixing bowl, beat the butter until light and fluffy. Sift in the icing sugar, and slowly mix. If you are using a stand mixer, a tea towel covering it will help prevent the icing sugar from billowing everywhere! Pour in the double cream and vanilla and mix well.

Keep the best-looking cake for the top.

On the bottom layer, carefully spread the jam. You can thin it a bit with a little warm water, which will make it easier to spread. Carefully spread the buttercream on the bottom side of the top layer. Sandwich the two cakes together with the jam and buttercream in the middle. Dust with icing sugar and serve with a nice cup of tea.

You can find additional teatime treats in the Admin. Chapter.

Adapted from: BBC Good Food   Contribution By: Afton Cochran

CARROT FRITTERS

Original receipt: Beat 2 or 3 boiled carrots to a pulp with a spoon; add to them 6 eggs and a handful of flour; moisten them with either cream, milk, or white wine, and sweeten them. Beat all together well, and fry in boiling lard. When a good color, take them off and squeeze on them the juice of a Seville orange, and strew over with fine sugar.
The Cook's Own Book, Mrs. N.K.M. Lee, 1832

Historical receipts, or recipes, assumed a lot; such as the cook having enough experience that measurements were not necessary. Fortunately for our intrepid readers and historians, we have corrected those assumptions below, with two slightly more modern takes on this classic recipe; a sweet and a savory option made with the same base of tempura-like beer batter.

Basic Batter Ingredients:
½ cup/ 2.29oz/ 65g Cake Flour or Low Protein Plain Flour
¼ cup/ 1.37oz/ 39g Rice Flour
½ teaspoon/ 0.07oz/ 2g Bicarbonate Soda
1 Egg, well-beaten
2 Large or 3 Medium Carrots, cut into chunks
½ cup/ 4fl.oz/ 120ml Light-Coloured Beer or Ale, White Wine, or Milk
Oil for frying, such as peanut, canola/ rapeseed, or even fine lard. Must have a high smoke point.

Boil carrots in enough water to cover in a small saucepan until just soft. Rinse with cool water until carrots are lukewarm. Place in a mixing bowl and mash.
Add beaten egg. Stir. Add flours and bicarbonate. Stir to incorporate.
Add liquid. Stir to make a batter.
Continue with ingredients and instructions for sweet or savory fritters.
Basic frying instructions:
Heat ½" of oil in a frying pan or skillet on high heat until quite hot. Test by dropping a small amount of batter into the oil. It should sizzle and rise immediately to the top of the oil, browning at the edges. Remove test dough and discard.
Carefully add a spoonful of batter to the skillet, using the back of the spoon to spread it thin. Repeat, spacing the fritters about an inch apart. The fritters should quickly fry to a rich, golden brown colour on one side; carefully turn the fritters and cook until golden brown on the other side. Remove to a plate with paper toweling to drain. Work quickly to fry up the rest of the fritters. Serve hot.

Sweet Carrot Fritters
Ingredients (add to basic batter):
1 Tablespoon/ 0.45oz/ 13g Sugar
1 Orange, zested and ½ juiced
1/8 teaspoon/ 0.008oz/ >1g Ground Nutmeg
1/8 teaspoon/ 0.008oz/ >1g Ground Clove
½ teaspoon/ 0.03oz/ 1g Ground Ginger
½ teaspoon/ 0.03oz/ 1g Ground Cinnamon

Add ingredients to the Basic Batter and stir to incorporate.
Continue with the basic frying instructions. After draining, a sifting of powdered sugar on the fritters is an attractive option. Serve while hot.

Savoury Carrot Fritters
Ingredients (add to basic batter, above):
½ teaspoon/ 0.11oz/ 3g Salt
Ground Black Pepper, to taste
1 Clove Garlic, minced
1 Shallot or ½ Small Onion, minced
½ teaspoon/ 0.07oz/ 2g Ground Ginger
1 teaspoon/ 0.07oz/ 2g Ground Cumin
2 Tablespoons/ 0.38oz/ 11g Grated Parmesan or Asiago cheese

Add ingredients to the Basic Batter and stir to incorporate.
Continue with basic frying instructions.
Garnish with minced parsley, herbs, or green scallion tops and serve up hot.

Photo and Contribution By: Merry Schepers

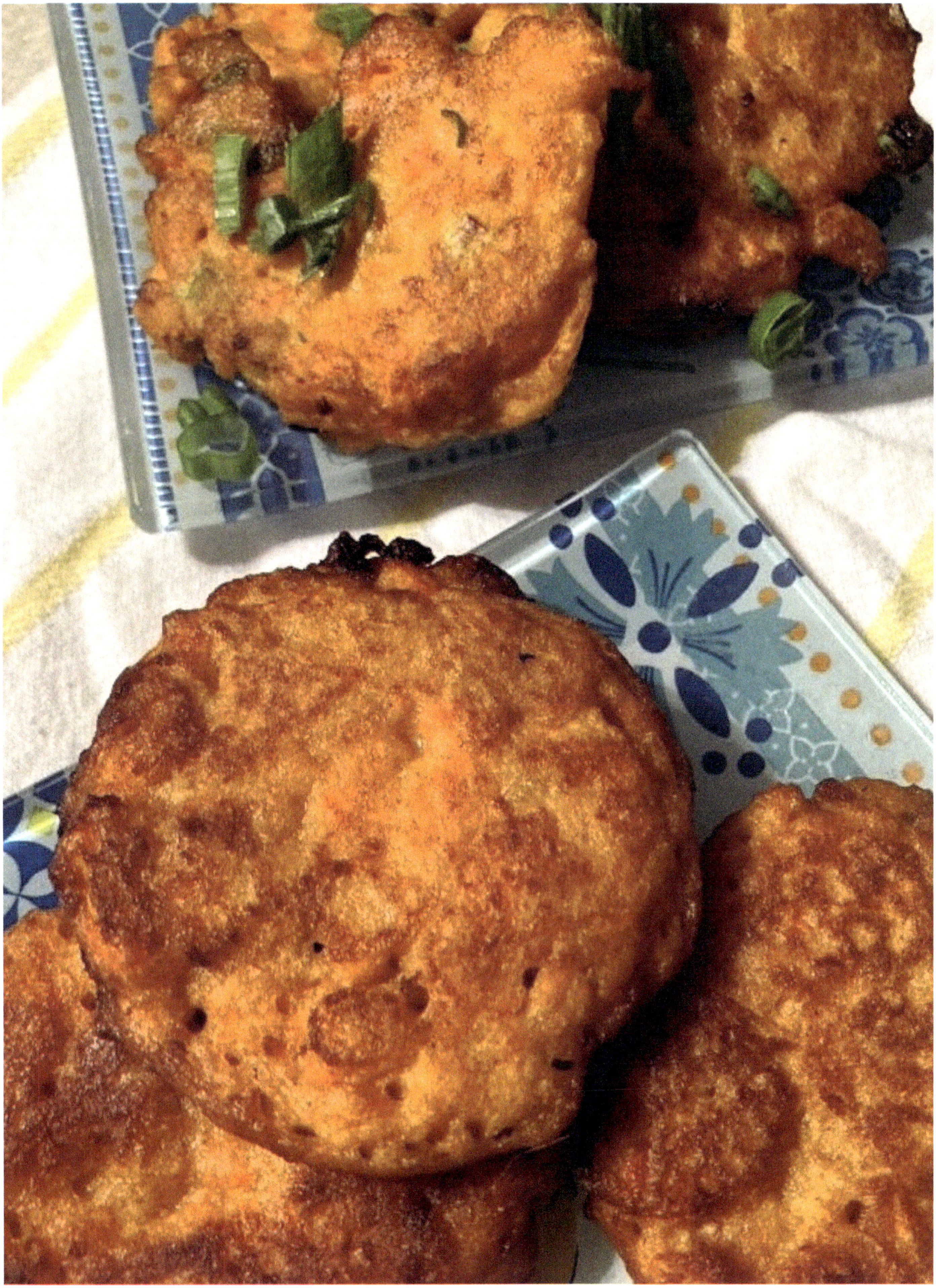

Upside Down Cakes

Cakes as we know them today are a very recent invention. There are many ideas on why this change happened; but lack of sugar, lack of raising agents such as bicarbonate of soda and improvements in oven design are listed high on the list for catalysts for changes in cakes. Honey Cakes were part of the diet in the middle east with the Ancient Egyptians eating a sweetened yeasted dough and early Romans baked barley loaves with honey, raisins, pine nuts and pomegranate seeds. By the 11th century a dense honey cake was being made in central Italy, this is thought to have spread across Europe and to have been the predecessor of gingerbread, and lebkuchen.

Honey Cake

Ingredients:
- 1 ½ cups/ 7.6oz/ 218g Plain Flour
- 1 ½ cups/ 7.6oz/ 218g Wholemeal Flour
- 1 cup/ 8fl.oz/ 237ml Honey
- ½ cup/ 4oz/ 113g Fat, such as Butter
- ½ cup/ 4fl.oz/ 118ml Single Cream

Preheat oven to 350 °F/ 180 °C/ Gas Mark 4
Line a 9 inch tin with baking parchment.
Mix warmed honey, melted butter and milk. Slowly fold in the flours until it is well combined. The dough will be very thick and closer to shortbread then modern cake batters.
Press or spread the batter across the bottom of the tin. Bake in the preheated oven for 30 to 35 minutes.
The cake is best when served warm.

Skillet cakes have been around and popular since the middle ages. These cakes did not use pineapple but rather apples, pears, cherries or some other local seasonal fruit.

Pear and Ginger Skillet Cake

Ingredients:
To prepare the tin:
- 1 Tablespoon/ 0.5oz/ 15g Butter
- 1 teaspoon/ 0.16fl.oz/ 5ml Vegetable Oil
- ¼ cup/ 1.7oz/ 50g Brown Sugar
- 2 to 3 pieces of Crystalized Ginger, sliced thinly
- 3 to 4 Pears, ripe and each sliced into eight pieces

For the cake:
- ¾ cup/ 6fl.oz/ 180 Stout Beer
- 1 teaspoon/ 0.17oz/ 5g Bicarbonate of Soda
- 2/3 cup/ 5.3fl.oz/ 158ml Dark Treacle
- ¾ cup/ 5.2oz/ 150g Brown Sugar
- 1 ½ cup/ 7.6oz/ 217g Plain Flour
- 2 Tablespoons/ 0.42oz/ 12g Gingerbread Spice (recipe in R&D)
- ½ teaspoon/ 0.07oz/ 2g Baking Powder
- 2 Eggs
- 1/3 cup/ 2.6fl.oz/ 78ml Vegetable Oil
- 1 Tablespoon/ 1 inch/ 2.5cm Ginger, freshly grated (optional)

Preheat the oven to 350 °F/ 180 °C (170°C fan)/ Gas Mark 4
Heat the butter and vegetable oil in an 8inch/ 20cm cast iron skillet/frying pan or cake tin just until butter melts. Add ¼ cup of brown sugar to the bottom of the pan making sure to evenly spread the sugar and butter. Core and peel 3 to 4 pears, and slicing each fruit into eight pieces. Arrange pear slices in spiral on top of the butter and sugar mixture. Slice the crystallized ginger very finely. Arrange thin slices of crystalized ginger in between the pear slices. Set to the side to cool.
In a saucepan bring the stout beer to a boil, immediately remove from the heat, and add the bicarbonate of soda to the beer. To this, add the dark treacle and brown sugar, stirring until combined and the sugar has melted into the beer. Set aside to cool.
In a large mixing bowl whisk together flour, spice and baking powder.
Once the beer and sugar mixture has cooled to the touch add the eggs, oil and freshly grated ginger, stirring to combine. Take care, if your beer mixture is too hot it will cook the eggs and will mean you will have to start over.
Slowly mix the beer mixture into your prepared dry ingredients until well combined.
Carefully pour the mixture over the pears and sugar in your pan. Bake in the oven for 35 to 45 minutes, or until a skewer poked into the middle comes out clean. Cool for 10 minutes then run a knife between the cake and pan to make sure it is not stuck. Place a large plate on top of your pan and very gently turn the pan and plate over keeping them together. This should allowing the cake to release and come away from the pan. Use extreme caution when doing this so you or those around you are not burnt or hurt.

Photo and Contribution By: Sara Robinson

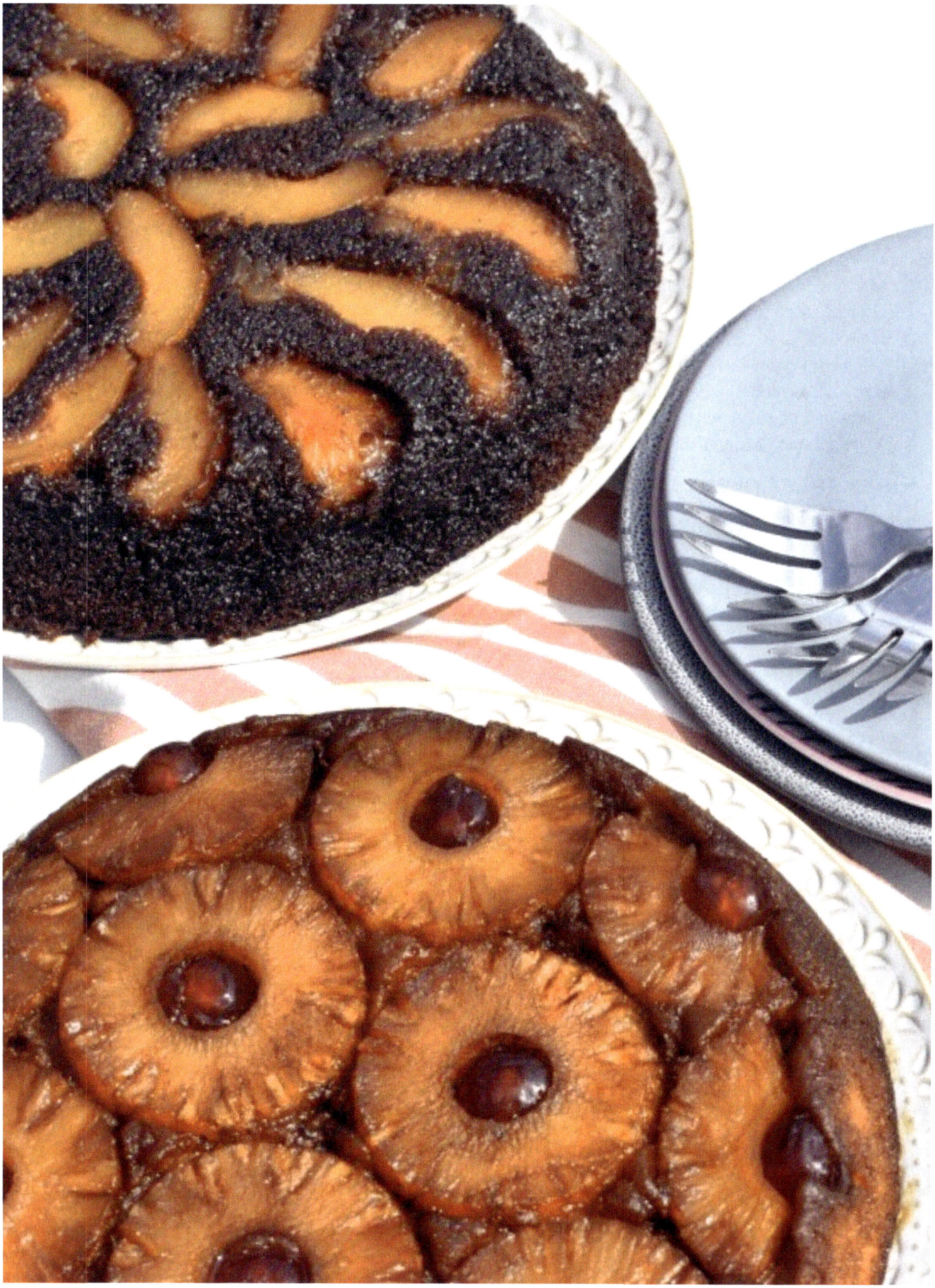

Upside Down Cakes

The skillet cakes were not generally cooked in an oven but rather with directional heat much like how a hob works today. Because of the layer of a sturdy fruit on the bottom with additional fats and sometimes sugar or honey, these cakes were less likely to burn and stick to the pan making them an ideal treat.

It wasn't until the 1800's that the skillet cake was starting to be referred to as an upside-down cake, where the beautiful arrangement of fruit on the bottom of the cake as it baked and then became the top of the cake when served. It wasn't until the 1910's that we started to see Pineapple upside down cakes. This does not mean that Pineapple was not used because pineapples were known in England from the mid-sixteenth century and were grown in hot houses. Pineapple was not the norm and it did not have the same success until the Hawaiian Pineapple Company began to manufacture sliced rings of pineapple in syrup in 1901. These beautifully coloured slices in tins were shipped worldwide. It was not until 1925 that the cake's popularity began to pick up with radio programs, newspapers, and magazines sporting recipes for Pineapple Upside Down Cake, and by 1950 it was well intrenched in culinary heritage.

Pineapple Upside Down Cake

Traditional Ingredients:
To make the upside:
¼ cup/ 2oz/ 57g Butter, vegan butters also work
½ cup/ 3.5oz/ 100g Brown Sugar
1 teaspoon/ 0.16fl.oz/ 5ml Vanilla Extract
8 Pineapple Rings, tinned is fine
15 Glacé Cherries
To make the cakey downside:
½ cup/ 3.5oz/ 100g Brown Sugar
¼ cup/ 2oz/ 57g White Sugar
½ teaspoon/ 0.07oz/ 2g Salt
1 ½ teaspoons/ 0.1oz/ 3g Baking Powder
1 ½ cups Plain Flour
1/2 cup Greek Yogurt
1 teaspoon/ 0.16fl.oz/ 5ml Vanilla Extract
½ cup/ 4fl.oz/ 118ml Milk, plant milks work well
2 Eggs
¼ cup/ 2oz/ 57g Butter, melted, vegan butters also work

Gluten Free Ingredients:
To make the upside:
¼ cup/ 2oz/ 57g Butter, vegan butters also work
½ cup/ 3.5oz/ 100g Brown Sugar
1 teaspoon/ 0.16fl.oz/ 5ml Vanilla Extract
8 Pineapple Rings, tinned is fine
15 Glacé Cherries
To make the cakey downside:
1 ¼ cups/ 5.3oz/ 153g Plain or Buckwheat Gluten Free Flour
2 Tablespoon/ 0.5oz/ 15g Cornflour
½ cup/ 3.5oz/ 100g Brown Sugar
¼ cup/ 2oz/ 57g White Sugar
1 teaspoon/ 0.01oz/ 3g Xanthan Gum
1 ½ teaspoons/ 0.1oz/ 3g Baking Powder
½ teaspoon/ 0.07oz/ 2g Salt
½ cup/ 4fl.oz/ 118ml Milk, plant milks work well
1 teaspoon/ 0.16fl.oz/ 5ml Vanilla Extract
3 Eggs
1/3 cup/ 2.7oz/ 76g Butter, melted, vegan butters also work

Preheat your oven to 350 °F/ 180 °C (160°C fan)/ Gas Mark 4

In a 10 inch/ 25cm cast iron frying pan melt your butter over medium heat. Remove from the heat promptly to not brown the butter, stir in brown sugar and vanilla. Return to the heat for a short time to melt the sugar. Evenly spread the mixture across the bottom and let cool slightly before arranging the pineapple and cherries on top of the melted brown sugar.

In a separate large bowl whisk together the flour, sugars, (xanthan gum), baking powder and salt. In a small bowl whisk together the wet ingredients milk, vanilla and eggs. Add the wet ingredients into the dry and give a quick stir, then slowly start adding the melted butter into the mixture. Whisk until well combined and few lumps remain.

Carefully pour the batter over the pineapple so as not to move the slices around. Let the cake rest for 10 to 15 minutes, then place in a preheated oven to bake for 40 to 45 minutes, until the cake bounces back when poked and a skewer placed in the centre of the cake comes out clean.

Let the cake cool for 15 to 20 minutes before running a spatula or knife around the inside of the tin. Place a plate on top of the frying pan and very carefully flip the cake over. Be exceedingly careful when doing this to prevent burns. Sometimes pineapple rings may stick to the bottom of the pan, this is normal and gently lift them out of the pan and replace them in the top of the cake.

Contribution By: Sara Robinson

TARTA DE SANTIAGO

The Santiago Di Compostela pilgrimage route is in the north-west of modern-day Spain and dates back to the 9th century C.E. In the 14th century the pilgrimage route began to decay due to war, epidemics and natural disasters. This route saw a resurgence in the 19th century and continues as a backpacking route today.
There is some academic debate as to whether the pilgrims that followed the route of 'St. James' were given this to sustain them through the gruelling journey, or if they brought it as an offering to the cathedral.
Traditionally the most pious did this pilgrimage on their knees, so we really hope that they were given this amazing cake to sustain them.

Ingredients:
2 ½ cups/ 8.8oz/ 250g Almond meal/ground
6 Large Eggs, separated
1 cup/ 7oz/ 200g Caster Sugar
1 teaspoon/ 0.07oz/ 2g Cinnamon (optional or use more)
Pinch Fine Sea Salt
Icing Sugar, to dust
Butter, to grease the tin

Preheat oven to 180/350/Gas 4
Grease and line with parchment paper a 24cm spring form tin.

To start place the egg whites and pinch of salt in a clean grease free bowl and whisk to soft peaks. Continue whisking as you gradually add half of the sugar to the egg whites, a tablespoon at a time. In a separate bowl whisk the egg yolks with the remaining sugar and cinnamon until thick and very pale in colour as well as an increased in volume from incorporating air into the mixture. Gently fold the ground almonds into the yolk mix. Then gently fold about 1/3 of the whipped egg whites into the nut/yolk mix into to loosen it. Then gently fold almond/yolk mixture into the remaining whipped egg whites mixture.

Spoon the mixture into the prepared baking tin. Bake in a preheated oven for around 35 minutes. Keep an eye on the cooking time as it can brown quickly. If it is getting too brown, cover with greaseproof paper for a further 10 minutes. Remove from the oven and cool in the tin for 10 minutes, then turn out on a rack to cool.
Dust with icing sugar to serve.

Note: Traditionally there is a stylized cross in the icing sugar across the top. If it is not included this does not affect the taste of the gorgeous cake.

Contribution By: Sara McKenna

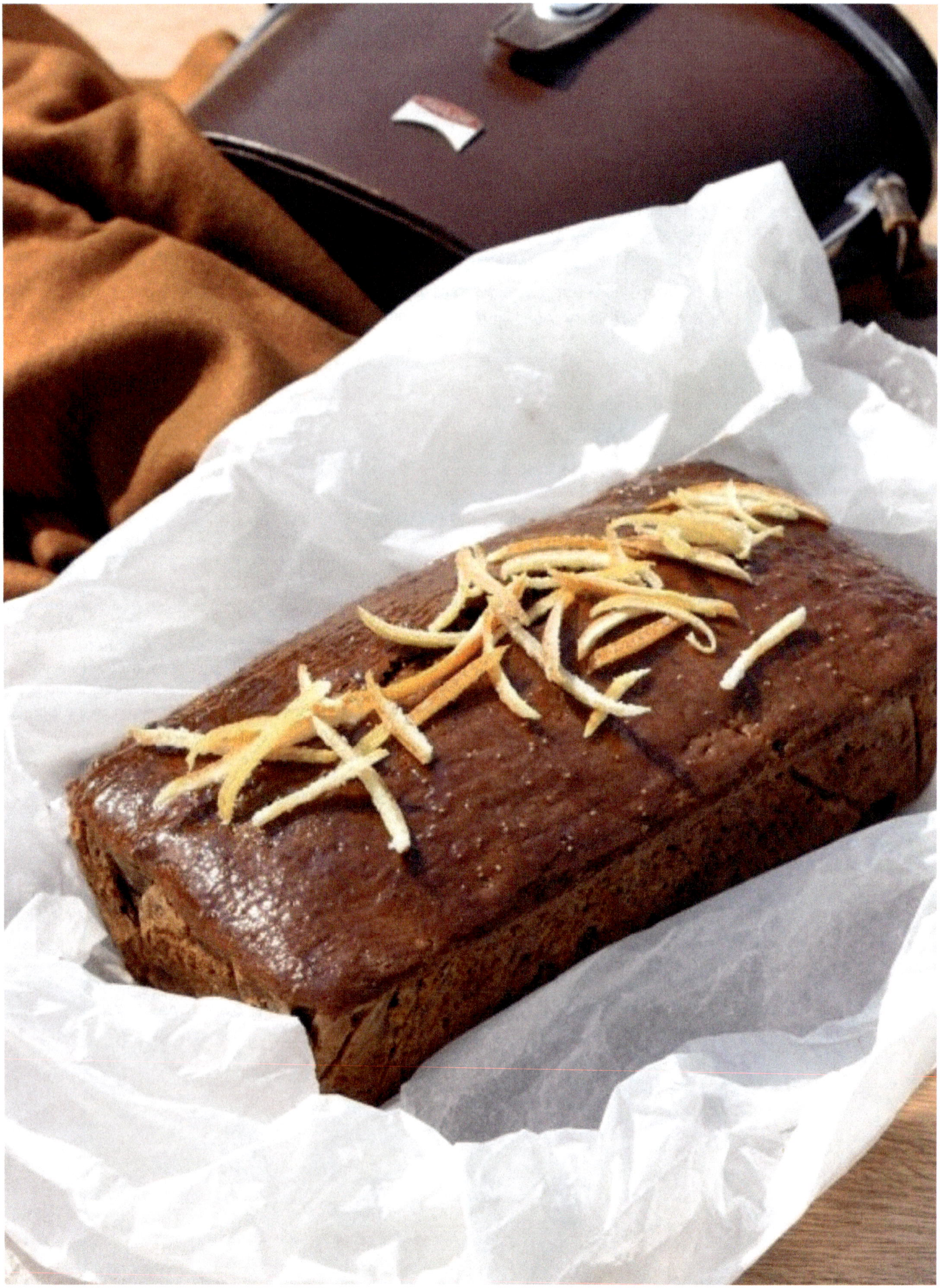

LOAF IN THE TIME OF CABLE STREET

The Battle of Cable Street was an event that took place in the east end of London on Sunday 4 October 1936. It started with a protest march lead by the British Union of Fascists and the Metropolitan Police were sent to protect the marchers and quell violence. The counter protesters comprised trade unions, communists, British Jews, Irish dock workers, socialists and anti-fascist groups, who built barricades to prevent the march from taking place. Marchers and police tried to clear streets, and were met by opposition hurling rotten vegetables, rubbish and brandishing makeshift weapons. Police were rained with contents of chamber pots and eventually convinced the marchers to disband as the anti-fascists continued to 'riot'. There were 150 anti-fascist protesters arrested and 175 people were injured. Not a single Fascist was arrested. This event is pointed to as when British Fascism was defeated.

Mrs McKenna from the Kitchen Department hurried into Hawking's with a small string bag holding a small item, wrapped in greaseproof paper and tied with string. "Rachel!" she shouted. "Rachel, wait! I heard you're off to Cable Street, to see the fascists being kicked out, so I thought you'd better have this."

Rachel took the string bag, and to her surprise, nearly dislocated her shoulder. How odd, she mused. The package is tiny, yet it's incredibly heavy! "Thanks, Mrs McKenna. What is it?"

"Well, you're going to 1936, and the East End was a really impoverished area. They were Make Do and Mending before it was fashionable - plus tea will be in short supply," said Mrs McKenna breathlessly. "And you're going to be seeing those fascists in the flesh...." Mrs McKenna grimaced, and added "So I've made you a tea bread!"

Rachel remembered Mrs McKenna's 'strong views' on fascists, so she knew that there was something important going on here. "It's food?!" Rachel swung the bag experimentally. "Why is it so heavy?"

"It's an old recipe, for them that don't have much." Mrs McKenna grinned with pleasure.

"Oh, I see. No, wait, I don't see! What's the date of the recipe got to do with it's heft-factor?"

"Well, you see, Rachel, when you're skint, you're effectively on rations." Mrs McKenna clarified. "Butter is really expensive, so this loaf is made with tea instead of butter!" Mrs McKenna nodded with the satisfaction of a good explanation, well explained.

"Ah, that makes sense." Rachel turned towards the pod. She stopped. "No, wait, it still doesn't explain the fact that this tiny package has the gravitational pull of a small moon."

"Poor people's recipe, Rachel. Poor people standing up for what's right!"

Rachel waited.

"It's delicious and nutritious, and it keeps really well."

"And the weight, Mrs Mack?" Rachel raised an eyebrow.

"Well, it's pretty much just solid fruit. And when you're facing off against fascists, it's always good to have a tea loaf on hand. You see, if you don't have time to eat it, you can just throw it at Mosley's head!"

"Food that doubles as a weapon? That's absolutely perfect!"

TEA LOAF

Ingredients:
1 1/4 cups/ 10fl.oz/ 300ml Strongly Brewed Tea
2 ¼ cups/ 17.6oz/ 500g mixed dried fruit
1 Egg, beaten
1/2 cup plus 2 Tablespoons/ 4.4oz/ 125g Brown Sugar
2 cups/ 8.8oz/ 250g Self Raising Flour
2 teaspoons/ 0.3oz/ 8g Mixed Spice or Apple Pie Spice

Make the strongly brewed tea and remove the tea bags. Add the mixed dried fruit to steep for at least 2 hours or better if left overnight.

Stir in the beaten egg, then mix in brown sugar, self raising flour and mixed spice. Pour mixture into a lined loaf tin and bake for an hour at 350°F/ 180°C/ Gas Mark 4. Cool in the tin for a bit, then on a wire rack. Wrap in greaseproof to "stodge up" for a day.

Serve with butter or on it's own, with tea, obviously.

To finish melt a little marmalade or apricot jam for a glaze and add some homemade candied peel on top.

Photo by: Sara Robinson　　　Story and Recipe Contribution By: Sara McKenna

Lemon Ketchup

Ketchup is an amazingly old dish that dates to 300BCE in China. The original sauce was not made from tomatoes but rather fish entrails and soybeans that were fermented. The love of the condiment was brought back by the English in the 1700's and experimenting to make the sauce ended with some interesting results.

The first recipes for ketchup included such things as oysters, mussels, mushrooms, pickled walnuts, lemons and many other types of fruit. Some of these recipes were quite fanciful in their writing with one calling for over 100 oysters, while others such as the "Prince of Wales" ketchup, combined elder berries and anchovies.

It was not until 1812 that a recipe for tomato ketchup was first published by James Mease in his book "Archives of Useful Knowledge, vol.2." He didn't refer to it as tomato but rather the colloquial 'love apples'. The 1800's also saw the rise of commercially made ketchups, and is a good reason why we have health and safety today. Some producers handled things poorly, resulting in food born illnesses, but others used such things as coal tar as a preservative. It is no wonder Pierre Blot called commercial ketchup, "filthy" in his cookbook in 1866.

It wouldn't be until 1876 when Dr. Harvey Washinton Wiley and Henry J Heinz started their production of ketchup, that the industry started to take off and recipes for ketchup started to disappear from cookbooks.

If you would like to try additional ketchup recipes, a recipe for Mushroom Ketchup is located in the R&D Chapter. Mushroom ketchup is known to be a favourite of Jane Austen.

Ingredients:
12 Lemons, zested and juiced
4 Tablespoons/ 1.5oz/ 44g White Mustard Seeds
2 teaspoons/ 0.21oz/ 6g Turmeric
1 Tablespoon/ 0.1oz/ 3g White Pepper
1 teaspoon/ 0.07oz/ 2g Ground Cloves
1 teaspoon/ 0.07oz/ 2g Ground Mace
2 Tablespoons/ 0.88oz/ 25g White Sugar
2 Tablespoons/ 1.1oz/ 34g Salt
1 to 3 Tablespoons/ 0.5 to 1.5oz/ 15 to 45g Fresh Horseradish, grated
1 teaspoon/ 0.07oz/ 2g Cayenne Pepper
1 Shallot, finely sliced or minced

Place all ingredients into a saucepan and let sit for 3 hours to infuse. Bring to a simmer and reduce heat. Simmer for 30 minutes, stirring occasionally. Remove from heat and allow to cool. Place in lidded jar or fermenting crock and leave for 2 weeks, stirring daily. Remove to a blender and blend until smooth, then pour into sterile containers. Place a small layer of oil on the top, and seal.

This Lemon Ketchup is amazing with meat and cheese in a Ploughman's lunch or is simply delicious in a cheese toastie.
This ketchup is not for the faint hearted as the horseradish can be quite strong.

Original Recipe from The Dominion Cookbook– 1899   Photo and Contribution By: Afton Cochran

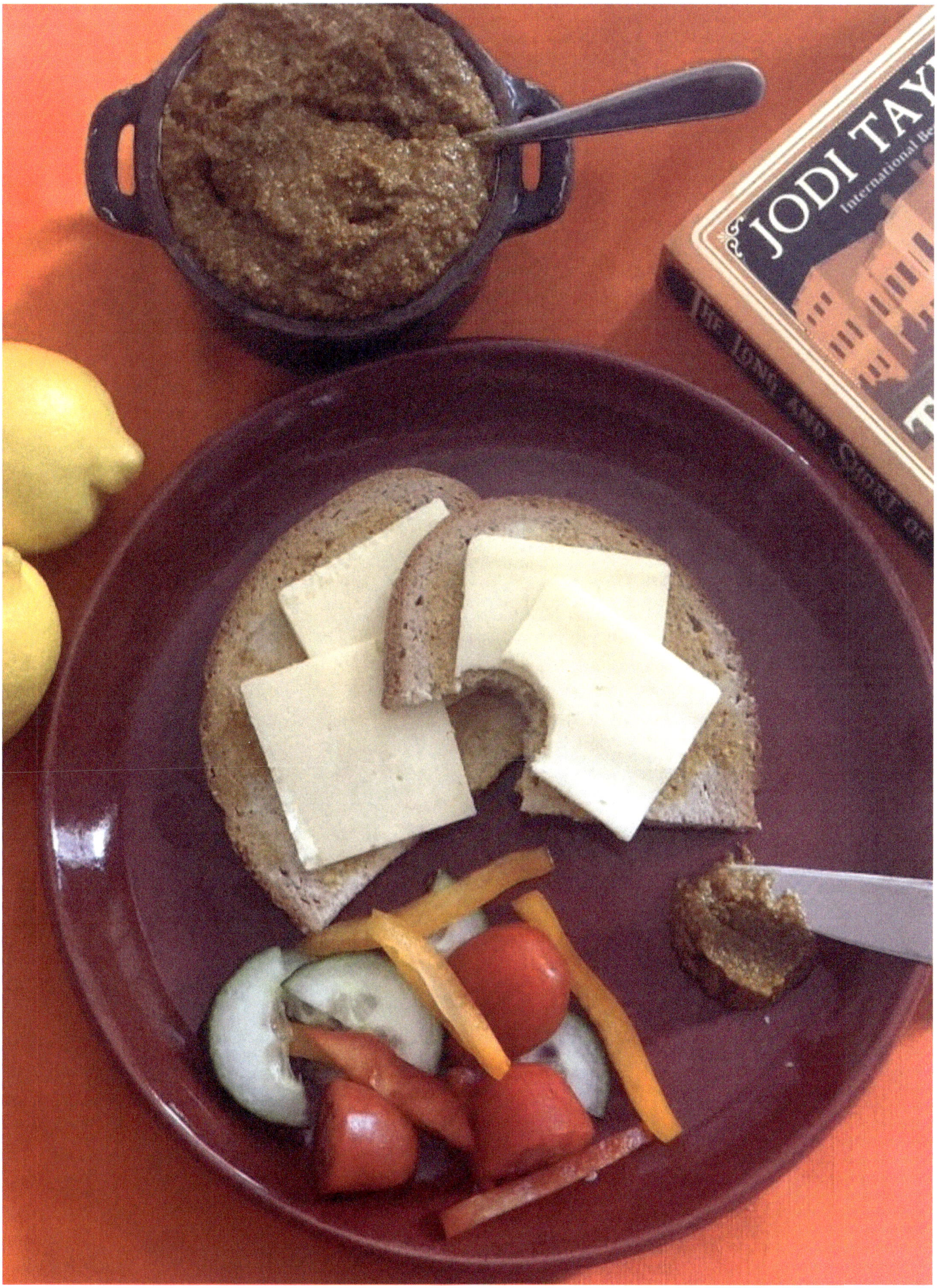
JODI TAY

Cheese Toasty/Grilled Cheese

Cheese Toasties or Grilled Cheese are one of the easiest and most satisfying things to make, as well as there being endless possibilities for customisation.

In finding the origins of this recipe we have looked far and wide. We found that the idea of combining cheese and bread have been enjoyed since at least Roman times. This does not mean that it was a cheese toastie, but it was the beginning of the idea for this amazing dish. In 1762, the cook for John Montagu, the 4th Earl of Sandwich, may have created the first official sandwich, but it was not a toasted sandwich.

So where did the recipe come from?

There were several other things that helped catapult this sandwich into the diet of so many people. In 1927 Otto Frederick Rohwedder designed a machine that would slice full loaves of bread, and by 1933 bakeries were selling more sliced bread then unsliced.

In 1916, James Kraft patented his processed cheese that was shelf stable and made excellent grilled cheese. Then there was also the travesty of World War II. One part of the war that was not a travesty was that many ideas were shared across cultures and were shared and reshared across the world. Grilled cheese or cheese toasties could be made with very few resources, so they were ideal for a quick, warm and filling meal.

Back to tracking the origins of the cheese toasty. A melted cheese sandwich made its debut in 1902 as part of the 'Mrs. Rorer's New Cookbook,' by Sarah Tyson Rorer. Another toasted cheese sandwich was the Croque Monsieur, which started to be found on menus in France starting in 1910. This is not the same, as there is ham and a bechamel-like sauce as well as two layers of cheese, but it is close.

(You can find a Croque Monsieur recipe in the Security Section's Chapter.)

During the depression of the 1930's the sandwich gained more favouritism by being cost effective and very filling.

By the time of World War II grilled cheese was a staple part in the cookbooks issued to US Navy chefs. Soldiers brought the knowledge of the sandwiches that they ate home with them and by 1950 it was part of the American and British diet.

Cheese Toastie/Grilled Cheese

Ingredients:
8 Thick Bread Slices, use your favourite
5 Tablespoons/ 2.5fl.oz/ 75ml Butter
12 Slices/ 13oz/ 360g Cheese, choose one or more cheeses

Any Extras: Bacon, Jalapenos, Sliced Chicken Breasts, Spinach, Roasted Peppers, Caramelised Onions, Tomatoes, Artichoke Hearts and so much more

Preheat oven to 425 °F/ 220 °C (200°C fan)/ Gas Mark 7
Slice the butter and place it on a rimmed baking sheet. Bake the butter 3 to 5 minutes or until the butter melts. Arrange the bread slices in a single layer on the baking sheet on top of the melted butter. Place one slice of cheese on each of the bread slices. Return the baking sheet to the oven for 5 minutes or until the cheese is melting and the bread has just begun to toast. Remove from the oven. Add any extras to half of the bread slices and assemble the sandwich using one slice of bread with one slice of cheese being sandwiched another slice of bread with one slice of cheese with any added extras being trapped in the middle. Replace the pan with the sandwiches to the oven for an additional 3 minutes.
Serve immediately.
Makes 4 sandwiches

Contribution By: Sara Robinson

Shooters Sandwich

Shooters sandwiches were created during the Edwardian era, 1901 to 1910, in England. It was meant as a way for a hearty meal to be had while out hunting, stalking, or shooting. While in the U.S. hunting is an all-encompassing term, there are distinct differences in the U.K. The term 'hunting' in the U.K generally refers to the hunting of foxes with the assistance of hounds. The term 'stalking' in the U.K. generally refers to deer stalking.
'Shooting' in the U.K. refers to the hunting of game birds but can also be used when referring to clay pigeon shooting and target shooting.
Shooting, hunting and stalking have long been the pass times of the rich and the aristocracy. Shooting changed in the latter part of the 1800's with the improvements to shotgun technology and the relaxation of game laws in 1831.
This relaxation meant that the wider public could obtain permits to shoot game birds, but as is still observed today, doing so without the landowner's permission is considered poaching.

Ingredients:
18oz/ 500g Mixed Mushrooms, Shiitake, Oyster, Chestnut, Porcini
7oz/ 200g Shallots, minced
2 Cloves Garlic, crushed and minced
1 Tablespoon Fresh Thyme Leaves
5 Tablespoons/ 2.5oz/ 75g Butter
2 Tablespoons/ 1fl.oz/ 30ml Brandy (optional)
1 teaspoon/ 0.16fl.oz/ 5ml Worcestershire Sauce (recipe in R&D)
2 Tablespoons/ 1fl.oz/ 30ml Double Cream
Salt and Pepper, to taste
2 Thick-cut Ribeye Steaks, evenly sized, with a good marbling of fat throughout
1 Round Crusty Bread Loaf, at least 8 inches/ 20cm in size
2 to 3 Tablespoons/ 1 to 1.5fl.oz/ 30 to 45ml Dijon Mustard, or Horseradish Sauce
0.75 to 1oz/ 20 to 30g Rocket/ Arugula, optional

Cut the top quarter off the crusty loaf and scoop out the soft middle bread, leaving the crust intact. You can save it for breadcrumbs or give it to any young disaster magnets nagging you to feed them. Leave the bread of the lid intact. Heat the butter in a frying pan and add the mushrooms. Fry until they have released their liquid, and it has been reabsorbed. Add the shallot, garlic, thyme, and a bit of salt and pepper and cook until the shallot is soft and translucent. Add the brandy and Worcestershire sauce and scrape up any brown bits off the bottom. Add the cream and reduce until thick. Your steaks can be seasoned and cooked the way you like. You can grill, BBQ, fry, or reverse sear them, the latter being preferable. Ideally you want a nice crust on the outside with the middle nice and pink. Spread the inside of the bread bowl with 1 to 2 Tablespoons/ 0.5 to 1fl.oz/ 15 to 30ml of the Dijon or horseradish. Place 1/3 of the mushroom mixture on top of the Dijon and then a bit of rocket, if you are using it. Then add a steak, 1/3 more mushrooms and more rocket, if using. Add another steak, a bit more rocket and the remainder of the mushroom mixture. Pour any remaining steak or mushroom juices on the top of the mushrooms. Spread a bit more Dijon on the inside of the lid and place the lid back on the bread. Wrap the bread in baking parchment and tie up like a parcel with the twine. Wrap in two layers of foil, place on a baking sheet with a cutting board on top of the sandwich. Weigh it down with heavy objects, such as books, tins, or small children. Place in a cool spot, but not in the refrigerator. Leave for 6 hours or overnight. When serving, cut into wedges like you would a cake. Serve with cheese and piccalilli (see R&D for a recipe).
Serves 6

Adapted from: 2 Fat Ladies, Tim Howard, and J Kenji Lopez-Alt   Contribution By: Afton Cochran

Cowboy Stew

Cowboys are icons and well known from books and stories to moving pictures. Few people know that Florida was the first area in the US to have cowboys. Cattle were being raised by the Spanish around Florida by the mid 1500's. These cowboys predated the ones in the American West by 350 years.

This recipe is what cowboys might have eaten around the campfire even into the 1800's.

Ingredients:
2 ½lbs/ 1.3kg Beef Mince
2 cups/ 14oz/ 400g Tomatoes, diced
4 cups/ 19oz/ 558g Potatoes, thickly cubed
3 Carrots, thickly cut
1 ½ cups/ 8.8oz/ 250g Peas
1 ½ cups/ 8.8oz/ 250g Sweet Corn
1 teaspoon/ 0.17oz/ 5g Salt
½ teaspoon/ 0.07oz/ 2g Black Pepper

Over medium to medium high heat, brown the beef mince in a large heavy bottomed pan. Do not drain any juices or oils from the pan. Add salt, pepper, and diced tomatoes. Reduce the heat to medium and cook for 10 minutes stirring often. Add potatoes and carrots. Cook for another 10 minutes, stirring frequently. Add peas and sweet corn and cook a further 10 minutes, or until the potatoes and carrots are well cooked and softened, stirring often.

Serves 6 and reheats very well.

Contribution By: Ann Morris

Nettle Soup

Not necessarily a long time historical recipe, but one that is immensely important to learn and may actually save your life on the dreaded outdoor survival exercise.

Ingredients:
3 ½ cups/ 28fl.oz/ 828ml Chicken Stock
¼ cup/ 1.7oz/ 50g Pearl Barley
1/3 cup/ 0.1oz/ 3g Nettles
Salt and Black Pepper to taste

Nettles are not your friend. When you are on the dreaded survival exercise you will need to gather young nettles from the high part of the wall where they are clean. Young nettles are less likely to have stingers, but you still need to be careful. Wash the tops in salted water and then chop or rip them very finely. Hopefully you listened to the security section and can start a fire. Place your soup pot in the fire and add the stock and barley. When the stock is boiling add the nettles, and simmer until they are tender and season to taste.

It is advised that you practice this recipe before it is needed. We really do not want you to poison yourself! As an added incentive while you are practicing the soup can be thickened with a little mashed potato, but that probably won't be available when you are dropped off in the middle of no where.
Good Luck!

(Adapted from the SWRI 1945 to 1971 cookbook)   Contribution By: Jane Oswald Ryan

Chapter Four:
The Kitchen Department
Or
Feeding the Ever Hungry Hordes
or
Comfort Foods

We are the Kitchen Department. We offer food every day of the year and the kitchens never close. We serve everyone from the Boss and the Admin. Department to the grounds keepers. We order the carrots that are used to tempt Turk into behaving, help the technical section with bacon rolls and pod restocking, serve delectable meals when we need to mend fences with the Parish Council and so much more. The hungry hordes never ever end and we triumph everyday against them.

Recipes:

Breakfast at St Mary's   56 to 61
   Perfect Porridge, Cooked Breakfast, Potato Scones, Bacon Butty, Overnight Oats, Muffins, Pancakes

Soup and Sandwiches   62 to 71
   Soups: Slow Cooker Ham and Lentil Soup, Mud Soup, Creamy Vegetable Soup, Cullen Skink, Tortellini Sausage Soup with Spinach, Mushroom Stew, White Bean and Orzo Soup, Brown Stock or Bone Broth, Cool as a Cucumber Soup, Leek and Potato Soup, Chunky Chicken and Noodles
   Sandwiches: Brioche Rolls, Cheese Puffs, Polenta Muffins, Sweet Potato Cheddar Scones, Cheese and Caramelized Onion Scones, Sandwich Fillings, Po' Boy

Swiss Beef and **Chorizo Orzotto**   72
Sausage Pasta and **Chicken and Rice Dish**   73
Just One Damn Casserole After Another   75
Fish Pie   76
Chicken and Vegetable Pie   78
Beef Stroganoff   81
Spicy Lamb Meatballs   82
Lancashire Hotpot   84
Big Murdoch Pie   85
Sausage and Bean Casserole   85
Nidi di Rondine   87
Toad in the Hole   88
Sunday Roast and sides   89 to 92

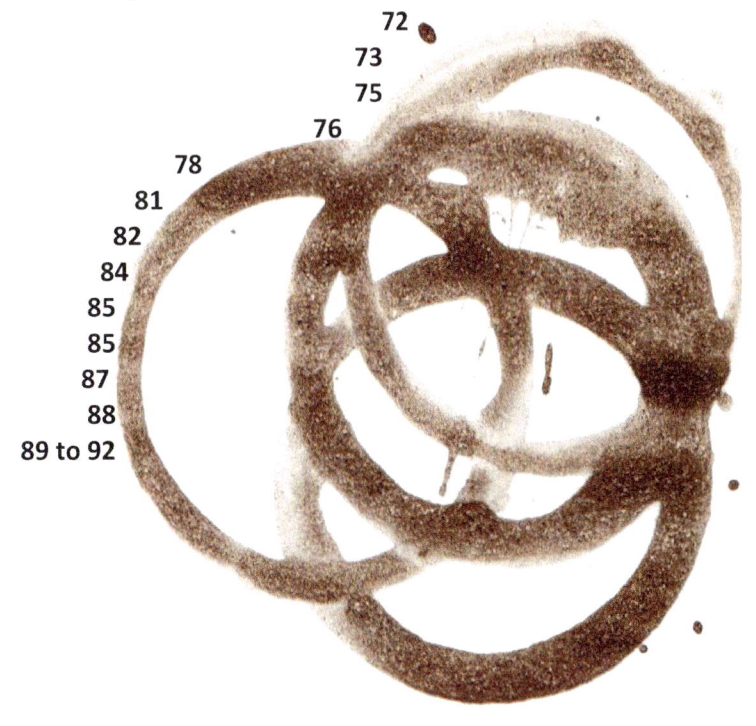

Breakfast At St Mary's

We are the first stop for everyone when they are starting their working days. We can and must have food available 24 hours a day, but breakfast is important as it is when and where people make peace from the grievances or vigorous academic debate from the night before.

Perfect Porridge

Ingredients:
¾ cup/ 4 ½oz/133g of Oats or Oatmeal
2 ½ cups/ 20.2fl.oz/ 600ml Cold Water, or half water and half milk
Pinch of salt
Brown sugar and cold milk to serve.

Put the oatmeal into a pan add the water or milk and water, bring to the boil and continue simmering, stirring continuously for 3 to 4 minutes. When the porridge is as thick as you want it, season with a pinch of salt. Place the porridge in a bowl and sprinkle over with the brown sugar and pour a little milk around the edge to make a moat.
Serves 2

Contribution By: Barb Ruddle

Cooked Breakfast

Scrambled Eggs

To Impress Visitors:
Ingredients:
2 Eggs
6 Tablespoons/ 3fl.oz/ 90ml Double Cream
Salt and Pepper, to taste
Hot Sauce (optional)
Chives, for garnish
2 nobs/ pats Butter

Crack your eggs into a mixing bowl, break up the yolks and lightly whisk. Add the cream a pinch of salt and pepper, and your hot sauce, if you're using it. Give it a good whisk. Set aside. In a small frying pan, over a medium low heat, add a nob of butter and let it melt gently until it starts to bubble. Give your eggs one last stir and pour them into the pan. Let them sit and cook for 20 seconds or so. Using a wooden spoon, slowly lift and fold the cooked egg from the bottom of the pan. Continue stirring gently until the eggs are almost cooked. Add the other nob of butter to add creaminess to your eggs and gently finish cooking. Do not overcook the eggs as they will go rubbery and no one likes a rubbery egg. Remove from the heat and serve garnished with chives.

The Lazy Everyday Way:
In a microwavesafe bowl, crack two eggs, add a splash of milk/cream and some salt and pepper and hot sauce. Cover with cling film and microwave for one minute. Carefully remove the cling film, give it a stir, recover it, stick it back in for another 30 seconds to a minute. Take it out, carefully uncover it, being careful not to burn yourself on the steam, give it another stir. And eat it, you culinary cretin.

Contribution By: Afton Cochran

Toast

Ingredients:
Thick Slices of Bread, as many as desired
Butter
Extras - Jam or Marmite or Marmalade

Sit in front of a good fire, impale your slice of bread on a toasting fork if you have one or a long-handled fork hold in front of the fire until golden brown, remove from fork and turn over, toast the other side. If you haven't got a fire put a slice in the electric toaster and wait for the timer to pop your toast up. If you don't have either of these you can make toast under a grill/ broiler turning it over when golden brown. Smother in lashings of butter and the extra topping of your choice.

Contribution By: Barb Ruddle

Bacon

Buy the best back bacon rashers you can find and afford. The cheaper ones are full of water and shrink. Allow 2 rashers for each person.
Place rashers in a single layer in a grill pan or frying pan and cook gently turning as necessary until they are cooked to the crispness you desire.

Contribution By: Barb Ruddle

Breakfast At St Mary's

Sausages

On the hob: Remove sausages from refrigerator 20 minutes before cooking. You don't want to put a cold sausage on a hot pan. Place a frying pan on medium heat. Add a tablespoon or two of oil or lard (Or duck or goose fat, if you're posh or pretentious.) Do not use olive oil. Place sausages in frying pan spaced evenly apart. Do not crowd the pan. Cook slowly and evenly keeping a constant heat on all the sausages.

Remember: Slow and low. When the sausages have reached an internal temperature of 158°F/ 75°C and are browned evenly all over, remove them to a plate, cover in foil and let them rest for five minutes before serving. For best results: do not bake or deep fry. Grilling is ok but it does not lend the same level of control over the sausages.

Contribution By: Afton Cochran

Sautéed Mushrooms

Ingredients:
- 2 Tablespoon/ 1fl.oz/ 30ml Bacon Grease or Olive Oil or 1 Tablespoon/ 0.5fl.oz/ 15ml Neutral Oil or Butter, melted
- 2 cups/ 17.6oz/ 500g Mushrooms of any kind (obviously not the poisonous ones), wiped clean and sliced
- Salt and Pepper, to taste
- Fresh Thyme, chopped, to taste (optional)

Mushrooms for breakfast are best cooked in the pan just after you have cooked the bacon, as it uses up all the flavourful bacon fat, and gets those lovely crispy bits off the bottom of the pan. Obviously, if you are a vegetarian or vegan you can't do this.

Heat whatever fat you are using in a frying pan over a high heat. Add the mushrooms and cook until they begin to brown, about 5 to 7 minutes, stirring occasionally. Season with salt, pepper and thyme, if using, and continue to cook until they begin to go crisp on the edges.

Check the seasoning and serve.

Contribution By: Afton Cochran

POTATO SCONES

Ingredients:
- 8oz/ 225g Potatoes, peeled, boiled and mashed or leftovers
- ½ cup/ 2 ½oz/ 65g Plain Flour
- 2 Tablespoons/ 1oz/ 30g Butter
- ½ teaspoon/ 0.1oz/ 3g Salt
- Black Pepper, to taste
- Pinch/ 0.03oz/ 1g Baking Powder

This is a great recipe for using leftover mashed potatoes!

If you are not using leftovers, peel and boil the potatoes in salted water until they are tender and easy to mash. Drain the potatoes and mash with butter, salt and pepper. If you are using leftovers, gently warm the potatoes to at least room temperature. Mix the baking powder through the mashed potatoes. Mix in the flour and this should make a very stiff dough. You may have to add a little more flour as this is dependant upon the type of potatoes used and the amount of butter or cream that might have been used in the mashed potatoes. Roll about ¼ of the dough on a floured surface into a round shape or cut out using a small plate as a guide. The dough should roughly be 6mm/ ¼ inch thick. Using a fork, dock or poke the rolled-out dough, marking at least two lines to mark 4 even edges. In a hot frying pan that has been lightly greased, add the rounds one at a time. Cook each side for about three to four minutes, or until the scones are a golden brown.

Contribution By: Sara Robinson

BACON BUTTY? ROLL? SARNIE?

There are many ideas on where this guilty pleasure was first made and for whom. Whatever you call it, it is delicious any time of day! This humble little sandwich keeps our Technical section happy and working!

Ingredients:
- 8 rashers of back Bacon (Not streaky bacon!)
- 4 Milk Rolls or another soft floury roll
- Brown Sauce or Tomato Ketchup
- Butter, at room temperature

Fry in a shallow pan or grill bacon until cooked to perfection. Split the rolls and generously butter each side. Add 2 rashers of bacon to each roll and then a generous amount of brown sauce or tomato ketchup. Serve immediately.

Serves 4 or 1 Hungry Technician.

Add a fried egg, sausages, Lorne sausage or all three to the roll!

Contribution By: Sara Robinson

Breakfast At St Mary's

Overnight Porridge

These are the ultimate grab and go breakfast for the busy historian that just might, and we understand might, be concerned about the nutrition that they eat daily. For those that are not concerned, well we can stuff them with chocolate too!

Container:
If you are really posh, then you can buy a special screw top lidded jar typically used in bottling, but you can use any clean jar with a screw top lid. Best not to use one that has had strong flavours in it previously unless you want to have Bolognaise-flavoured oats. You can also use a plastic container with a lid.

Basic ingredients:
Oats, plain oats. Not the fancy steel cut, or quick oats, just boring rolled oats
Milk (cow, almond, soy, coconut, oat, rice)
Yoghurt - Greek is best, as it has a higher amount of protein, and it is thick, kind of like the Security Department.
Any kind or flavour will work, this includes non-dairy.
Chia seeds - these little things are amazing. Full of goodness and soak up liquid.
Sweetener - honey, maple syrup, agave, jam, and even those coffee syrups!

You will need:
1 part Rolled Oats
1 part Milk
1 part Yoghurt
¼ part Chia Seeds
Sweetener, to taste
Pinch of Salt

Ratios are important because you need to size it to your container.

Add oats, chia seeds, yoghurt and sweetener to the container. Add milk and stir well. Cover and refrigerate for 2 hours or overnight. Stir well and add desired toppings.
Additional ingredients - some of these may or may not defeat the idea of a healthy breakfast, but it is your breakfast, so do what you like. We are just here to enable.

Toppings Ideas:

Fresh fruit * Apple, grated or chunks * Pears, grated or chunks
Dried fruit * Berries * Nuts
Cookie butter * Peanut Butter * Nut Butters
Hazelnut spread * Cocoa Nibs * Chocolate chips
Double cream * Whiskey or Rum (we will not judge)
Vanilla * Cinnamon * Instant Coffee
Cocoa Powder * Protein Powder * Peanut Butter Powder
Raisins * Shredded Coconut * Flax Seeds
Hemp Seeds * Pumpkin Seeds * Sunflower Seeds

Piña Colada Overnight Oats
Coconut Milk, Shredded Coconut, Pineapple Chunks

PB-J Overnight Oats
Peanut Butter or Powdered Peanut Butter, Your Favourite Jam.

Apple Pie Overnight Oats
Apple Chunks, Chopped Pecans or Walnuts, Maple Syrup, Cinnamon

Scottish Cranachan Overnight Oats
Fresh Raspberries, Honey, Whipped Double Cream

Contribution By: Afton Cochran

Breakfast At St Mary's

Vegan Gluten Free Banana Muffins

Ingredients:
2 Tablespoons/ 1oz/ 30g Chia Seeds, mixed with
    1/3 cup/ 2.6fl.oz/ 78ml Warm Water
½ cup/ 4fl.oz/ 118ml Coconut Oil, softened or melted
1/3 cup/ 2.6fl.oz/ 78ml Maple Syrup or Golden Syrup
2 Large Ripe Bananas, mashed
1 teaspoon/ 0.14oz/ 4g Baking Powder
1 teaspoon/ 0.14oz/ 4g Bicarbonate of Soda
½ teaspoon/ 0.07oz/ 2g Salt
1 teaspoon/ 0.07oz/ 2g Apple Pie Spice (recipe in R&D)
½ cup/ 4fl.oz/ 118ml Water
1 cup/ 2.8oz/ 80g Rolled Gluten-Free Oats
1 cup/ 6oz/ 170g Buckwheat Flour
½ teaspoon/ 0.07oz/ 2g Xanthan Gum
½ cup Almonds, or other nuts, chopped

Preheat oven to 375 °F/ 190 °C (170°C fan)/ Gas Mark 5
Line a 12-cup muffin pan with paper liners.

Mix the chia seeds with the warm water. Set aside for at least 5 to 10 minutes.
In a medium sized bowl, mash the ripe bananas. Add the coconut oil, maple syrup and chia seed mixture and mix well to combine. In a separate bowl add the flour, oats, xanthan gum, spices, salt, baking powder and bicarbonate of soda. Whisk the dry ingredients to combine. Add the banana mixture and the water to the dry ingredients and stir well to combine. Fold in the chopped nuts. Using an ice cream scoop, measure the batter and divide evenly between the muffin cases. Sprinkle batter with the crumble topping (recipe below).
Bake for 20 to 25 minutes, being careful not to open the door because it can cause them to deflate. They have completed cooking when a toothpick inserted in centre of muffins comes out clean.

Spiced Apple Muffins

Ingredients:
2 cups/ 10.5oz/ 300g Plain Flour or Gluten Free Flour
1 cup/ 5.2oz/ 150g Wholemeal Flour or Buckwheat Flour
1 Tablespoon/ 0.21oz/ 6g Apple Pie Spice (recipe in R&D)
2 teaspoon/ 0.28/ 8g Baking Powder
½ teaspoon/ 0.07oz/ 2g Bicarbonate of Soda
¼ teaspoon/ 0.03oz/ 1g Salt
4 Large Eggs
1 cup/ 8fl.oz/ 250ml Vegetable Oil
2 cups/ 14oz/ 400g Granulated Sugar
4 to 5/ 5 cups/ 20.4oz/580g Apples, finely diced or grated

Preheat oven to 350 °F/ 180 °C (160°C fan)/ Gas Mark 4
Line 24 muffin cups with paper cases.
Dice or grate the apples.
Mix flours, sugar, baking powder, bicarbonate of soda, apple pie spice and salt in a large bowl. In a separate smaller bowl beat together the oil, and eggs. Mix the dry and wet ingredients together. Using a measuring cup or ice cream scoop, divide the mixture evenly between the 24 cases and bake for 15 to 20 minutes or until the top springs back when lightly touched.
Cool for 5 minutes before serving.

Crumble Topping for Muffins

Ingredients:
2 Tablespoons/ 0.63oz/ 18g Plain Flour
    or Gluten Free Flour
1½ teaspoons/ 0.1oz/ 3g Apple Pie Spice (recipe in R&D)
½ cup/ 3.5oz/ 100g Brown Sugar
½ cup/ 4.4oz/ 125g Butter or Coconut Oil, melted

In a small bowl combine the melted butter, flour, apple pie spice and brown sugar in a small bowl. Crumble over the unbaked muffins. Bake as directed.

Muffins Contribution By: Sara Robinson

Breakfast At St Mary's

English Pancakes

Ingredients:
½ cup/ 4oz/ 100g Plain Flour
Pinch of Salt
1 Egg
1 ¼ cups/ 10fl.oz/ 285ml Milk

Sieve flour and salt together in a basin. Drop in egg and beat mixture well. Gradually beat in just enough milk to make a stiff smooth batter. Allow to stand for a few minutes then whisk or beat in the rest of the liquid. Put in cool place for at least 30mins or until needed. This batter is also used for Yorkshire Pudding.
To make pancakes. Whisk your mixture and put in a jug for easy pouring.
Put a little oil or butter into a pan. Heat until a blue haze is seen. Pour enough of the mixture into the hot pan to give a paper-thin layer. Cook quickly until one side is golden brown (lift edge of pancake to see) toss or turn and cook on the other side.
Remove from pan and serve with lemon and sugar.

Contribution By: Barb Ruddle

Drop Scones (Scottish Pancakes)

Ingredients:
2 teaspoons/ 0.34 oz/ 10g of Baking Powder
1 cup/ 7.6oz/ 220g Plain Flour
Pinch Salt
¼ cup/ 1.76oz/ 50g Caster Sugar
2 Eggs
1 cups plus 1 Tablespoon/ 9.5fl.oz/ 280 ml Milk
1 Tablespoon/ 0.5fl.oz/ 15ml Vegetable Oil

In a large bowl whisk together flour, baking powder, salt and sugar. In a separate bowl whisk the eggs and milk together. Whisk the eggs and milk into the flour mixture and then add the oil and whisk or stir until just combined.
Heat a frying pan or griddle and lightly oil it before spooning the batter onto the surface. You are looking for about 3 Tablespoons/ 45ml of batter for each pancake. Flip the pancake when the small bubbles around the edge begin to pop and continue cooking until both sides are a golden brown, usually about a minute on each side. Serve with the topping of your choice, but we love golden syrup on these.

Contribution By: Sara Robinson

American Style Pancakes

Ingredients:
1 cup/ 7.7oz/ 220g Plain Flour
¾ cup/ 5.2oz/ 165g Wholemeal Flour, Buckwheat Flour or Plain Flour
2 Tablespoons/ 0.88oz/ 25g Granulated Sugar
1 Tablespoon/ 0.5oz/ 15g Baking Powder
¼ teaspoon/ 0.07oz/ 2g Salt
1 Egg, beaten
1 ½ cups/ 12oz/ 355ml Milk or Buttermilk
3 Tablespoons/ 1.5fl.oz/ 45ml Vegetable Oil

In a large bowl whisk together flour, sugar, baking powder and salt. In a separate bowl whisk together egg, milk and oil. Add the egg mixture to the flour mixture and stir until just combined. The batter may be a little lumpy but that is normal.
Heat a large skillet or griddle and grease lightly with vegetable oil or butter. Pour about ¼ cup/ 2fl.oz/ 60ml of the batter onto the hot surface. Spread the batter if necessary. Cook the pancake over medium heat for about 2 minutes on each side. It is time to flip the pancake over when the bubbles at the edges pop and the edges are golden brown. Repeat with remaining batter.
Top with maple syrup and serve.
Makes about 12 pancakes.

Contribution By: Afton Cochran

Other Breakfast Ideas

Pots of Plain and Flavoured Yoghurts   *   Leftovers
Fresh Fruit (Yes, even Historians like apples!)   *   Melon Balls
Croissants and Pastries   *   Sausage Rolls   *   Doughnuts
Muesli   *   Granola   *   Boxed Cereals with Milk
Wait, we are supposed to eat breakfast?

Photo By: Sara Robinson

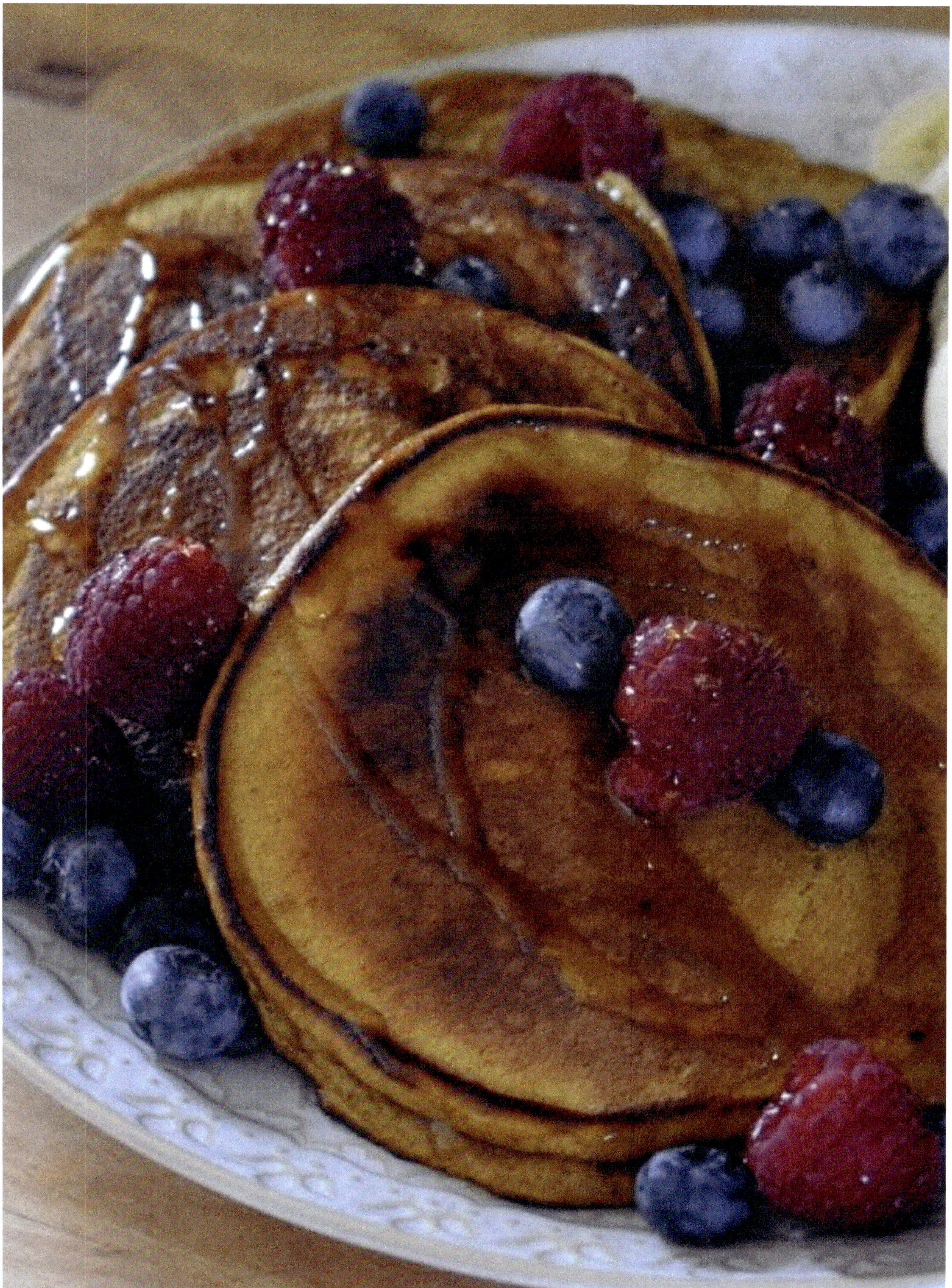

Soup and Sandwiches

Soup and sandwiches are a great way to get everyone at St Marys a mid day meal. We serve whenever they are hungry. There is no specific time.
They are easy to make and easy to eat, as well as portable so they can be eaten in the dining area, in an office or on the go.

Slow Cooker Ham and Lentil Soup

Ingredients:
- 17.6oz/ 500g Dry Lentils
- 2.2 pounds/ 1kg Lean Ham
- 1 Large Onion
- 1 Large Carrot
- 2 to 3 Stalks Celery
- 2 Stock Cubes
- 2 teaspoons/ 0.14oz/ 4g Basil
- 2 teaspoon/ 0.1oz/ 3g Onion Seasoning (recipe in R&D)
- 1 teaspoon/ 0.07oz/ 2g Rosemary
- 1 teaspoon/ 0.07oz/ 2g Oregano
- ½ teaspoon/ 0.03oz/ 1g Black Pepper
- ½ teaspoon/ 0.07oz/ 2g Salt
- ½ teaspoon/ 0.01oz/ >1g Fennel

If the ham is frozen, remove from freezer and set on plate to defrost overnight in the refrigerator.

5 to 6 hours before meal time.
Weigh and then rinse lentils well.
Chop vegetables into medium size chunks and dice ham to 1-1.5cm chunks.
Combine vegetables, ham, lentils, water, and stock cubes in slow cooker
Add 150 to 200ml of additional water.
Set slow cooker to high and let cook, stirring occasionally.
Once the mixture is simmering nicely, add herbs and spices and mix in.
Continue to visit your concoction periodically to stir the soup.
After about the 4-hour mark, test the lentils occasionally to see if they are still firm. Once they are soft, turn down the heat to low until you are ready to eat.
Serve the soup with a nice roll and a salad (if you are not in the History Department).
Serves 6

Contribution By: Sara Robinson

Mud Soup
Egyptian Lentil Soup or Shurit Ads

Ingredients:
- 7 cups/ 57.4fl.oz/ 1.7 litres Chicken or Vegetable Stock
- 2 cups Brown Lentils
- 1-14 oz/411g Tin Diced Tomatoes or Fresh Tomatoes, peeled and diced
- 4 Cloves Garlic, roughly chopped
- 2 Medium Onions, roughly chopped
- ¼ cup Dried Parsley
- ¼ teaspoon Ground Black Pepper
- 2 teaspoons Ground Cumin
- Lemon Juice, to taste
- Fresh Chives or Scallions and Lemon Wedges to garnish

Place stock, lentils, tomatoes, garlic, onions and parsley into a large pot. Bring the mixture up to a simmer, stirring ever so often until the lentils are softened, about 45 minutes.

Add the black pepper, ground cumin and lemon juice, to taste. You may need a bit of salt as well depending on your stock but put the lemon juice in first and taste. Using an immersion blender purée until smooth. It is nice served with chopped chives or scallions on the top and lemon wedges on the side.
Serves 4

Shhh..... don't tell anyone, but for Sick Bay, we also stick in additional vegetables such as shredded carrots, zucchini/ courgette or even spinach and cook them with the lentils. Once the soup is puréed, the veggies disappear and none of the Historians are any wiser.

Contribution By: Constantina Mead

Soup and Sandwiches

Creamy Vegetable Soup

Ingredients:
2 Tablespoons/ 1oz/ 30g Butter
2 Cloves Garlic, minced
2 Shallots, finely chopped
2 pounds/ 32oz/ 0.9kg Tinned Tomatoes, chopped
1 2/3 cups/ 14fl.oz/ 400ml Vegetable Stock
1 teaspoon/ 0.7oz/ 2g dried basil
Salt and Pepper, to taste
7oz/ 200g Baby New Potatoes, quartered
4 Small Carrots, diced
6 Large Radishes, diced
3 ½oz/ 100g Mangetout Peas
½ cup/ 4.22fl.oz/ 125ml Single Cream
Garnish with grated Parmesan Cheese

Add the butter, garlic and shallots to a large saucepan. Over medium heat gently sauté the mix until the shallots become translucent and have softened. Usually this takes 2 to 3 minutes stirring occasionally. Add the diced radishes, diced carrots and quartered potatoes. Continue to sauté the veggies for a further 4 to 5 minutes or until the vegetables are starting to soften.

Add the tomatoes and their liquid, vegetable stock, basil and a pinch of salt and pepper. Then cover, and simmer for 15 minutes.

Trim and half the mangetout and add them. Simmer for another 5 minutes. Stir in the cream, and season to taste. Serve immediately sprinkle with the cheese.

Serves 2 to 3

Contribution By: Barb Ruddle

Cullen Skink

This Scottish soup is amazingly warm and comforting. It has been a favourite over the years with many of the Scots working at St. Mary's. We aim to get real Arbroath Smokies several times a year to give a more authentic flavour and show them some love.

Ingredients:
2 Tablespoons/ 0.88oz/ 28g Butter
1 Onion or 2 Leeks, finely chopped
2 2/3 cups/ 14oz/ 400g Floury Potatoes, cubed
2 fillets/ 10oz/ 300g Smoked Haddock
1 cup/ 8fl.oz/ 250ml Whole Milk
1/3 cup plus 1 Tablespoon/ 3.3fl.oz/ 100ml Double Cream
1 ¼ cups/ 10fl.oz/ 300ml Fish Stock

Place the smoked haddock in a frying pan skin side up, and just cover with milk. Let sit while you continue to prepare the soup. Start your fish stock heating on the hob. Wash, peel and finely chop the onion or leeks and peel and cube the potatoes. Add butter to a large heavy bottomed pan and over a medium heat fry the onions for about 5 minutes until the onion is soft but not brown. Add the potatoes near the end before pouring 300ml of boiling fish stock over the veggies. Cover and allow to simmer for 15 minutes. Heat the milk and haddock very gradually, over a maximum of a medium heat but don't scald the milk! This should take about 5 minutes. Simmer the milk and fish for a further 5 minutes. Remove the haddock from the milk with a slotted spoon and keep the milk to one side, adding the cream to the pan. Cool the fish slightly and discard skin and/or bones and break the fish into large flakes. Remove and mash about ¼ of the potatoes before returning them to the pot. Add the milk and cream to the pan of stock and veggies. Stir for a few minutes to combine. Add your flaked haddock and stir gently. Add salt and pepper to taste. Serve with crusty wholemeal bread.

Serves 4 to 6

(Adapted from SWRI) Contribution By: Jane Oswald Ryan and Sara Robinson

Soup and Sandwiches

Tortellini Sausage Soup with Spinach

Ingredients:
4 Tablespoons/ 2fl.oz/ 60ml Olive Oil
1 Onion, diced
2 Carrots, diced
2 Stalks Celery, diced
1 Bulb Fennel, fronds and base removed, diced
5 Cloves Garlic, crushed and minced
18oz/ 500g Italian Sausage, or a good quality sausage meat (see R&D for recipe)
1 Tablespoon/ 0.21oz/ 6g Fennel Seed
2 teaspoons/ 0.24oz/ 7g Red Pepper Flakes, or to taste
1 Tablespoon/ 0.14oz/ 4g Fresh Oregano, chopped
Salt and Pepper, to taste
2 Tablespoon/ 1fl.oz/ 30ml Tomato Purée/ Paste
1 cup/ 8fl.oz/ 250ml White Wine
6 ½ cups/ 50fl.oz/ 1.5L Chicken or Vegetable Stock
2 14oz/ 400g Tins Peeled Plum Tomatoes
Pinch of Sugar
1 cup/ 8fl.oz/ 250ml Double/ Heavy Cream
17.6oz/ 500g Tortellini, fresh or homemade with your preferred filling
14oz/ 400g Baby Spinach
Parmesan, to garnish
Fresh Parsley, finely chopped to garnish

In a pot or a Dutch oven, heat 2 tablespoons/ 2fl.oz/ 30ml olive oil over medium heat. Add your sausage meat and brown it, breaking it up into smaller pieces until it has a nice brown crust on it. Lightly season with salt and pepper. Remove with a slotted spoon and set on a plate lined with kitchen roll. Add the final 2 tablespoons/ 2 fl.oz/ 30ml olive oil, or add less oil if you have a lot of residual fat from the sausage meat. Add the onion, carrot, celery and fennel and cook down until the onion is translucent. Add the garlic, fennel seeds, chilli flakes and a bit of salt and pepper. Stir and cook for a minute or two. Turn heat up and add your wine and deglaze the pan, scraping up all the yummy brown bits from the bottom. When the wine is almost all absorbed, add the tomato purée/ paste and stir well. Add the stock. Stir well. Open your tins of plum tomatoes, pour them into a bowl, and, with clean hands, crush the tomatoes. Pour the tomatoes into your Dutch oven. Add a pinch of sugar, the oregano and a bit of salt and pepper. Bring to a simmer and simmer for 10 to 15 minutes. Add your sausage meat and cook for another 10 minutes. Add the double cream and bring back to the simmer. Add your fresh tortellini and cook it for a minute less than the package requires, or if using homemade, for as long as it takes for them to almost cook. When your tortellini is almost cooked, add in your spinach and heat through, adjust seasoning and serve, garnished with Parmesan and parsley along with crusty bread.
Serves 4 to 6

Photo and Contribution By: Afton Cochran

Mushroom Stew

Ingredients:
0.5oz/ 15g Dried Porcini Mushrooms
32oz/ 900g Fresh Mushrooms, assorted varieties, wiped and chopped in half
2 Tablespoons/ 1fl.oz/ 30ml Olive Oil
1 Onion, finely chopped
2 Garlic Cloves, minced
1 teaspoon/ 0.03oz/ 1g Thyme
Pinch of Ground Cloves
Salt and Pepper, to taste
25oz/ 700g Tomatoes, chopped

Soak the dried mushrooms in a small bowl of hot water for 20mins. Drain saving the mushrooms and liquid. Heat the oil in a large saucepan and add the onions. Cook gently until softened add the garlic, thyme and cloves and continue cooking for 2 minutes.
Add all the mushrooms and cook until the mushrooms have softened, stirring often. Season to taste with salt and pepper and add the tomatoes and the saved liquid. Simmer, partly covered over a low heat for about 20 minutes until thickened. Taste and add more seasoning if needed.

Contribution By: Barb Ruddle

Note: to use dried mushrooms, rehydrate and prepare them according to the package. If using porcini, use 15g and rehydrate with 175ml of boiling water. Let them sit for 1/2 an hour then remove with a slotted spoon. Strain the liquid through a cheesecloth and set aside.

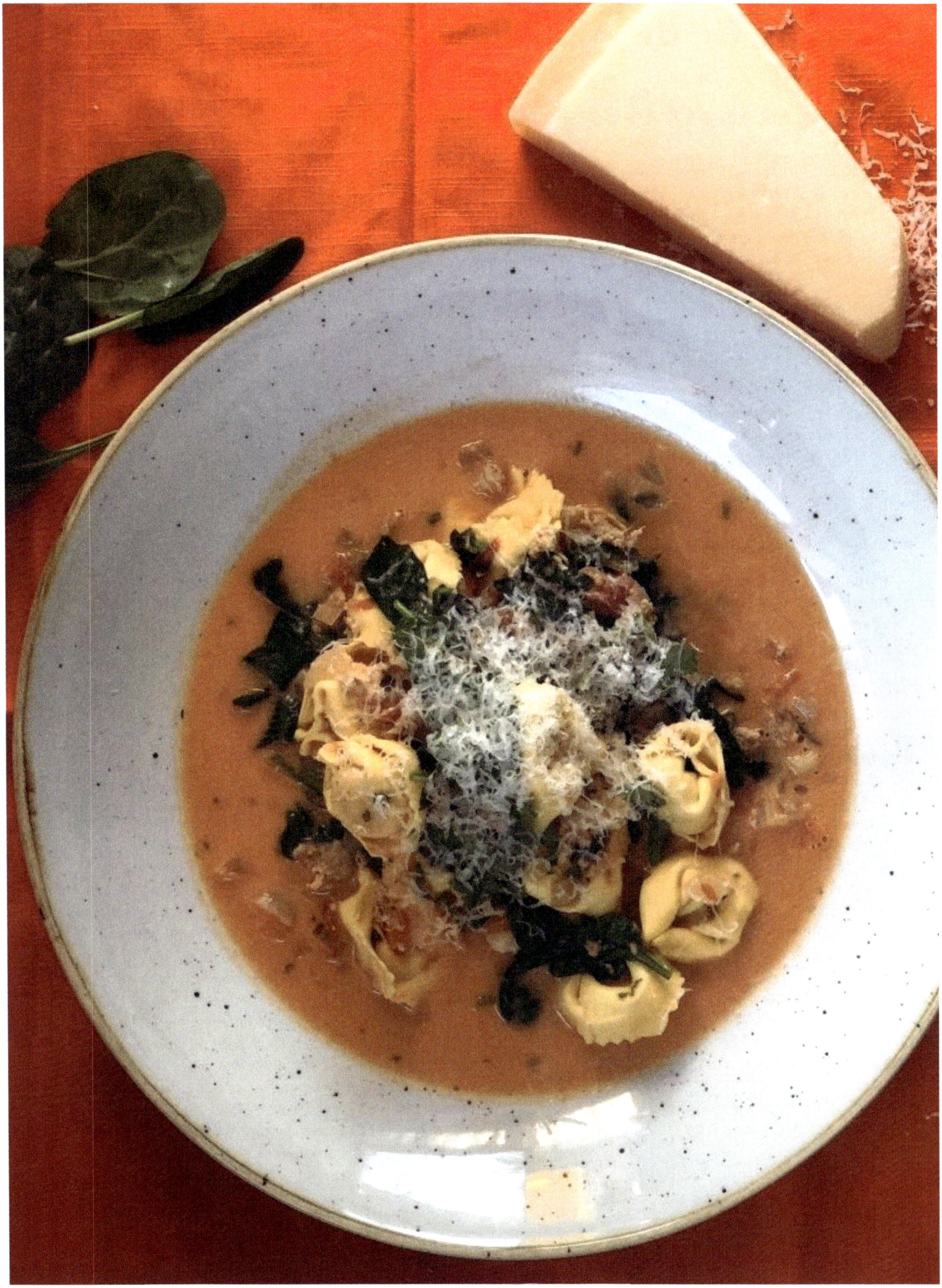

Soup and Sandwiches

White Bean and Orzo Soup

Ingredients:
3 15oz/ 400g Tins Cannellini Beans, Navy Beans or other white bean
1 15oz/ 400g Tin Chickpea/ Garbanzo Beans
13 cups/ 103fl.oz/ 3L Vegetable Stock, divided
2 Tablespoons/ 1fl.oz/ 30ml Olive Oil
1 Large Onion, chopped
3 Carrots, chopped
2 Stalks Celery, chopped
4 Cloves Garlic, minced and crushed
2 Bay Leaves
2 Lemons, zested and juiced
2 Tablespoons Fresh Rosemary Leaves, chopped
250 g Leafy Greens, such as kale, chard, frisée, or spinach
9oz/ 250g Orzo Pasta
Salt and Pepper
Parsley, to garnish
Italian Hard Cheese, to garnish

Heat 2 tablespoons/ 1fl.oz/ 30ml olive oil in a skillet or Dutch oven. Add the onion, carrot, and celery and a pinch of salt and pepper and cook until the onions are soft and translucent. Add in your bay leaves, lemon zest, rosemary and garlic. Cook for a minute more. Remove 2 cups/ 16fl.oz/ 500 ml stock, set aside and add the remainder to the pot. Add 1 tin of drained and rinsed chickpeas and 1 can of drained and rinsed white beans, stir well and cook 20 min. In a blender add the remainder of the stock with 2 tins of drained and rinsed white beans. Blend until smooth. Add blended cannellini beans to the stock pot and heat through. Stir in 9oz/ 250g orzo pasta, cook for 5 min. Add in greens and lemon juice. Cook for 2 min and adjust seasoning. Garnish with parsley and Italian hard cheese.
Serve with crusty bread.

Serves 4 to 6

Note: To make this a vegetarian or vegan dish do not include the Italian hard cheese, but rather use an acceptable alternative. This is because most Italian hard cheeses like Parmesan or Grana Padano use animal rennet in their production, so the addition of this would make the dish non vegetarian or vegan.

Contribution By: Afton Cochran

Brown Stock or Bone Broth

Ingredients:
1 to 1 ½ pounds/ 500 to 600g Good Quality Bones, such as: beef or lamb shanks or joint bones; pig trotters or neck bones; chicken or turkey necks, back bones, wings, or feet; or any combination of these
1 Large Onion, peeled and halved
6 Cloves Garlic
2 Large Carrots, whole
2 Stalks Celery, whole
1 Tablespoon/ 0.5fl.oz/ 15ml Tomato Purée/ Paste
2oz/ 30g Dried Mushrooms, or
    6oz/ 170g Fresh Mushrooms
1 Tablespoons/ 0.59oz/ 17g Sea Salt
1 teaspoon/ 0.07oz/ 2g Whole Black Peppercorns
1 Bay Leaf
1 cup/ 8fl.oz/ 250ml Dry Marsala Wine
2 Tablespoons/ 1fl.oz/ 30ml Worcestershire Sauce
Water

Heat oven to 400°F/ 200°C (180°C fan)/ Gas Mark 6
Place meat bones on a baking sheet. Cover one side of bones, face up, with tomato paste. Roast in oven until browned, about 10 to 15 minutes. When browned, remove from baking sheet and place into a large stockpot or Dutch oven.
Place onion, garlic, carrots and celery on the same baking sheet (tuck garlic cloves between larger vegetables to keep them from burning), turning the vegetables in the meat juices from the bones to coat and roast in the oven till brown, about 15 to 20 minutes. Add to stockpot with the bones.
Add all other ingredients to the stockpot. Fill pot to within 1 inch (2.5 cm) off the top with water.
Turn stove burner to high setting until the pot contents come to a rolling boil, then reduce heat to a simmer. Simmer contents for 6-8 hours. Do not add more water.
Remove pot from heat and remove bones and vegetables from the pot with a slotted spoon. Skim extra fat and any scum from the surface of the broth. Ladle stock through a sieve into freezer-safe containers with tight lids.
Store in freezer until ready for use.

Contribution By: Merry Schepers

Soup and Sandwiches

Cool as a Cucumber Soup

Ingredients:
1 Large Cucumber
4 Tablespoon Fresh Mint, chiffonade
17.6oz/ 500g Natural Greek Yoghurt
2/3 cup/ 5fl.oz/ 150ml Single Cream
2 Tablespoons White Wine Vinegar
Salt and Black Pepper, to taste
Fresh Mint, for garnish

Trim rinse and dry the cucumber and grate it coarsely with skin on into a large bowl. Add the mint to the cucumber. Stir in the yoghurt, cream and vinegar, season well and stir again. Serve in cooled bowls. Garnish with small sprigs of mint.

Contribution By: Barb Ruddle

Leek and Potato Soup

Ingredients:
3 ½ Tablespoons/ 2oz/ 50g Butter
16oz/ 450g Leeks, trimmed and finely sliced
1 ½pounds/ 700g Potatoes, peeled and cubed
3 ¾ cups/ 31.6fl.oz/ 900ml Vegetable Stock
1 ¾ cups plus 2 Tablespoons/ 15.8fl.oz/ 450ml Whole Milk
Salt and Pepper, to taste

Melt the butter in a large saucepan, add the leeks and cook gently for 5 minutes. Add the potatoes, vegetable stock and milk. Bring to the boil, then reduce the heat, cover and simmer gently for 20 to 25 minutes or until the vegetables are soft.
For a smooth soup texture: Cool for 10 to 15minutes pour into a food processor or blender to form a smooth soup. Return the soup to a clean saucepan and add salt and pepper to taste. Reheat gently without boiling and serve.
Serves 2 to 3

Contribution By: Barb Ruddle

Chunky Chicken and Noodles

Ingredients:
3 to 4 Boneless, Skinless Chicken Breasts, cubed 1inch/ 2cm pieces
4 Celery Stocks, diced
1 Medium Onion, diced
3 Carrots, diced
1 Large Bell Pepper, diced
8 Rashers Bacon, diced
Salt and Pepper, to taste
1 Tablespoon/ 0.14oz/ 4g Italian Seasoning (recipe in R&D)
1 Tablespoon/ 0.25oz/ 7g Onion Seasoning (recipe in R&D)
33.8fl.oz/ 1Liter Chicken Stock or Brown Stock
14fl.oz/ 400g Pasta, uncooked
2 Tablespoons/ 1fl.oz/ 30ml Oil (use only with stove top method)

Add a little oil to a frying pan over medium heat and brown chicken and bacon. Remove meat to a plate and set to the side. Add a little oil to the frying pan and brown celery, carrots, onion and bell pepper. Place browned meat and veggies into a large stock pot and cover with stock and spices. Simmer for 30 to 40 minutes. Add in uncooked pasta to the stock mixture. Cook pasta to timing on the package directions. If you desire a thinner soup, more stock can be added with the pasta.

If making in a slow cooker: Dice all meat and veg before adding it to the slow cooker. Add stock and spices then mix well. Cook until bubbly and the onions are translucent; 6 to 10 hours on low and 4 hours on high but individual appliance times may vary. 20 to 30 minutes before time to serve, mix the dry pasta through the slow cooker dish and turn heat level up to high. Serve when pasta is fully cooked.
Serve with garlic bread.

Serves 4 to 6

Contribution By: Sara Robinson

Soup and Sandwiches

Brioche Rolls for Sandwiches

Ingredients:
2 cups/ 16.9oz/ 480g Strong Flour
1 teaspoon/ 0.28oz/ 8g Salt
2 Tablespoons plus 1teaspoon/ 1oz/ 30g Castor Sugar
1 Tablespoon/ 0.42oz/ 12g Active Dry Yeast
¼ cup/ 2fl.oz/ 57ml Water, room temperature
4 Eggs, beaten plus 1 for an Egg Wash.
¾ cup plus 2 Tablespoons/ 7oz/ 200g Butter, room temperature but not melted

This is easiest to do in a stand mixer with the dough hook attachment but can be done by hand.
Whisk together flour, salt and sugar into a bowl. Dissolve the yeast in the water and add to the dry ingredients. Add the beaten eggs and mix well. Knead the dough until smooth. Beat in the soft butter making sure that it is all incorporated, the dough should be elastic and shiny. Rest the dough in a covered bowl in a warm place until it has doubled in size
Weigh into 70g balls or about the size of your fist. Roll these on an un-floured worktop to a lovely ball, place on a baking sheet that has been lined with baking paper. Slightly smash the rolled balls into disks.
Cover loosely and prove again until doubled in size. Egg wash each roll lightly. Bake in preheated oven at 425°F/ 210°C (fan 200°C)/ Gas Mark 7 for 15 to 20 min or until golden brown.

Contribution By: Sara Robinson

Cheese Puffs

Ingredients:
1 Egg
½ cup/ 4fl.oz/ 125ml Milk
1 cup/ 5.2oz/ 150g Self Raising Flour
2/3 to ¾ cups/ 5.2 to 7oz/ 150 to 200g Cheddar Cheese, grated
Pinch of Salt
1 teaspoon/ 0.07oz/ 2g Onion Powder
Pinch of Cayenne
¼ teaspoon/ 0.03oz/ >1g Ground Dry Mustard
2 or 3 Spring Onions, finely sliced

Beat the egg into the milk.
Add salt, herbs and any other flavourings to the flour and cheese and mix together well. Mix dry ingredients with the milk mixture until well combined.
Drop six to eight spoonsful onto a baking tray, covered in baking paper. Or drop into a lightly greased muffin mould. Bake for 20 minutes in an oven preheated to 350°F/ 180°C / Gas Mark 4.
If you use an ice cream scoop to shape the dough you get about 12 smaller puffs which works well. The cooking time remains the same.
You could make them bite-sized as well but you would need to reduce the cooking time by about 5 mins.

Variations:
¼ tsp of paprika or smoked paprika or
¼ tsp of garlic granules or chives instead of onions or
replace some of the Cheddar with other cheeses
Add in two cooked rashers smoked bacon finely chopped.

Contribution By: Mort Reading

Soup and Sandwiches

Polenta Muffins

Ingredient:

2 cups/ 11.2oz/ 320g Course Ground Polenta
2 cups/ 8 ½oz/ 240g Plain Flour
1 1/3 cup/ 10.5oz/ 300g Caster Sugar
1 teaspoon/ 0.25oz/ 8g Salt
1 teaspoon/ 0.17oz/ 5g Bicarbonate of Soda
2 cups/ 17.2oz/ 490g Sour Cream
1 cup/ 8oz/ 227g Butter, melted or Neutral Oil
4 Eggs
2 teaspoons/ 0.25oz/ 8g Onion Seasoning (optional, recipe in R&D)
1/4 cup/ 2oz/ 60g Parmesan Cheese, finely grated (optional)

Preheat oven to 375°F/ 190°C/ Gas Mark 5. Butter or line a muffin tin with paper cases.
Whisk together polenta, flour, sugar, salt, spices and baking soda together in a large bowl. Tip in the sour cream, butter and eggs; stir until fully incorporated. The batter may be a little lumpy, but that is okay. Pour batter into the prepared muffin tin, filling each case about ¾ full.
Bake in the preheated oven until a toothpick inserted in the centre of the muffin comes out clean, about 12 minutes.
Makes about 18 muffins.

Contribution By: Sara Robinson

Sweet Potato Cheddar Scones

Ingredients:

1 cup/ 7oz/ 200g Sweet Potatoes, peeled, cooked and mashed
2 cups/ 8oz/ 250g Plain Flour (plus extra for dusting)
2 Tablespoons/ 1oz/ 30g Baking Powder
1 teaspoon/ 0.211/ 6g Salt
5 Tablespoons/ 2.4oz/ 70g Butter, cubed and cold
1 teaspoon/ 0.03oz/ 1g Italian Seasoning (recipe in R&D)
½ cup/ 3.5oz/ 100g Strong Cheddar Cheese, finely grated
2 Eggs
4 Tablespoons/ 2fl.oz/ 60ml Milk (plus additional to brush on scones)

Line a baking tray with baking parchment.
Preheat oven to 425°F/ 220°C (200°C fan)/ Gas Mark 7.
Place peeled and diced sweet potato in a saucepan and cover with water. Boil for 10 to 15 minutes or until the pieces are very tender. Drain and mash the sweet potatoes. Set aside to cool.
Whisk together the flour, baking powder and salt. Add the butter and rub in until well combined and the flour resembles a fine sand. Add in the sweet potato mash and rub that into the butter and flour mixture. It is important to do this well because you do not want large lumps of butter or sweet potato in the mixture.
Stir in the Italian seasoning and the cheddar cheese.
Quickly beat the eggs and stir in the milk. Add the egg mixture to the flour mixture and stir until just combined. Over mixing will make for a chewier texture. Do not over mix!
Place the dough on a well-floured surface. Flour your hands to keep the dough from sticking to them. Flatten the dough to about 1 inch/ 2cm in thickness and cut out rounds or use a knife to make square scones.
Bring together the scraps and continue until all of the dough has been used. 2¼ inch/ 58mm round or square will yield about 12 scones. Brush the top of each scone with milk.
Bake for 10 to 15 minutes, until well risen and golden brown.
Remove and cool on a wire rack.
Serves 12 to 16 scones

Contribution By: Sara Robinson

Soup and Sandwiches

Cheese and Caramelised Onion Scones

Ingredients:
6 Tablespoons/ 3.5oz/ 85g Butter
1 Small Onion, very thinly sliced
1 cup plus 2 Tablespoons/ 9.5oz/ 270g Plain Flour
2 Tablespoons/ 0.88oz/ 25g Granulated Sugar
1/4 cup/ 2oz/ 60g Strong Hard Cheese such as Parmesan, finely grated
2 teaspoons Baking Powder
a Pinch of Salt
1 Egg
¼ cup/2.1oz/ 60g Mascarpone
1/3 cup/1.4oz/ 40g Plain Yogurt
1 Tablespoon/0.7fl.oz/20mls of Milk

Place 1 Tablespoon/ 0.5oz/ 15g butter into a frying pan and slowly cook the onion over medium low heat until it is brown and sticky. Put aside to cool. Rub the remaining butter into plain flour and then stir in granulated sugar, baking powder, cheese and salt. Then add the cooked onion and mix well. In another bowl, beat the egg and add and in the mascarpone and plain yoghurt. Add 20mls of milk then beat until less lumpy (smooth is optimistic). Tip the wet ingredients into the dry and mix well. Tip the mixture onto a lightly floured board and knead. You might not think it will combine all the dry ingredients in but kneading it will do it. Divide the mix into eight and shape those into flattened rounds of about 7 to 8cm across.

Put a sheet of baking paper on a big-enough tray, don't let the scones touch each other. Brush the tops with milk and sprinkle a little extra cheese on each top.

Bake for 15 to 20 minutes at 425°F/220°C/ Gas Mark 7
After the scones have cooled, split and butter or dunk in your soup.

Contribution By: Caroline Price and Sara Robinson

Sandwich Filling Ideas—For filling Rolls, bread or …

Egg Mayo (Chopped Hard Boiled Eggs with Mayo) * Ham * Smoked Salmon * Pepperoni * Chicken or Turkey Breast * Beans in a Tomato Sauce * Chicken Tikka * Piri Piri Chicken * Coronation Chicken * Salt Beef * Corned Beef * Steak and Kidney Pie * Any Cheese You Enjoy * Flavoured Cream Cheese * Piccalilli * Mayo * Mustard * Ketchup * Butter * Tuna Mayo (Well drained tinned Tuna, with Mayo) * Avocado * Sweet Pickle Relish * Chutney * Hummus * Grilled Peppers * Peanut Butter * Jam * Honey * Nutty Chocolate Spread * Smooth Cookie Spread * Tahini Spread * Almond Butter * Marshmallows * Wine Gums * Chocolate * Mac and Cheese * Mac and Cheese Pie * Chips * Crisps * Pickled Onion * Pickled Cabbage * Jalapeños * Sliced Tomato * Sliced Gherkins * Sliced Cucumbers * Green leafy things called Lettuce * Water Cress

Po' Boy Sandwich

The best dressed sandwich in New Orleans, Louisiana.
This "Poor Boy" sandwich originated at Martin Brothers' French Market Restaurant and Coffee Stand in New Orleans during the 1929 streetcar strike. The Po' Boy roll is a distinctive one. It is a type of French bread native to New Orleans with a crisp outside, and a fluffy interior.

Spice Blend Ingredients:
2 teaspoons/ 0.14oz/ 4g Paprika
2 teaspoons/ 0.14oz/ 4g Cayenne
1 teaspoon/ 0.03oz/ 1g Dried Oregano
1 teaspoon/ 0.03oz/ 1g Dried Thyme
1 teaspoon/ 0.1oz/ 3g Garlic Granules
1 teaspoons/ 0.1oz/ 3g Onion Powder
1 teaspoon/ 0.21oz/ 6g Salt
1 teaspoon/ 0.07oz/ 2g Ground Black Pepper

Shrimp Ingredients:
1½ pounds/ 680g Raw Jumbo Prawns/Shrimp, peeled and deveined. (See Note)
1½ cups/ 7.7oz/ 220g Plain Flour
1½ cups/ 6.3oz/ 180g Polenta/ Cornmeal
1½ cups/ 11.8fl.oz/ 350ml Buttermilk
Oil for frying (peanut is best, but not suitable for nut allergy sufferers).

Remoulade Ingredients:
¼ cup/ 2fl.oz/ 60ml Prepared Mustard, preferable creole
1 ¼ cups/ 10fl.oz/ 300ml Mayonnaise
2 teaspoons/ 0.33fl.oz/ 10ml Prepared Horseradish
1 teaspoon/ 0.15fl.oz/ 5ml Dill Pickle Juice or Vinegar
1 teaspoon/ 0.15fl.oz/ 5ml Louisiana Style Hot Sauce, or more to taste
2 Cloves Garlic, crushed and minced

To Finish:
Sandwich 4 Po' Boy rolls, sub rolls, or 4 lengths of French bread baguette cut to 10 inch/ 25cm lengths
4 Tablespoons/ 2fl.oz/ 60ml Unsalted Butter, melted
2 to 4oz/ 60 to 120g Shredded Iceberg Lettuce
2 Beef/ Beefsteak Tomatoes, sliced
Sliced Dill Pickles (optional), plus 1 teaspoon/ 0.15fl.oz/ 5ml juice reserved for remoulade.

Prepare remoulade: mix all remoulade ingredients together, adding 1 Tablespoon of the spice blend. Season to taste. Cover with cling film and refrigerate for at least an hour for the flavours to meld. In a medium bowl, toss the shrimp in the buttermilk and 1 Tablespoon of the spice blend. Cover with cling film and refrigerate for an hour.
Heat oil to 180°C/350°F in a large saucepan or a deep fat fryer.
In another medium bowl, mix the flour, cornmeal and remaining spice mix. Line a plate with kitchen roll.
Remove the shrimp from the buttermilk and drain off the excess. Working in batches, dredge the shrimp in the flour mixture, fry in small batches for about a minute or until they are golden brown. Do not overcrowd the pan or it will lower the temperature and give you soggy shrimp. Remove cooked shrimp with a spider strainer to a paper towel lined plate. Allow the oil to come back to temperature between each batch.
To assemble the sandwiches, brush the inside of each roll with the melted better. Spread a layer of the remoulade on top of the butter. Place about 5 of the fried shrimps on the bottom half of the roll. Top with tomato, shredded lettuce and dill pickle slices, if desired. Serve with a cold beer and potato chips (crisps).
Serves 4

Note: The size of the shrimp is important. You want about 15 count prawns to the pound (500g) in weight. This size helps ensure the shrimp stay crisp and do not go rubbery. This recipe will give you about 5 shrimp per sandwich.

Contribution By: Afton Cochran

Swiss Beef

Miss Perkins loves this one and usually has seconds when it is on the menu!
Despite the name this one is from the U.K.

Ingredients:
- 1/3 cup/ 2.4oz/ 70g Plain Flour, or as much as is needed to cover the beef
- 2 Tablespoons/ 1fl.oz/ 30ml Olive or Vegetable Oil
- 3 Small Onions, chopped
- 1 Clove Garlic, minced
- 1 14oz/ 400g tin Chopped Tomatoes
- 1 Tablespoon/ 0.5fl.oz/ 15ml Tomato Purée/ Paste
- 2 to 4 Tablespoons/ 1 to 2fl.oz/ 30 to 60ml Worcestershire Sauce
- ¼ to ½ pint Beef Stock
- 1 to 1 ½ pounds/ 500 to 750g Lean Beef, cut into slices
- Salt and Pepper, to taste

Serve with home made sour cream!
(Found in R&D)

Flour and season the beef slices.
Heat the oil and fry in batches till nicely browned.
Remove to a casserole with a close-fitting lid.
Do not clean the frying pan!
Add more oil, fry the onions, scraping up all the gubbins, till softened. Add the garlic, cook till lightly browned.
Remove to the casserole with the meat.
Mix the stock, tomatoes, tomato purée and Worcestershire sauce, then stir a small amount into the pan to deglaze and thicken.
Pour this and all the stock into the casserole and stir well to combine.
Cover and cook at 325°F/ 165°C/ Gas Mark 3 for 2 to 2.5 hours. Stir occasionally and check your seasoning.

Serve with jacket potatoes, sour cream, and a nice green vegetable such as spring greens or kale.

Serves 4

Contribution By: Sara McKenna

Chorizo Orzotto

Ingredients:
- 8oz/ 225g Spanish Chorizo, chopped
- 2 Fillets/ 10.5oz/ 300g Chicken Breasts, boneless skinless, cubed
- 3 Cloves Garlic
- 17.6oz/ 500g Orzo Pasta
- 2 cups/ 17fl.oz/ 500ml Vegetable or Chicken stock, boiling
- 1 cup/ 4.5oz/ 130g Peas, frozen

Roughly chop up the chorizo up into half-moon shapes, about 1/2 inch/ 1cm thick and cube the chicken into 1inch/ 2.5cm. In a frying pan, gently fry the chorizo and chicken until lovely and golden; usually there is no need to add additional oil, but if it is needed, add a little olive oil. Add the garlic at the last minute. Pour in the orzo and stir it in to coat it with all the lovely golden oils. Add the peas and enough boiling stock to just cover the orzo. It is important not to stir the orzo too much. Keep an eye on it though because you do not want it to burn either. The mixture will go thick and gooey, let it simmer away until the water is almost gone, then test the grains and add more boiling stock if necessary, but a little bit of a tooth or bite it a good thing.
Serve it up in a big bowl, each with a spoonful of butter inside. This means the desired amount of butter is placed in the middle of the bowl to melt and coat the mixture.

Serves 4

Contribution By: Gina Burnside

Sausage Pasta

This is a favourite to have on the late, or super late shift. It can be scaled up or down very easily to feed one lonely historian or the whole IT department. It is also very forgiving and we swap out vegetables for whatever is in season.

Ingredients
Half a Small Onion, diced
Clove of Garlic, crushed
Half a Large Courgette, chopped
2 teaspoons/ 0.33fl.oz/ 10ml of Dijon Mustard
1 Tablespoon/ 0.5fl.oz/ 15ml of Crème Fraiche
1 Well Flavoured Sausage
Oven-Dried Tomatoes - a handful
Pinch of Chilli Flakes (optional)
Fresh Basil, chopped
¾ cup/ 2.6oz/ 75g Pasta, of choice

Cook pasta to the instructions on the packet.
Take the sausage meat out of the skins and rolls into small balls. Fry them gently until they start to brown. If the sausage is very lean you may need to add just a little olive oil to keep it from sticking.
Add the onion, garlic and courgette and fry until soft and golden.
Add the mustard and stir until the other ingredients are coated. Add the crème fraiche and the tomatoes, stirring gently so you do not break the tomatoes up. It will take a few minutes to warm through, do this slowly on a lower heat setting so that the crème fraiche does not break or curdle. If it is too thick, you can add a little of the pasta water.
When it is ready, stir through most of the chopped basil and sprinkle the rest on top. I like to add lots of black pepper and some chilli flakes.
Serves 1

Contribution By: Sara Pickering

Chicken and Rice Dish

This recipe is truly bananas! No seriously, it is one of those recipes that puts some strange things together and they come out lovely and so tasty! We would blame Professor Rapson for this one if he ever finished the recipe, but it was definitely Miss Lingoss.

Ingredients:
2 cups/ 16fl.oz/ 473ml Water
2 cups/ 16fl.oz/ 473ml White Wine or Sherry
1 Onion, sliced
1 Tomato, sliced
2 teaspoons/ 0.38oz/ 11g Salt
1 Chicken, approximately 5lb/ 2.27Kg
2 cups/ 18oz/ 500g Rice, cooked
½ cup/ 1.7oz/ 50g Celery, finely chopped
2 cups/ 8oz/ 127g Mushrooms, roughly chopped and browned
½ cup/ 1.8oz/ 52g Onion, finely chopped
1 cup/ 7.9oz/ 225g Banana, sliced
¼ cup/ 1oz/ 30g Parsley, chopped
¼ cup/ 2oz/ 57g Butter, melted
1 teaspoon/ 0.17oz/ 5g Salt
Sauce:
2 Tablespoons/ 0.98oz/ 28g Butter
1 clove Garlic, finely chopped
2 Tablespoons/ 0.5oz/ 15g Plain Flour
3 cups/ 24oz/ 709ml Chicken Stock
¼ cup/ 1.9fl.oz/ 59ml Creamy Milk or Single Cream
½ teaspoon/ 0.08oz/ 2g Salt

Cut chicken into similar sized pieces. Using a large roasting pan add the chicken, water, wine, sliced onion, tomatoes and 2 teaspoons of salt. Roast in the oven at 400°F/ 200°C/ Gas Mark 6 uncovered, for 35-40 minutes until tender. Use a meat thermometer to check they are thoroughly cooked through. Allow the chicken to cool slightly then remove the skin and set the skin aside for later. Remove any bones and cut the chicken into thin slices. Mix together the rice, celery, mushrooms, 1/2 cup of onion, banana, parsley, melted butter and 1 teaspoon of salt. In a greased casserole dish, place alternate layers of the chicken slices and the rice mixture. The top layer should be meat.
Sauce: Melt the butter in a pan and lightly brown the garlic and flour. Add the chicken stock, milk and 1/2 teaspoon of salt. Heat and stir diligently until the mixture is thick and smooth. Pour half of the sauce over the layered mixture in the casserole dish and bake in a moderate oven 350°F/ 180°C/ Gas Mark 4 for 30 minutes. Fry the chicken skin in a pan until crisp. When the casserole dish has baked for 30 minutes, remove it from the oven and pour over the remaining sauce. Crumb the crispy chicken skin over the top. Serve hot.

Contribution By: Jacqui Ryder

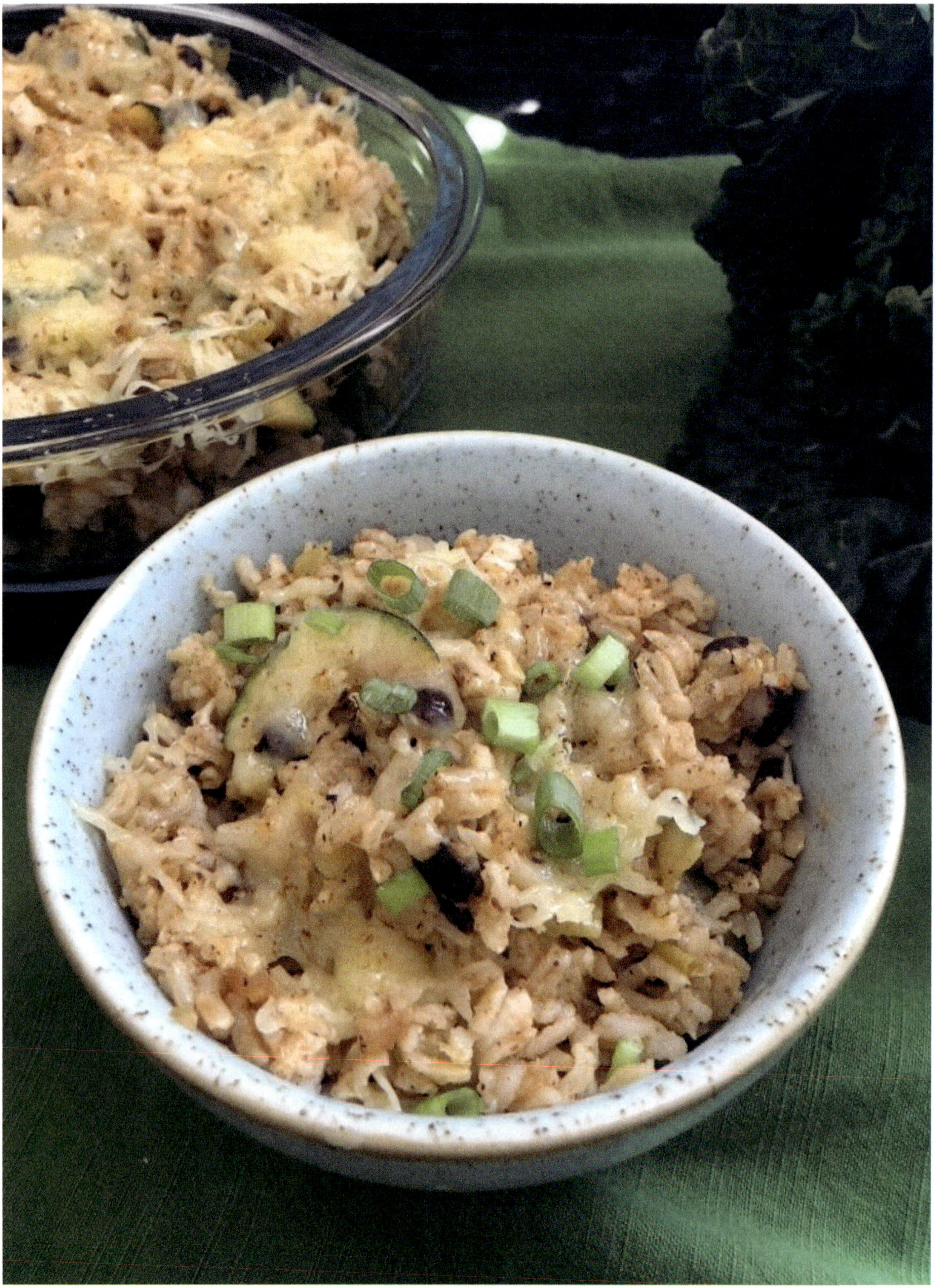

JUST ONE DAMN CASSEROLE AFTER ANOTHER

Life in the Kitchen department is never knows a dull moment.
With section heads popping through to discuss reloading pods,
the Security Section demanding chips at all hours and
the technicians wanting just one more bacon butty ...
Sometime it never ends!
So when Mrs Mack lost her temper about getting the 'damn casserole' in the oven,
well the name just stuck.

Ingredients
2 cups/ 11.8oz/ 340g Brown Rice
4 cups/ 32.1fl.oz/ 950ml Vegetable or Chicken Stock
1 Tablespoon/ 0.5fl.oz/ 15ml Olive Oil
1/2 Onion, diced
2 Medium Courgettes (Zucchini), thinly sliced
3 cooked Chicken Thighs, diced. You can use any leftover cooked chicken in this.
1/2 cup/ 2.4oz/ 70g Mushrooms, sliced (optional)
1/2 teaspoon/ 0.03oz/ 1g Ground Cumin
Salt to taste
Ground Cayenne Pepper to taste
1 -15oz/ 425g tin Black Beans, rinsed and drained
1 -4oz/ 114g can diced Green Chilli Peppers, drained - these are mild and are quite difficult to get in the UK. You can add green pepper or seeded and diced fresh green chillies, or just omit it, if you like.
1 to 2 cups/ 3 to 6oz/ 85-170g shredded Cheese, shredded (Cheddar, Monterey Jack, or Pepper Jack)

Place the stock in a pot and bring to a boil. Add rice and stir. Reduce heat to low, cover and simmer until rice is tender. Remove from heat but leave the lid on. Open, drain and rinse beans. Preheat oven to 350 °F/ 180 °C (160 °C Fan)/ Gas Mark 4. Lightly grease a large casserole dish.

Heat the olive oil in a skillet over medium heat and cook the onion until tender. Mix in the courgette and mushrooms. Sauté for a few minutes until the courgette is browned. Add chicken and heat through. Season with cumin, salt and ground cayenne pepper.

In large bowl, mix the cooked rice, onion, courgette, chicken, mushrooms, beans, chillies and 1/2 the cheese. Transfer to the prepared casserole dish and sprinkle with remaining cheese. Cover casserole loosely with foil and bake for 30 minutes in the preheated oven. Uncover and continue baking for 10 minutes, or until bubbly and lightly browned.

Serves 4

This would also make a great vegetarian dish!
Simply by omitting the chicken and use vegetable stock.

Photo and Contribution By: Afton Cochran and Sammie Backham

Fish Pie

There is a big debate on how fish pie should be served. Is it correct to serve it with a potato mash top? Is it correct to serve it with a pastry top? At St. Mary's we serve it both ways so there is no fighting, or vigorous academic debate.

Ingredients:
Filling
12oz/ 350g of Fish, recommended:
- 1 Salmon fillet, deboned and skin removed
- 12 Small Prawns/ Shrimp, deveined and shells removed
- 1 Smoked Haddock fillet, deboned and skin removed
- 1 White Fish fillet, deboned and skin removed

1 Onion or 2 Leeks, diced (optional)
½ teaspoon/ 0.02oz/ 1g Dill or to taste
Salt and Black Pepper to taste
1 ¼ cups/ 9.6fl.oz/ 285ml of Milk
2 Tablespoons/ 0.64oz/ 18g Plain Flour
2 Tablespoon/ 1oz/ 30g Butter

Add the fish to the bottom of a heavy bottomed pan and cover with the milk. Over a gentle heat, poach the fish but not the prawns, in the milk with dill, salt and pepper for 5 to 10mins or until the fish flakes easily with a fork. Remove the fish from the milk and put to one side. Sieve the milk to catch any little bits. Add half of the butter, leeks or onions to the pan if using and gently fry until soft and translucent. Remove from the pan and set aside.

Make a roux by adding half the butter to a frying pan over a medium heat and melt the butter. Add flour to the butter stirring and scraping the bottom of the pan. Add the sieved milk and cook until the sauce is lovely and thick. Flake the fish into largish pieces, add the prawns, leeks or onions and stir into the white sauce.

Pastry Fish Pie

Ingredients:
1 ¾ cups/ 8oz/ 227g Plain Flour
8 Tablespoons/ 4oz/ 113g Butter, Margarine, Lard or a mixture
Pinch of Salt
Cold Water
1 Egg Yolk

Rub the butter into the flour and salt until it resembles fine sand. Slowly add the cold water 1 Tablespoon/ 1fl.oz/ 15ml at a time and begin to bring the mixture together into a dough. Wrap the dough in clingfilm and cool in fridge for 20 to 30 minutes. On a lightly floured surface roll out and line a dish or tin with half the pastry. Blind bake the bottom crust at 350°F/ 180°C/ Gas Mark 4 for 10 minutes and allow to cool. Pour the filling into the pastry case, roll out remaining pastry and cover. Coat top of the pastry with beaten egg yolk wash. Bake in oven at 375°F/ 190°C/ Gas Mark 5 until golden. Allow to cool, serve warm or cold

Mash Topped Fish Pie

Ingredients
16oz/ 453g Floury Potatoes, peeled and cubed
½ cup/ 4fl.oz/ 118ml Cream, or Plant-Based Cream
1 Tablespoon/ 0.5oz/ 15g Butter, or Margarine
1/4 cup/ 0.79oz/ 22g Parmesan Cheese, grated
Salt and Black Pepper, to taste

*Be creative and use chips, or crisps on the top!
There are loads of possibilities!*

Peel, cube and place potatoes in a large saucepan and cover well with water. Bring to a simmer over medium-high heat. Reduce heat and cook until the potatoes are tender and can easily be poked with a fork, about 15 minutes. Drain potatoes well. Return the potatoes to the pot and add cream, butter, parmesan cheese and salt and pepper to taste. Mash potatoes as best as you can while mixing in the butter, cheese and cream. Pour the filling into a 9x9inch/ 23x23cm solid bottom pan and cover with the mashed potatoes. Add additional parmesan cheese to the top of the pie. Place pie on baking dish before placing it in the oven. Bake in the oven at 375°F/ 190°C/ Gas Mark 5 until well heated. About 20 to 25 minutes depending on the temperature going into the oven.

Serve warm with peas.

Photo by: Sara Robinson Contribution By: Barb Ruddle

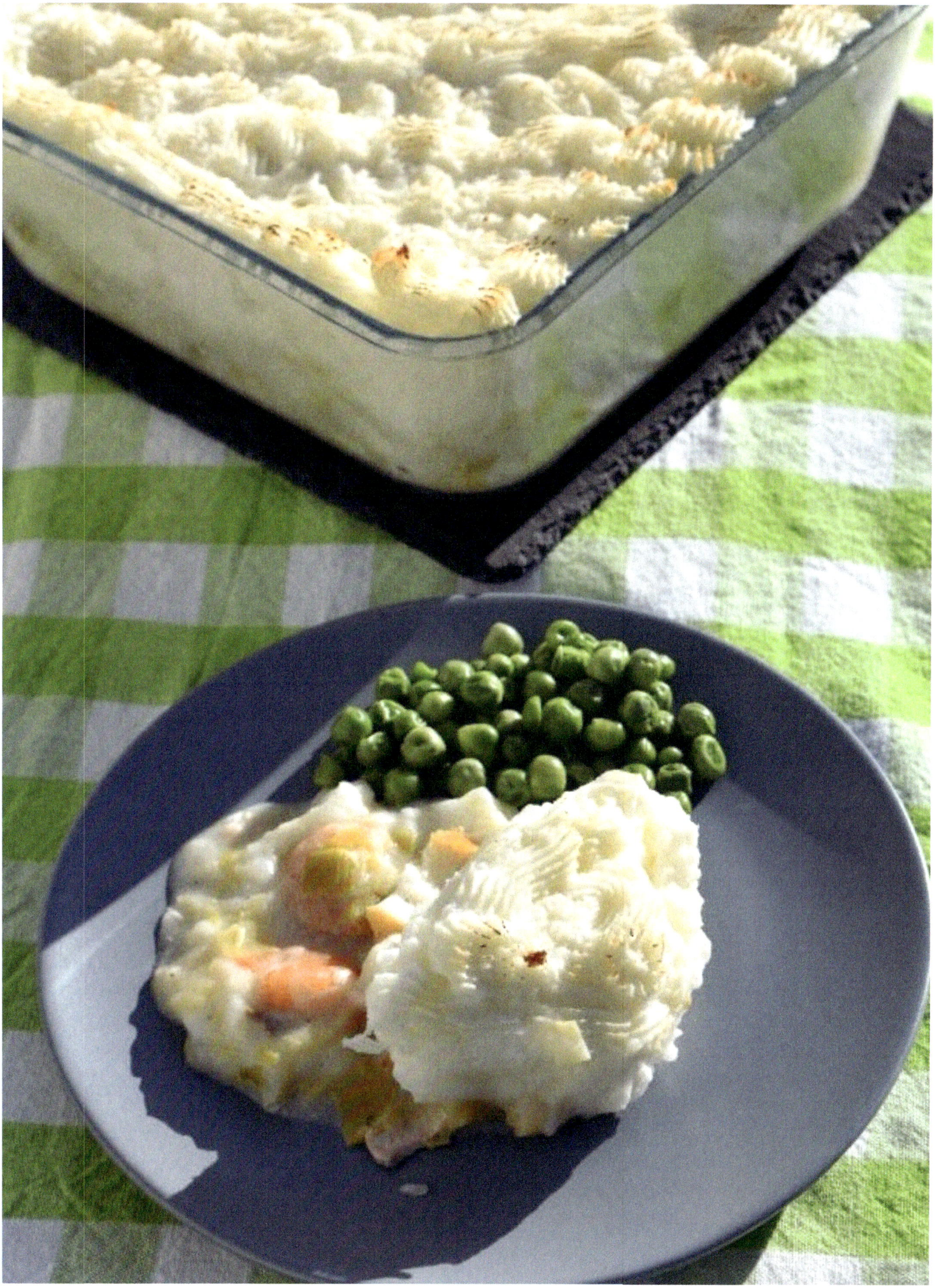

CHICKEN AND VEGETABLE PIE

Historians are not known for their culinary prowess and tend to gravitate to the comforting and familiar especially after a hard jump. This pie is amazingly so tasty and so comforting to eat.

Ingredients:
Pastry:
3 2/3 cups/ 16oz/ 453g Plain Flour
1 cup/ 8oz/ 227g Butter or Margarine, cold and cut into small cubes
Pinch Salt
2 Tablespoons/ 1fl.oz/ 30ml Cold Water

Filling:
2 ¼ cups/ 10.5oz/ 300g Chicken, cooked, deboned and then diced
5 1/2 cups/ 28oz/ 800g Vegetables, fresh or frozen
    We recommend a good mixture including carrots, peas,
    swede, bell pepper, sweet corn, leeks and potatoes

Gravy:
3 1/2 cups/ 28fl.oz/ 828ml Chicken or Vegetable Stock
1 teaspoon/ 0.2fl.oz/ 6ml Soy Sauce or Worcestershire Sauce to taste
1 Tablespoon/ 0.3oz/ 9g Cornflour to thicken, or more to achieve desired thickness

Great for Leftover Chicken!

Pastry:
Use a 9x13 inch pan
Sift the flour in a large bowl and add a pinch of salt. Cube the butter or margarine into small pieces and add to the flour. Rub together using fingertips until it resembles breadcrumbs, add cold water 1 Tablespoon/ 0.5fl.oz/ 15ml at a time to form a dough, wrap in clingfilm and cool in the fridge for at least a half hour. Remove from the fridge and divide into 1/3 and 2/3. Roll out the larger portion of dough to fit your dish so it covers the bottom, sides and over the edge so you can crimp it with the top when you have filled it.
Lay a piece of parchment paper over the dough in the dish and fill with pie weights or dried beans. Blind bake the pastry at 400°F/ 200°C (180°C fan)/ Gas Mark 6 for 10 minutes.
Remove and allow to cool.

If using fresh vegetables you will need to dice and then parboil veg for 10 minutes. Once it is done, drain in a colander and set aside. If you are using frozen veg make sure it is well defrosted and drained of moisture.

To make gravy:
In a small saucepan add chicken or vegetable stock, soy sauce or Worcestershire sauce and bring to a simmer. Make a slurry with the cornflour and a little water before adding it to the saucepan. Increase the temperature a little and whisk until it becomes lovely and thick. If it is too thin repeat making the cornflour slurry.

Mix the chicken and vegetables together and place in the pan over the bottom crust. Pour the gravy over the chicken and veg.

Roll out the smaller piece of dough so it fits over the top of your dish and edge. Dampen the edge of the pastry in the dish with a little water and lay the top over, crimp together by pressing your thumb on the edge all the way round. Trim off any excess. Wash the top of the pastry with milk, or a well beaten egg. Bake in oven 350°F/ 180°C/ Gas Mark 4 for 25 to 35 minutes or until golden.

Serves 6

This recipe can easily be made vegan by using margarine, vegan chicken, vegetable stock and soy sauce as an alterative in the ingredients.

Photo By: Sara Robinson   Contribution By: Barb Ruddle

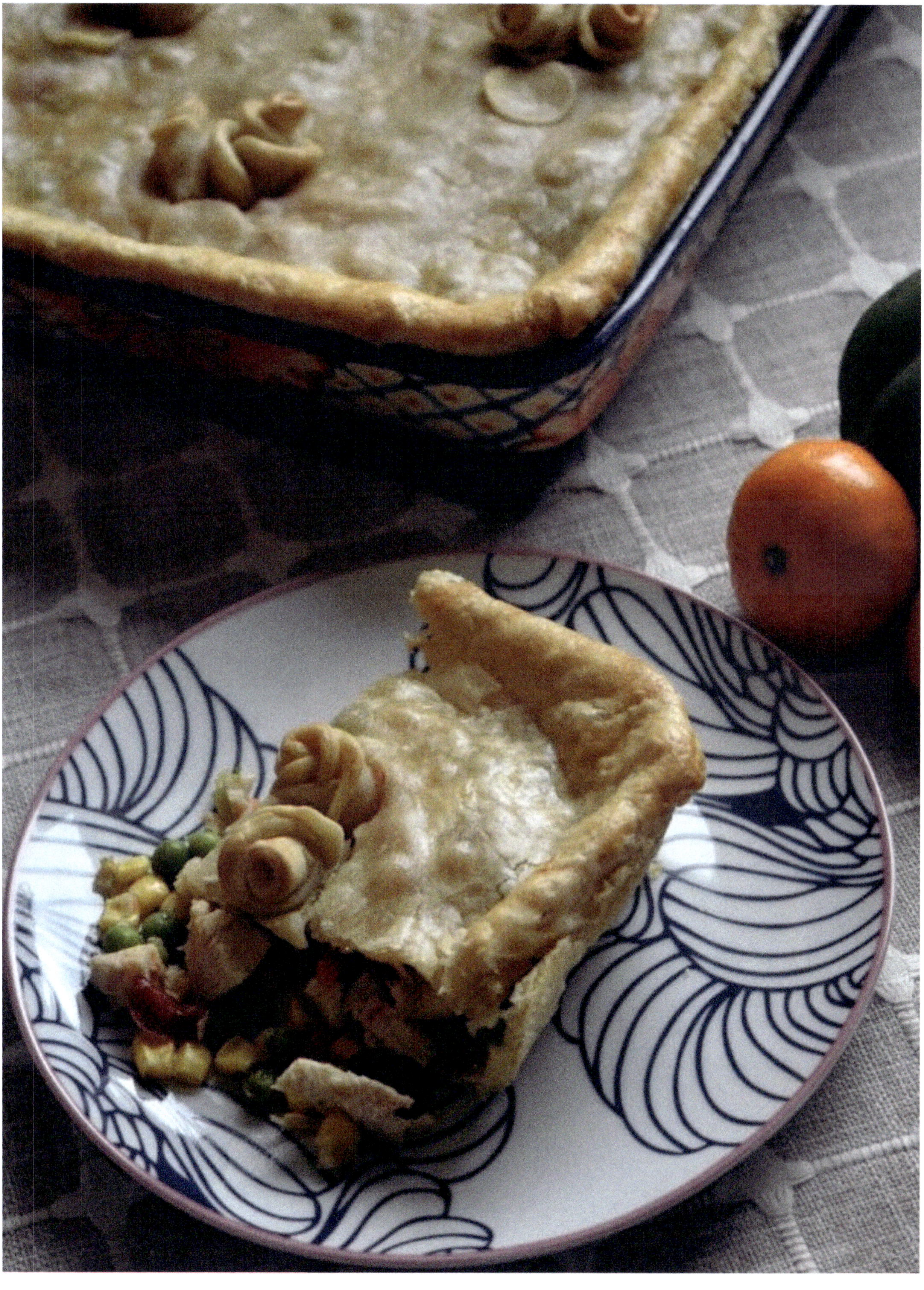

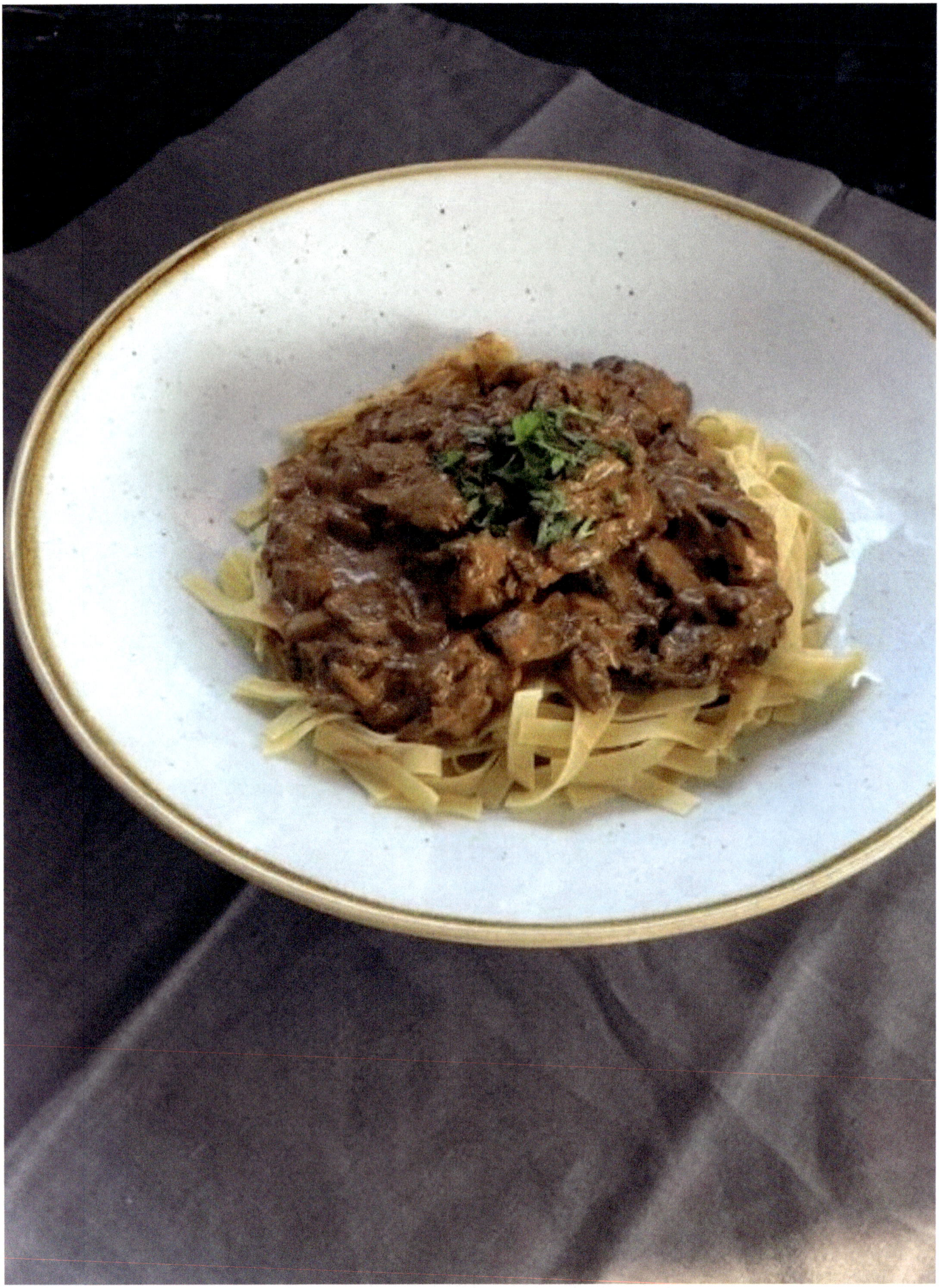

Beef Stroganoff

*Our team would fight through the harshest winter for this one.
It is so creamy and just delicious.*

Ingredients:
For marinade:
5 Tablespoons/ 2.5fl.oz/ 75ml Soy Sauce or GF Tamari Sauce
2 Tablespoons/ 1fl.oz/ 30ml Fish Sauce or Worcestershire Sauce
½ cup/ 4.2fl.oz/ 125ml Red Wine
2 Cloves Garlic, crushed and minced
1 Shallot, minced
2 Tablespoons/ 1 fl.oz/ 30ml Olive Oil
2.2pounds/ 1kg Lean Beef, such as rump steak

For the sauce:
1 Medium Onion, minced
5 Tablespoons/ 2.5oz/ 71g Unsalted Butter, divided into individual tablespoons
3 Tablespoons/ 1.5fl.oz/ 45ml Neutral Vegetable Oil
1 Tablespoon/ 0.21oz/ 6g Mild Paprika
1 Tablespoon/ 0.21oz/ 6g Smoked Paprika
1 Tablespoon/ 0.21oz/ 6g Aleppo Pepper, if unavailable, use an additional 1 Tablespoon/ 0.21oz/ 6g Smoked Paprika
2 teaspoons/ 0.17oz/ 5g Fresh Ground Pepper
1 cup/ 8fl.oz/ 250ml Good Quality Beef Stock
16oz/ 450g (1 lb) Mushrooms, any type and preferably a good mix and match of varieties Make sure they are cut into even sizes. See note if using porcini or dried mushrooms.
1 cup/ 8fl.oz/ 250 ml Marsala or dry white wine
2 Tablespoons/ 1fl.oz/ 30ml Tomato Purée/ Paste
3 Tablespoons/ 1.5fl.oz/ 45ml Dijon Mustard
1 Tablespoon/ o.5fl.oz/ 15ml Worcestershire Sauce
1 Tablespoon/ 0.5fl.oz/ 15ml Soy sauce or GF Tamari Sauce
1 teaspoon/ 0.5oz/ 15g Anchovy Paste (optional)
1 Tablespoon/ 0.08oz/ 3g Fresh Thyme, chopped
1 Bay Leaf
14fl.oz/ 400 ml Good Quality Sour Cream
1 Small Bunch Parsley, stems removed, finely minced
Cornflour slurry as needed.

Cooked Wide Egg Noodles, to serve

For marinade:
Thinly slice your meat. In a non-reactive container mix all your marinade ingredients. Add your meat, cover and refrigerate for at least three hours, but overnight is preferable.
Remove the meat from the marinade. Discard the marinade and pat the meat dry. Allow it to come to room temperature.
Mix the paprika, smoked paprika, Aleppo pepper and black pepper together and sprinkle evenly over the meat.
In a skillet or a Dutch oven, heat 2 Tablespoons/ 30ml oil with 1 of the tablespoons/ 15ml of butter. Brown your meat in batches, being careful not to overcrowd your pan. Do not cook the meat all the way through. Remove to a plate, cover with foil, and set aside.
In the same skillet, add another tablespoon of the oil and another tablespoon of the butter. Sauté your mushrooms until they release their liquid, absorb it again and start to brown. Add in another tablespoon of butter and add your minced onion. Sauté together with the mushrooms until the onions are soft and translucent. Turn the heat down a bit and add the tomato purée, Dijon mustard and anchovy paste, if using. Stir well to coat all the mushrooms and onions. Cook for a minute or two. Add the juices from the meat, the soy sauce, and Worcestershire sauce and cook for another minute or until the mushrooms have absorbed the liquid. Turn up the heat and your Marsala or white wine, thyme, and bay leaf. Bring it to a simmer and give it a good stir, scraping up any of the nice crusty bits off the bottom of the pan. Cook until almost all the liquid has been absorbed.
Pour 75 ml (1/3c) of the beef stock into the sour cream. Mix well and set aside.
Add the remaining stock to your mushroom mixture and reduce down by half. When it has reduced, drizzle your sour cream mixture slowly into the pan, stirring well. Thicken with a cornflour slurry. Add your meat back in right at the end, so it doesn't overcook. Check and adjust your seasoning. It shouldn't need any extra salt. Add your parsley, saving some for garnish.
Serve over wide egg noodles or rice and garnish with parsley.

Serves 5

Note: if using dried mushrooms, such a porcini (which lend a meaty earthy flavour) rehydrate them according to the package instructions. When ready to use, lift them out of any liquid with a slotted spoon to keep out any sediment at the bottom. Use as stated in the recipe.

(based on a recipe by Jennifer Eremeeva)   Photo and Contribution By: Afton Cochran

Spicy Lamb Meatballs

Such a lovely warming meal. Mrs De Winter is known for her lamb dishes and this one doesn't disappoint. The meatballs are easy to make and can be either fried or baked. It is just so tasty!

Ingredients:
For the meatballs:
2.2pounds/ 1kg Lamb Mince
¼ Onion, minced
1 teaspoon/ 0.07oz/ 2g Ground Ginger
1 teaspoon/ 0.07oz/ 2g Ground Coriander
1 teaspoon/ 0.07oz/ 2g Ground Cumin
2 Cloves Garlic, crushed or minced
1 Tablespoon/ 0.1oz/ 3g Fresh Thyme, chopped
Zest of 1 Lemon
Salt and pepper to taste
2 Tablespoons/ 1fl.oz/ 30ml Vegetable Oil, if frying

For the sauce:
4 Cloves Garlic, crushed or minced
¾ Onion, minced
18oz/ 500g Tomatoes, preferred are baby plum/ cherry/any small tomatoes
14fl.oz/ 410ml Double Cream (heavy cream)
4 Tablespoons/ 2fl.oz/ 60ml Tomato Paste/ Purée
Hot Pepper Sauce, to taste
Salt and pepper to taste

To finish:
6 Tablespoons/ 3fl.oz/ 90ml Greek Yoghurt
Juice of half a Lemon
Fresh Parsley, chopped

For the meatballs:
Put the lamb mince in a bowl, add ginger, coriander, thyme, cumin, zest, 2 cloves garlic, and the 1/4 minced onion. Mix well and shape into balls. Place on a baking tray on parchment and refrigerate for one hour. Heat oil over medium heat in the skillet in which you will make the sauce. Carefully fry the meatballs in batches until they are browned evenly. Set on a plate lined with kitchen roll to remove excess fat. Remove excess oil (carefully) and wipe the pan. If you would prefer not to fry the meatballs to brown them, place in a 400°F/ 200°C (180°C fan)/ Gas Mark 6 for 10 to 15 minutes, turning once to brown evenly.

For the sauce:
Heat olive oil in the large skillet over a medium heat. Add the ¾ onion, garlic and fry until translucent. Add baby tomatoes and fry for 5 minutes. They may burst, this is fine. Add your double cream, tomato paste/ purée, your favourite hot sauce (as much or as little as you like!) and salt and pepper. Stir well and add in your meatballs. Simmer for 5 to 10 minutes or until your meatballs are cooked through. Add the yoghurt and lemon juice, heat through and adjust the seasoning.

Serve over pappardelle, tagliatelle/fettuccine or crusty bread.

Serves 4

Photo and Contribution By: Afton Cochran

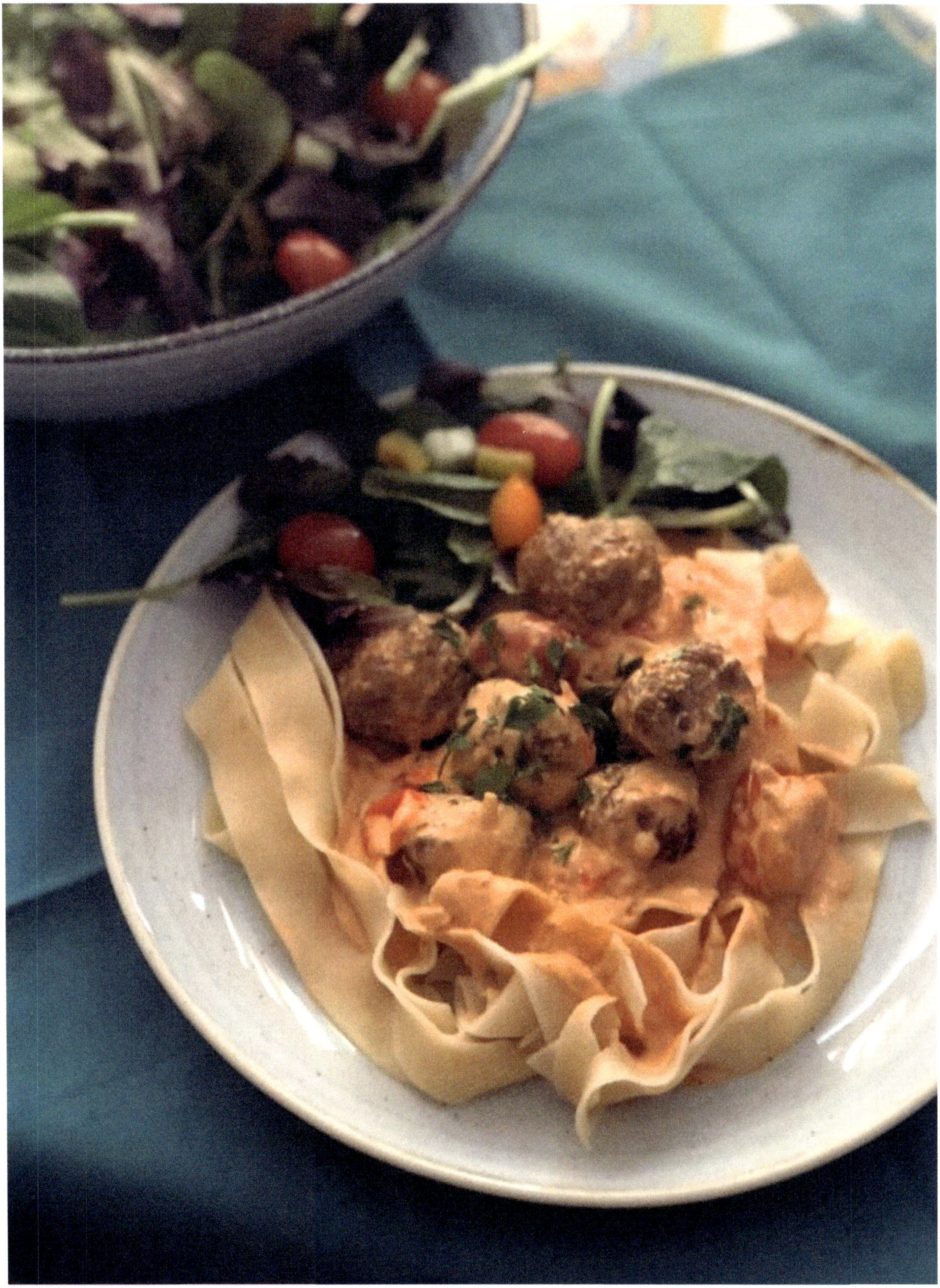

Lancashire Hotpot

It is a not the prettiest dish but it holds a special place in our hearts. Hotpot is eaten across the U.K. and is always a big hit at St Mary's.

Ingredients:
7 Tablespoons/ 3.5oz/ 100g Butter (or 3½ Tablespoons/ 1.7oz/ 50g Butter plus
 3½ Tablespoons/ 1.7oz/ 50g Fat/Drippings)
2 pounds/ 900g Stewing Lamb, roughly cubed about 1inch/ 2cm in size
2 Medium Onions, diced
1 to 2 Bay Leaves
3 to 4 Carrots, diced
4 to 6 Tablespoons / 1.2 to 1.9oz/ 36 to 54g Plain Flour
2 cups/ 17fl.oz/ 500ml Lamb Stock
2 Tablespoons/ 1fl.oz/ 30ml Red Wine
2 Tablespoons/ 1fl.oz/ 30ml Worcestershire Sauce
2.2 pounds/ 1kg Floury Potatoes
 sliced 3/22 to 1/8inch/ 3 to 5mm thick
Salt and Pepper, to taste

Preheat oven to 325°F/ 160°C/ Gas Mark 3

Season the lamb generously. Add a little butter or fat to a frying pan, let it melt slightly before adding a portion of the stewing lamb. Brown the meat in batches so not to over crowd the pan, adding more butter or fat as needed to prevent sticking. Place browned meat on a plate and set to the side.
Add a little more butter or fat to the frying pan and gently sauté the onions so that they slightly caramelise. Remove the onions to a plate and set aside.
Add additional butter or fat to repeat the process with the carrots, removing them to the side as well. The carrots should be slightly browned and just starting to soften.

There needs to be enough oil in the frying pan to be absorbed into the flour, a small amount of butter or fat might need to be added. Make a roux by adding the plain flour to the frying pan. Slightly toast the flour while briskly stirring all the cooked bits and oil into the flour, ensuring it is relatively lump free. Gradually add in the stock and red wine while whisking to form a beautiful gravy, bring to a boil to thicken to desired consistency. Whisk in Worcestershire sauce to give the gravy a nice umami flavour.

In an oven-safe dish or oven-safe frying pan, add in the bay leaves, meat, onions, carrots and gravy. Form a lid with the sliced potatoes by slightly overlapping the slices so that there are no gaps of the meat mixture showing, drizzle the potatoes with the remaining butter or fat and season with salt and pepper.

Cover the dish well and place on a baking tray before setting it into the oven. Cook for an hour and check the potatoes. If they are not yet soft when pierced with a knife, allow an additional 15 to 30 minutes cooking time with the pan well covered.

Remove the lid and brush the potatoes with a little butter or fat. Place the dish back in the oven or under the grill/ broiler for about 6 minutes or until the potatoes are golden and browned.
Serve with savoy cabbage or a braised red cabbage.
Serves 4

Note: traditional recipes add 2 to 3 chopped kidneys (1 inch/ 2cm pieces) which are browned after the browning of the lamb meat. If you like this flavour that is fine, but we do not serve it that way at St. Mary's.

Contribution By: Sara McKenna

Big Murdoch Pie

This one has survived from before Mrs Mack joined St. Mary's. Big Dave Murdoch had dinner duty one night and not knowing what to make, rummaged through the meagre kitchen cupboards and came up with his signature pie.

Ingredients:
14oz/ 400g Sausage Meat, or 16 Sausages
2 -14oz/ 400g tins Tomatoes, chopped
1 -14oz/ 400g tin Chickpeas
2 Bell Peppers, chopped
½ Onion, chopped
1 teaspoon/ 0.07oz/ 2g Paprika
1 teaspoon/ 0.03oz/ 1g Basil
1 teaspoon/ 0.03oz/ 1g Oregano
½ teaspoon/ 0.03oz/ 1g Ground Cinnamon
Salt and Pepper to taste
Your favourite shortcrust recipe or shop-bought shortcrust
1 Egg

Preheat oven to 350 °F/ 180 °C/ Gas Mark 4
Brown the sausage meat, or cut up the sausages with bell pepper and onion. Empty tins of tomatoes and chickpeas into the pan. Mix in all spices and heat until it is bubbly and smells good. Transfer the mixture to a pie dish and top with shortcrust pastry. Be sure to leave a vent hole in the middle! Paint the pastry well with a beaten egg wash. Bake for 20 to 25 minutes or until the pastry is golden and crispy.

Contribution By: Gina Burnside

Sausage and Bean Casserole

Mr Irving from the Security Department loves this dish because it reminds him of home and comfort. Please, don't let him eat it before a jump. This would be for the nasal comfort of everyone on the jump, it is worse then Eau de Pod!

Ingredients:
1 -14oz/ 400g tin Tomatoes, chopped
1 Garlic Clove, minced
1 teaspoon/ 0.03oz/ 1g Italian Herb Blend
1 Red Onion, finely chopped
1 -9oz/ 265g tin of Mixed Beans
Olive Oil for frying
Salt and Pepper to taste
Sausages - 2 Pork and 2 Chorizo or any 4 Sausages of choice.

Preheat oven 350°F/ 180°C/ Gas Mark 4.
Put olive oil and minced garlic in a pan, then add the chopped onion and cook on low heat, do not allow to brown. Add tomatoes, beans and herbs allow to simmer for 5 to 10 minutes. Season with Italian herb blend and salt and pepper to taste. Put the sausages into a casserole dish pour the sauce over and cook in oven for 20 minutes.
Add a little water if sauce is too thick or if it seems to be too dry.
Serve with garlic bread or crusty rolls.
Serves 2

Additions like ½ cup/ 1.5oz/ 42g grated cheese of choice added 5 to 10 minutes before the end of cooking in the oven, and/ or a fried egg on top when served are tasty!

Contribution By: Barb Ruddle

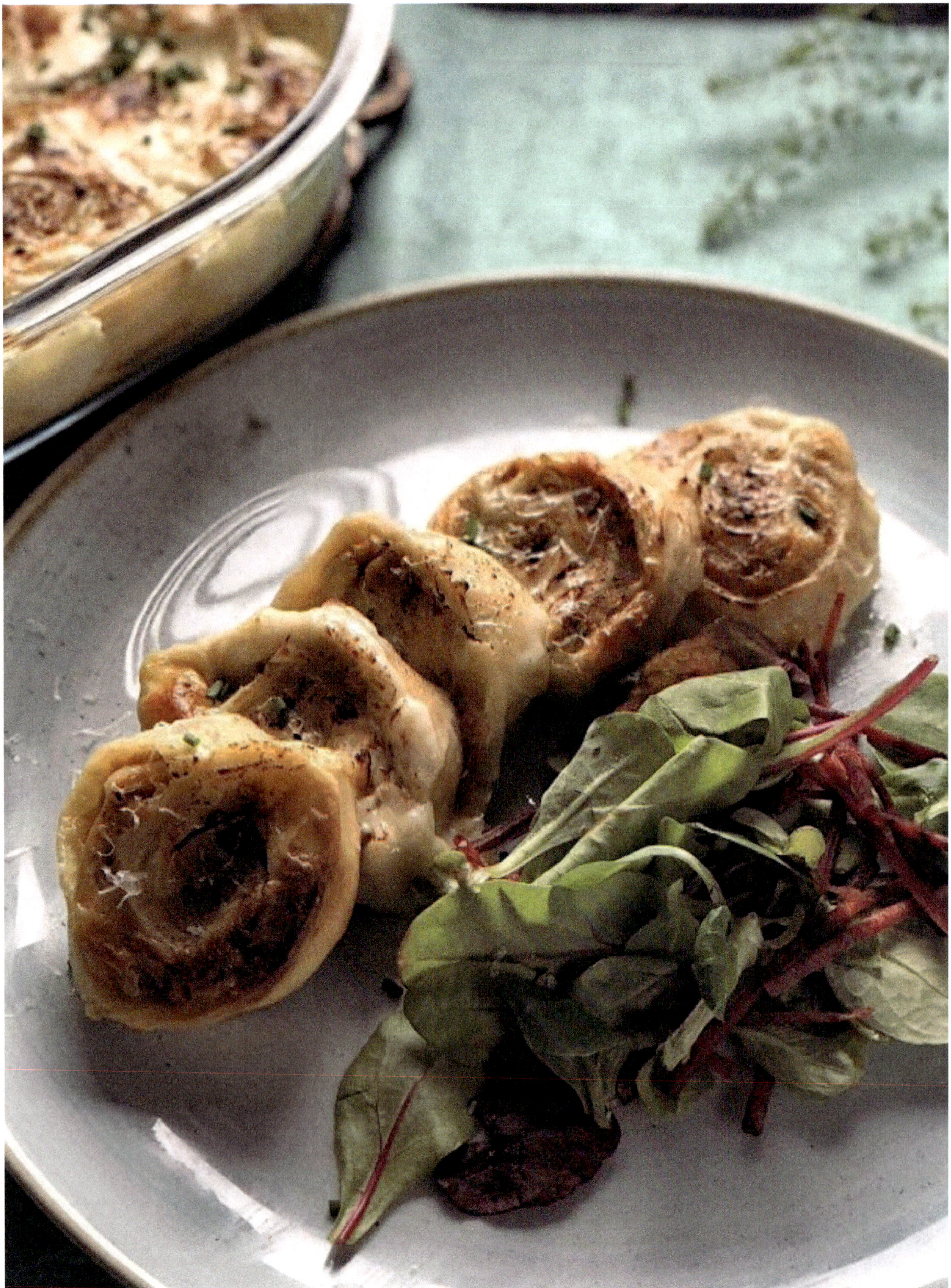

NIDI DI RONDINE
SWALLOW'S NESTS

You would think as this was a recipe containing pasta, that it would be Italian. Nope. This recipe comes from the tiny country of San Marino.

PASTA

Ingredients:
Pasta:
1 ¼ cups/ 7oz/ 200g 00 (Pasta) Flour
2 Eggs

Place the flour in a medium sized bowl. Crack the eggs into the bowl and mix with a fork and then with your hands, until you get a smooth and homogeneous dough. Wrap the dough in cling film and leave it to rest at room temperature.

It is essential that you use 00 (pasta) flour. It is the finest milled flour and is best to produce a smooth, silky pasta.

FILLING

Ingredients:
1 Shallot, finely minced
14oz/ 400g Sausage Meat
2 Tablespoons/ 1fl.oz/ 30ml Olive Oil
20 Courgette Flowers
5.2oz/ 150g Provolone Sliced
½ cup/ 1.7oz/ 50g Parmigano Reggiano
10fl.oz/ 300ml Béchamel (recipe below)
Salt and Pepper to taste

In a skillet over a medium heat, add the olive oil. When the olive oil is hot, add the shallot and gently fry for a minute. Add the sausage meat and brown it through. Add the courgette (zucchini) flowers, and a bit of salt and pepper. Cook for about 5 minutes. Remove the mixture to a bowl and allow it to cool.

*Ideas for additional fillings: Ham * Emmental * Sausage * Courgette flowers * Provolone * Salami * Ricotta Mozzarella * Spinach * Rocket (arugula) * Spinach and Ricotta * Porcini or other mushrooms (Sautéed and finally minced) Courgette/Zucchini (thinly sliced and sautéed)*

BÉCHAMEL

Ingredients:
5 teaspoons/ 0.88oz/ 25g Butter
3 ¼ Tablespoons/ 0.88oz/ 25g Plain Flour
1/2 Onion, studded with cloves and
    bay leaves (Onion Pique)
1 ½ cups/ 12.6fl.oz/ 375ml Whole Milk
Freshly Grated Nutmeg

Gently warm the milk with the pique in a pan over a medium heat. Do not bring it to the boil. The milk should be hot, but not boiling. Remove it from the heat and leave the pique in to infuse while you prepare the roux.
In a skillet over a medium heat, melt the butter until it begins to bubble, but not brown. Add the flour and a pinch of salt and mix well until the flour and butter are combined. Stir occasionally, allowing the flour to cook. This step is essential because you do not want your béchamel to taste like raw flour. Cook for 2-5 minutes, stirring often. Carefully strain the milk into a jug and discard the pique. Slowly add the milk to the roux, a bit at a time, stirring well to avoid lumps, ensuring it's well mixed and smooth in between additions of milk. When you have used all the milk and have a nice smooth sauce, cook for a few more minutes, then grate some fresh nutmeg into the sauce. Stir well, pour into a jug and cover with cling film, ensuring that the film is completely covering the surface of the béchamel so it does not form a skin as it cools. Set aside to cool.

ASSEMBLY

On a lightly floured surface, roll out the pasta into a thin, even rectangular shape. Cover the surface with about 2 tablespoons/ 30ml of the béchamel.
Lay the slices of provolone evenly over the pasta, place the sausage and courgette flower mixture evenly over the cheese. Grate a third of the Parmesan on top of the meat.
Carefully and tightly roll the pasta up from the long side of the rectangle, wrap it tightly in cling film and put in the freezer for 45 minutes to an hour to make it easier to cut.
Heat the oven to 350 °F/ 180 °C (160°C fan)/ Gas Mark 4.
In a baking dish, add a couple of tablespoons of the béchamel and distribute it evenly over the base.
Slice the roll of pasta into 20 slices about 2cm (1in) thick. Place them in the baking dish, overlapping slightly if needed. Cover evenly with all the remaining béchamel, grate the remaining Parmesan on the top.
Bake for 20 to 30 minutes or until the internal temperature reaches 167°F/ 75°C and is golden brown on the top.

Contribution and Photo By: Afton Cochran

Toad In The Hole

Vortigern the famous kitchen cat is known for looking for tasty treats and for bringing 'gifts' to the kitchen crew. On Jenny Fields' first day she jumped higher then the toad he gifted her! Luckily the toad wasn't seriously hurt and she released him down by the lake.

Ingredients:
Toad:
8 Toads (ahem, Sausages) of your choice.
2 Tablespoons/ 0.45oz/ 13g Lard or
    2 Tablespoons/ 1fl.oz/ 30ml Vegetable Oil

Hole:
1 cup/ 8oz/ 227g Plain Flour
Pinch of Salt
2 Eggs
2 cups/ 16fl.oz/ 475ml Whole Milk

Pre-heat your oven to 400°F/ 200°C (180°C fan)/ Gas Mark 6

In order to have a place to put your toads, you need a hole.

Sift your flour into a mixing bowl. Add a pinch of salt. Make a well in the centre of the flour and crack your eggs into the well. Slowly stir the eggs together, gradually incorporating the flour into the eggs. Once they're combined, slowly add your milk until the mixture becomes smooth and lump free. It should be the consistency of double (heavy) cream. You can even do this the night before and cover and refrigerate it. In a large roasting pan (30x12x6cm/ 9x13inches), place your toads (ahem, sausages). Put the pan in your preheated oven for 12 minutes or until they ~~start jumping around~~ are just cooked. Remove your pan from the oven. Turn the oven up to 425°F/ 220°C(200°C fan)/ Gas Mark 7. Add the knob of lard or veg oil and put back in the oven to heat up for 3 to 4 minutes. Get your batter out, and give it a good stir. When the oil in the pan is hot and smoking, (be careful because hot fat spits and burns!) carefully rearrange your toads (sigh, your sausages) so they are well spaced. Pour your batter evenly through the pan and place it back in the oven for a further 20 minutes, or until the batter is cooked through and has risen and is crispy. DON'T OPEN YOUR OVEN DOOR (or else the toads will escape) until it's cooked, or it won't stay nice and puffy. Serve with a lovely onion gravy, and fresh steamed vegetables.
Serves 4 to 6

Red Onion Gravy

Ingredients:
1 ¾ Tablespoons/ 0.88oz/ 25g Butter
2 Tablespoons/ 1fl.oz/ 30ml Olive Oil
1 Bay leaf
4 Sprigs Fresh Thyme
4 Onions or 8 Shallots, these can be a combination or red, white, or brown, thinly sliced
2 cups/ 18oz/ 500 ml Beef Stock
1 teaspoon/ 0.14oz/ 4g Brown Sugar
2 teaspoons/ 0.33fl.oz/ 10ml Red Wine Vinegar
1 teaspoon/ 0.16fl.oz/ 5ml Worcestershire Sauce
¾ cup plus 1 Tablespoon/ 6.7fl.oz/ 200 ml Red Wine, good quality
2 Tablespoons/ 0.5oz/ 15g Plain Flour **OR**
2 Tablespoons/ 0.7oz/ 20g Cornflour
Salt and pepper to taste

In a heavy bottomed skillet, heat the oil and butter on a medium heat. When the butter has melted and is bubbly, add your bay leaf and thyme. Let them gently fry for a minute to infuse the flavour of the herbs into the butter. Add your onions, turn the heat to medium and gently fry for 10 minutes until translucent and soft. Do not allow them to brown or burn. Turn your heat to low add sugar and a pinch of salt and pepper, stir well and slowly cook the onions until they are soft and caramelised, stirring occasionally. This will take about an hour. Good things take time. When the onions are nice and caramelised, turn up the heat to medium and sprinkle the flour over. Add a little salt and pepper. Stir it well, so that those yummy onions are nicely coated in the flour and cook for a couple minutes to get rid of the flour taste. Slowly add your red wine and stock and stir well until it thickens and has no lumps. Add your Worcestershire sauce and vinegar and season to taste.

"To make this a cheap dinner, you should buy 6d or 1s worth of bits or pieces of any kind of meat, which be to be had cheaper at night when the day's sale is over." - Charles Esme Francatelli, "No. 59. Toad in the Hole", from: A Plain Cookery Book for the Working Classes, 1861

Contribution By: Afton Cochran and Barb Ruddle

Sunday Roast

Sunday Roast is a tradition in most houses in the U.K. and is something that St. Mary's takes great pleasure in. The menu changes a little bit with the season but the same incredibly tasty and simple foods shine like jewels in a crown, or dishes on the table.

Defrosting:

Defrosting: Defrost your meat in a cool room or refrigerator (under 10 to 15C/50 to 59F) to ensure the outside of the meat remains cold. Never defrost meat in a warm room, as it can lead to food poisoning. Ensure poultry is completely defrosted before cooking. For turkey: defrost in a cool room under the temps stated above for 3 to 4 hours per kilo/2lbs or, ideally in a fridge at 10 to 12 hours per kilo/2lbs.

Rib of Beef

Ingredients:
Rib of Beef
3 Carrots, peeled and chopped
3 Celery Stalks, chopped
1 Onion, cut into wedges
1 Leek, trimmed and sliced
2 Bay Leaves
6 Peppercorns
Red Wine
Brown Stock (pg 54) or Water
Corn Flour Slurry
Salt and Pepper, to taste
Mustard or Garlic Powder (optional)

This is the mother of all roasts, a real treat for your Sunday roast!

Remove the beef from the refrigerator and allow to come to room temperature.
Remove all packaging and pat dry with kitchen roll.
Season the meat all over with salt and pepper. You can also coat the layer of fat on the top with garlic or mustard powder. This will help give it a crust on the top.
Preheat the oven to 425°F/ 220°C (200°C fan)/ Gas Mark 7.
In a roasting tray, place the vegetables, bay leaves and peppercorns in the bottom and stand the rib on the vegetables, ribs pointing up. Add a splash of red wine to the bottom, but don't allow the meat to get wet. Place the tray on the bottom rack of the oven and allow it to cook for 20 minutes.

Turn the heat down to 350°F/ 170°C (150°C fan)/Gas Mark 3 and cook, using the guide below:
Rare: 10 to 15 min per 500g (per pound) or internal temp 50°C/125°F
Medium rare: 15 min per 500g (per pound) or internal temp 54°C/130°F
Medium: 20 min per 500g (per pound) or internal temp of 58°C/136°F

Always insert your meat thermometer into the middle of the joint without it touching any bones. When the desired internal temperature is reached, remove the tray from the oven, place the joint on a plate and cover with a foil tent. Allow it to rest for 20 to 30 minutes, depending on the size of your joint. Slice your beef, serve with Yorkshire pudding, horseradish sauce, roast potatoes, your favourite vegetable side dishes and plenty of jus or gravy.

Notes:

A rib of beef should have the bones in, be aged at least 21 days, a good layer of fat on the top, and a good marbling of fat throughout. Do not remove the fat before cooking as it is needed to keep the meat moist and full of flavour.
A rib of beef should be cooked from room temperature, at a high heat initially, which allows a nice crust to form and seals the juices inside.
Knowing the weight of the beef is vital to ensuring your cooking times are accurate for the level of doneness you desire for the meat.
An instant read thermometer is incredibly helpful in ensuring your beef is cooked to the internal temperature you desire. Remember, do not allow the probe to touch the bone. You will not get an accurate reading.
Also remember that the outer layers of the meat will be more done than the middle, which allows for people to have a variety of doneness.
Resting the meat after cooking is vital. Do not skip this step. Resting allows the meat to reabsorb the juices and makes the meat easier to carve.

Contribution By: Afton Cochran

Sunday Roast

Roast Chicken

Ingredients:

1 Whole Free-Range Corn-Fed Chicken, about 3.3 pounds/ 1.5 kg
5 Tablespoons/ 2.6oz/ 75g Butter
1 bunch of Fresh Thyme, Fresh Rosemary, or Fresh Parsley, or a combination of your choosing.
4 cloves Garlic, 2 crushed and minced finely and two crushed
3 Carrots, peeled and chopped
3 Celery Stalks, chopped
1 Leek, trimmed and sliced
2 Onions, peeled and cut into wedges
2 Bay Leaves
8 Peppercorns
White Wine
300 ml Chicken Stock

Remove your chicken from the refrigerator and allow it to come to room temperature before cooking. Remove all the packaging and pat dry with kitchen roll.

Remove the leaves from half of the herbs and finely chop them. Set the remainder aside. In a bowl, add butter, the 2 cloves of finely minced garlic, the chopped herbs and salt and pepper. Mix well.

Heat your oven to 400°F/ 200°C (180°C fan)/Gas Mark 6.

Place the carrot, celery, leek, remaining onion, bay leaves and peppercorns in a roasting tin.

Using a clean hand, gently loosen the skin away from the chicken breasts being careful not to rip or remove it. Carefully push half the butter mixture under the skin of the breasts and the remainder on top of the thighs and drumsticks. Place the remaining 2 whole crushed cloves of garlic into the cavity of the chicken, along with the remaining herbs on the stems and one of the onions that you cut into wedges. Place the chicken, breast side up on the nest of vegetables, add a splash of white wine to the bottom of the pan, and place in the oven for 20 minutes plus 20 minutes per 500g (per pound), basting every 20 minutes with the lovely buttery juices. The chicken will be done when a thermometer put in the thickest part of the thigh (not touching the bone) reaches 167°F/ 75°C. Remove onion, garlic and herbs from the carcass, pouring the juices from the chicken back into the pan. Put the chicken on a plate, cover it with a foil tent and allow it to rest for 15 to 20 minutes before carving.

Use the vegetables, drippings, wine and stock to make the jus or gravy using the method on page 102.

Photo by: Sara Robinson   Contribution By: Afton Cochran

Roast Leg of Lamb

Ingredients:

1 Leg of Lamb, approximately 2.5kg /5 lbs
1 Bulb Garlic
1 Bunch Fresh Rosemary
Salt and Pepper
1 Onion, peeled and cut into wedges
3 Carrots, peeled and chopped
2 Stalks Celery, chopped
1 Leek, trimmed and sliced
2 Bay Leaves
6 Peppercorns
Red Wine
Lamb or Brown Stock
2 teaspoons/ 0.04fl.oz/ 10ml Mint Sauce, plus more to serve

Note: Meat sliced near the outside of the joint will be more well done than that nearest the bone. This allows you to have a variety of doneness to suit your guests.

Remove the lamb from the refrigerator and allow it to come to room temperature. Remove all packaging and pat dry with kitchen roll. Make 36 small incisions all over the lamb, spaced evenly. Remove all the cloves of garlic from the bulb and peel each one. Slice half of the cloves of garlic into thin slices. Put these slices into the incisions you made into the lamb. Pull or cut small sprigs of the rosemary off the stem (saving a few stems for the roasting tray), and put these in the incisions with the garlic. Season the lamb generously with salt and pepper. Heat oven to 220C/200fan/425F. In a large roasting tray, place the onion, carrot, celery, leek, the remainder of the garlic and rosemary, the bay leaves and the peppercorns. Place the leg of lamb skin side up, on top of the vegetables. Add a large splash of red wine to the pan, and place on the middle rack of the oven. Cook for 20 minutes. Turn the heat down to 350 °F/ 180 °C (160°C fan)/ Gas Mark 4 and cook: Medium rare: 20 minutes per 500g (per pound) or until the internal temperature reads 150°F/ 65°C Medium: 25 minutes per 500g (per pound) or until the internal temperature reads 160°F/ 70°C Well done: 30 minutes per 500g (per pound) or until the internal temperature reads 165°F/ 75°C. Remove the roast from the oven, set the lamb on a plate or cutting board covered in a tent of foil and allow it to rest. Drain the juices from the roast back into the roasting tray and make the gravy or jus as listed on page 88, adding a few teaspoons of mint sauce for added flavour. Serve with roast potatoes or new potatoes, your choice of vegetables, and plenty of mint sauce or jelly.

Contribution By: Afton Cochran and Sara McKenna

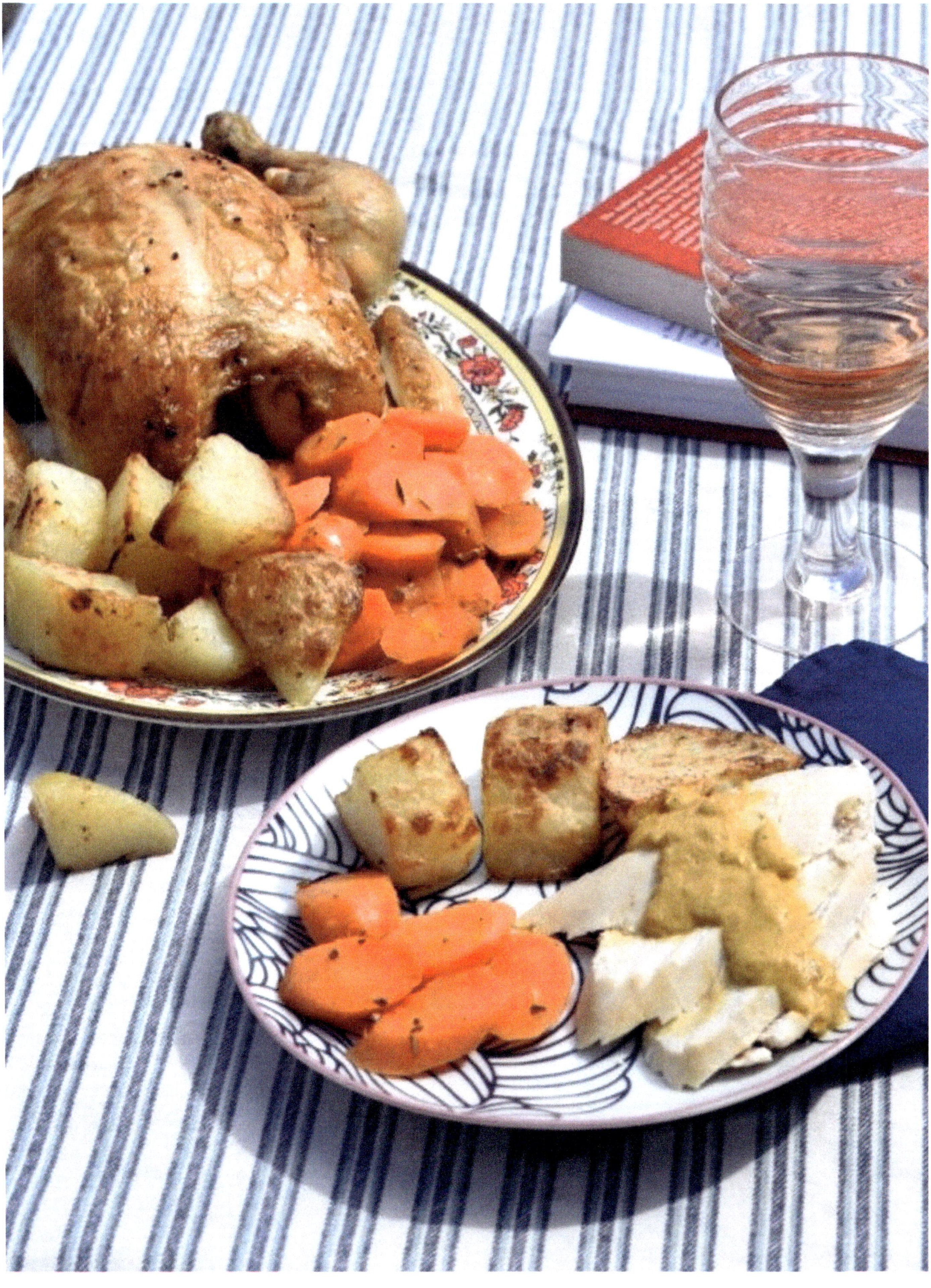

Sunday Roast Sides

What is a roast without some of the accompaniments?

Jus/ Gravy

While the meat is resting, place your roasting tray on the hob on a high heat. Deglaze the pan with red or white wine, depending on the roasted meat, making sure to scrape up any of those nice, crusty bits off the bottom. When this is done, strain the liquid into a pot from the solids and dispose of the solids. Add as much of the brown stock, or water as you need for gravy, bring to the boil and reduce to desired level for jus, or thicken with a cornflour slurry for gravy.

Contribution By: Afton Cochran

Roast Potatoes

Ingredients:
- 2.2 pounds/ 1kg Large Potatoes, such as Maris Piper, washed and peeled and cut into 6 to 8 pieces
- 1 1/4 cup/ 10fl.oz/ 300ml Olive Oil
- 2 teaspoons/ 0.17oz/ 5g Onion Seasoning (recipe in R&D)
- Salt and Pepper, to taste

Clean, peel and cut the potatoes into large pieces. In a large pan submerge the potato pieces into water. Bring the potatoes up to a boil for 5 to 8 minutes. The potatoes should have a soft exterior and a raw interior. Drain the potatoes in a colander immediately and dry the potatoes as well as you can. In a large roasting pan place the oil, coating the bottom of the pan, before adding the potatoes and then sprinkling the salt, pepper and onion seasoning over the top of the potatoes. Coat the potatoes well in the oil. Make sure there is only 1 layer of potatoes.
Preheat the oven 425 °F/ 220 °C (200°C fan)/ Gas Mark 7
Roast in a hot oven for about 30 minutes. Remove from the oven and turn the potatoes coating them again in the oil. Return the potatoes to the oven for an additional 15 to 20 minutes or until the outside is the desired crispiness and they clang against the roasting pan. Drain on a little kitchen roll before serving.

Contribution By: Gina Burnside and Sara Robinson

Citrus Roasted Carrots

Ingredients:
- 17.6oz/ 500g Large Carrots, washed, peeled, and sliced into ½inch/ 1.3cm pieces
- 6 Tablespoons/ 3fl.oz/ 90ml Butter, melted
- 2 teaspoons/ 0.14oz/ 4g Thyme, leaves
- 1 Orange, zested and juiced
- Salt and Pepper to taste

Preheat the oven 400 °F/ 200 °C (180°C fan)/ Gas Mark 6
Clean, peel and slice the carrots. Place the melted butter into a deep roasting pan add the carrots, thyme, orange zest, salt and pepper to the pan. Toss the carrots in the butter mixture. Roast in the oven for 25 minutes, remove from the oven, toss the carrots and return to the oven for a further 10 to 15 minutes. Remove from the oven, toss again in the butter and about half of the orange juice. Serve hot.

Contribution By: Sara Robinson

Yorkshire Puddings

Ingredients:
- 4 Eggs
- 1 ½ cups/ 11.8fl.oz/ 350ml Milk
- 1 ½ cups/ 7.9oz/ 225g Plain Flour
- Pinch of Salt
- Lard or Goose Fat or Vegetable Oil.

Crack the eggs into a jug and gently whisk together with the milk.
In another bowl, mix the flour and salt. Pour the egg and milk mixture into the flour, stir well. There may be some lumps left over. This is fine.
Pour the mixture back into the jug you mixed the egg and milk in, cover and refrigerate for 4 hours or overnight.
Preheat your oven to 395°F/ 200°C (180°C fan)/ Gas Mark 6
In a deep Yorkshire pudding tin, or deep muffin pan, add a teaspoon of your chosen fat into each of the holes. Remove the batter from the fridge. It may have scum on the top. Do not worry about this, just give it a good stir.
Place your pan in the oven for 5 minutes or until the fat is smoking.
Remove the pan from the oven. Take care because the fat will be extremely hot. Carefully pour the batter into each hole, about halfway up the sides. Be careful of the fat splattering.
Carefully put the tin in the oven and cook for 20 minutes without opening the door. After the 20 minutes, you can carefully open the door to check if they are done. If they are not done, close the oven and cook for another 2 to 3 minutes.
Serve with some mushroom ketchup and gravy alongside your roast beef and favourite vegetables!

Contribution By: Afton Cochran

Chapter Five:
The Security Department
Or
Those Worldly Lovable Scamps
Or World Foods

Where would we be without the Security Department? They have saved our bacon more often then anyone can count. They are the best at their jobs. They are also our lovable scamps and keep us on our toes!

Recipes:

Thai Corn Fritters	94
Sri Lankan Dhal	96
Bombay Aloo/ Bombay Potatoes	96
Cashew Chicken	97
Salt and Pepper Prawns and Curry Udon	99
Lahmacun/ Turkish Pizza	101
Tabbouleh and Jollof Rice	102
Bobotie and Geelrys	103
Mafe Stew	104
Shakshuka	106
Greek Fish Stew and Horiatiki/ Greek Village Salad	108
Pollo Alla Caccitore	109
Mediterranean Baked Cod	109
Carbonnade Flamande	110
Soupe à l'Oignon de ma Mère/ My Mothers Onion Soup	112
Croque Monsieur	112
Chicken and Mushroom Fricassee	114
Tartiflette	114
Red Onion Tarte Tatin	115
Hope for the Best, Plan for the Wurst	116
Borscht	118
Verlorene Eier in Kräutersoße/ Lost Eggs in a Herb Sauce	120
Peppercorn– Pothast	120
Hungarian Goulash	121
Pastel de Choclo	123
Slow Cooked Pork Carnitas	124
Guacamole	127
Canja	128
Ensalada de Portos con Cebolla/ Chilean Bean and Onion Salad	128

Thai Corn Fritters

These golden nuggets are perfect to make for a jump. Perfect, because they keep nosey historians munching instead of asking questions or worse yet, placing blame on the totally professional Security Department.

Ingredients:
2.2 lbs/ 1kg Sweetcorn, fresh or frozen
2 Tablespoons/ 1.2 oz/ 35g Red Curry Paste
1 quart/ 1 Litre Neutral Oil, for frying
2 Eggs
1 ½ cups/ 7.5 oz/ 213 g Rice Flour
2 teaspoons/ 0.3 oz/ 10g Baking Powder
1 Tablespoon/ 0.5 oz/ 15g Salt
6 Kaffir Lime leaves or a small bunch of fresh Thai Basil Leaves
    (Do not use Mediterranean Basil)
Sweet Chilli Sauce for dipping

If you are using frozen corn, ensure that it is completely defrosted and patted dry.

Heat the oil in a large pan to 150C (300F). Never fill a pan with oil more then half full and never leave a pan of hot oil unattended. Line a baking sheet with kitchen roll. Set it aside. Set aside half the corn kernels in a large mixing bowl. Place the other half in a food processor or blender with the curry paste, the eggs, the rice flour, baking powder and salt. Blitz it up until it forms a smooth paste. Transfer this paste to the bowl with the whole corn kernels.

Make a chiffonade from your kaffir lime leaves (or the basil leaves). Fold the strips into the corn batter. Using a tablespoon and being very careful, we don't want to see any oil splatter burns in Sick Bay, drop the corn batter into the hot oil. Don't overcrowd the pot. Once the fritters float, give them a flip to ensure they cook on both sides. Remove when they're a nice golden brown on the outside and are cooked completely in the middle. Using a slotted spoon, carefully remove them from the oil and let them drain on the baking sheet lined with kitchen roll. Repeat until you run out of batter.

Serve with sweet chilli sauce for dipping.

These are best prepared and eaten alone, so you aren't forced to share with others.

Serves 4

History Tip:

Maize has been a staple for centuries in the Americas, but wasn't introduced to South East Asia until Spanish and Portuguese traders brought it to trade in the late 16th century. It thrived well in some of the drier regions, thereby becoming a staple in places such as Indonesia and Thailand.

Although the corn cake was invented by Pre-Colombian Native American peoples, the frying of the corn cake most likely originated with white colonials in the Southern United States.

Both Indonesia and Thailand each have their own savoury corn cakes, filled with spices and aromatics, which differ from the sweet version of the American South.

(Adapted from Serious Eats.)   Contribution and Photo By: Afton Cochran

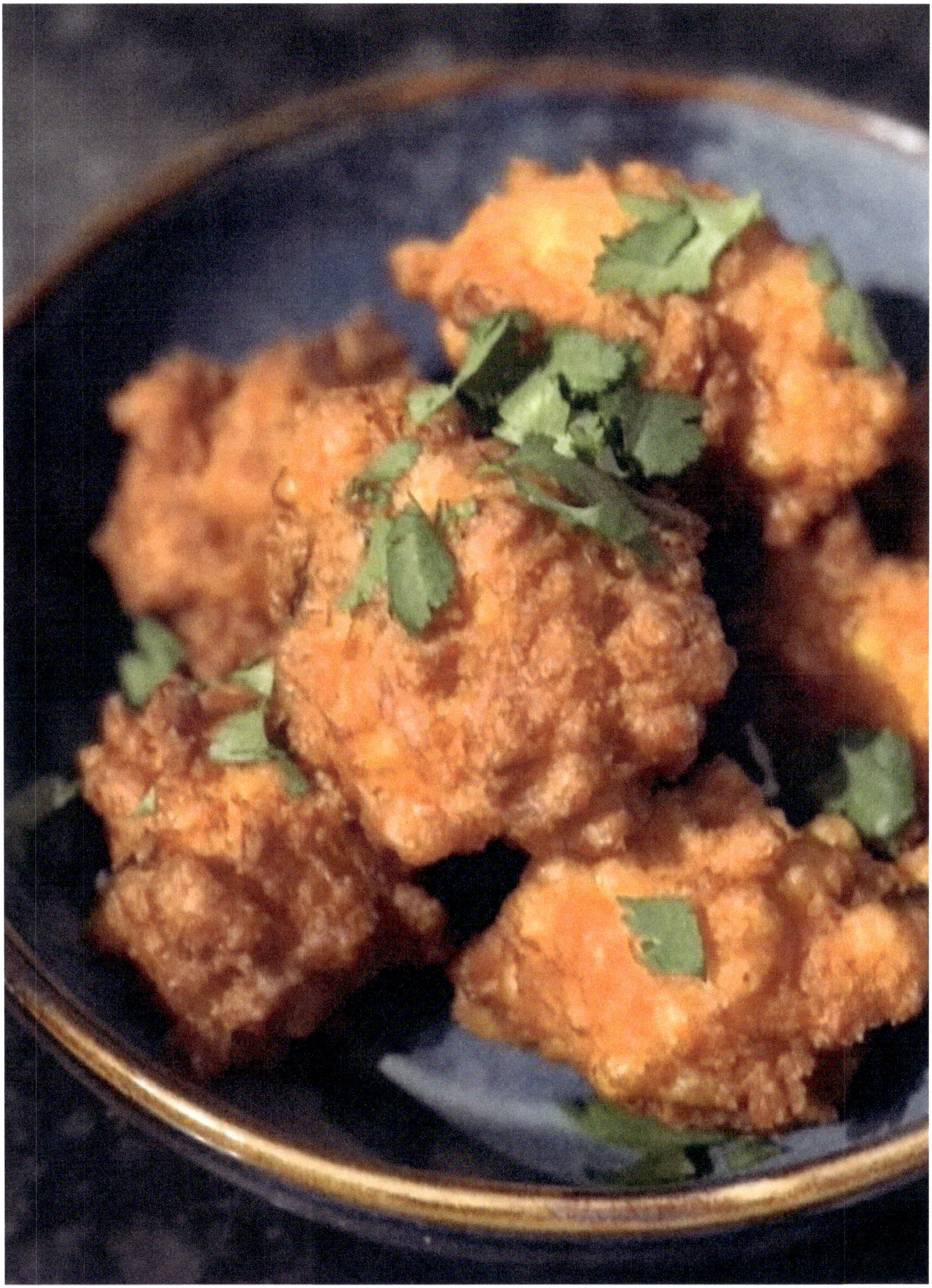

Sri Lankan Dhal

Those new security personnel, or half wits as most of us have been calling them (but even then that is trying to be generous), anyway, the half wits burst into the kitchen and caused a major catastrophe knocking more chilli powder into the dhal than was legally permissible. Mrs Mack bellowed and everyone in the kitchen was ready for battle. The half wits turned tail and are now hiding in the Security Command Centre. They really need to learn that you do not mess with the admin. staff and especially do not mess with the kitchen staff!

Ingredients:
- 2 Tablespoons/ 1fl.oz/ 30ml Rice Bran Oil
- 1 to 2 Medium Onions, chopped
- 2 Cloves Garlic, finely chopped or crushed
- 1 teaspoon/ 0.1oz/ 3g Turmeric
- 2 teaspoons/ 0.14oz/ 4g Ground Cumin
- 1 teaspoon/ 0.07oz/ 2g Chilli Powder, or to taste
- 1 to 2cm Piece of Fresh Ginger, peeled & finely chopped or grated (optional)
- 1 Stick Curry Leaves
- 1 ¼ cups/ 7.9oz/ 225g Red Lentils, rinsed thoroughly in cold water & drained
- 1 Cinnamon Stick or ½ teaspoon/ 0.03oz/ 1g Ground Cinnamon (optional)
- Approx 2 cups/ 17.5fl.oz/ 500ml Hot Water with a Stock Cube added
- 2.2oz/ 65g Coconut Milk, tinned

Heat oil in pan, add onion & fry until soft. Add garlic and fry for another minute or two, then stir in the powdered spices and ginger (if using) and curry leaves. Add lentils and cinnamon, with enough water to cover them. Bring to boil, stirring occasionally, then turn down the heat and cover. Simmer for about 15 to 20 minutes stirring occasionally until lentils are soft but not mushy. Remove cinnamon stick, add coconut milk.
Sprinkle with chopped coriander and serve with other curries, rice, naan bread etc.

Contribution By: Jen Pietersz

Bombay Aloo
(Bombay Potatoes)

Ingredients:
- 2 Medium Potatoes, peeled and cut into 1inch/ 2cm (1 in) cubes
- 1/2 Green Chilli, seeded and roughly chopped
- 1 inch/ 2cm Piece Fresh Ginger
- 3 Garlic Cloves
- 2 Medium Tomatoes
- 1 Onion, thinly sliced
- 1 teaspoon/ 0.1oz/ 3g Turmeric
- 2 teaspoon/ 0.14oz/ 4g Ground Coriander
- 1 teaspoon/ 0.07oz/ 2g Ground Cumin
- 1 teaspoon/ 0.07oz/ 2g Garam Masala
- 1 teaspoon/ 0.07oz/ 2g Chilli Powder, or to taste
- Salt, to taste
- Handful of freshly chopped coriander (cilantro)

Place the cubed potatoes in a saucepan, cover in cold water with a pinch of salt. Bring the potatoes to a boil and boil only for 5 to 7 minutes. They need to be just tender. Do not overcook. They need to hold their shape. Drain, pour back in the pan, cover in cold water and allow the potatoes to completely cool. Drain again. Set the potatoes aside in a bowl.
Chop one tomato into quarters and wedge the other. Put the chopped tomato, the garlic, ginger and green chilli in a blender and blend until smooth. Set aside.
In the same pan that you cooked the potatoes, heat the oil. Add the onion and fry over a medium heat until they are translucent, about 5-6 minutes. Add your tomato, garlic, ginger and chilli mixture and a pinch of salt. Stir well. Let cook for 3 to 4 minutes. Add your tomato wedges and spices. Stir well. Check your seasoning. Add a bit of salt if it needs it.
Add your potatoes back in, and stir gently, so you do not break up the potatoes. Heat through thoroughly, stirring occasionally. You can add a little water if you feel it needs it.
Season to taste and stir in your coriander.
Serve immediately.

Contribution By: Afton Cochran

CASHEW CHICKEN
BLESS YOU!

Who would have ever guessed that sneezes can be contagious? Well please don't talk to Markham about it, he is really upset. Sneezing all over the village mafia when we are trying to mend fences again, wasn't what was expected from a section head. So please be careful with those dashes of white pepper, they can cause a chain ... achoo! Oh no! Not again!

Ingredients:
1.1lb/ 500g Boneless, Skinless Chicken Thighs, cut into 1inch/ 2.5cm cubes
3 Tablespoons/ 1.5fl.oz/ 45ml Vegetable Oil
¾ inch/ 2cm Piece Fresh Ginger, peeled and thinly sliced
1 Bell Pepper seeded and cut into the same size cubes as the chicken
½ Onion, chopped and cut into the same size cubes as the chicken
2 Sticks Celery, chopped.
1 cup/ 5.2oz/ 150g Unsalted Cashews

Chicken Marinade:
1 Tablespoon/ 0.3oz/ 9g Cornflour
1 Tablespoon/ 0.5fl.oz/ 15ml Shaoshing (Chinese Rice Wine)

Sauce:
1 Tablespoon/ 0.5fl.oz/ 15ml Oyster Sauce
1 ½ teaspoon/ 0.25fl.oz/ 7ml Soy Sauce
6 Tablespoons/ 3fl.oz/ 90ml Chicken Stock
1 teaspoon/ 0.14oz/ 4g Brown Sugar
1 teaspoon/ 0.16fl.oz/ 5ml Shaoshing (Chinese Rice Wine)
2 teaspoons/ 0.33fl.oz/ 10ml Sesame Oil
5 Dashes Ground White Pepper (about ¾ teaspoon/ 0.07oz/ 2g)
Salt to taste

Be sure that you have prepared all your ingredients before you begin. Place the raw, cubed thighs in a bowl with the cornflour and Shaoshing, stir well to ensure it's well combined. Set aside. Mix all the ingredients for the sauce together and set aside. In a wok, heat up 1 ½ tablespoons of the oil. Stir fry the chicken until it's white all over. Do not let the chicken fully cook or brown on the outside. You want it just white and partially cooked. Remove from the wok and set aside on a plate. Add the remaining oil to the wok, add the ginger, peppers, onion and celery to the wok and stir fry until the peppers and ginger become aromatic. Add your chicken (and any juices) back in, stir fry for a minute or so before adding the sauce. Stir continuously until the chicken is cooked through, and the sauce is thickened. Add cashews, stir well and season to taste. Serve with steamed rice.

Note: You can substitute chicken breasts for the thighs in this recipe. We find that thighs retain their moisture better, as well as being cheaper. You can use any colour pepper that you wish instead of the green pepper. Should you feel that the sauce isn't thick enough, you can thicken it further with a cornflour slurry.

(Adapted from Rasa Malaysia)   Contribution By: Afton Cochran

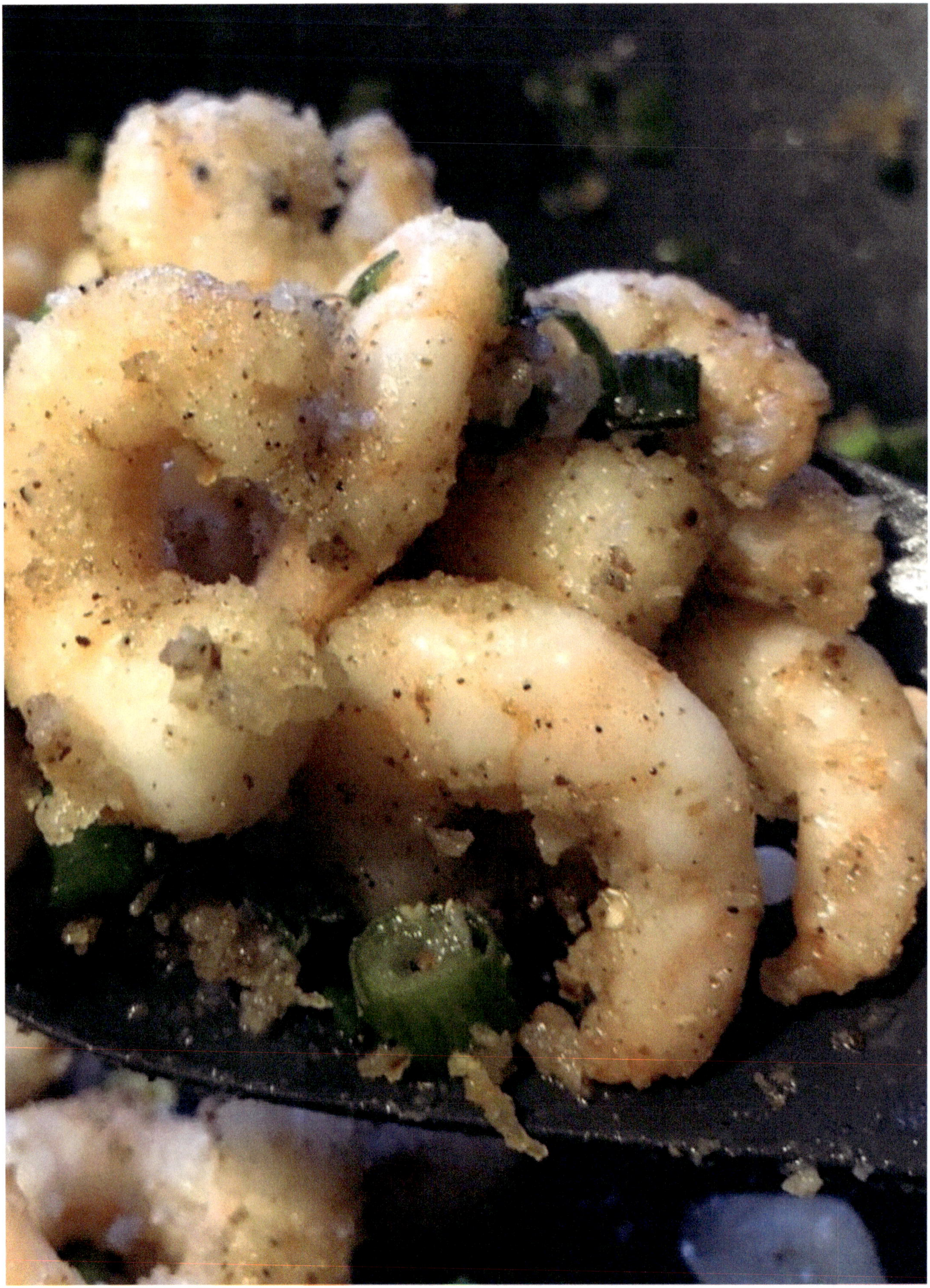

Salt and Pepper Prawns

Please, please don't mention the pepper incident to Major Guthrie. We're sure that he will eventually forget about it, but in our defence some ashes and white pepper do look a lot alike!

Ingredients:

For the prawns:
1.1 lb/ 500g Raw King Prawns/ Jumbo Shrimp, shelled and deveined
1/2 teaspoon/0.1 oz/ 3g Fine Salt
1/2 teaspoon/ 0.07 oz/ 2g Ground White Pepper
1/2 cup/ 60g Cornflour
Pinch of Flour or Rice Flour
Oil for Frying

For the stir fry:
1 Green Chilli, sliced
1 Red Chilli, sliced
3 Cloves Garlic, minced
3 Spring Onions, chopped
Fine Salt and White Pepper to taste

Heat oil in a frying pan to 350°F/ 180°C. You'll need enough to deep fry the prawns. This would be around 2 cups/500ml of oil, depending on size of pan, but don't overfill the pan! Oil should never be more than half filling a pan.
Slice the chillies, mince the garlic and slice the spring onions. Set aside.
Make sure your prawns are as dry as possible. If they're wet, pat them dry with kitchen roll (paper towel). Mix the flours and the salt and pepper together well. Coat the prawns with the cornflour mixture.
In small batches, fry the prawns in the oil until they're pink and cooked through. Let them drain on some kitchen roll on a plate. Heat a few tablespoons of oil in a wok or additional frying pan to a high heat. Add the chillies, garlic, and onion and fry quickly until they're aromatic. Don't let them burn. Add the prawns back and heat through until thoroughly mixed and piping hot. Season to taste with fine salt and white pepper.
Serve with sticky rice and stir fry vegetables.

Serves 4

Contribution and Photo By: Afton Cochran

Curry Udon

Ingredients:

7 oz/ 200g Thinly Sliced Pork Belly, Chicken, Beef, or whatever protein you fancy
1 Tablespoon Vegetable Oil
1 Onion, thinly sliced
42 fl.oz/ 1.2 L Dashi, Chicken, or Vegetable Stock
1 Tablespoon Mirin
1 Tablespoon Soy Sauce or Tamari
4 cubes of Japanese Curry Roux Mix (your choice of heat)
12 oz/ 320g Precooked Udon Noodles, or Dried Udon Noodles
1 Finely Minced Spring Onion (Scallion), or Chives
Cornflour Slurry, to thicken if needed

Dashi is an essential base stock used by the Japanese in their cuisine. It is the foundation of many dishes. It's made from water, seaweed, and dried bonito flakes (a type of fish). Most Japanese households use ready-made or powdered dashi. If it is unavailable, you can substitute chicken or vegetable stock. Thinly slice your desired protein and your onions. Heat the oil in a large saucepan on a medium heat and fry your onion and choice of protein until it is no longer pink. Add your dashi (or chicken stock), mirin, and soy sauce and bring to the boil. Reduce the heat and continue to cook until the onion is soft. Crumble your curry roux blocks into the pot and stir until it's dissolved and thickened. If you want it a bit thicker, use a cornflour slurry to thicken the curry to your desired thickness. If you're using dry Udon noodles, cook and drain them according to the package directions. If using pre-cooked noodles, you can blanch them in boiling water to quickly heat through or microwave should the packaging allow. Divide the noodles between 4 bowls, ladle on the soup and garnish with spring onion or chives. Japanese curry roux blocks, dashi powder, mirin, and Udon noodles are available in most Asian supermarkets, some larger grocery stores, or online.

To make this vegetarian, cube tofu and fry it separately from the onions, then add with the vegetable stock. Use the appropriate curry roux mix.
To make this gluten free use appropriate stock, tamari, curry roux mix and gluten free noodles.

Contribution By: Afton Cochran

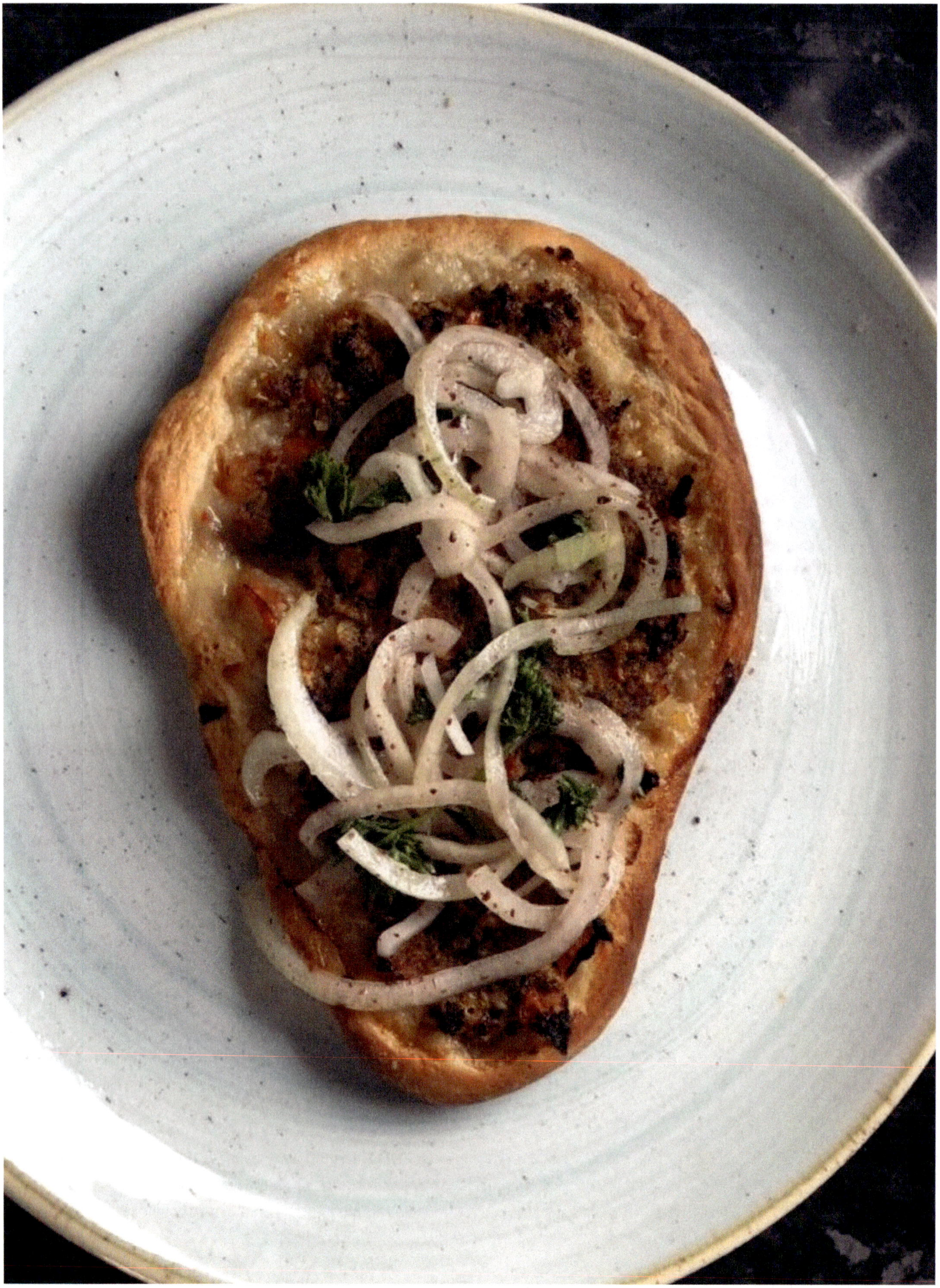

Lahmacun
Turkish Pizza

This is a great dish with many subtle flavours. The base is usually thin and crispy, but we like it thick ... You know, kind of like the History Department.

Ingredients:

Dough Base:
- 3 cups/ 17.6 oz/ 500g Plain Flour
- 1 ¼ cups/ 10fl.oz/ 300 ml Water, Room Temperature
- 2 ¼ teaspoons/ 0.2 oz/ 7g Instant Dry Yeast
- 1 ½ teaspoons/ 0.3 oz/ 10g Salt
- Olive oil

Onion Salad:
- 2 Onions
- 4 Tablespoons/ 2fl.oz/ 60ml Lemon Juice
- ½ teaspoon/ 0.1oz/ 3g Fine Sea Salt
- 2 teaspoons/ 0.14oz/ 4g Dried Sumac
- 1 medium Tomato
- ¼ cup/ 0.5 oz/15g Fresh Curly Parsley

Lamb Meat Topping:
- 4.5 oz/ 130g Lamb Mince
- ½ Red Pepper, de-seeded
- 1 Medium Tomato, de-seeded
- 1 Onion, Minced
- 4 Garlic Cloves Crushed
- 1/8 cup/ 0.25 oz/ 7g Fresh Parsley, chopped
- 2 teaspoons 0.14oz/ 4g Aleppo Pepper (substitute half Hungarian Sweet Paprika, and half Cayenne)
- ½ teaspoon/ 0.03oz/ 1g Dried Mint
- ½ teaspoon/ 0.03oz/ 1g Ground Cinnamon
- 1 teaspoon/ 0.07oz/ 2g Smoked Paprika
- ½ teaspoon/ 0.03oz/ 1g Ground Cumin
- 1 teaspoon/ 0.07oz/ 2g Ground Allspice
- ½ teaspoon Fine Sea Salt

For the dough: Mix together flour, yeast, salt, and water until no lumps remain. You can do this in a stand mixer or by hand. When you're at this point, knead the dough for 8 min in your stand mixer with a dough hook, or about 15 minutes by hand. Put your dough in a bowl that has been oiled. Cover with a tea towel or cling film, place in a warm spot and allow to double in size.

During this time, you can make the onion salad. Slice your onions thinly with a knife or a mandolin. Make sure you don't slice your fingers. We don't want finger chunks in the salad. Or blood. Add the onions to a bowl. Cut your tomato in half and scoop out the seeds and discard them. Finely dice the tomato and add to the onions. Finally, add the sumac, lemon juice and sea salt. Mix well, cover and refrigerate. You can make this well in advance, should you choose. It allows the flavours of all the ingredients to meld. Don't put the chopped parsley in until you're ready to serve.

For your lamb meat topping: For this stage, a food processor comes in handy, but it's not necessary. It just means more chopping. You can blitz up the onion, garlic, red pepper and parsley into fine pieces. If you're not using a food processor, chop it all up really finely. Add this to a bowl. Halve and seed the tomato. Chop it really finely and add it to the bowl. Add your lamb mince, Aleppo pepper, the rest of the herbs, spices and seasoning. Mix well.

Tip your dough on to a lightly floured work surface. Divide your dough into 8 equal pieces. Roll out to desired thinness (5mm or 0.2 inches). Cover with oiled clingfilm if you want to have a puffier base and leave to prove for an hour. If you prefer a thinner base, carry on to the next step. Preheat your oven to 390°F/200°C (180°C fan)/ Gas Mark 6. Divide your meat topping into 8 parts and spread evenly over the dough, leaving about 5 mm (0.2 in) gap at the edges. Bake for 12 minutes on a sheet lined with parchment, or a pizza stone. Keep an eye on it, especially if you're opting for the thinner crust, to ensure it doesn't burn. Mix your chopped parsley into the sumac onion salad. Spoon over the flatbreads.

Serves 8, or 4 hungry people.

Contribution and Photo By: Afton Cochran

Tabbouleh

This dish dates back to the Middle Ages from the region of Lebanon and Syria. Traditionally the dish is made with bulgur wheat. This recipe uses pearl cous cous or Israeli cous cous to make it more substantial.

Ingredients:
16oz/ 450g Pearl Cous Cous
3 cups/ 23.6fl.oz/ 700 ml Vegetable Stock or Water
5 Plum Tomatoes
1 Red Onion
Fresh Parsley, a large bunch
Fresh Mint, a small bunch
3 Lemons, zested and juiced
5 ½ Tablespoons/ 2.7fl.oz/ 80 ml Good Quality Olive Oil
Sea Salt

In a large pot, bring your vegetable stock to the boil. Add your Pearl cous cous and boil for 25 minutes, it should be just cooked. Drain, and rinse under cold water. Set aside. Seed and finely dice your tomatoes. They need to be very small, about the size of the Pearl cous cous. Finely chop your parsley and mint. Finely mince your onion. Mix the cous cous with the tomato, onions, herbs and lemon zest. In a small bowl whisk 3oz/ 80ml good quality olive oil with the juice of the three lemons. Season with a little salt and pour over the tabbouleh. Chill the salad until ready to serve.

Serve on romaine lettuce leaves with a little diced green chilli, and wedges of lemon

Serves 4

Contribution By: Afton Cochran

Jollof Rice

*Jollof Rice is a popular rice dish throughout the African continent with each country thinking that their way of making Jollof is the best.
This recipe is based on the Ghanaian way of making it.*

Ingredients:
For the purée:
1 Red Pepper, seeded and cut into large chunks
1 Onion, peeled and cut into chunks
1 inch/ 2cm Fresh Ginger, peeled and cut into chunks
1 14oz/ 400g Tin Chopped Tomatoes or 14oz/ 400g Fresh Tomatoes, chopped
5 Cloves Garlic
2 Scotch Bonnets or Habaneros, or a milder red chilli of choice
2 to 3 Tablespoons/ 1 to 1.5fl.oz/ 30 to 34ml Vegetable Oil, to fry the purée.

For the rice:
3 ¾ cups/ 26oz/ 750g Basmati Rice, rinsed several times and drained
6 Tablespoons/ 4.3fl.oz/ 125ml Vegetable Oil
2 Onions, peeled and finely chopped
5 Cloves Garlic, crushed and minced
2 Tablespoons/ 1fl.oz/ 30ml Tomato Purée/ Paste
1 Tablespoon/ 0.5oz/ 15g Vegetable or Chicken Bouillon Powder
1 Tablespoon/ 0.4oz/ 12g Curry Powder, preferably an African or Jamaican blend
1 Tablespoon/ 0.14oz/ 4g Fresh Thyme
2 Bay Leaves
2 cups/ 17.5fl.oz/ 500ml Chicken or Vegetable Stock
Salt and Pepper, to taste

For the purée:
In a blender, add the pepper, garlic, tomatoes, chillies, and onion. Purée until smooth. Add enough water to bring the amount to 4 1/2cups/ 1Litre of purée. Heat the oil in a pan over medium heat. Add your purée and stir. Bring to the boil, cover and cook for 15 to 20 minutes or until it's reduced by a third. Set aside.

For the rice:
Heat oil in a pan. Add your onions and gently fry until they are translucent. Add the garlic and cook for a minute more. Add the tomato purée, the curry powder and the bouillon powder and cook until the curry powder is fragrant and the tomato purée has darkened. Add in the purée you cooked earlier, the thyme, bay leaves and rice. Season. Stir well, turn down the heat to very low, cover the pot with foil and put a lid on it. Allow it to steam for 30 to 35 minutes. Remove the pot from the heat, leave the foil and lid on for a further 15 minutes. Fluff the rice with a fork. There may be some crusty bits of rice on the bottom. This is normal. Remove bay leaves. Taste and adjust seasoning. The rice should be an orange red colour and the grains should be fluffy.

Serve with chicken and fried plantains.

Contribution By: Afton Cochran

Bobotie

This South African dish first appeared in a Dutch cookbook in 1609, but variations may date back to Roman times. The tasty dish is also the national dish of South Africa.

Ingredients:
For the meat:
2 Slices White Bread, crusts removed
½ cup/ 4fl.oz/ 120ml Milk
2 Tablespoons/ 1oz/ 30g Butter
2 teaspoons/ 0.3fl.oz/ 10ml Olive Oil
1 Large Onion, finely chopped
4 Cloves Garlic, crushed and minced
2.2 pounds/ 1kg Lean Minced Beef
1 ½ Tablespoons/ 0.33oz/ 10g Madras Curry Powder
1 teaspoon/ 0.11oz/ 3g Ground Turmeric
2 teaspoons/ 0.11oz/ 3g Coriander Seeds or 1 teaspoon/ 0.07oz/ 2g Ground Coriander
3 Whole Cloves or ½ teaspoon/ 0.038oz/ 1g Ground Cloves
2 teaspoons/ 0.14oz/ 4g Cumin Seeds or 1 teaspoon/ 0.07oz/ 2g Ground Cumin
4 Whole Allspice Berries or 1 teaspoon/ 0.07oz/ 2g Ground Allspice
2 teaspoons/ 0.07oz/ 2g Dried Mixed Herbs
1 Granny Smith Apple, cored and grated
4 Tablespoons/ 3.5oz/ 100g Peach or Mango Chutney
¼ cup/ 1.7oz/ 50g Sultanas or Raisins
¼ cup/ 1oz/ 30g Slivered Almonds, toasted (optional)
1 Lemon, zested and juiced
1 Tablespoon/ 0.5fl.oz/ 15ml Worcestershire Sauce
Salt and pepper to taste
For the topping:
½ cup/ 4fl.oz/ 124 ml Double Cream
4 Eggs
½ teaspoon/ 0.05oz/ 1.5g Ground Turmeric
Pinch of Salt
6 Bay Leaves

Heat oven to 350°F/ 180°C (160°C fan)/ Gas Mark 4.
Soak the crustless slices of bread in the milk. Add the grated apple, the chutney, sultanas, almonds (if using), lemon juice and zest, Worcestershire sauce and salt and pepper. Stir well and set aside.
If using ground spices, skip this step.
We would highly recommend you using whole spices, however. In a dry frying pan, toast the cumin seeds, coriander seeds, allspice berries and cloves until fragrant. Do not allow them to burn. Remove to a plate, allow to cool and crush in a mortar and pestle or grind in a spice grinder.
In a Dutch oven, melt the butter and olive oil. Fry the finely diced onion until it is soft and translucent. Add the garlic, curry powder, spices, herbs and a bit of salt and pepper. Mix well. Add the beef and continue to cook, breaking up any large chunks, until the beef is browned. Remove from the heat and mix in the bread and milk mixture. Mix well.
Check the seasoning and add more if needed. Press this mixture well into the bottom of the Dutch oven. Place in the oven for 40 minutes. In a mixing bowl, crack the eggs, add the cream, a bit of seasoning and the 1/2 teaspoon of turmeric. Whisk well. When the 40 minutes is up, remove the Dutch oven from the oven, press the meat down again with the back of a spoon. Pour on the egg mixture. Arrange the bay leaves on the top, place back in the oven for 15-20 minutes or until the egg has set.
Serve with Geelrys (recipe below) and vegetables.
Serves 4

Geelrys (Yellow Rice)

Ingredients:
2 cups/ 14oz/ 400g Basmati or Long Grain Rice
1 Tablespoon/ 0.5oz/ 15g Butter or Vegetable Oil
3 cups/ 20fl.oz/ 600ml Chicken or Vegetable Stock
2 teaspoon/ 0.21oz/ 6g Ground Turmeric
½ teaspoon/ 0.45oz/ 1.3g Ground Cinnamon
1 teaspoon/ 0.74oz/ 2g Madras Curry Powder
2 Tablespoon/ 0.93oz/ 26g Brown Sugar (optional)
1 Cinnamon Stick
1 Bay Leaf
3 Tablespoons/ 1oz/ 30g Sultanas or Raisins
Pinch of Salt

Rinse and drain the rice well.
In a saucepan, heat the butter or oil over a medium heat. Add the rice until it starts to turn opaque. Add the sultanas, turmeric, curry powder and ground cinnamon. Stir well. Slowly add the stock, a pinch of salt, the cinnamon stick, brown sugar, and bay leaf. Cover. Bring to the boil. Reduce heat and cook until the water has been absorbed, about 20 minutes. Remove from heat. Leave for 10 minutes before removing the lid.
Serve with Bobotie (recipe above).

Contribution By: Afton Cochran

MAFÉ
WEST AFRICAN PEANUT STEW

This recipe is not suitable for those with nut allergies.
This is a traditional Senegalese recipe cooked with peanut butter and root vegetables. It is often made with lamb, beef, or in this instance, chicken.
You can also use any root vegetable you wish in this dish. Swede (rutabaga), turnip, carrot, potatoes, sweet potatoes, etc are all appropriate. Green cabbage is a must, as it's a traditional component of the dish.
Scotch bonnets are the chilli of choice for this dish, but you can substitute a milder red chilli if a scotch bonnet is too hot.

Ingredients:
For the chicken marinade:
8 Cloves Garlic
2cm/ 1inch long piece of Ginger, peeled and cut into large chunks
Chilli Flakes, to taste
Salt and Pepper, to taste
2.2pounds/ 1kg Chicken Legs, bone in, with skin removed

For the stew:
4 Tablespoons/ 2fl.oz/ 60ml Vegetable Oil
1 Onion, finely diced
8 Cloves Garlic, crushed and minced
4 Tablespoons/ 2fl.oz/ 60ml Fish Sauce
¾ cup/ 6oz/ 170 ml Tomato purée (paste)
1 cup/ 9oz/ 260g Unsweetened Peanut Butter, can be crunchy or smooth
4 carrots, peeled and cut into 4cm/ 2inch chunks
1 large Sweet Potato, peeled and cut into 2cm/ 1inch chunks
1 Swede, peeled and/ or 12 waxy new Potatoes cut into 2cm/ 1inch chunks
1 large Green Cabbage, cut into quarters and core removed.
Salt and pepper to taste
3 Scotch Bonnet, habanero, or other milder red chilli to serve.
Chopped peanuts for garnish

In a blender, add the garlic for the marinade, ginger, red chilli flakes, pepper and blend, adding a bit of water to form a paste. Carefully poke your chicken legs all over, season with salt, and then coat the chicken all over with the marinade paste. Place in on a tray, cover with cling film, and refrigerate for four hours or overnight.

In a pot over a medium heat, add your oil. When it is hot, add your onion and fry until it is translucent but not brown. Add the garlic and some salt and fry for another 2 minutes. Stir in the fish sauce and tomato purée and cook until the tomato purée turns a darker colour and it is well combined with the onions.

Add 6 cups/ 50fl.oz/ 1.4L of water, the chicken and marinade, scrape up any brown bits from the bottom of the pan, and bring to the boil. In a separate bowl, add your peanut butter. Using a ladle, add bits of the water from the chicken into the peanut butter to loosen it up a bit and turn it into a paste. Add this back to the pot with the chicken. Stir well. Cover and simmer for 20 min.

Add cabbage and carrots, stir, and cook for another 20 minutes.

Add sweet potato, swede, and/or potatoes and cook for another half an hour until the vegetables are cooked, the chicken is falling off the bone, and the sauce is thickened. If the sauce is too runny for your taste, you can thicken it with a cornflour slurry or remove the chicken and vegetables and let it cook down.

Season to taste. Serve with steamed rice or cous cous and top with scotch bonnet slices and chopped peanuts.

Serves 5 to 7

Note: the oil will separate from the sauce. This is normal.

(Adapted from a recipe by Rama Dione and Papa Diagne.)   Photo and Contribution By: Afton Cochran

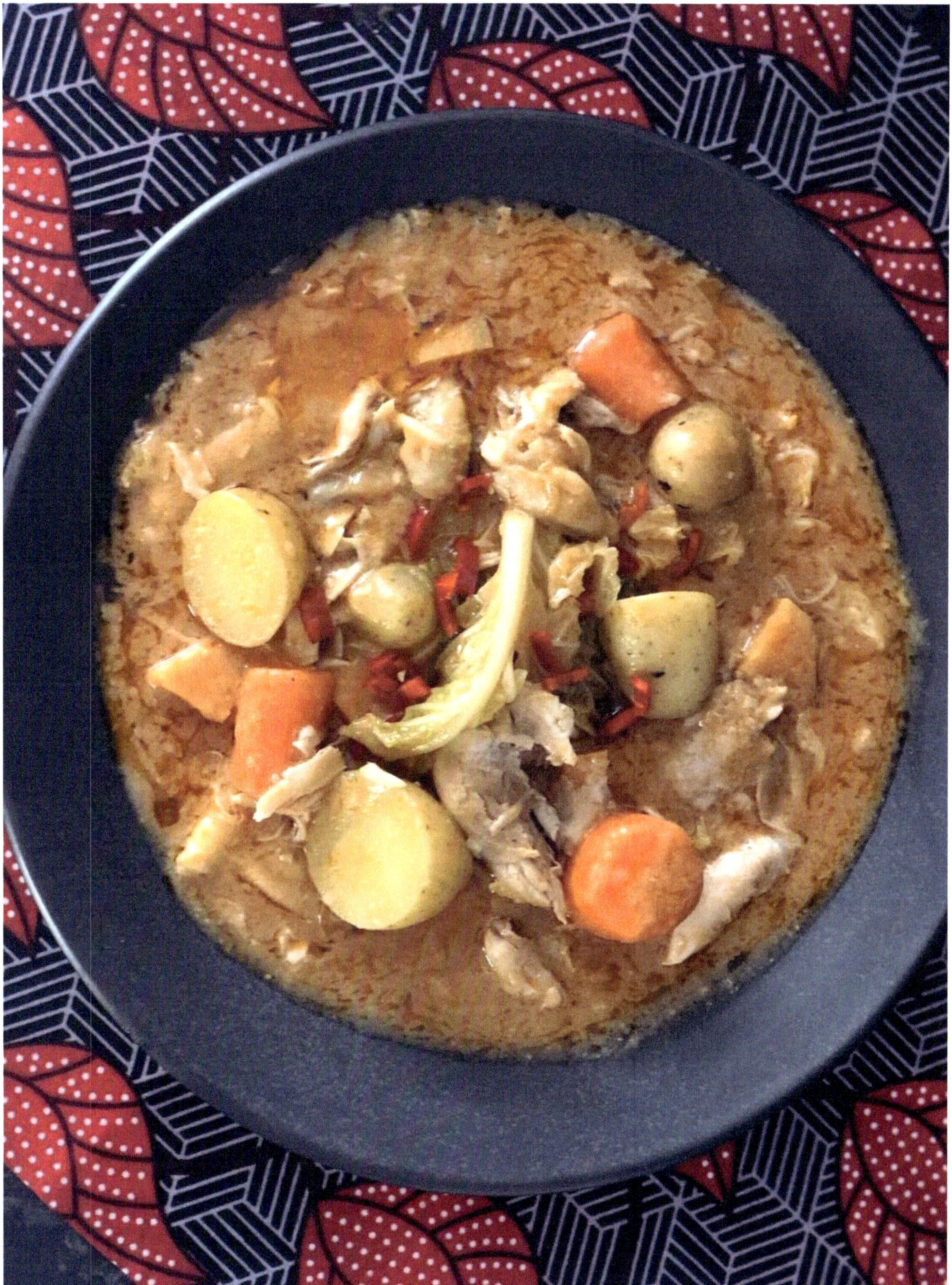

SHAKSHUKA

Eggs are the best protein, especially when you are hungry. Mr. Evans has the unprecedented knack for finding eggs, and I don't mean just chicken eggs. Ducks, Swans, Platypus ...
In the recent Time Police cock-up
he was very nearly trampled for the Platypus one...

Ingredients:
2 to 3 Tablespoons/ 1 to 1 1/2fl.oz/ 30 to 45ml Olive Oil
3 to 5 Green Chillies: Anaheim or Jalapeño, stemmed, seeded, and finely diced
2 Red, Yellow, Orange Bell Pepper, or a combination of each, stemmed, seeded and diced
1 Small Onion, diced
8 Cloves of Garlic, crushed or minced
2 teaspoons/ 0.14oz/ 4g Ground Cumin
1 Tablespoon/ 0.24oz/ 7g Smoked Paprika
2-400g or 1- 28oz Tin Peeled Plum Tomatoes/ Whole Peeled Tomatoes
1 teaspoon Granulated Sugar
Hot Sauce, such as Tabasco, to taste
8 Eggs
1 1/3 cups/ 7oz/ 200g Crumbled Feta Cheese
2 Tablespoons Fresh Flat Leaf Parsley, finely chopped
Salt and Pepper to taste
Flatbreads, Tortillas, Pitta, or toast to serve.

In a 30 cm (12") Dutch Oven or a skillet, heat your olive oil on a medium high heat. Add chillies, peppers, and onion and cook through until soft, stirring occasionally. This should be about 10 minutes or until the onion is translucent and starting to go golden brown. Add the garlic and cook for a few seconds before adding the paprika, cumin and a bit of salt and pepper. This next bit is a bit messy. Open your tin(s) of tomatoes and pour into a bowl. Carefully squish the tomatoes with your hands (make sure they're clean, Markham, and don't splatter tomato juice everywhere like it's a crime scene!) Put this tomato stuff in the pan with about 120ml (1/2 cup) water. Give it a good stir. Turn the heat down. Add the sugar to reduce the acidity of the tomatoes. Give it a good stir again. Check the seasoning and add hot sauce to taste, or not. It's up to you. It can be mild, or hotter than the blazes of hell, but if it burns your mouth off, don't go crying to Sick Bay. Let this simmer for 20 minutes or so. When the sauce has reduced a bit, take your spoon and make 8 little wells in the sauce. Crack an egg into each well. Make sure they're separated evenly around the pan. Cover the pan and let the eggs cook for about 5 minutes. Carefully remove the lid and baste the eggs with the sauce, but don't break the yolks. If for some odd reason you like yolks to be more solid, cook them for longer. Remove from the heat, sprinkle with the feta and parsley. Enjoy with a flatbread, toast, tortillas, any bread products you like to scoop up this yummy sauce.

Serves 4 to 8

History Tip:
Shakshuka is one of the most popular breakfast foods in Israel today. This humble dish is a working-class dish with roots that date back to the early days of the Ottoman Empire.
There is some academic debate as some people say that it
originated in North Africa.
All we know until Dr B approves the jump, is that this is an amazing dish
no matter what time of day you eat it!

(Adapted from Saveur.) Photo and Contribution By: Afton Cochran

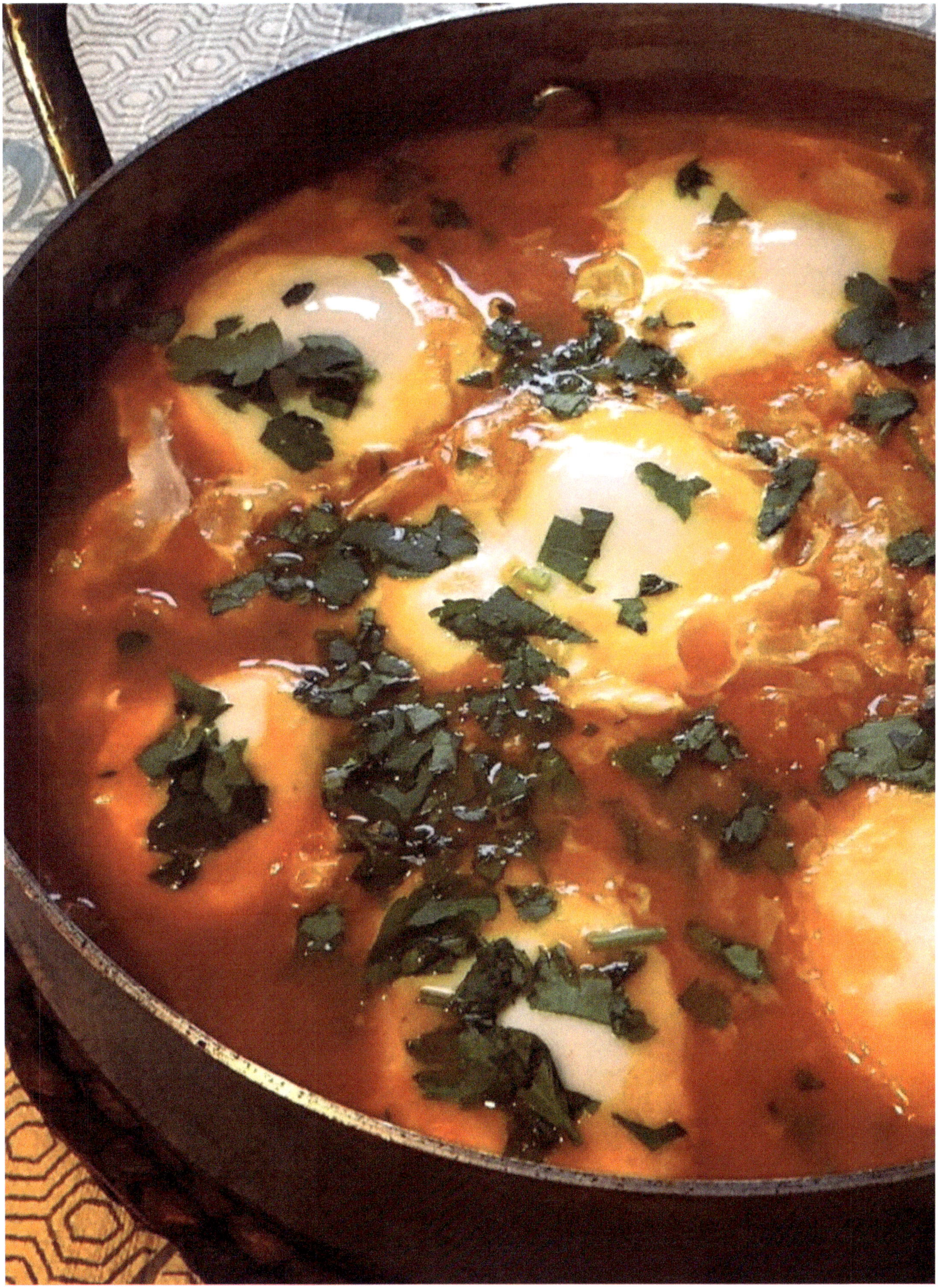

Greek Fish Stew

Ingredients:
1 Tablespoon/ 0.5fl.oz/ 15ml Extra Virgin Olive Oil
1 Onion or 6 Shallots, finely chopped
1 to 2 Garlic Cloves, crushed
2 3/4 cups/ 1lb 2oz/ 500g Fresh Tomatoes, peeled and chopped
1/3 cup plus 2 Tablespoons/ 3 ½fl.oz/ 100ml Dry White Wine
1/3 cup plus 2 Tablespoons/ 3 ½fl.oz/ 100ml Water
3 1/2 cups/ 1lb 9oz/ 700g Sea Fish, Boneless, and cut into chunks, eg. Swordfish, Sea trout, Prawns and Mussels
3 Tablespoons/ 0.5oz/ 15g Fresh Parsley, chopped
Juice of 1 Lemon
Salt and Pepper to taste

In a large frying pan, heat the oil. Cook the onion and garlic over a low heat for 5 mins, stirring often. Add the tomatoes, wine and water and cook for 8 to 10 mins, until the tomatoes are soft. Add the fish and/or shellfish and return to the boil, cooking over a medium heat for 5 minutes or until just tender. Avoid overcooking.
Remove from the heat and stir in the parsley and lemon juice. Season to taste and serve at once.

Contribution By: Becky Parsons

Horiatiki
Greek Village Salad

*They say it takes a village to raise a child.
Apparently, it takes a Greek village to make a salad.*

Ingredients:
3 Ripe Vine Tomatoes
1 Medium Cucumber
1 Green Pepper
1 Red Onion
16 Kalamata Olives or Green Olives, do not use pitted black olives
7oz/ 200g Greek Feta Cheese
2 Tablespoons/ 1fl.oz/ 30ml Red Wine Vinegar
5 Tablespoons/ 3fl.oz/ 85ml Greek Olive Oil, good quality, plus a little for drizzling
1 teaspoon/ 0.03oz/ >1g Dried Oregano
Salt and Pepper, to taste

Cut the tomatoes into wedges. Slice the onion thinly into rings. De-seed the pepper and cut it into thin slices. Cut the cucumber in half and then into thick half-moon shapes. Place these, along with the olives into a large shallow bowl. In a small bowl, mix your vinegar and olive oil with freshly cracked pepper and a little bit of salt. Do not add too much salt, as the feta is very salty. Pour this over the salad. Place the block of feta on the top of the salad and drizzle with a bit of olive oil and black pepper. Sprinkle the salad with the oregano. Serve in a shallow bowl with bread, not pitas, and a lot of good wine

Serves 4

Contribution By: Afton Cochran

Pollo alla Cacciatore

The security section is cultured and knows its compass directions, unlike the historians we shepherd around. Well, 'when in Rome' as the old saying goes.... We know that this version is inspired from the south of Italy where using red wine is the norm. Should you come across a recipe using white wine, the recipe comes from the north. Easy to tell where you are right?

Ingredients:
For the chicken:
1 Corn Fed, Free Range Chicken, skin on, jointed
Save the remaining carcass for chicken stock
3 Tablespoons/ 1.5fl.oz/ 45ml Vegetable Oil

For the Cacciatore
6.5oz/ 180g Smoked Pancetta, chopped into lardons
1 glass/ 10fl.oz/ 270ml Red Wine
2 Tablespoons/ 1fl.oz/ 30ml Olive Oil
1 Onion, minced
1 Carrot, peeled and diced
1 Stalk Celery, diced
3 Cloves Garlic, crushed and minced
2 Tablespoons/ 0.28oz/ 8g Fresh Rosemary, chopped
3 Juniper Berries, crushed
7oz/ 200g Wild Mushrooms, sliced (optional)
3 Tablespoons/ 1.5fl.oz/ 45ml Tomato Purée/ Paste
2 cups/ 18fl.oz/ 500ml Chicken Stock
Handful of pitted Black Olives (optional)
1 Tablespoon/ 0.28oz/ 8g Baby Capers (optional)
Salt and Pepper to taste

In an enamel or stainless-steel pan, heat your oil for the chicken over a medium heat. Brown your chicken in batches. Do not overcrowd them or they will poach, not fry. You want a nice browning on all your pieces of chicken. Remove, and set aside on a plate. In the same pan, add your lardons and fry until cooked, but not crisp. Remove to a plate. Remove any excess oil from your pan and dispose of safely. Put your pan back on the heat, add your red wine and deglaze, scraping up all the crusty bits off the bottom of the pan. Simmer gently for 5 minutes until reduced by 2/3. Remove to a bowl, and set aside. Add the olive oil to your pan. Add your onions, carrots, celery, juniper berries, rosemary, and mushrooms if using. Gently fry until the onions are translucent. Add in your garlic and fry for a further minute. Add your chicken pieces and lardons back to the pan with the tomato purée/ paste. Cook for 5 minutes. Add back your wine reduction and your chicken stock, (and olives and capers if using) and gently cook on a low heat for an hour or until the chicken is cooked through. Taste your sauce before adding extra salt and pepper. If your sauce isn't thick enough, you can add a cornflour slurry to thicken it to your liking. Serve with mashed potatoes or pasta and a salad or steamed vegetables.

Note: Be mindful of adding in extra salt if you use the capers and olives. You don't want your sauce to be too salty.

Serves 4

Contribution By: Afton Cochran

Mediterranean Baked Cod

Ingredients:
4 x 6oz/ 175g Cod or Hoki Fillets; skinless and thick
1lb/ 450g Charlotte Potatoes, cooked and sliced
1/2 cup/ 4oz/ 110g Black Olives, stoned/pitted
1 1/3 cups/ 9oz/ 250g Tomatoes
3 Tablespoons/ 1.5fl.oz/ 45ml Olive Oil
2 Tablespoons/ 1oz/ 30g Fresh Basil, chiffonade
Salt and Pepper to taste

Preheat oven to 375°F/190°C (180°C fan)/ Gas Mark 5. Lay fillets in a large, shallow, ovenproof dish and season well. Scatter with potatoes, olives and tomatoes. Drizzle over oil. Bake in the centre of the oven for 25 to 30 mins. Sprinkle with chopped basil before serving.

Contribution By: Becky Parsons

Carbonnade Flamande

Okay, try not to laugh. This dish is amazing and is so much like the security section. See, the frites that everyone thinks are French, they are actually from Belgium. It was just the other day those snobs in IT were saying that Beef Burgundy was better, because it has good red wine, and no beer in it. Can you believe that? Sounds rather snooty don't you think? Seriously, beer is the food of the gods!

So just like the hard working security section who elevate all the other departments, with no acclaim. Beer gets too little acclaim.

Ingredients:
- 2.2 pounds/ 1kg Braising or Stewing Steak, cut into 4 cm/1.5 in cubes
- 2 Bay Leaves
- 2- 11 ½fl.oz/ 340ml Bottles Sour or Dark Flemish Ale
- 3 cloves Garlic, crushed
- 5 Tablespoons/ 1.32oz/ 38g Plain Flour
- Salt and Pepper, to taste
- 8.8oz/ 250g Pancetta or Bacon, diced
- 4 Carrots, cut into 3 cm/ 1.2 in chunks
- 1 Large Onion, thinly sliced
- 1 Leek, thinly sliced
- 1 Tablespoons/ 0.5fl.oz/ 15ml Tomato Purée/ Paste
- 1 Bouquet Garni
- 1 Tablespoon/ 0.5fl.oz/ 15ml Whole Grain Mustard
- 1 Tablespoon/ 0.48oz/ 14g Dark Brown Sugar
- 1 ½ cups/ 11.8fl.oz/ 350 ml Good Quality Beef Stock
- 1 Fresh Parsley, a large bunch, finely chopped

Marinade your beef in both bottles of ale, the garlic and the bay leaf. Cover and refrigerate for at least three hours, preferably overnight.

Drain the marinade from the meat and reserve the marinade. You will need it later.

Pat the meat dry with some kitchen roll. Toss the meat with the flour and salt and pepper. Set aside.

In a Dutch oven, heat a little of the oil on a high heat. Brown your beef well, so there is a nice brown crust on each piece. Do this in batches and do not overcrowd your pan, or you will not get that nice crust on each piece. You may need to add a bit of the oil in between each batch. Do not worry if you get bits stuck to the pan. We will deal with that in a bit. Place the browned meat on a plate and set aside.

Now fry off your pancetta until it is crisp. Remove the pancetta with a slotted spoon to the same plate as the beef, leaving any oil in the pan.

Heat your oven to 325°F/ 160°C (140°C fan)/Gas Mark 3. Lower your heat on the hob a bit and add the onions, carrots, and leek. If you need a bit more oil, feel free to add it. Fry them off until the leek and onion are soft and all the vegetables are starting to brown. This will take 10 to 12 minutes.

Add the tomato purée/ paste, mix well, and cook for 2 minutes.

Turn the heat up, add the marinade you set aside earlier, using it to scrape up those lovely brown bits on the bottom of your pan. Bring to the boil. Reduce by half.

Add the beef stock, the beef and pancetta, together with the bouquet garni. Season and stir well. Remember that your pancetta will already add saltiness to your dish.

Cover and place in the oven for an hour and a half. After this time, remove it from the oven, stir in the brown sugar, mustard and 3/4 of your chopped parsley. Check the seasoning and put it back in the oven for a further 30 minutes. Remove from the oven.

Garnish with the remaining parsley and serve with frites.
Serves 4

Photo and Contribution By: Afton Cochran

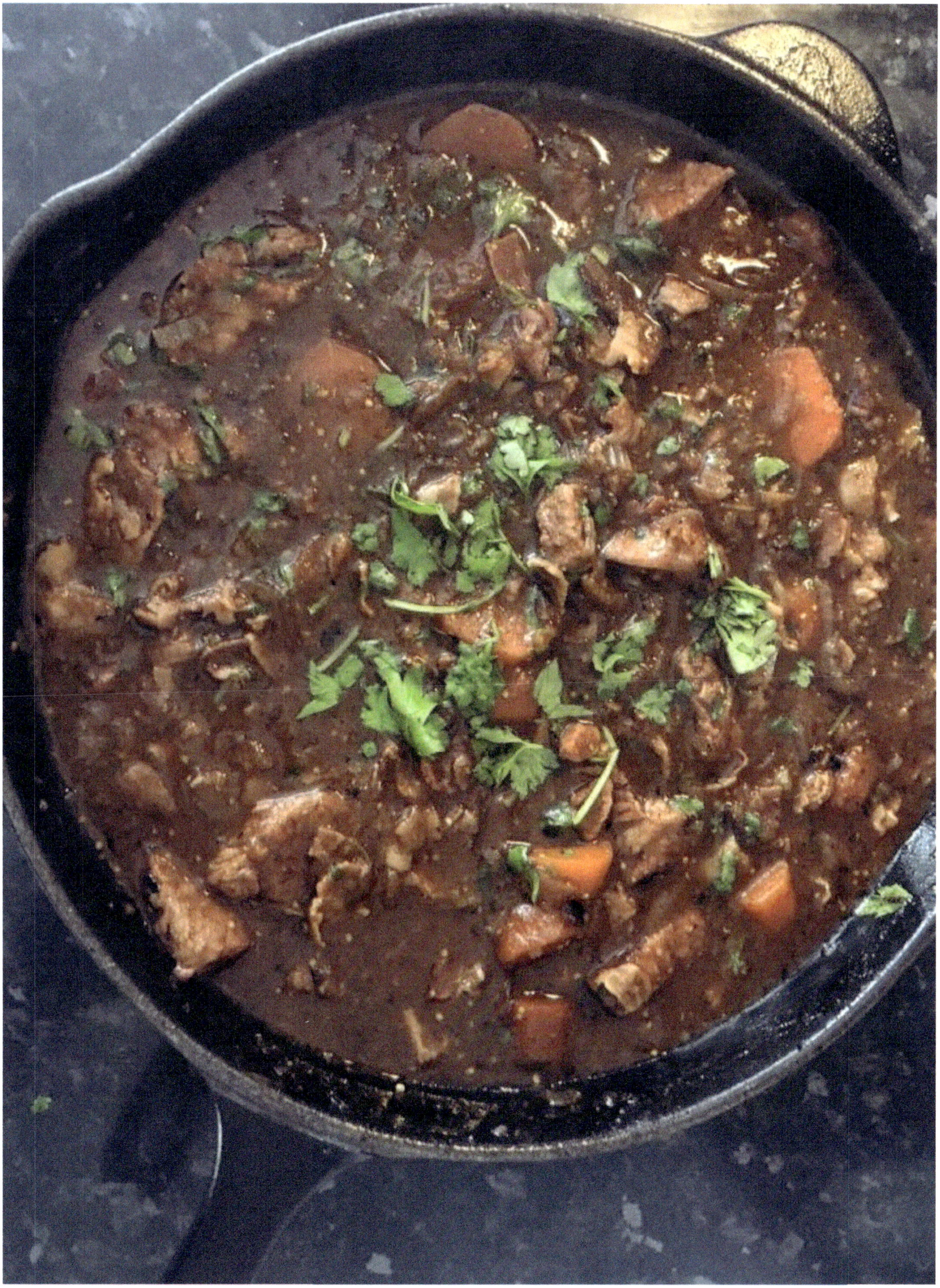

Soupe à l'oignon de ma mère
My Mother's Onion Soup

Leon doesn't often talk about his family from before. We try to be understanding because it is very hard on him to think about those times. One thing that he has told us is that his mother would make onion soup with the onions she grew in the back garden. He looked forward to the times when there was a crusty bread slice and cheese to go with it!

Ingredients
1 to 2 Tablespoons/ 15 to 30oz/ 15 to 30g Butter
6 Onions, peeled and sliced thinly
1 Garlic Clove, peeled and sliced thinly
1 Tablespoon/ 0.3oz/ 10g Fresh Thyme Leaves
8 1/2 cups/ 68fl.oz/ 2ltr Vegetable or Chicken Stock
Salt and Pepper to Taste
4 Thick Cut Slices of Bread, Toasted (optional)
1 1/2 cup/ 4.2oz/ 120g Grated Swiss Gruyère Cheese (optional)

Traditional French Onion Soup is made with a rich beef broth, but this can be costly to make or to buy.

Peel and slice the onion as thinly as possible. Melt the butter in the bottom of a heavy-based saucepan and add the onions and garlic. You may have to work in batches. Sauté for 20-25 minutes over a very low heat until golden brown. This is where a lot of flavour for the soup is made and there is no way to rush it.

Gently warm the stock and thyme before adding both to the onions. Bring the mixture to a boil and simmer for about 10 to 15 minutes.

Season the soup and divide between 4 soup bowls. If using the bread, place one piece in the top of each bowl and top with the grated cheese. These can then be placed under the grill/ or broiler to melt the cheese, usually about 5 minutes. Serve immediately.

Serves 4

Contribution and Photo By: Sara Robinson

Croque Monsieur

Ingredients:
Béchamel Sauce:
7fl.oz/ 200ml Milk
0.6oz/ 20g Plain Flour
0.6oz/ 20g Butter
Salt and Pepper to Taste
Sandwich:
4 thin slices of bread
1 Tablespoon Dijon Mustard
4 slices of Carved Ham
4 slices or about 200g grated Swiss, Gruyère or Emmental Cheese
3.1oz/ 90g Cheddar Cheese or Parmesan Cheese, grated

Preheat the grill/broiler 425°F/ 220°C (200°C fan)/ Gas Mark 7. Add milk, flour and butter to a saucepan, whisking continuously bring the mixture to a boil for a thick and silky sauce. Reduce the heat and simmer for about 4 minutes making sure the flour has fully cooked. Remove from the heat and set to the side.
Toast bread by placing on a baking sheet under the grill until golden. Begin with your toasty bread and layer toast, thin layer of dijon mustard, béchamel sauce, gruyère cheese, ham slices, and top with a second slice of toast for two sandwiches. Across the top piece of toast spread a layer of the Béchamel Sauce and sprinkle with Parmesan cheese. Grill for 5 to 10 minutes until golden brown and the cheese is melted and bubbly. Allow to cool slightly before serving.
It is also excellent with a fried egg on top!

Serves 2

Contribution By: Sara Robinson

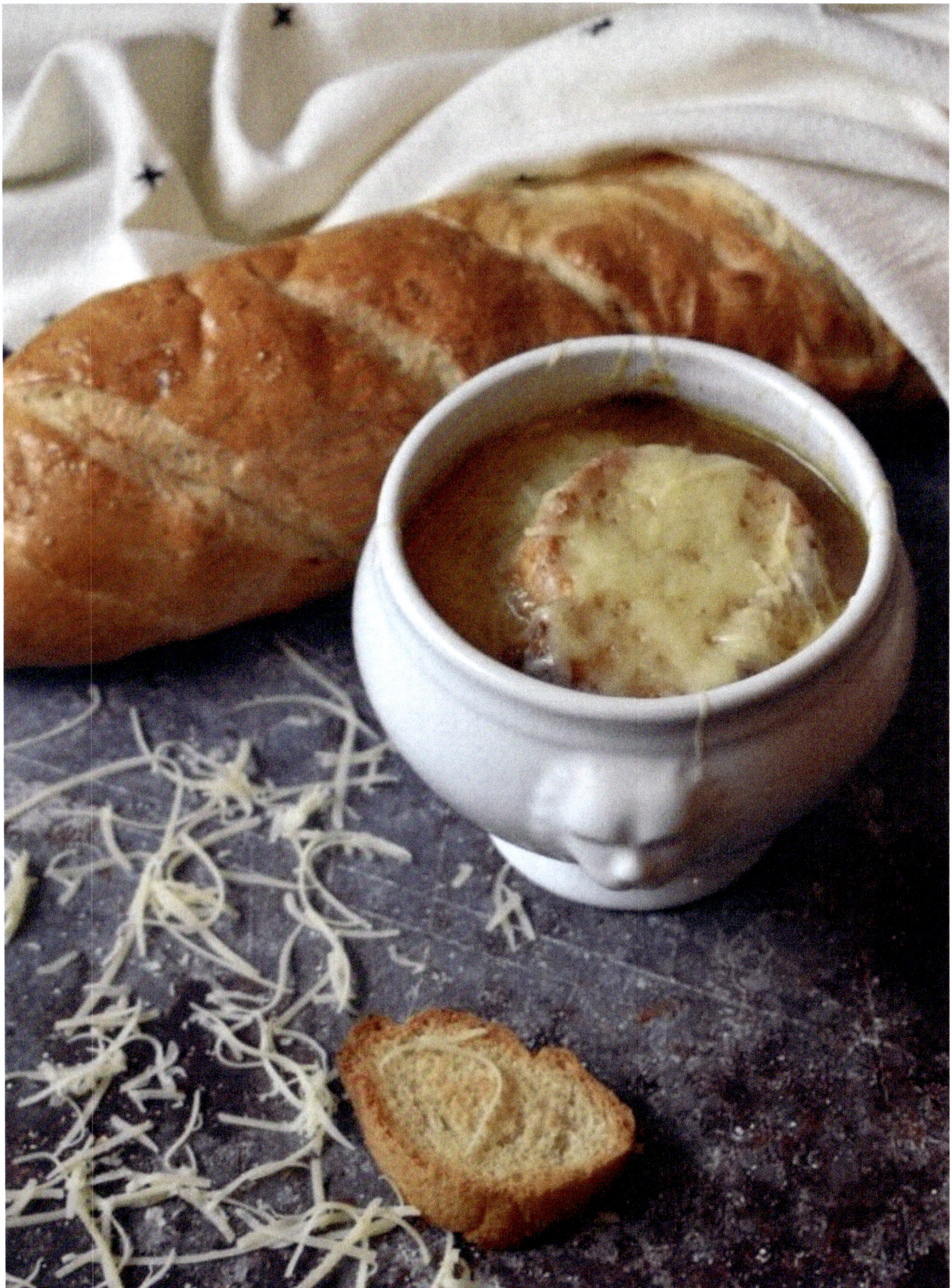

Chicken and Mushroom Fricassee

Ingredients:
20oz/ 566g Chicken Thighs or Breast, boneless, skinless
Salt and Pepper, to taste
3 Tablespoons/ 1.5oz/ 45g Butter
2 Large Leeks, diced
1 Garlic Clove, minced
3 Large Carrots, peeled and diced
1 Celery Stalk, diced
1lb Chestnut Mushrooms, chopped
¼ cup/ 1.1oz/ 30g Plain Flour
½ cup/ 4.1fl.oz/ 118ml White Wine
2 cups/ 16.6fl.oz/ 474ml Chicken Stock
1/3 cup/ 2.7fl.oz/ 78ml Double Cream
1 Tablespoon/ 0.5fl.oz/ 15ml Lemon Juice
2 Tablespoons Fresh Flat-leaf Parsley, chopped
½ teaspoon/ 0.03oz/ 1g Thyme leaves
½ teaspoon/ 0.03oz/ 1g Tarragon

Generously season the chicken with salt and pepper. In large heavy bottomed pan melt 2 tablespoons of the butter over a medium-high heat. Cook the chicken in butter 2 to 4 minutes on each side or until browned; transfer to plate.

Melt remaining butter in the large pan. Cook leeks, garlic, carrot and celery in butter for 5 to 6 minutes, stirring frequently, until the vegetables are softened. Add mushrooms; cook 8 to 10 minutes, stirring occasionally, until mushrooms brown.

Make a rue by stirring the flour into the cooked vegetables. Continue cooking the flour for about 1 minute until flour coats vegetables. Add in wine; simmer 1 to 2 minutes, stirring constantly until thickened. Stir in the stock. Bring the temperature up to a boil and add the chicken back into the sauce. Reduce the heat and simmer an additional 10 to 15 minutes, or until the chicken is fully cooked. (Internal temperature of 165°F/ 74°C or the juices run clear when you poke the thickest point.) At this point the sauce should have greatly thickened. Add the double cream, lemon juice and herbs. Heat through. Serve over mashed potatoes or rice.

Serves 4 to 6

Contribution By: Sara Robinson

Tartiflette

Ingredients:
1 pound/ 2.2kg Potatoes, preferably thin skinned
6 Onions, peeled and thinly sliced
500g Smoked Bacon or Lardons
4 Tablespoons/ 2fl.oz/ 60ml Double Cream
2 Tablespoons/ 1fl.oz/ 30ml White Wine
2 Reblochons or about 17.6oz/ 500g Soft Cheese such as Brie
Salt and Pepper, to taste

Cook the potatoes in water for 20 minutes, allow to cool slightly and then peel and cut into thin slices. Thinly slice the onions. In a large frying pan melt butter and add the sliced onions. Cook until the onions are translucent and brown. Cut the bacon into bit-sized pieces adding them to the onion mixture. Cook an additional ten minutes, stirring often. Use a large baking dish or two 12inch pie plates. Place a layer of potatoes in the bottom of each dish. Then split the onions and bacon between the two dishes. Smooth to an even layer and add a final layer of sliced potatoes.

Season generously with salt and pepper. Pour the wine and double cream over the dishes. If it is looking a little dry then add additional cream.

Preheat the oven to 375°F/ 190°C/ Gas Mark 5.

Slice the cheese thinly and layer across the potatoes. Bake for about 20 to 30 minutes. Serve immediately with a sprinkle of chopped parsley, crusty bread and the wine you used to make the dish.

Serves 4 to 6

Contribution By: Sara Robinson

Red Onion Tarte Tatin

This one is nice and sweet and so good to eat. Be forewarned, don't let Evans anywhere near it unless you want it to disappear quicker than a blink of the eye!

You will need a cast iron frying pan (9 inch/ 23cm) or other suitable solid based pan or tin that can be used on the hob and in the oven.

Ingredients:
Pastry:
1 cup/ 5oz/ 125g Plain Flour
3 Tablespoons plus 2 teaspoons/ 2oz/ 50g Butter, cold
1/4 cup/ 1oz/ 25grams Cheddar or Parmesan Cheese, grated
Water

Filling:
2lb 8 oz/ 1.15kg Red Onions
1 3/4 Tablespoons/ 1oz/ 25g Butter
1 teaspoon/ 0.14oz/ 4g Caster Sugar
1 Tablespoon/ 0.5fl.oz/ 15ml Balsamic Vinegar
A few shavings of Parmesan cheese to serve
Sea Salt and Ground Black Pepper to taste

Pre-heat the oven to 350°F/ 180°C/ Gas Mark 4 and preheat a solid baking sheet as well.
Skin the onions and cut in half lengthways from top to bottom. Place the pan over a medium heat and as soon as it is hot adding the butter and rolling it in the pan until melted, then add the sugar and the balsamic vinegar. When it starts to sizzle fit the onions in cut side down so there is no space left. You may have to cut a few onions to make sure there are no open spaces. Season well with the salt and pepper. Turn the heat down and cook very gently for about 10 minutes. Remove from heat, cover the dish with foil and place on the heated baking sheet in the oven for 50 to 60 minutes.
Make the pastry by rubbing the fat into the flour until it resembles breadcrumbs and mix in the grated cheese. Add cold water to make a soft dough. Wrap in cling film and put in the fridge for 30 minutes.
Test the onions with a skewer, they should be cooked through but still retain some texture. Remove dish from oven turn the oven up to 400°F/ 200°C/ Gas Mark 6 and if necessary, place your pan back on the hob over medium to low heat to reduce the juices (about 10 minutes). Watch the onions carefully so they don't burn.
Roll out the pastry in a circle of about 10 inches/ 25½cm then turn the heat off under the dish. Carefully fit the pastry over the onion, pushing down and tucking the edges all around the inside of the dish, so there are no large air bubbles and no onions showing. Return the dish to the oven placing on the baking sheet and cook for 25 to 30 minutes until the pastry is crispy and golden.
When done, remove from the oven and allow to cool for 20 minutes before turning it out. You need to have a completely flat plate or board to do this. Place plate or board on top the pan like a lid and turn both pan and board together upside down then give them a good shake. Be very careful when doing this and make sure you have a firm grip on both pan and board because if they come apart, they can splash you. If some of the onions are left in the pan don't worry just lift them out of the pan gently and fit back into correct place in the tart. Serve warm with a few shavings of parmesan over the onions together with a salad.

Serves 4 as a main course or 6 as a starter.

A good shortcut is to use store bought puff pastry that has been well docked. Cut it to the correct size and proceed as above.

Contribution By: Barb Ruddle

Hope For The Best, Plan For The Wurst

Markham, Evans and Peterson were stopped before they could make it out of Hawking. Their plan was to jump back to 1949 to witness how curry wurst was invented. Dr Bairstow was not amused, that jump would have broken the 100-year rule!
Peterson always hopes for the best but Markham was planning for the wurst!
They will just have to get to Germany another way.

Ingredients:
For the Curry Ketchup:
1 Tablespoon/ 0.5fl.oz/ 15ml Vegetable Oil
1 Medium Onion, finely diced
2 Cloves of Garlic, minced
2 Tablespoons/ 0.98oz/ 28g of a Good Curry Powder – use your favourite curry powder and adjust spice to your taste.
1 Tablespoon/ 0.5oz/ 14g Sweet or Hot Paprika (not smoked)
1/8 teaspoon/ 0.007oz/ 0.2g Ground Cloves
1/8 teaspoon/ 0.007oz/ 0.2g Ground Cinnamon
1 cup/ 7.9oz/ 225g Tomato Ketchup
1 Tablespoon/ 0.5fl.oz/ 15ml Tomato Purée/ Paste
1 teaspoon/ 0.14oz/ 4g Brown Sugar
1 teaspoon/ 0.2fl.oz/ 5.9ml Worcestershire Sauce
¼ Tablespoon/ 0.14oz/ 4g Prepared Mustard
5 Tablespoons/ 2.5fl.oz/ 75ml Beef Stock/ Broth
1 Tablespoon/ 0.5fl.oz/ 15ml Apple Cider Vinegar
1 Tablespoon/ 0.5fl.oz/ 15ml Honey
Salt and Pepper to taste

Sausages:
4-8 genuine Bratwurst, Weißwurst, Bokwurst, or Rotwurst.

To Serve:
Curry Powder or cayenne to sprinkle
Fries, chips or Brötchen (bread rolls).

First, prepare the ketchup. This is best made the day before.

Heat the oil in pan on a medium heat. Add the onions and fry gently until they're translucent and soft. Do not allow them to go brown. Then, add your garlic and fry for another minute. Add the curry powder, paprika, cloves, and cinnamon. Stir well and fry for another minute. Add the remaining ingredients for the curry ketchup, stir well until all ingredients are incorporated, season to taste and let simmer for 10 to 15 minutes. Transfer the contents to a blender or use an immersion blender to purée until smooth. Remove to a container, let cool, cover and refrigerate until needed.

If your sausages are not already pre-cooked, poach them lightly in water that is barely simmering, until cooked through Remove from the water, drain well, and pat dry.

Then you can finish the sausages off in one of two ways: You can pan fry them in some oil until they are crispy and brown on the outside, or you can grill them until you achieve the same effect.

To serve: heat up your curry ketchup until it is piping hot, slice your wurst into chunks. Mix your chunks of wurst into the curry ketchup. You can either serve it with chips (chunky fries), fries, or on bread rolls (brötchen). Sprinkle curry powder or cayenne on top to finish! Mahlzeit!

Serves 4 to 6 people

Contribution and Photo By: Afton Cochran

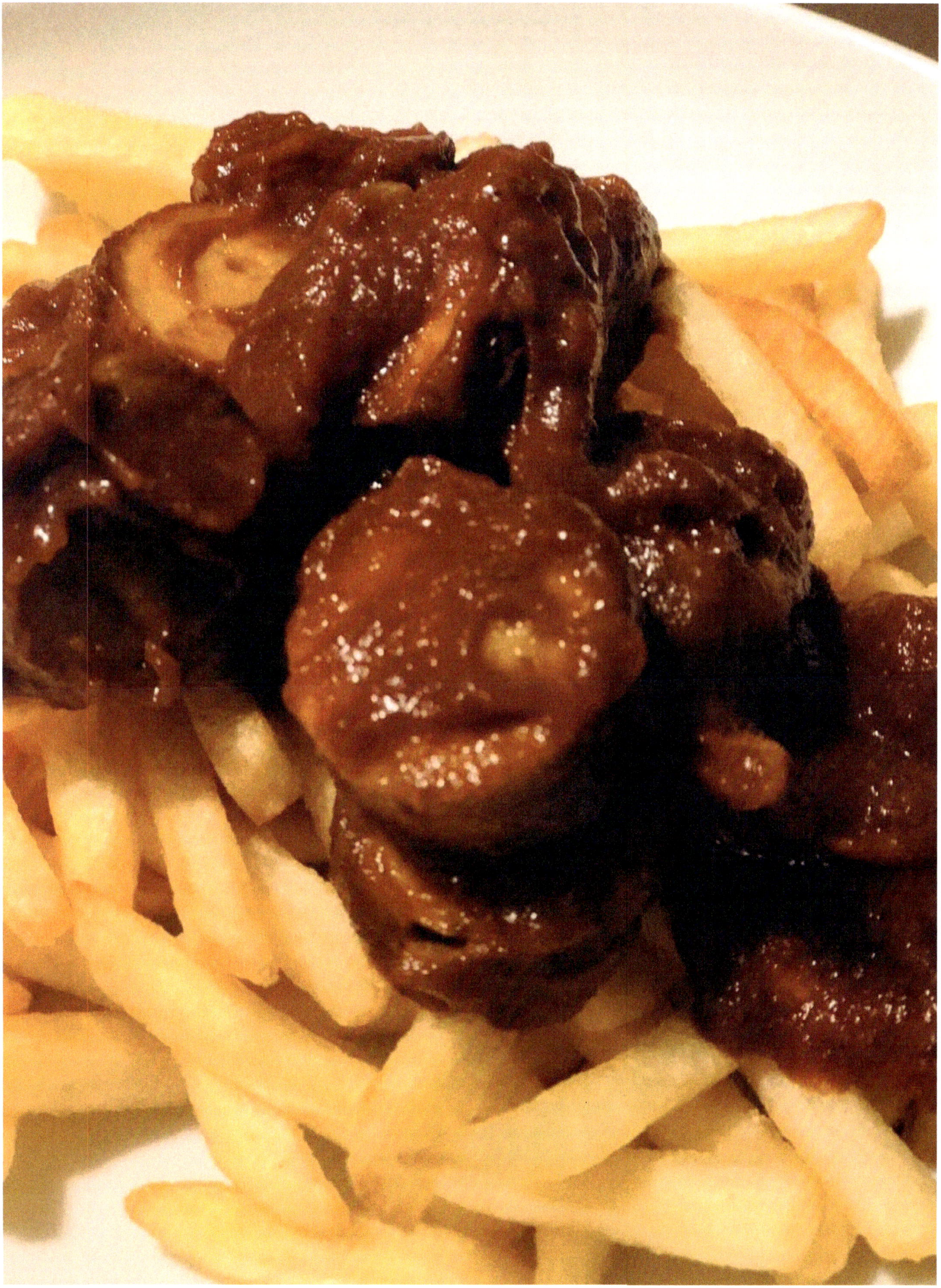

BORSCHT

Mr Evans would really like to know what those in the History Department have against beetroot! Borscht is a perfect example of good and filling food, but namby pamby historians like Bashford won't even try the delicious soup!
Their loss, more for us!

Ingredients:
16oz/ 500g Beef or Pork Shoulder, cut into 1inch/ 2 ½cm cubes
1 Red onion, coarsely chopped
2 to 3 Carrots, peeled, cut into ½inch/ 1 ¼cm pieces
2 Cloves Garlic, minced
3 to 4 Beetroots, peeled, cut into ½inch/ 1 ¼cm pieces
1/3 Red Cabbage, sliced thinly cross-wise to shred
1 Tablespoon/ 0.5oz/ 15g Sweet Hungarian Paprika
1 teaspoon/ 0.07oz/ 2g Dried Dill Leaf
2 teaspoons/ 0.42oz/ 12g Salt
Black Pepper, to taste
1 Tablespoon/ 0.5fl.oz/ 15 ml Worcestershire Sauce, shop bought or use our recipe
4 cups/ 34fl.oz/ 947ml Bone Broth, or a Good Stock of Beef or Vegetable
1- 28oz/ 794g Tin of Diced Tomatoes
1 Tablespoon/ 0.5fl.oz/ 15 ml Lard, Butter, or Oil
Sour cream or Greek Yoghurt to serve (optional)

In a large stockpot or Dutch oven, melt fat or oil over medium heat. Add onions and cook till soft, about 10 minutes. Add garlic on top of onions until just fragrant. Add spices and warm till fragrant. Do not burn the paprika or it will turn bitter. Add tomatoes and stir to scrape any brown bits off the bottom of the pot. Add bone broth.
While onions cook, place cubed meat on a cooking sheet and brown in a hot oven 400°F/ 200°C, (180°C fan)/ Gas Mark 6 about 15-20 minutes or until brown. Add meat to pot, reserving any juices on the cooking sheet. Keep the same heat going in the oven.
Place carrot cubes on one side of the baking sheet, beets on the other. Roll them in the meat juices to coat, then put in the hot oven and roast for 10 to 15 minutes until they start to brown. Add the vegetables and all the juices to the stock pot.
Cook for 1 ½ hours. Reduce heat to a simmer, then add slivered cabbage and cook another 15 minutes or until the cabbage just softens.
Dish into bowls and add a generous dollop of sour cream or Greek yoghurt. Serve with egg noodles, mashed potato, or a warm bread and butter on the side. Or just enjoy by itself.

Serves: 6, or just 1 Mr. Evans

This makes a fabulous Vegan dish by using vegetable broth or stock and by leaving out the meat and sour cream.

Photo and Contribution By: Merry Schepers

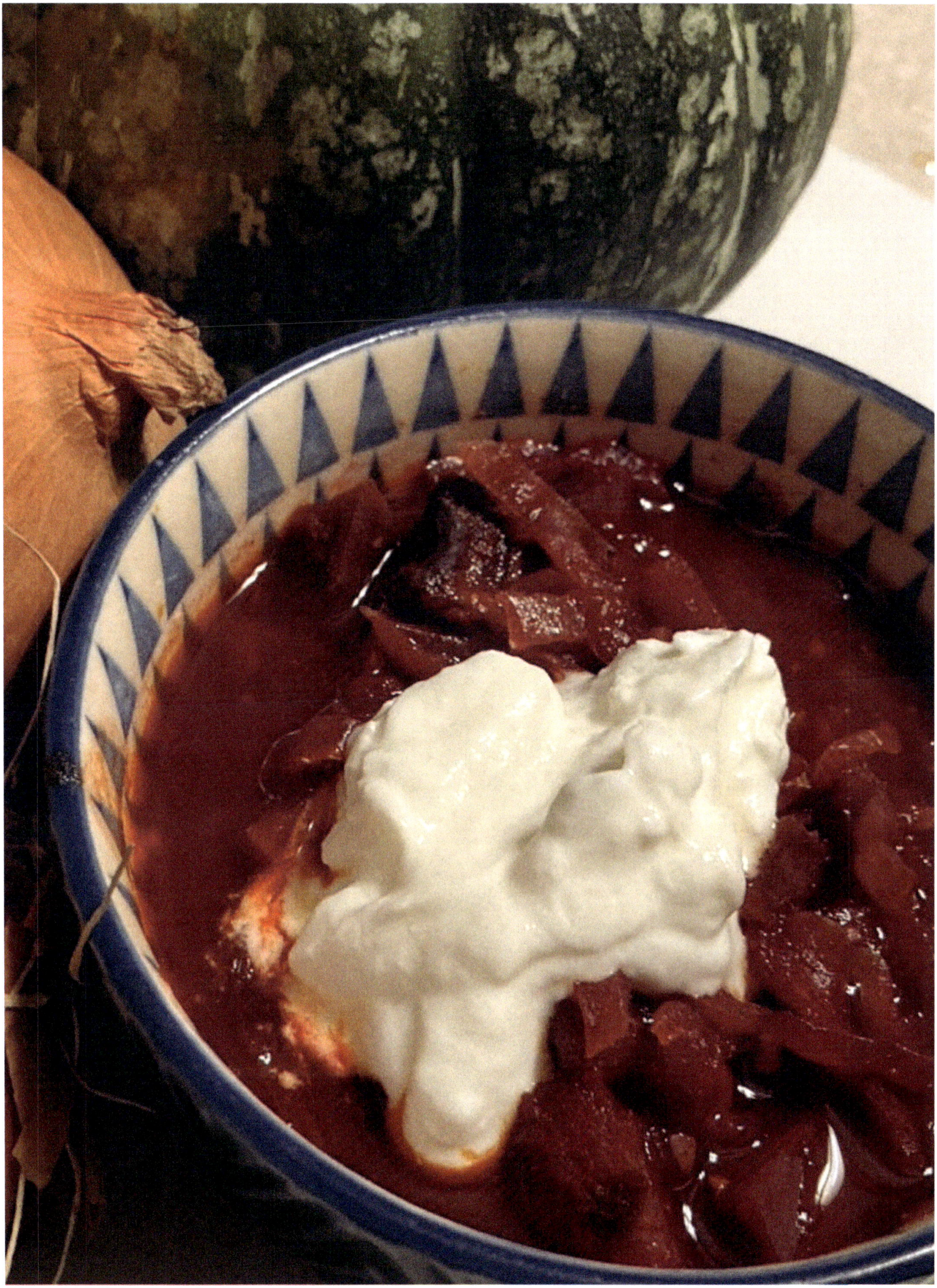

Verlorene Eier in Kräutersosse
Lost Eggs in a Herb Sauce

First off, no jokes about the security section being lost, or losing historians. Most historians don't know where we parked the pod let alone what they had for lunch. Second, the security section wasn't on that jump. Third, these eggs are filling and great for keeping everyone happy.

Ingredients:
- 2 ¼ Tablespoons/ 1oz/ 30g Butter
- 3 1/3 Tablespoons/ 1oz/ 30g Plain Flour
- 1 cup/ 8fl.oz/ 250ml Vegetable Stock, simmering
- 1 cup/ 8fl.oz/ 250ml Milk
- Pinch Ground White Pepper
- Pinch Ground Nutmeg
- 1 Bunch Fresh Parsley, chopped
- 1 Bunch Fresh Chives, chopped
- Prepared Mustard to taste
- 8 Eggs

In a medium pan, melt the butter then stir in the flour to make a roux. Cook over a low heat, then stir in the milk and stock bit by bit, not stopping stirring, to avoid lumps. To this sauce, add pepper and nutmeg, bring to the boil and simmer for 5 minutes.

Wash, drain and finely chop the herbs and set aside.

Hard boil the eggs and peel (alternatively poach them in boiling water).

Put the eggs into a warmed bowl.

Stir the herbs and mustard into the sauce, which should taste mustardy. Pour the sauce over the eggs.

Serve with boiled or mashed potatoes.

Serves 4

Contribution By: Becky Parsons

Peppercorn– Pothast

This one we discovered in the market on that one jump. Peace with Westphalia? That can't be right, wasn't there a van named after that? It was in the north-west of Germany area, 1648? Anyway give this a try! The line for food can't be wrong!

Ingredients:
- 1 ½ pounds/ 750g Beef, cubed
- 4 to 5 Onions, thinly sliced
- 1 teaspoon/ 0.28oz/ 8g Salt
- Fresh Black Pepper, to taste
- 1/3 teaspoon/ 0.02oz/ >1g Allspice
- 2 Bay Leaves
- 1 Lemon, sliced
- 4 to 6 cups/ 32 to 47fl.oz/ 950 to 1400ml Good Quality Beef Broth, or Water
- 1 Tablespoon/ 0.28oz/ 8g Breadcrumbs
- 2 Tablespoon/ 0.63oz/ 18g Plain Flour or Rusk Flour (Zwieback)
- Lemon Juice

Cube the meat, into ¾ to 1 inch/ 2 to 3 cm cuts and thinly slice the onions. In a large pot place the cubed beef and onions. Add all the spices/herbs and lemon slices. For a better taste, keep the black pepper as course as possible. Add broth or water to cover the meats and slow cook over medium heat for 1 hour. Add extra water when necessary.

Add breadcrumbs and zwieback, cook for another 10 min. Remove bay leaves and lemon slices.

Sauce should now be quite creamy. Taste and adjust the seasoning if necessary.

Serve with boiled potatoes and gherkins or beetroot.

Serves 4 to 6

Contribution By: Sara Robinson

Hungarian Goulash

*How were we supposed to know there were going to be shepherds?
Or how were we to know there would be so many sheep?
Or that one would bite Markham, it probably has rabies.
Can we not talk about Bashford tripping over one either. Is he awake?*

Ingredients:
1kg/ 2.2 pounds Beef or Pork Shoulder, cut into ¾inch/ 2 cm cubes
2 Tablespoons/ 1oz/ 30g Lard, Butter, or Neutral Oil, not olive oil
3 Cloves Garlic, minced
2 Medium Onions, finely chopped
2 Carrots, finely diced
2 Cloves Garlic, minced
2 Stalks Celery, diced
2 Red Bell Peppers, cored, seeded, and chopped
2 Fresh Tomatoes, cored, seeded, and chopped
2 Tablespoons/ 1fl.oz/ 30ml Tomato Purée/ Paste
2 cups/ 16fl.oz/ 500ml Beef Broth
1 Bay Leaf
2 Tablespoons/ 0.42oz/ 12g Sweet Hungarian Paprika, and only Hungarian paprika
¼ tsp/ 0.01oz/ >1g Smoked Paprika
¼ tsp/ 0.01oz/ >1g Caraway Seeds
Salt and Pepper to taste

Cut the meat into cubes, pat dry and set aside. Chop onions, carrots, garlic, pepper, fresh tomatoes and celery. Set aside.

In a non-reactive Dutch oven or stock pot, melt some of the lard until shimmering hot. Fry the meat cubes on medium high heat in 2 or 3 batches for about 5 minutes, or until all sides are browned. Add a little lard as needed for each batch. When browned, remove meat cubes to a plate and set aside.

Add the rest of the fat to the pot, melt, then add onions and carrots, cooking until the onions are slightly coloured, about 5 to 7 minutes, stirring occasionally to keep from burning. Tip: keep the carrots and onions in a heap in the center of the pot. The trapped steam will help keep them from burning. After stirring, gather back into a heap in the centre.

Add garlic, red peppers, celery tops, tomatoes, tomato paste and bay leaf to the onions and carrots, cooking further for another 5 minutes, stirring occasionally. Use a spoon to scrape up any delicious brown bits from the bottom of the pot.

Add the paprika and caraway and stir in, cooking for 1 minute. Add meat cubes back to the mixture in the pot. Add beef stock. Stir well and cover pot.

Bring the stew to a boil, then reduce to a simmer for 1 ½ to 2 hours, or until the meat is very tender.

Remove pot lid and continue to simmer until the goulash thickens a bit more, about 15 minutes, stirring occasionally. Taste, then add salt and pepper as needed. Discard bay leaf. This stew also freezes well for future use.

Serve with buttered egg noodles, spaetzle noodles, or mashed potatoes.

Serves 4 to 6

History Tip:
Hungarian Goulash is a traditional thick and hearty soup that has been traced back to the 9th century.
It is also the original hiking food. The stew was made by the Magyars and then dried in the sun to make an easy meal, just add water and simmer over the campfire.

Contribution By: Merry Schepers

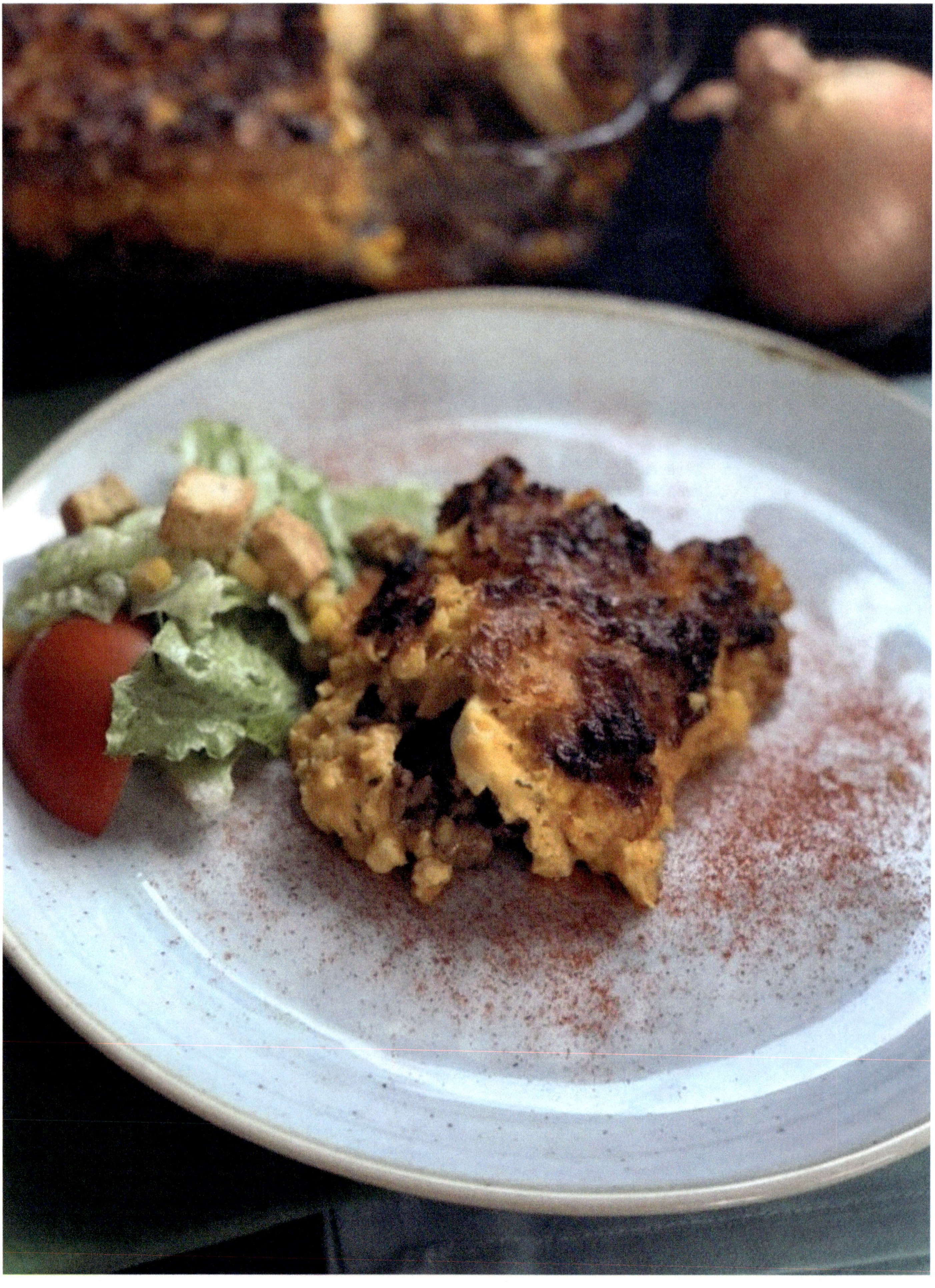

Pastel de Choclo

This is a dish that is quintessentially Chilean. It is Chile's answer to Britain's Cottage Pie. The beef mince is flavoured with Merkén, ground Goat Horn Chile (aji cacho de cabra) which is native to Chile, and similar to Paprika or the stronger Chipotle powder. The topping is made with the starchy Chilean summer corn instead of potato. It is quite a delightful dish. You can use sweet paprika, or chipotle chile powder in place of Merkén, and corn (thickened at the end with cornflour).

Ingredients:
For the beef:
- 2 Tablespoons/ 1fl.oz/ 30ml Vegetable Oil
- 1 kg/ 2.2 pounds Beef, minced or ground
- 2 cups/ 16fl.oz/ 474ml Beef Stock
- 3 Yellow Onions, diced
- 1 to 2 Tablespoons/ 0.24 to 0.49oz/ 7 to 14g Merkén, Sweet Paprika or Chipotle Powder
- 1 teaspoon/ 0.07oz/ 2g Cumin, ground
- Salt and Pepper to taste (a smoked sea salt goes nicely!)
- 1 cup/ 4.9oz/ 140g Chicken, cooked and shredded (optional)
- 2 Tablespoons/ 0.5oz/ 15g Cornflour dissolved in ¼ cup/ 2.1fl.oz/ 63ml Water or Beef Stock
- 4 Hardboiled Eggs
- 8 to 10 Black Olives, whole and pitted
- 10 to 20 Raisins (optional)

For the corn topping:
- 10 cups/ 3.6pounds/ 1.65kg Sweetcorn, frozen
- 3 Tablespoons/ 2.1oz/ 60g Butter
- ¾ cup/ 6fl.oz/ 180ml Whole Milk
- 1 bunch Basil, stems removed, chiffonade
- 2 Tablespoons/ 0.5oz/ 15g Cornflour dissolved in ¼ cup/ 2.1fl.oz/ 63ml Whole Milk, to form a slurry
- Merkén or Sweet Paprika or Chipotle Powder to taste
- Salt and Pepper to taste

In a large skillet, heat your oil on a high heat. Add your minced beef all at once, (don't break it up) and let it sear for 3-4 minutes until it gets a nice crust on the side. Flip it over and allow it to sear on the other side. Add the Merkén (or paprika or chipotle), cumin and salt and pepper. Add the stock and slowly and carefully break up the meat. Turn the heat down, cover and simmer for 30 minutes. Ensure it doesn't go dry. If it starts to go dry, add a bit more stock. After the half an hour, add in your diced onions, stir well, cover and simmer for a further 30 minutes.

If you are using your cooked chicken, add it now, cook until it's heated through.

Your mixture should be quite thick, if it is not, use your cornflour slurry to thicken.

You can prepare your meat to this point ahead of time and cool and refrigerate, or use immediately.

For the corn topping: In a large pan, melt the butter. Add the corn and cook for 8-10 minutes, ensuring the corn has defrosted and is coated in the butter.

Add your milk, the basil, Merkén (or paprika or chipotle powder) and salt and pepper, and cook for a further 10 minutes.

With an immersion (stick) blender or in a normal blender (in batches), blend up your corn mixture. You don't want it completely smooth. You want some texture in this mixture. How much is down to you. When you're happy with the consistency, add your cornflour and milk slurry and cook for a further 5 minutes or until it's thickened. Adjust your seasoning to your liking.

To assemble: Heat your oven to 400°F/ 200°C (180°C fan)/ Gas Mark 6. In a 9x13inch or 23x33cm pan or dish, evenly spread your meat and onion mixture. If you're using the hard boiled eggs, olives and raisins (or any combination), now is the time to add them to the dish. Slice your eggs, and distribute them evenly over the top of the meat. Now carefully spread the corn mash layer over the meat and egg/olive/raisin layer so not to break up or disturb those ingredients. Place on a baking sheet and cook for 40 to 60 minutes or until the corn mash has a nice crunch to it and the food is piping hot (167°F/ 75°C). Let it stand for 10 minutes before serving.

(Adapted from Pilar Hernandez)   Photo and Contribution By: Afton Cochran

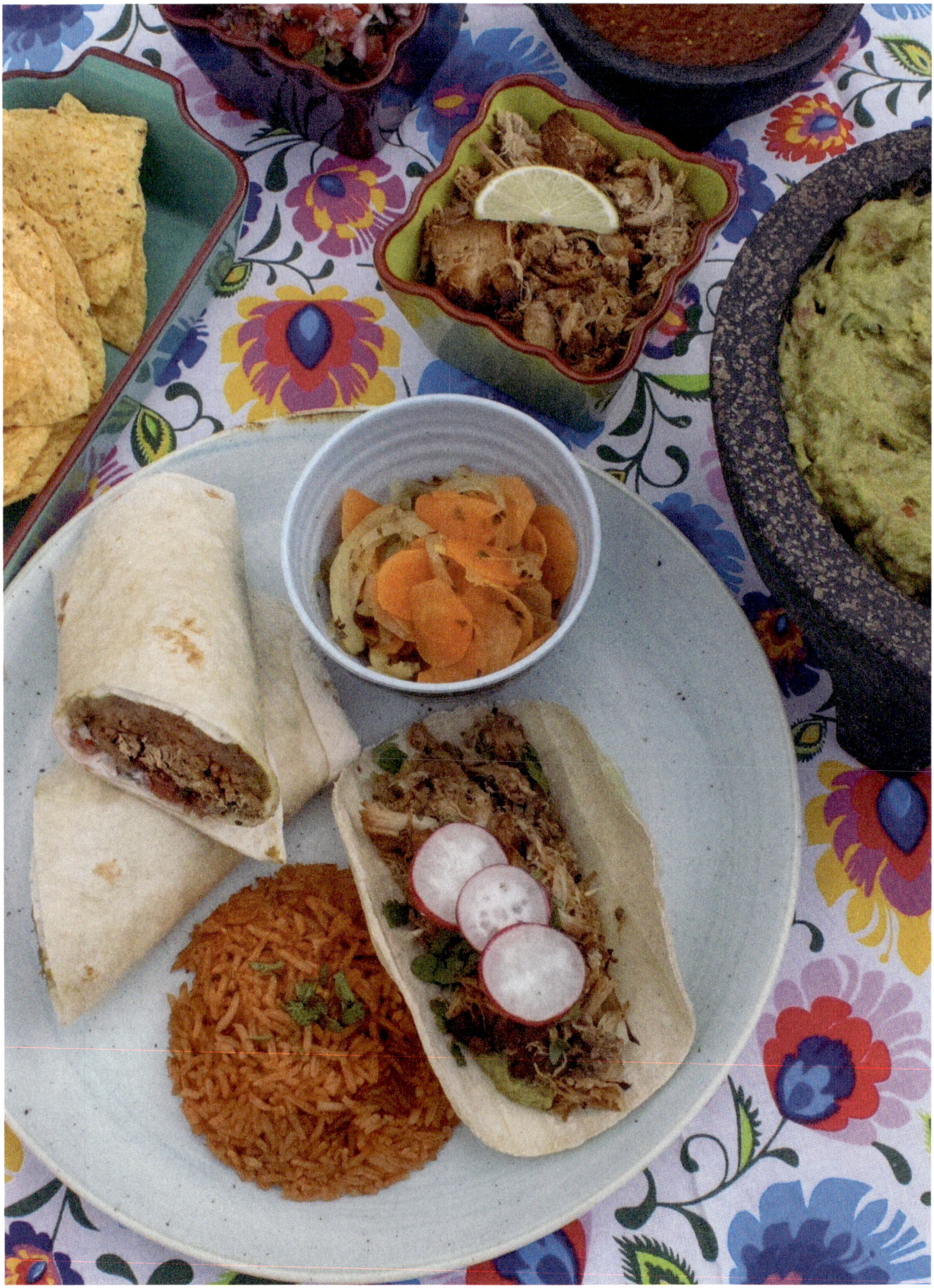

Slow Cooked Pork Carnitas

Back when travel was much easier and you could come home clutching your duty frees, our Mr. Markham went to Mexico. How he made it back was anyone's guess because he isn't telling. But he brought back a fabulous new dish that has delighted all of St. Mary's.

Ingredients:
2 kg/4lbs Pork Shoulder
2 teaspoons/ 0.4oz/ 11g Salt
1 teaspoon/ 0.07oz/ 2g Cracked Black Pepper
1 to 2 Tablespoons/ 0.1 to 0.2oz/ 3 to 6g Dried Oregano, preferably Mexican
1 Tablespoon/ 0.2oz/ 6g Ground Cumin
1 Large Onion, cut into wedges
8 Cloves Garlic, minced
2 Limes, zested and juiced
2 Large Oranges, zested and juiced or ¾ cup/ 6.2fl.oz/ 175ml Orange Juice
¾ cup/ 6.2fl.oz/ 175ml Cola with sugar, preferably Coca-Cola - if you can get Mexican/Full sugar Coke, it will be so much better.
2 Bay Leaves
2 Tablespoons/ 0.5oz/ 13g Lard or 2 Tablespoons/ 1.1fl.oz/ 35ml Vegetable Oil, if you're using the frying method and not the grill.

Remove the skin from the shoulder if it has it. Cut the meat into large manageable chunks. Pat the pork shoulder dry, coat it all over with the salt, pepper, oregano and cumin. Place in a 6 litre (6 quart) slow cooker. Add remaining ingredients, apart from the lard/oil. Put the lid on it and cook on low for 8-10 hours or high for 4-5 hours.

If you don't have a slow cooker, you can cook the pork on the hob. You will need a heavy pot, ideally 8L (8 qt). Add all your ingredients, apart from the oil/lard, bring to the boil, turn down and simmer 2 to 3 hours. You want the liquid to slowly cook down to next to nothing, but you don't want it to go dry and stick to the bottom of the pan. If you find you have too much liquid, but the pork is completely cooked, you can use your battle ladle to take out the excess. Save it, just in case. When the pork is thoroughly cooked, you can finish it off as listed in the recipe above.

When the pork is cooked, remove and shred. Keep the juices. Season the pork well with salt.

There are different options for finishing the Carnitas:

Option 1: Grill/Broiler
Place the shredded meat on a foil lined baking sheet (the foil helps with clean up!). Add 1 cup of the liquid to the meat. Place under a medium grill/ broiler and cook for 10 to 15 minutes until the pork is crispy. Season to taste.

Option 2: Hob/Stove Top
Place 2 tablespoons of the lard or oil in a frying pan, wok, or skillet and bring to a high heat. Working in batches, fry the pork until it is just starting to get crisp. When all the pork has been fried, add all the meat back into the pan, add about ½ cup/ 120ml or so of the juices and cook the liquid down until the pork is once again crispy. Season to taste.

Use as a taco, burrito, tostada filling, or have it on its own with rice, beans and a salad

Photo by: Hannah Holt   Contribution By: Afton Cochran

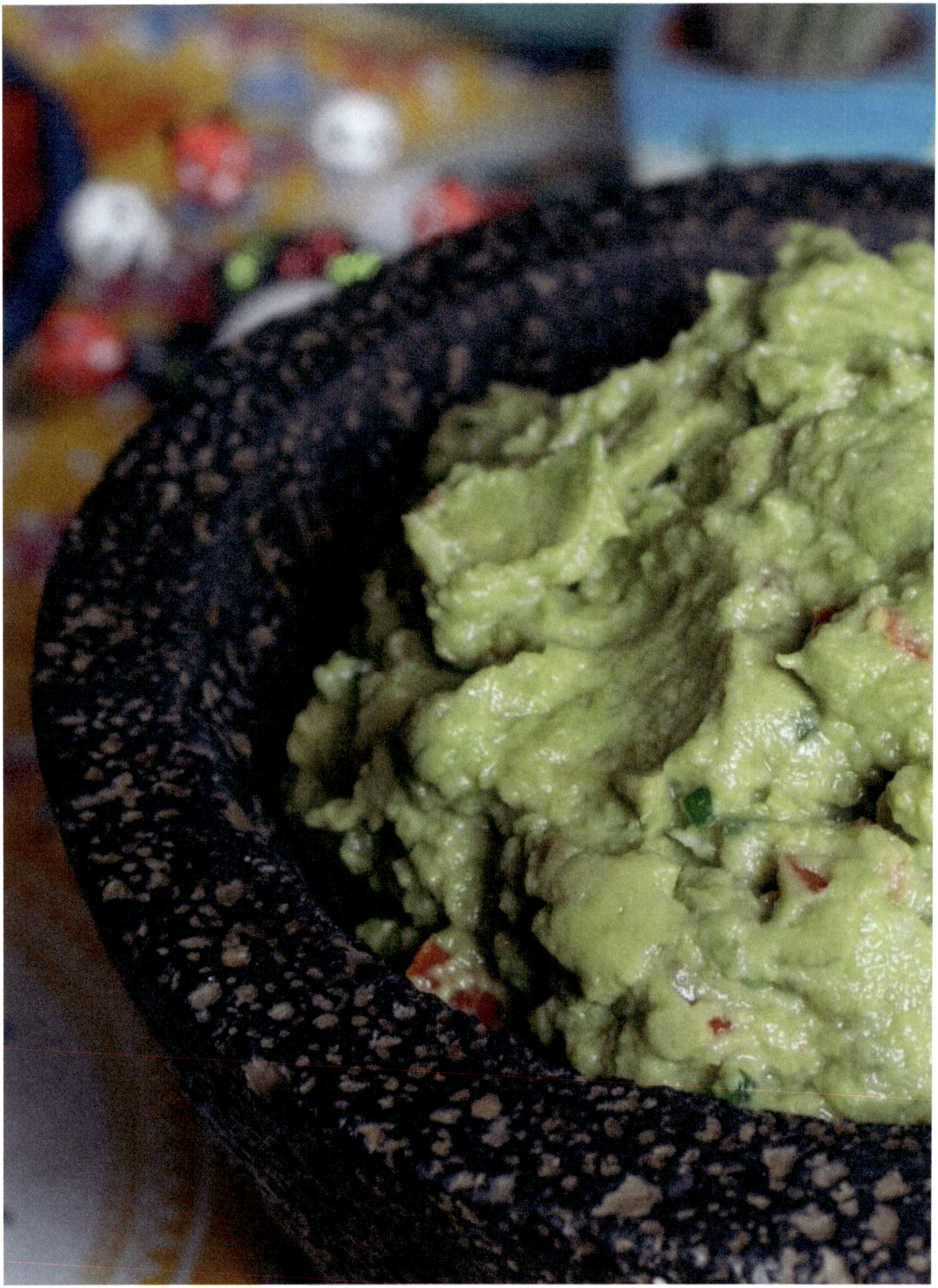

Guacamole

The history of this awesome dish dates back to the Aztec Empire in Central America and was recorded by the Spanish in the early 1500's. Aztecs loved the 'ahucca-mulli' or avocado mixture.

Ingredients:
3-4 Ripe Avocado
Salt
1 Jalapeno
1 Plum Tomato
Garlic
Hot Sauce
Juice of 1 Lime
Sour Cream (optional)

Make sure your avocados are ripe, they shouldn't be as hard as rocks. You won't be able to mash them if they are. Carefully slice your avocados in half and twist the pit out with the sharp edge of your knife. And please be careful, we don't want any trips to Sick Bay with sliced hands, thank you. Scoop out the flesh of the avocado and place in a bowl. Do this with all the avocados. If there are any black bits, scoop them out and throw them in the bin. Take your jalapeño and if you can handle the heat, leave the seeds in, if not, cut the top off and scoop the seeds and membrane out. Do not rub your eyes. In fact, go wash your hands thoroughly with warm soapy water. And did I mention not to rub your eyes? Don't. Again, we don't want another trip to Sick Bay because someone has burning eyes. Finely dice the jalapeño and put it in the bowl with the avocado. Who would have thought making guacamole would be so perilous?

Now we mash. Choose your implement. It could be a fork, or a pastry cutter, or a potato masher. Just don't use your fists. Do not use a stick blender or a food processor or any kind of mixer. You want this guacamole to have texture from the avocado, not be some runny slop. Mash away. Add a bit of salt while you're at it. Mash it to how you like it. Just make sure there are no bloody great big chunks of rock hard avocado. Next, cut your tomato in half. Scoop out all the seeds and membrane. Leaving it in would make for very wet guacamole and no one has time in their life for that kind of negativity. Carefully dice up the tomato as small as you can. Put it in the bowl. Do you see a pattern here?

Now we have to deal with the garlic. Get a clove of garlic. Make sure that there aren't any green shoots coming out of the end, as it will make it bitter. If it is, throw it in the bin and get one that isn't. Crush it and remove the skin and the dry bit at the top of the bulb. We don't want that in there, now do we? And now what do we do? We mince it up finely and put it in the bowl with everything else. You can also use a garlic press. Add the juice from half a lime at this point. Save the other half for later. Here you'd also add a little dollop of the sour cream. The combination of the lime juice and the sour cream keeps it from going brown so quickly. If you don't like it, don't add it. Pick your hot sauce. Or don't, if you're a wimp. This needs to be something like Tabasco of any colour, Valentina, Tapaito, something like that, but not sweet chilli. Add as much or as little as your heart(burn) desires. Remember, this is your guacamole.

Now give it a really good mix. You can add more salt, hot sauce, lime juice, sour cream, if you think it needs it. Serve it up (or eat up yourself) with tortilla chips, put it on tacos, or any Mexican food you fancy, or just eat it with a spoon. We won't judge.

Photo by: Hannah Holt   (Adapted from Dandelion Mama)   Contribution By: Afton Cochran

CANJA
Brazilian/Portuguese Chicken and Rice Soup

Supposedly Mr Whissell learned this from a bloke that grew up in Brazil, or was it born in Portugal? We can't remember and no one wants to track him down. Good thing is the recipe is wonderful and has outlasted the pillock.

Ingredients:
For the chicken stock:
Whole Corn-Fed Chicken
6 Sticks Celery
4 Carrots
1 Onion
Bunch of Parsley
Handful of Peppercorns
2 Bay Leaves

For the soup:
Meat from the chicken
25 cups/ 211fl.oz/ 6L of the above Stock (strained and skimmed)
2 Large Vine Tomatoes, seeded and minced
9oz/ 250g Smoked Bacon Lardons
1 Onion, finely chopped
3 Carrots, peeled and chopped
7oz/ 200g White Basmati Rice
1 Small Bunch Parsley, stems removed and finely chopped
Salt and Pepper to taste.

In a large stock pot place your chicken, onion, parsley, peppercorns, bay leaves, carrots, and celery. Cover in cold water (at least 6L/25 cups) Bring to a boil, cover, and gently simmer until the chicken is fully cooked. Remove from the heat and allow the chicken to cool in the stock. Remove the chicken from the stock and place on a plate. Strain the solids from the stock and discard the solids. Skim the fat from the stock and set aside. Pick the chicken meat from the bones, discarding the skin and bones. Set aside. Clean and dry the stock pot. Fry onions and bacon lardons together in the stock pot. Remove any excess oil when onions are soft and bacon is cooked. Add the stock, carrots, tomatoes and rice. Season. Be aware that if you used smoked bacon, you would need to be mindful of the amount of salt you put in. Simmer on a low heat for 25 min. When the rice is fully cooked, add your chicken to the pot. Heat through. Season to taste.
Garnish with parsley.
Serve with crusty bread and butter.

Serves 4

Contribution By: Afton Cochran

ENSALADA DE POROTOS CON CEBOLLA
Chilean Bean and Onion Salad

Bashford and Markham in little pod with beans, onions - and we are praying the toilet still works. The cabbage smell might be pleasant after this one.

Ingredients:
1 cup/ 6oz/ 170g Dried Pinto Beans
3 cups/ 24fl.oz/ 710ml Boiling Water
1 teaspoon/ 0.28oz/ 8g Salt
1 Bay Leaves
1 Medium Onion, thinly sliced
1 Tablespoon/ 0.5fl.oz/ 15ml Good Quality Olive or Canola Oil
1 Tablespoon/ 0.5fl.oz/ 15ml Lemon Juice or White Wine Vinegar
1 Green Bell Pepper, seeded and diced
Salt and Pepper, to taste
½ cup/ 1oz/ 30g Fresh Parsley or Chives, chopped

Pick through the beans, making sure there are no bad beans or debris. Rinse, place in a bowl and cover in cold water overnight. Drain. In a medium pot, cover the beans with the 3 cups/ 750ml of boiling water. Add the salt and bay leaf. Bring back to the boil and cook for 20 to 40 minutes. The beans should be firm but cooked through. Drain and allow the beans to cool. Thinly slice the onion, place in a bowl, and cover with boiling water. Allow it to sit for 10 min or so, then drain, rinse under cold water and pat dry with kitchen roll. Seed and dice the green pepper. Place the beans, onions and green pepper in a bowl. Whisk together the oil and lemon juice or vinegar and salt pepper. Mix the dressing into the salad. Garnish with the parsley or chives.

Serves 4 as a side

Contribution By: Afton Cochran

Chapter Six: The Medical Department or What St. Mary's Struggles To Eat. Eat Your Greens!

The Medical Staff pick us up and put us back together whenever there is a problem. The biggest problem with them is that they expect us to eat vegetables. Granted, in the future we know that there will be vegetarians and maybe even vegans at St. Mary's, so the kitchen staff need to start planning for them today!

Recipes:

Vegan Sweet and Sour Cauliflower	130
Vegetarian Wellington	130
Vegan Burrito	131
Mujadara/ Middle Eastern Lentils, Rice and Onions	132
Sweet and Sour Lentils	133
Leek and Cheese Pie	133
Tossed Cauliflower with a Mustard Vinaigrette	135
Lentil and Vegetable Pie	136
Saag Paneer	138
Syracuse Salt Potatoes	139
Lemon Orzo with Asparagus	139
Caesars Tossed Greens	140
Vegan Mexican Style Bean and Lentil Stew	141
Roasted Vegetables	143
Roasted Vegetable Soup, Mushroom and Roasted Squash Risotto	
Red Lentil and Mango Dahl	144
Vegetarian Lasagne	144
Vegetable Stock or Broth	145
Vegetarian Shepherds Pie	145
The Great St. Mary's Salad and Oven Chips and Jacket Potatoes	146
Steamed Vegetables	147 to 148
Vegan Gluten Free Vanilla Cake	149

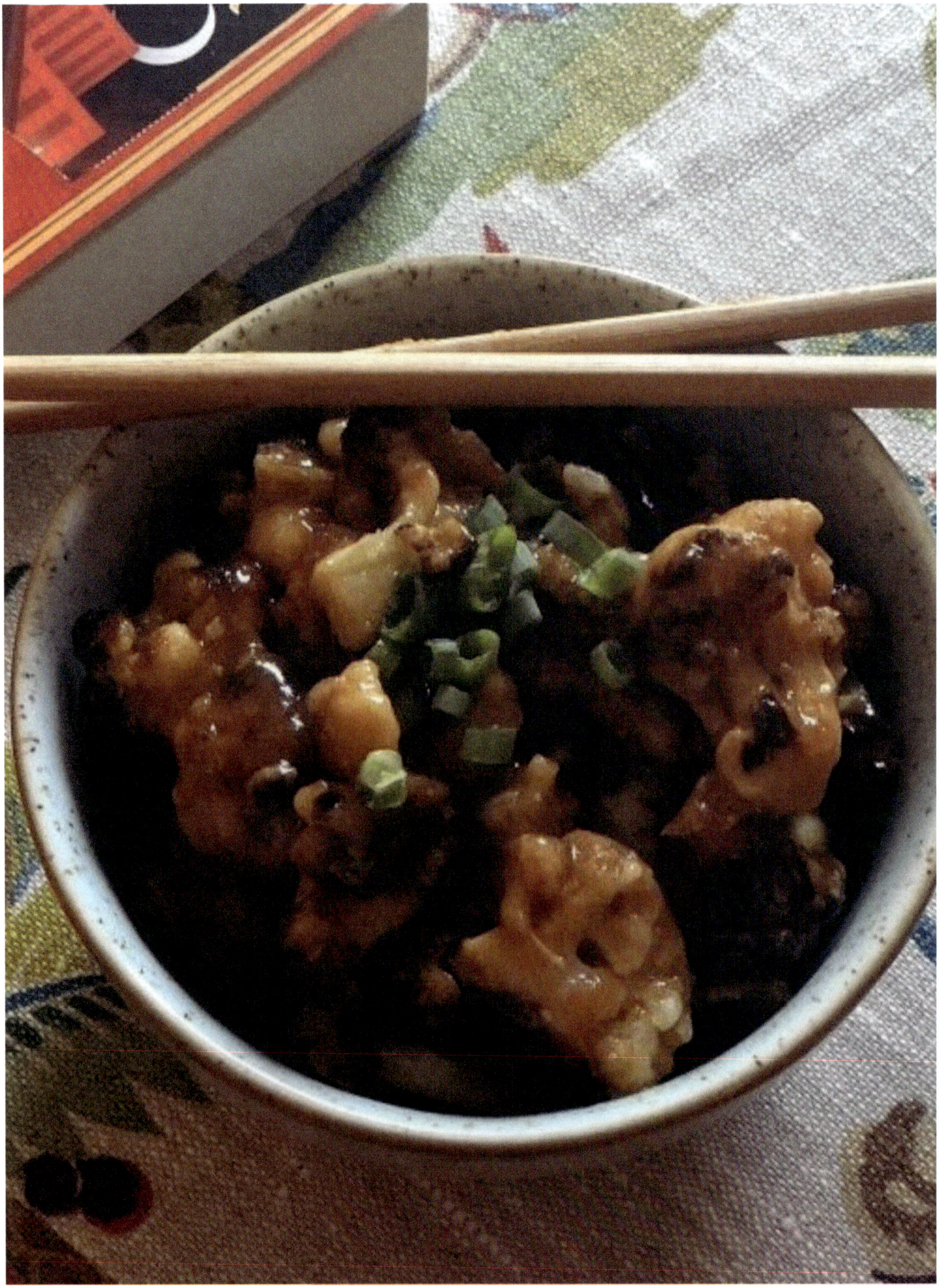

VEGAN SWEET AND SOUR CAULIFLOWER

This recipe is as sweet as how Markham thinks about the time with Nurse Hunter and his little family. Time with family is always sweet, but having to go back to work after time away can be a little sour.

Ingredients:
1 Large or 2 Small Heads of Cauliflower, cut into large florets
3 to 4 Tablespoons/ 1.5 to 2fl.oz/ 45 to 60ml Olive Oil
6 Tablespoons/ 1.5fl.oz/ 45g Cornflour, Rice Flour, Potato Flour, or any combination. Rice flour gives a crispier coating.
¾ cup/ 5.9fl.oz/ 175ml Vegetable Stock
2/3 cup/ 2.7fl.oz/ 80ml Soy Sauce or Gluten Free Tamari
3 Tablespoons/ 1.4oz/ 41g Brown Sugar
½ teaspoon/ 0.07oz/ 2g Chilli Flakes, or more to taste
3 Tablespoons/ 1.5fl.oz/ 45ml Tomato Ketchup
6 Cloves Garlic, finely minced
1 Tablespoon/ 0.5fl.oz/ 15ml Rice Vinegar
Cornflour Slurry, if needed

Preheat the oven to 425°F/ 220°C (200°C fan)/Gas Mark 7.
Combine the cauliflower florets and olive oil in a zip seal bag or a mixing bowl. Mix well. Add the corn flour and mix well to coat evenly. Place on a grease baking sheet. Bake for 20-25 minutes, turning occasionally to ensure it does not burn. While the cauliflower is cooking, add the stock, soy sauce, ketchup, sugar, chilli flakes, garlic, and vinegar into a small saucepan. Bring to the boil. Allow it to reduce slightly. Should you wish it to be thicker, mix up a cornflour slurry, and thicken it to desired consistency. In a heat safe bowl, mix the cauliflower and the sauce. Garnish with freshly snipped chives and serve with steamed jasmine rice.
Serves 2 as a main

Contribution and Photo By: Afton Cochran

VEGETARIAN WELLINGTON

This recipe is amazing! The subtle flavours and easy construction is a hallmark of the creator Mort Reading. We miss her and are proud to add some of her recipes to this book.

Ingredients:
1 -18oz/ 500g Pack of Puff Pastry, pre-rolled
Half a pack of precooked Basmati Rice
    (5/8 cup/4.4oz/ 125g)
1 Lemon, zested
Handful of finely chopped parsley (1/2 cup/ 1oz/ 30g)
5 to 6/ 6oz/ 175g Baby Leeks, trimmed and halved
1 – jar 16oz/ 450g of Roasted Red Pepper or
    12oz/ 350g Roasted Peppers, skins removed
1/3 cup/ 2oz/ 57g Blue Cheese
1 ¾ cups/ 8oz/ 225g Mushrooms
1 ¼ cups/ 6.3oz/ 180g Hulled Chestnuts, chopped
2 Tablespoons/ 1oz/ 28g Butter
1 Onion, finely chopped
1 Garlic Clove, minced
Salt and Pepper to taste
1 Beaten Egg to glaze
1 x 2lb Loaf Tin. lined with a strip of baking parchment to help with turning out the wellington.

You may need to roll out the puff pastry a little so that it fits the tin. Lay it into the tin so that the excess falls to one side to create the lid.
Mix the rice with the lemon zest and parsley and half the chopped onion and press into the bottom of the wellington. Slice and sauté the mushrooms in the butter with the garlic and the other half of the chopped onion. Allow to cool and then add 1 cup/ 3.5oz/ 100g of chestnuts. Drain the jar of peppers and reserve the oil as this is great for dressings. Slice the leeks in half and lay cut side up lengthways down the tin. Season with salt and pepper. Crumble the blue cheese on top of the leeks. Place a layer of peppers on top of this. Cover with the mushrooms and chestnuts. Brush the overhanging edges of the pastry with a little of the egg then fold over the top and seal around the edges with a fork. Make a couple of cuts into the lid to allow the steam to escape and glaze with the egg.
Bake at 400°F/ 200°C/ Gas Mark 6 for 45 mins

Contribution By: Mort Reading

Vegan Burrito

Burritos were not an instant success in the U.K. One Edinburgh food critic even wondered who has already chewed the food he ordered. This has changed so much over the years and burritos are seen as tasty food now.

Ingredients:
Rice:
1 cup/ 7oz/ 200g Brown Basmati Rice
2 cups/ 16fl.oz/ 500ml Vegetable Stock
Beans:
1- 15oz/ 425g Tin Black, Pinto, or Black-Eyed Beans, rinsed and drained
1 teaspoon/ 0.1oz/ 3g Sazon Seasoning
1 cup/ 8oz/ 250ml Water
Toppings:
1 Head Romaine Lettuce, finely shredded
2 Tomatoes, seeded and diced
8oz/ 250g Sweet Corn, preferably fresh off the cob
½ Onion, finely minced or two Spring Onions, chopped
1 Red Pepper, stemmed, seeded and diced
1 Avocado, peeled, seeded and diced
1 cup/ 4.2oz/ 120g Vegan Cheese, shredded
1 small bunch of Coriander/ Cilantro, leaves removed and chopped
½ cup/ 4fl.oz/ 120 ml Salsa or Pico de Gallo
Chipotle Sauce:
2/3 cup/ 13oz/ 375g Silken Tofu
1 Chipotle Pepper in Adobo Sauce
1 teaspoon/ 0.16fl.oz/ 5ml Adobo Sauce
2 Cloves Garlic, minced
½ Lime, juiced
¼ teaspoon/ 0.01oz/ 0.03g Ground Cumin
4 Large Flour Tortillas or 8 Small Flour Tortillas or 8 Hard or Soft Corn Tortillas.

In a saucepan, bring the vegetable stock to the boil. Add the rice, stir, reduce heat, cover, and allow to simmer gently until the water is absorbed. Remove from the heat and leave the lid on the rice for 10 minutes. In another small saucepan, add the beans, sazon, and water. Bring to the boil, turn the heat down to a simmer and cook until the water is almost fully evaporated. Do not allow it to boil dry. Set aside. In a blender, add the tofu, chipotle, adobo sauce, garlic, cumin, and lime juice. Blend until smooth. Season to taste. Warm your tortillas (apart from hard corn shells) in the microwave (wrapped in kitchen roll) or the oven (wrapped in foil). Fill with desired toppings and sauce. You could also omit the tortillas and have this as a burrito bowl.
If you want a vegetarian version, swap sour cream for the silken tofu and regular cheese of your choice.
Serves 4

The burrito filling can also be used as a taco filling, or on its own as a burrito bowl. Make sure to check the ingredients on tortillas or taco shells be sure they are appropriate as many have animal by products in the ingredients.

Adapted from The Garden Grazer   Contribution By: Afton Cochran

MUJADARA
MIDDLE EASTERN LENTILS, RICE AND ONIONS

This dish is also often made with bulgur instead of rice. Most types of lentils will do in this recipe, apart from red lentils, which go mushy faster than the others. If you can find Egyptian rice, it works best in this recipe, but if not, basmati or other long grain rice will work.

Ingredients:
Caramelised Onions:
3 Large Brown Onions
½ cup/ 4oz/ 120ml Vegetable Oil
1 teaspoon/ 0.14oz/ 4g Sugar
Salt and Pepper, to taste
Lentils:
2 cups/ 14oz/ 400g Dried Black, Brown, or Green Lentils
2 teaspoons/ 0.14oz/ 4g Ground Cumin
3 cups/ 25fl.oz/ 700ml Water
Pinch of Salt
Rice:
1¼ cup/ 7oz/ 200g Egyptian, Basmati, or other long grain rice
¼ teaspoon/ 0.01oz/ 0.03g Ground Cinnamon
1 teaspoon/ 0.07oz/ 2g Ground Coriander
1 teaspoon/ 0.07oz/ 2g Coriander Seeds
2 teaspoons/ 0.14oz/ 4g Ground Cumin
2 Tablespoons/ 1fl.oz/ 30ml Olive Oil
1 teaspoon/ 0.2oz/ 6g Salt
2 cups/ 17fl.oz/ 475ml Vegetable Stock
To Garnish:
Bunch of Parsley, finely chopped, or 1 cup/ 0.75oz/ 20g Rocket/Arugula
1 Pomegranate, seeded, or 75g (1/2c 2.6oz) Raisins

Onions: Thinly slice the onions (Don't cry for me, mujarada).
Heat the vegetable oil in a large skillet or frying pan on a medium high heat. Add the onions, stir to coat well in the oil. Add a bit of salt and pepper. Reduce heat to low and cover. Stir occasionally. Cook for 15 minutes, or until the onions are soft and translucent. Remove the lid and add the sugar. Stir well. Turn the heat up to medium and continue to cook the onions until they are a nice dark caramel colour. If they are starting to stick, turn the heat down and add a little bit of water to deglaze the pan. The caramelisation process will take at least half an hour, so you can prepare your rice and lentils during this time.

Rice: Rinse and drain the rice well. Heat the olive oil for the rice in a saucepan over a medium heat. Add the spices and stir well. Cook for 30 seconds, until the spices become fragrant and have darkened slightly. Add the rice and salt and stir well to coat the rice in the spices. Carefully add in the stock, as it might splatter. Stir well and bring to the boil, it may do this immediately. Cover and turn the heat down to a slow simmer. Allow it to cook until the water is absorbed. Keep an eye on it to ensure it does not boil dry and stick to the pan. When rice is cooked, remove from the heat, and let it sit for 10 minutes with the lid on.

Lentils: Pick through the lentils, rinse and drain well. In a saucepan, add the water, cumin and salt and bring to the boil. Add the lentils and cook for 15 minutes or until they are al dente. Be attentive as you do not want the lentils to go mushy. Drain, set aside and keep warm.

Assembly: Combine the lentils, rice, 2/3 of the caramelised onions and parsley, or rocket (arugula). Check seasoning and heat through. Place on a serving platter and garnish with the remaining caramelised onions and pomegranate seeds (or raisins), if desired.

Serves 4

Adapted and inspired by Palestine on a Plate and Sarah Jampel	Contribution By: Afton Cochran

SWEET AND SOUR LENTILS

We don't think anyone would ever make the mistake of saying that Helen Foster is sweet, but these lentils will knock your socks off! They are so tasty!

Ingredients:
Sauce:
2 cups/ 16.7fl.oz/ 475ml Vegetable Stock
1/4 cup/ 1.9fl.oz/ 59ml Soy Sauce or Tamari
2 Tablespoons/ 0.9oz/ 28g Jaggery or Brown Sugar
2 Tablespoons/ 1.4oz/ 40g Concentrated Tamarind Paste
2 Garlic Cloves, peeled and minced
¾ inch/2 cm piece of Fresh Ginger, peeled and minced
1 teaspoon/ 0.16fl.oz/ 5 ml Sesame Oil
1 teaspoon/ 0.07oz/ 2g Chilli Pepper Flakes
Lentils:
1 Tablespoon/ 0.5fl.oz/ 15ml Vegetable Oil
½ Onion, minced
1 cup/ 6.7oz/ 190g Red Lentils
2 Spring Onions (or 3 Tablespoons Chives), chopped

Mix all your sauce ingredients together. Set aside. In a pot on a medium heat, add your vegetable oil, and gently fry your onion until soft and translucent. Do not let them go brown. Add the lentils and stir well. Pour in your sauce, stir well and cover until cooked, about 10-15 minutes. Keep an eye on it to ensure the lentils don't boil dry and stick to the pan. Add more water or stock if the lentils aren't quite cooked. Adjust your seasoning as desired. You can add more jaggery, chilli flakes, or tamarind, should you desire a stronger flavour. Garnish with the spring onion, or chives and sesame seeds. Serve with jasmine rice. Should you not have access to concentrated tamarind paste, you can substitute lime juice to taste.

Serves 4

Contribution and Photo By: Afton Cochran

LEEK AND CHEESE PIE

Ingredients:
7 to 8 Slim Leeks
Salt and Black Pepper
9oz/ 250g Store Bought Puff Pastry
1 Tablespoon/ 0.5fl.oz/ 15ml Dijon Mustard
1 Egg
1.75oz/ 50g Cheddar Cheese, grated

Thaw the puff pastry if frozen.

Preheat the oven to 450°F/ 230°C/ Gas Mark 7.
Trim the leeks to a length of about 7inches/ 18cm and rinse them. Fill and boil the kettle. Arrange the leeks in a single layer in a large frying pan and pour on boiling water and add a pinch of salt. Bring the leeks and water back to a boil. Reduce the heat and simmer gently for 6 to 8 minutes, until the leeks have softened.
While that is cooking, roll out the puff pastry to a 10inch/ 25cm square then transfer the pastry to a baking sheet. Cut a ½inch/ 1cm strip of pastry from each of the four sides, dampen the area around the edge of the square of pastry with water and fit the cut off strips on the pastry square so that is resembles a picture frame.
Drain the leeks and cool them under cold running water. Drain again and put between clean tea towels, gently squeeze to remove any remaining water.
Arrange the leeks inside the picture frame of the pastry and brush them with the mustard.
Beat the egg lightly and brush the egg over the border of the tart. Spread the grated cheese evenly over the leeks.
Bake on the top shelf of the oven for 15 minutes or until the pastry has risen and golden and the cheese has melted and is bubbling.

Contribution By: Barb Ruddle

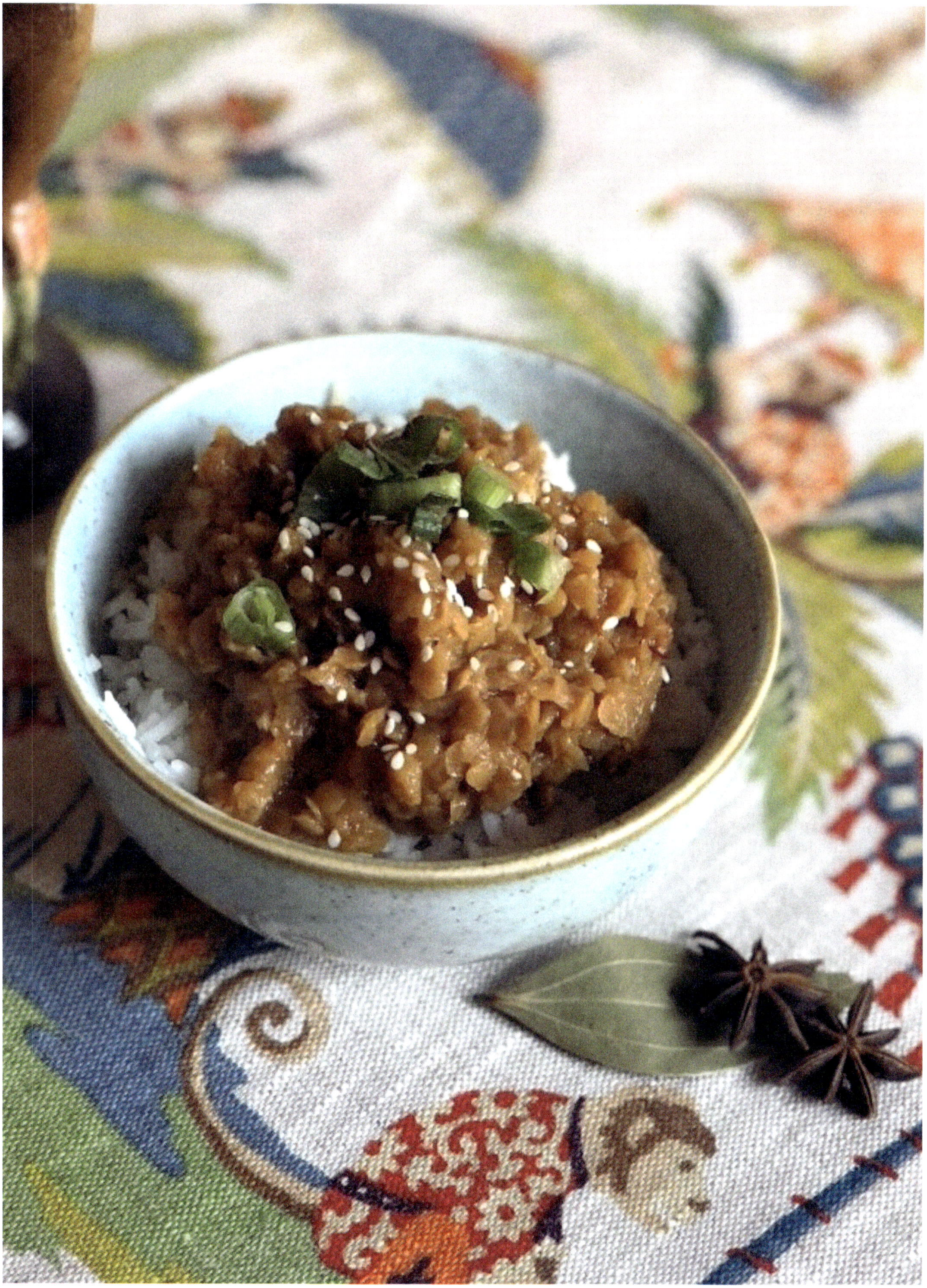

Tossed Cauliflower with a Mustard Vinaigrette, Caraway and Cheese

What is so objectionable with caraway? We know it was first used medicinally in the Middle East in 1500 BCE. It was used to freshen breath, and as a palate cleanser. This isn't good enough for the big rufty toughdies in the Security section when they were asked to eat this gorgeous dish, and let me tell you some of them need the help to freshen their breath!
Oh, well more for us!

Ingredients:
1 Cauliflower, broken into small florets
1 recipe Mustard-Caper Vinaigrette
3 Celery Stalks, diced finely
Small Handful of Celery Leaves, slivered
1 Small Bunch of Salad Onions, white part and half of firm greens, thinly sliced
½ cup/ 4fl.oz/ 120ml Small Cubes of Havarti, Goat, Cheddar or Other Firm Cheese
2 teaspoons/ 0.6fl.oz/ 20ml Caraway Seed, toasted lightly in a dry skillet
Salt and Pepper to taste
Lemon Juice

Put the cauliflower florets in a steaming rack over boiling water, cover and steam for about 6 minutes. The cauliflower will be slightly tender; it will continue to cook in residual heat. When the cauliflower is ready, toss it in a shallow bowl with the vinaigrette. Add celery, celery leaves, green onions, cheese and caraway seeds and toss again. Add salt, pepper and lemon juice to taste.

Serve warm.
Serves 4

Mustard-Caper Vinaigrette

Ingredients:
2 Tablespoons/ 2fl.oz/ 60ml Red Wine, Sherry Vinegar or Lemon Juice
1 Large Shallot, finely diced
1 Clove Garlic, minced
Sea Salt, to taste
2 teaspoons/ 0.6fl.oz/ 20ml Dijon Mustard
1 teaspoon/ 0.3fl.oz/ 10ml Coarse Mustard
1/3 cup/ 2.7fl.oz/ 79ml Olive Oil
Freshly Ground Pepper
2 Tablespoons/ 2fl.oz/ 60ml Chives, snipped
1 Tablespoon/ 1fl.oz/ 30ml Parsley, chopped
3 Tablespoons/ 3fl.oz/ 90ml Capers, rinsed and coarsely chopped

Combine vinegar, shallot, garlic and salt in a small bowl. Let stand for 10 minutes. Whisk in the mustard and oil briskly until thick and smooth. Grind in a bit of pepper, then stir in chives, parsley and capers.

Adjust to taste.

Contribution By: Merry Schepers

Lentil and Vegetable Pie

Nurse Katie loves this one! She makes it both ways with a bag of those chicken like pieces from the grocery, or with a couple of tins of lentils. It is so filling and helps keep her on her toes for a full shift in medical.

Ingredients:
Pastry:
3 2/3 cups/ 16oz/ 453g Plain Flour
1 cup/ 8oz/ 227g Vegan Margarine, cold and cut into small cubes
Pinch of Salt
Cold Water

Filling:
3 1/2 cups/ 17.5oz/ 500g Red Lentils, tinned or cooked and well drained or a Vegan Protein Alternative
5 1/2 cups/ 28oz/ 800g Vegetables, fresh or frozen
    We recommend a good mixture including carrots, peas,
    swede, bell pepper, sweet corn, leeks and potatoes

Gravy:
3 1/2 cups/ 28fl.oz/ 828ml Vegetable Stock
1 teaspoon/ 0.2fl.oz/ 6ml Soy Sauce or Tamari Sauce to Taste
1 Tablespoon/ 0.3oz/ 9g Cornflour to thicken, or more to achieve desired thickness

Pastry:
Sift the flour in a large bowl and add a pinch of salt. Cube the vegan margarine into small pieces and add to the flour. Rub together using fingertips until it resembles breadcrumbs, add enough cold water to form a dough, wrap in clingfilm and cool in the fridge for half an hour. Remove from the fridge and divide into 1/3 and 2/3. Use a 9x13 inch pan. Roll out larger portion of dough to fit your dish so it covers the bottom, sides and over the edge so you can crimp it with the top when you have filled it. Lay a piece of parchment paper over the dough in the dish and fill with pie weights or dried beans. Blind bake the pastry at 400°F/ 200°C (180°C fan)/ Gas Mark 6 for 10 minutes.
Remove and allow to cool.

If using fresh vegetables, you will need to dice and then parboil vegetables for 10 minutes. Once it is done drain in a colander and set aside. If you are using frozen veg make sure it is well defrosted and drained of moisture.

To make gravy:
In a small saucepan, add the vegetable stock, soy sauce or tamari sauce and bring to a simmer. Make a slurry with the cornflour and a little water before adding it to the saucepan. Increase the temperature a little and whisk until it becomes lovely and thick. If it is too thin repeat making the cornflour slurry.

Mix the lentils and vegetables together and place in the pan over the bottom crust. Pour the gravy over the lentils and veg.

Roll out the smaller piece of dough so it fits over the top of your dish and edge. Dampen the edge of the pastry in the dish with a little water and lay the top over, crimp together by pressing your thumb on the edge all the way round. Trim off any excess. Wash the top of the pastry with milk, or a well beaten egg. Bake in oven 180°F/ 200°C/ Gas Mark 4 for 25 to 35 minutes or until golden

Serves 6

Contribution By: Barb Ruddle

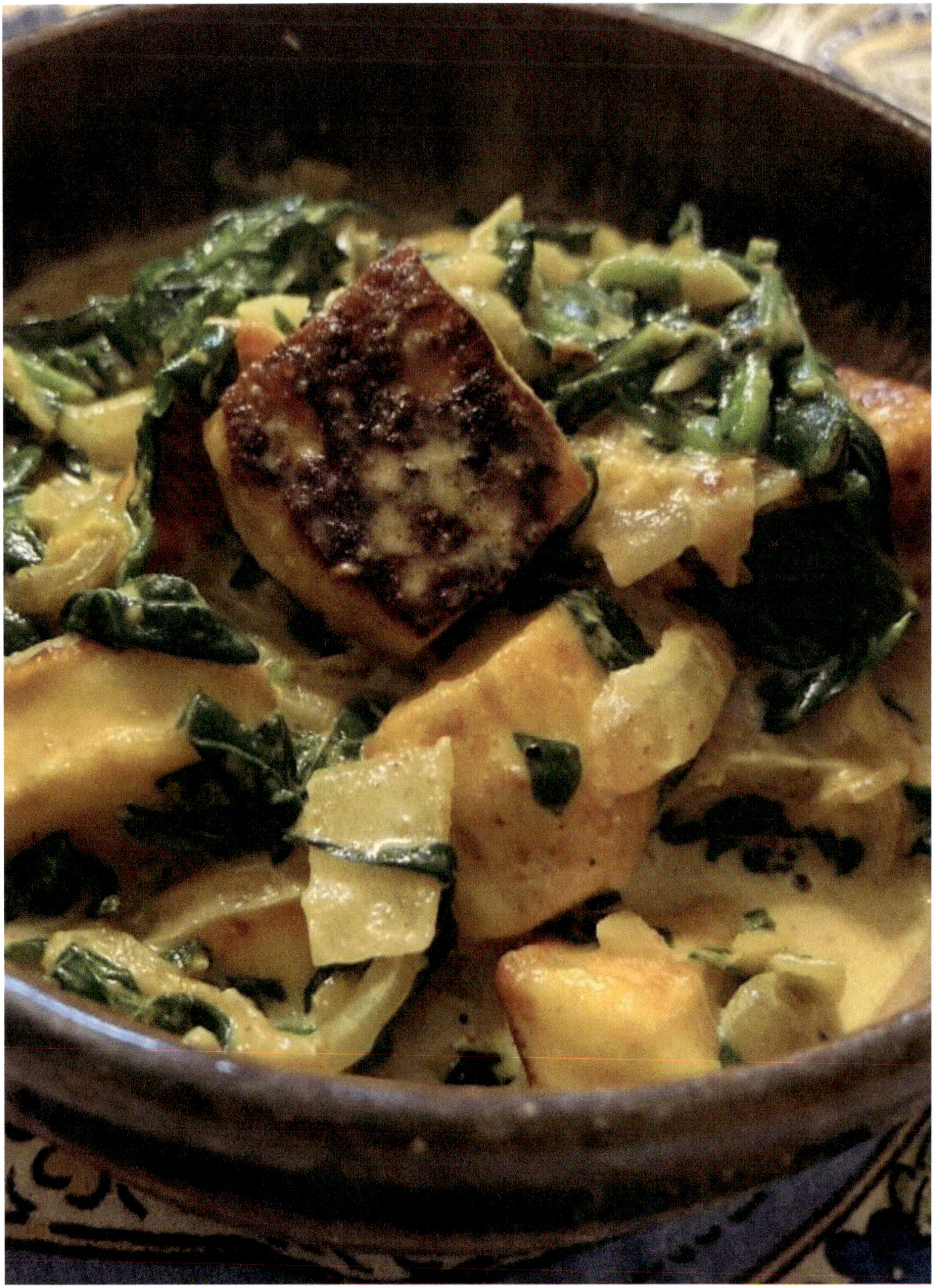

SAAG PANEER

This recipe reminds Miss North of home and better days. Traveling with her parents and long hot holidays in India, where her father was working for a time. She always asks for it to be served after a long assignment.

Ingredients:
16oz/ 450g Frozen Spinach or 1pound 12oz/ 800g Fresh Spinach Leaves, cleaned
8oz/ 228g Paneer or Halloumi Cheese, rinsed with water, cut into ¾inch/ 86cm chunks
3 Tablespoons/ 1.5fl.oz/ 45ml Ghee or Oil
¼ cup/ 2fl.oz/ 60g Water
1 Medium Onion, diced
4 Cloves Garlic, minced
1inch/ 2.5cm piece of Fresh Ginger, peeled and minced
1 teaspoon/ 0.07oz/ 2g Chilli Powder, mild or hot
1 teaspoon/ 0.07oz/ 2g Ground Turmeric
1 teaspoon/ 0.07oz/ 2g Ground Cumin
Sea Salt, to taste (the cheese can vary in saltiness. Taste dish before adding any salt)
1/3 cup/ 2fl.oz/ 60ml Double Cream

Marinade for Paneer/Halloumi:
2 teaspoons/ 0.3fl.oz/ 10ml Oil
½ teaspoon/ 0.03oz/ 1g Ground Turmeric
½ teaspoon/ 0.03oz/ 1g Chilli Powder
½ teaspoon/ 0.03oz/ 1g Ground Coriander (optional for those who do not like Coriander or Cilantro)
½ teaspoon/ 0.03oz/ 1g Ground Cumin

In a bowl or sealable bag, combine marinade ingredients and mix to incorporate. Add cheese chunks and stir. Marinate for 3 to 24 hours.

Heat 1 tablespoon/ 5ml ghee or oil in a large skillet or a saucepan on medium-high heat. Add cheese, large side down. Cook for 1 minute or until toasty brown. Add a little more oil as needed to do the browning. Flip and brown the opposite side. Remove to a plate and set aside.

Add 1 tablespoon/ 5ml oil to the pan and reduce heat to medium. Add onions and cook till they begin to turn clear. Add garlic, ginger, turmeric, chili and cumin. Cook until the onions turn light brown and the spices are fragrant, about 3 to 5 more minutes. Add water.

Add spinach, stirring to incorporate with the onion and spice mixture. Fresh greens will cook down considerably in volume, frozen will not. Add the cheese. Cook till greens are fully hot, about 5 to 8 minutes. Taste for salt and add more if needed. Turn off the heat. Pour the cream into the mixture slowly while stirring so that the cream does not curdle. Serve with rice or naan, or as a side dish. It makes a perfectly satisfying main dish.

<u>Tips and options:</u>

Substitute part of the spinach with other greens such as chard or kale, for a more complex flavour.

Stir 2 Tablespoons/ 30ml yoghurt with the cream to form a thick, tangy mixture, add <u>very</u> slowly to the cooked greens and cheese mixture to incorporate without curdling. The tanginess of the yoghurt balances the richness of the cheese and cream.

In a hurry? Had a long day and everyone is hungry? It is ok to use a good curry mix instead of making your own masala. Really. It is just fine.

Photo and Contribution By: Merry Schepers

Syracuse Salt Potatoes

The origin of salt potatoes can be traced to the 19th century in the Syracuse, NY area where Irish immigrants working in salt mines prepared the dish on their lunch break. Throughout the Onondaga Lake region, miners would boil small, unpeeled potatoes in the brine that was mined from salt springs.

Ingredients:
3 pounds/ 1.5kg Baby Potatoes, preferably Baby Red Potatoes, scrubbed clean, but not peeled
1 cup/ 10oz/ 290g Kosher Salt
7 Tablespoons/ 3.5oz/ 100g Unsalted Butter
Bunch of Parsley or Chives
1 gallon/ 3.7L Water

Do not use salted butter in this recipe. Wash and gently scrub clean the potatoes. Pat dry. In a large stock pot, add the water. Pour in the salt and stir well until all the salt is dissolved and none remains on the bottom of the pot. Add the potatoes and cover. Bring to a full rolling boil. Reduce the heat and boil for 25 minutes or until the potatoes are tender but still firm. Drain the potatoes into a colander and allow to them to dry. This is essential to allow the salty crust to form on the potatoes. Transfer to a serving dish. Melt the butter, pour over the potatoes, sprinkle with chopped parsley or chives.

Contribution By: Afton Cochran

Lemon Orzo with Asparagus

Ingredients:
Dressing:
1 Lemon, juiced and ½ zested
4 Cloves Garlic, crushed and minced
60ml (1/4c) Olive Oil
Salt and Pepper, to taste
Asparagus:
16oz/ 500g Asparagus
2 Tablespoons/ 1fl.oz/ 30ml Butter or Olive Oil
1 Lemon, ½ zested or the other half from the lemon in the dressing
Salt and Pepper, to taste
Orzo:
4 cups/ 32fl.oz/ 950ml Vegetable Stock
1 teaspoon/ 0.07oz/ 2g Ground Turmeric
1 Tablespoon/ 0.5oz/ 17g Salt
2 cups/ 12oz/ 340g Orzo Pasta
Small bunch of Parsley or Dill, finely chopped

To make the lemon dressing: Mix the dressing ingredients in a bowl or jug and set aside.
For the asparagus: Snap off the woody bits of the asparagus and cut into 5cm (2 in) pieces. Heat butter or oil in a frying pan until it begins to bubble. Add the asparagus, lemon zest and a bit of salt and pepper. Sauté until the asparagus begins to soften and brown. Add the lemon juice. Mix well and set aside.
For the orzo: Place the stock, turmeric, and salt in pot and bring to the boil. Boil the orzo for 7 minutes, or until al dente. Drain.
To assemble: Place the hot orzo in large bowl. Add the asparagus, the dressing, and the parsley or dill. Stir well, adjust the seasoning, and serve.
Other options to try as ingredients or toppings: Spring Onions, Spinach, Spring Peas, Cherry Tomatoes, Shallots, Pine Nuts, Sautéed Mushrooms, Crumbled Feta, Kalamata Olives, or Garlic Toasted Panko.

Adapted or inspired from Jo Cooks and Garden Grazer   Contribution By: Afton Cochran

Caesar's Tossed Greens

We all know how that assignment went! Bowls in the air, asps and our team running from the mob, again. Really the sonic scream was the inevitable ending to a trying jump.

Ingredients:
For the salad:
3 Heads Romaine (cos) Lettuce
Block of Parmigiano Reggiano (you won't need all of it, just enough for shavings for the salad)
Garlic Croutons, recipe below
Caesar Dressing, recipe below
11oz/ 300g Shredded Cooked Chicken, optional

Croutons:
Medium Sized Ciabatta Bread Loaf
3 Tablespoons/ 1.5fl.oz/ 45ml Olive Oil
6 Cloves Garlic, minced
Salt and Pepper, to taste

Dressing:
3 Cloves Garlic, minced
1 teaspoon Anchovy Paste
2 Tablespoons/ 1fl.oz/ 30ml Fresh Lemon Juice
1 teaspoon/ 0.16fl.oz/ 5ml Dijon Mustard
1 teaspoon/ 0.16fl.oz/ 5ml Worcestershire Sauce
1 cup/ 8fl.oz/ 250ml Mayonnaise, good quality and made with pasteurised egg
Salt and Pepper, to taste
¼ cup/ 1.4oz/ 40g Parmigiano Reggiano, finely grated

For Croutons: Heat your oven to 400°F/ 200°C (180 Fan)/ Gas Mark 6. Cut or rip the bread into crouton size chunks. Place the chunks in a bowl and drizzle over with the olive oil. Sprinkle over with sea salt, pepper and the minced garlic. Mix well and place on a baking sheet. Bake for 8 to 10 minutes, turning occasionally so the croutons brown evenly. Remove from the oven and allow to cool.

For Dressing: In a bowl, whisk together lemon juice, anchovy paste, Worcestershire sauce and Dijon. Add in the mayonnaise and whisk until combined. Add the finely grated Parmigiano Reggiano. Taste and season with salt and pepper.

To assassinate Caesar (assemble the salad): Wash the romaine lettuce and pat dry with kitchen roll then tear up into bite-sized pieces. Or, rip up the lettuce, wash and use a salad spinner; those are worth stabbing someone for! Toss lettuce, salad dressing and chicken (if using) together. Top with the croutons and freshly shaved Parmigiano Reggiano

Serve with 23 knives.
Serves 4 to 6

Most Caesar salad is made with raw egg. This is a recipe made with mayonnaise so it is suitable for those who are unable to have raw eggs.

Contribution By: Afton Cochran

Vegan Mexican Style Bean and Lentil Stew

Our technical department could never be considered smooth, but they like all of St Marys have charm in spades. Our Mr Lindstrom has decided to set his cap for the new primary teacher in the village. When he found out she was vegetarian, he had to do some research! We guess there are worse things to eat on a date then beans, but he might need a bit of gentle guidance.

Ingredients:
2 Tablespoons/ 1fl.oz/ 30ml Olive Oil
1 Red Onion, diced
2 Stalks Celery, diced
2 Carrots, peeled and diced
1 Leek, thinly sliced
8 Cloves Garlic, crushed and minced
1 Tablespoon/ 0.17oz/ 5g Ground Cumin
1 teaspoon/ 0.07oz/ 2g Ground Coriander
1 Tablespoon/ 0.2oz/ 6g US Style Chilli Powder Seasoning (found in R&D)
1 Tablespoon/ 0.5fl.oz/ 15ml Chipotles En Adobo (optional, but gives a nice smoky flavour)
2 Tablespoon/ 1fl.oz/ 30ml Tomato Purée/ Paste
1 -15oz/ 425g tin Black Beans, drained and rinsed
1- 15oz/ 425g tin Black Eye Beans, drained and rinsed
1-15oz/ 425g tin Pinto Beans, drained and rinsed
1-15oz/ 425g tin Sweet Corn, drained
1 Sweet Potato, peeled and chopped into 1inch/ 2cm chunks (optional)
1-15oz/ 425g tin Fire Roasted Diced Tomatoes or Plain Chopped Tomatoes
2 Jalapeños, seeded, deveined and minced finely (optional)
4 1/3 cups/ 35fl.oz/ 1L Tomato or you know that '8 Vegetable Juice'
2 cups/ 7oz/ 200g Red Lentils
1 -13.5fl.oz/ 400ml tin Coconut Milk, full fat
2 Bay Leaves
1 Lime, zested and juiced
Salt and Pepper
Pinch of Sugar
Vegetable Stock (optional)
Toppings: Corn Tortilla Chips or Strips, Vegan Soured Cream, Vegan Shredded Cheese, Sliced Jalapeños, Chopped Coriander

Heat the oil in a large pot over a medium high heat. Add the onion, leek, carrot, celery and a pinch of salt and pepper. Cook until the leek, celery and onion are soft.
Add the garlic, cumin, chilli powder, ground coriander, chipotles en adobo, jalapeños, if using and tomato paste. Cook for another minute.
Add all the beans, corn, sweet potato (if using), tomatoes, coconut milk, vegetable juice and bay leaves. Season with salt and pepper to taste and add a pinch of sugar if needed. Bring to the boil, cover, reduce heat to a simmer and cook for 20 minutes or until your sweet potato is soft but still retains its shape.
Add the lentils and cook for a further 5 minutes or until the lentils are cooked through. Stir often to make sure nothing sticks to the bottom of the pan. Add the lime zest and juice and check the seasoning again. If you want this to have a more soup-like consistency, feel free to add vegetable stock to thin it to your desired consistency.
Garnish with your choice of toppings listed above.

Serves 4 to 6

Photo by: Hannah Holt   Contribution By: Afton Cochran

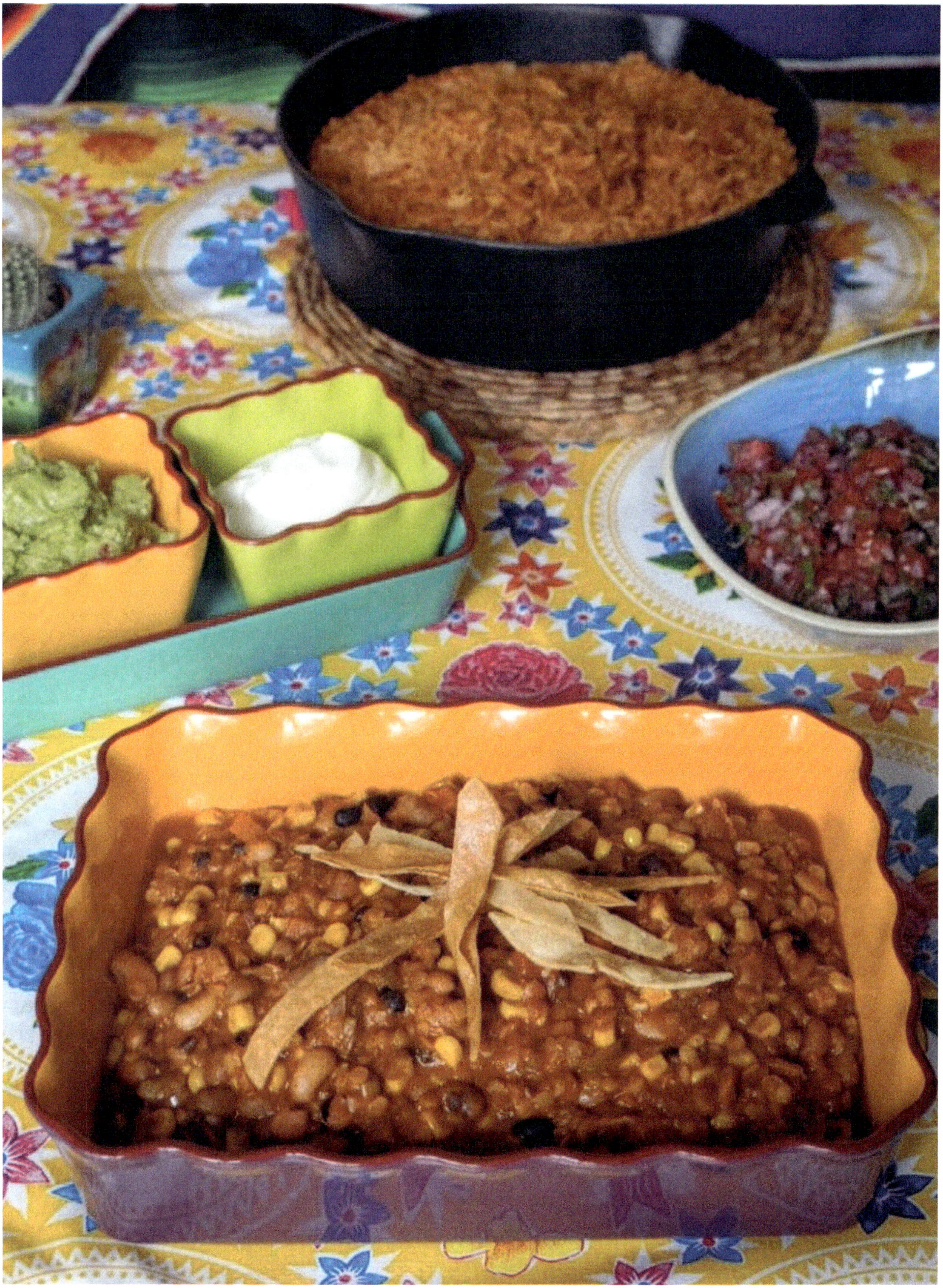

ROASTED VEGETABLES

Nurse Hunter swears that roasting the vegetables gives them a lot more flavour, and that no one has ever died from eating a vegetable. So here it goes ...
Oh! Yum!

Roasted Vegetable Soup

Ingredients:
1 Butternut Squash cut into 16 pieces
2 Red Onions, quartered
1 Red Pepper, deseeded and cut into 6 pieces
1 Yellow Pepper, deseeded and cut into 6 pieces
2 Cloves Garlic chopped finely
1 to 2 Tablespoons/ 0.5 to 1fl.oz/ 15 to 30ml Olive Oil
Salt and Pepper to taste
Ground Coriander, to taste
Rosemary, to taste
Aleppo Chilli Flakes, (optional).
2 litres/ 68fl.oz/ 3-3.5 pints Vegetable Stock

Toss all of the cut vegetables in olive oil ensuring they are all coated. Put all vegetables in a single layer in roasting dishes, sprinkle with garlic, pepper and rosemary.
Roast in a hot oven 400°F/ 200°C/ Gas Mark 6 for about 25 minutes.
Let the vegetables cool slightly so that you don't burn yourself as you remove the butternut squash skin carefully with a sharp knife and discard. Put all the veg into the stock in a large saucepan and simmer over a medium heat for 15 mins. Using an immersion blender, blitz the mixture to your desired creaminess and add salt, chilli and coriander to taste.
Serves 4

Contribution By: Caroline Price

Mushroom and Roasted Squash Risotto

Ingredients:
2 to 3 Tablespoons/ 1 to 1.5fl.oz/ 30 to 45ml Olive Oil
Half a Butternut Squash, peeled, deseeded and cut into 1-2cm cubes
1 Onion, peeled and finely chopped
1 cup/ 7oz/ 200g Mushrooms, chopped
¾ cup/ 3.8oz/ 110g Arborio or other Risotto Rice
Thyme, fresh, to taste
2 ¼ cups/ 16.9fl.oz/ 500ml Chicken or Vegetable Stock, hot
½ cup/ 3.1oz/ 90g Parmesan Cheese, or other Cheese of choice, grated

Coat the squash in a tablespoon or two of oil, then roast in a preheated oven at 350°F/ 180°C/ Gas Mark 4 for about 45 to 50 minutes until tender and slightly caramelised. They do benefit from being turned halfway through cooking.
Heat 1 tablespoon of oil in a suitable risotto-making pan. Add the onion and cook gently until translucent. Add mushrooms then cook until the mushroom juices start flowing.
Meanwhile put your stock in a pan over a medium heat to keep simmering. Turn down if it starts boiling.
Add the rice to the mushrooms and stir to coat then remove the leaves from the thyme sprigs and stir in.
Stir in the stock ladleful by ladleful, waiting for each addition to be fully absorbed before adding the next.
When fully cooked but still retaining a little bite, stir in the grated cheese then gently stir in the squash.

Serve with a few gratings of Parmesan cheese and rocket leaves.
Serves 4

Contribution By: Beckie Parsons

RED LENTIL AND MANGO DAHL

Ingredients:
3 Tablespoons/ 1.5fl.oz/ 45ml Vegetable Oil
3 Leeks, thinly sliced
1 Large Sweet Potato, peeled and diced
8oz/ 225g Smoked Tofu, diced
1 teaspoon/ 0.07oz/ 2g Garam Masala
2 teaspoons/ 0.14oz/ 4g Ground Turmeric
½ teaspoon/ 0.01oz/ 0.3g Ground Coriander
½ teaspoon/ 0.01oz/ 0.3g Ground Cardamom (optional)
2 to 3 Chillies of Your Choice, diced. You can choose to leave the seeds in if you want the heat.
1 ½ cups/ 11oz/ 300g Dry Red Lentils
2½ to 3 1/3cups/ 20 to 27fl.oz/ 600 to 800ml Vegetable Stock (see note)
¾ cup/ 7oz/ 200 ml Coconut Cream (see note)
¾ cups/ 7oz/ 200ml Mango Purée (see note)

Rinse and drain the lentils. Set aside. In a large saucepan, heat the vegetable oil on a medium high heat. Add the leeks and sweet potatoes and a bit of salt and pepper until the leeks are soft and the sweet potatoes are beginning to soften. Add the tofu, garlic, ginger, spices and chillies, if using and a pinch of salt. Stir well and cook for a further minute. Add 600 ml of the stock, the mango purée, the coconut cream and the lentils and stir well. Reduce the heat and cook for 20 to 25 minutes, stirring occasionally to keep the lentils from sticking to the pan. You can add small amounts of stock should you need to (see note). When the lentils are soft, but not mushy, remove from the heat and adjust the seasoning. Serve with steamed rice.
Serves 4.

Note: The amount of stock you will need is dependent on how wet the coconut cream and mango purée are. The more liquid they are, the less stock you will need. You can add a little bit of stock throughout the cooking process if you think it's too dry. You do not want this dish to be overly wet.

Adapted from Nensi Baram. Contribution and Photo By: Afton Cochran

VEGETARIAN LASAGNE

We had to jump to the future St. Mary's for this one! The boss asked us to thank whomever started this recipe, but we forgot to ask when we were there. So who invented this recipe? That's like asking who invented investigating major historical events in contemporary time, or the pods. We could be here for a while.

Ingredients:
9 x 9inch/ 23cm Square Solid Bottomed Pan
14 Dried Lasagne Pasta Sheets
1 ¾ cups/ 7oz/ 200g Parmesan and Cheddar Cheeses, grated

Bolognese:
1 ½ Sweet Potatoes
1 ½ Red Onions, finely chopped
1 Garlic Clove, finely chopped
6 Tomatoes, large, chopped
1 -600g Tin Tomatoes, chopped
Olive Oil
1 cup/ 5.2oz/ 150g Feta Cheese, crumbled
Basil

Béchamel Sauce:
2 1/3 cups/ 20fl.oz/ 568ml Milk
1 Carrot
½ Onion
6 Peppercorns
1 Bay Leaf
6 Tablespoons/ 3oz/ 85g Butter
3 Tablespoons/ 2oz/ 57g Plain Flour

Bolognese: Peel and dice the sweet potato and finely chop the onion and garlic. Add olive oil to a frying pan and over medium heat, fry potato, onion and garlic until soft. Mix in all the tomatoes. Simmer for 5 minutes and add the feta and basil.

Béchamel Sauce: In a heavy bottom pan, add milk, a few slices of carrot and onion, peppercorns and bay leaf. Bring the mixture to a boil and then, turning off the hob, leave to infuse for about 15 minutes. Remove the peppercorn, bay leaf, onion, and carrot. In another pan melt the butter and add the plain flour, whisk until the flour and butter are well combined. Continue to whisk as you gradually add in the infused milk. Stir over a medium low heat until it just starts to thicken.

Lasagne sheets are generally not cooked before adding them to the layers.

Assemble in layers: Bolognese, lasagne sheets, Béchamel sauce, Bolognese, lasagne sheets, Béchamel sauce, Bolognese, lasagne sheets, Béchamel sauce, grated cheese over the top.

Place in a preheated oven at 350 °F/ 180 °C/ Gas Mark 4 for 20 to 30 minutes or until well heated through and the cheese is melted.

Contribution By: Kenneth Hay

Vegetable Stock or Broth

Broth and stock has been used for ages to help in healing. It is nutritious, helps with hydration and forms the essential ingredient for so many recipes. There is no substitution for making your own!

Ingredients:
3 Onions, peeled and halved
6 Whole Cloves Garlic, peeled
4 Large Carrots, Whole
3 Stalks Celery, whole
1 Tablespoon/ 0.5fl.oz/ 15ml Tomato Puree/ Paste
2 oz/ 28g Dried Mushrooms or 6oz/ 170g Fresh
2 Tablespoons/ 1fl.oz/ 30 ml Red Miso Paste
1 Tablespoon/ 0.59oz/ 17g Sea Salt
1 teaspoon/ 0.07oz/ 2g Whole Black Peppercorns
1 Bay Leaf
1 cup/ 8.4fl.oz/ 240 ml Dry Marsala Wine
Water

Preheat oven to 400°F/ 200°C (180°C fan)/ Gas Mark 6
Place onion, garlic, carrots and celery on a baking sheet (tuck garlic cloves between larger vegetables to keep them from burning), and roast in the oven till brown, about 15-20 minutes.
In a large pot, add all ingredients. Fill pot to within 1" (2.5 cm) of the top of the pot with water.
Turn the hob on to a high setting until the pot contents come to a rolling boil, then reduce heat to a simmer. Simmer contents for 4 hours. Do not add more water.
Remove pot from heat and remove the vegetables from the pot with a slotted spoon. Ladle stock through a sieve into freezer-safe containers with tight lids. Store in freezer until ready for use.

Contribution By: Merry Schepers

Vegetarian Shepherd's Pie

Shepherding historians around is definitely a full time job. The security staff may keep them safe but they have nothing on the medical staff. We have to resolve complex issues with chewing gum and a paperclip and did we mention getting them to eat more than chocolate?

Ingredients
16oz/ 453g Floury Potatoes, peeled and cubed
½ cup/ 4fl.oz/ 118ml Cream, or Plant-Based Cream
1 Tablespoon/ 0.5oz/ 15g Butter, or Margarine
Salt and Black Pepper, to taste
1 Tablespoon/ 0.5fl.oz/ 15ml Olive Oil
1 Onion, diced
½ cup/ 2.2oz/ 64g Carrot, diced
½ cup/ 2.4oz/ 70g Green Peas
1 Tablespoon/ 0.5fl.oz/ 15ml Water
¾ cup/ 3.5oz/ 100g Sweet Corn Kernels, tinned or thawed if frozen
3 1/3 cups/ 3.5oz/ 100g Fresh Spinach, coarsely chopped
½ teaspoon/ 0.01oz/ 0.46g Thyme
3 Tablespoons/ 0.88oz/ 25g Plain Flour
1 ¾ cups/ 14fl.oz/ 414ml Vegetable Broth
1 Tablespoon/ 0.5fl.oz/ 15ml Tomato Paste
1 1/2 cups/ 3.9oz/ 113g Lentils, cooked or tinned

Peel, cube and place the potatoes in a large saucepan and cover well with water. Bring to a simmer over medium-high heat. Reduce heat and cook until the potatoes are tender and can easily be poked with a fork, about 15 minutes. Drain potatoes well. Return the potatoes to the pot and add cream, butter and salt and pepper to taste. Mash potatoes the best you can while mixing in the butter and cream.

Preheat Oven Grill / Broiler
Place an oven-safe 8 inch solid-bottomed pan on a baking tray. Oil the pan lightly with butter or olive oil. Placing a baking try under the pan is important as the shepherd's pie can bubble over and make a mess.

Heat oil in a large heavy-bottomed frying pan over medium heat. Add onion, carrot and water. Cover and cook, stirring occasionally until softened, about 3 to 5 minutes. Stir in corn, peas, thyme, spinach, tomato paste and season with salt and pepper. Stir well and allow to cook, stirring every 2 minutes or so. Sprinkle the flour across the mixture and combine. Stir in broth and simmer, stirring occasionally to prevent it sticking to the bottom. Bring to a simmer and add the lentils, cooking for an additional 3 to 4 minutes stirring continuously.

Place the lentil mixture in the bottom of the prepared pan, spreading to an even layer. Top with spoonsful of the mashed potatoes for a smooth layered topping. Place in the oven for 10 to 15 minutes or grill (broil) the potatoes for 5 to 10 minutes. The potatoes will be slightly browned and everything will be hot and bubbly.

Serves 4 to 6

(Adapted from Eating Well) Contribution By: Sara Robinson

The Great St. Mary's Salad

Made you look!

Did you honestly think we would eat salads?

OVEN CHIPS

Chips are the perfect vegetable, at least according to the Security Section. Chips are tasty and go well with so many different dishes, or on their own as a snack. The fried version can be high in calories and saturated fats. By making oven chips we are trying to make things just a little bit healthier. Why not try this recipe with carrots or parsnips?

Ingredients:
2 to 3/ 28oz/ 800g Baking Potatoes or Sweet Potatoes
2 Tablespoons/ 1fl.oz/ 30ml Oil
Sea Salt
Fresh Ground Black Pepper

Pre-heat oven to 475°F/ 245°C (fan 230°C)/ Gas Mark 9
Clean and cut each of the potatoes into 1cm by 1cm slices. Blanch in a pan of boiling water for about 2 to 3 minutes. They should still be firm but have a little give to them. Drain and dry the slices with a kitchen towel. Shake the potatoes onto a baking tray and toss with the oil. Make sure that the potatoes are in a single layer, so they roast instead of steam. Bake at high heat for 15 to 20 minutes. Turning the potatoes at least twice while they are cooking. The potatoes are done when they are golden and crisp. Season and serve as quickly as possible. Serves 2 to 3 or maybe 1 security personnel.

Contribution By: Sara Robinson

JACKET POTATOES

Jacket Potatoes or Baked Potatoes are wonderfully diverse and can be the main part of a meal or a side dish. Jacketed Potatoes are one of the easiest things to make.

Ingredients:
1 Large Baking Potato
Neutral Oil
Salt and Pepper

Heat oven to 425°F/ 220°C (200°C fan)/ Gas Mark 7
Wash and clean the potato well. Dry the potato with a tea towel, rub the potato with a little oil, salt and pepper. Place the potato on a baking tray and then into the preheated oven. Bake for 20 to the 30 minutes. Reduce the heat to 375°F/ 190°C (170°C fan)/ Gas Mark 5. Bake for about 1 hour more or until it is slightly squishy and tender, and the skin is crispy.

For a quicker version. Clean and wash the potato well. Take a fork and pierce the potato very well. Take a length of kitchen paper and scrunch it into a ball and run warm water over it until it become slightly damp and more pliable. Smooth out the paper and wrap it around the outside of the potato. Place in the microwave for 8 to 10 minutes or until the potato is softened.

To serve, cut across the potato exposing the inner flesh and add your favourite toppings.

Contribution By: Sara Robinson

Steamed Vegetables

We are not talking about how upset with you the medical section is going to get if you don't eat some of your vegetables. Steaming vegetables is super easy and a nutritious way to fix vegetables. Yes Maxwell, you need to eat vegetables.

The key to steamed vegetables is uniform size. You want the pieces of whatever vegetables you use to be relatively the same dimensions.
If you are steaming a mix of vegetables, be aware that some vegetables, such as cauliflower or broccoli will cook faster than denser vegetables like carrots.
If steaming a mix of vegetables, make sure you start the denser vegetables first and then add the less dense vegetables later, or cut the denser vegetables into smaller pieces than the less dense vegetables.

You do not want soggy veggies. Vegetables with a bit of a bite to them retain more nutrients. The softer they are, the less nutrients there are. Have you noticed when you have boiled vegetables that the water often changes colour? That means the nutrients have left the vegetables and gone into the water. This is fine for things like soups and stews, but not for vegetables to be served on their own. It is the same with steaming. Over cooking defeats the point of steaming vegetables.

If you are using an electric steamer, follow the directions as indicated in the user manual. If using a collapsible steamer basket, put 1 inch/ 2cm of water in the bottom of a saucepan, unfold the steamer and place it in the saucepan. Add another couple of cm (an inch or so) so the water comes just under the basket. If it comes above the basket, pour some out. Bring to the boil, add your veggies, cover, reduce heat to a simmer and steam for the time stated in the chart. Also, remember, hobs can be temperamental, so use your judgment.

If you have a tiered saucepan with a steamer insert, or a bamboo steamer, again ensure the water remains underneath the bottom of the pan. If using multiple layers with multiple vegetables, put the denser vegetables on the bottom.

Using a microwave, place the vegetables in a bowl with 1 to 2 tablespoons/ 1fl.oz/ 15 to 30ml water. Cover with cling film, and microwave for the time stated. If you do not have a steamer or a microwave, you can make a trivet using three balls of foil, add the water, and place a heat proof plate on top of it and steam as normal. Use a timer. This is one of the key things you need to get your veggies just right. Use your judgment. Cooking times can vary due to differences in hobs (stoves). If you are not sure if they are cooked, insert the point of a knife, or a cocktail stick in the middle. Again, steamed veggies should not be overly soft or soggy. When the vegetables have been steamed, season with salt and pepper, citrus juice, herbs or spices, as desired, or you could just slather them in butter.

We will not judge. Just eat your vegetables!

Steamed Vegetables

Asparagus	Whole thick spears	5 to 7 minutes
Asparagus	Tips	3 to 5 minutes
Baby Corn	Whole	5 to 6 minutes
Broccoli	Florets	5 to 7 minutes
Brussel Sprouts	Cleaned and Trimmed	8 to 10 minutes
Cabbage, Green	Shredded	4 minutes
Cabbage, Green	Wedges	10 minutes
Cabbage, White	Shredded	5 to 6 minutes
Cabbage, White	Wedges	10 to 12 minutes
Carrots	Baby	5 to 8 minutes
Carrots	Batons	10 to 12 minutes
Carrots	Slices	6 to 8 minutes
Cauliflower	Florets	5 to 8 minutes
Corn on the Cob	Whole	7 to 10 minutes
Green Beans	Whole	4 to 5 minutes
Greens, Leafy	Kale or Callard	5 to 7 minutes
Leeks	Baby	8 minutes
Mangetout	Whole	3 minutes
Okra	Whole	5 to 7 minutes
Parsnip	Batons	12 to 15 minutes
Peas	Fresh	3 minutes
Potatoes	Baby	20 to 40 minutes (depends on size)
Potatoes	Peeled 1 inch/ 2cm dice	20 to 30 minutes
Rocket/ Arugula/ Spinach		3 minutes
Sugar Snap Peas		5 minutes
Swede/ Rutabaga	1 inch/ 2cm dice	10 to 12 minutes

All vegetables in this chart are from fresh. Frozen vegetables will take longer.

Vegan Gluten Free Vanilla Cake

Just to show we are not unreasonable, even though some people say other wise!
We are looking at you Markham.
We wanted to show that even sweets can be made to cover dietary requirements
and be enjoyed in moderation.
Yes, we said moderation Maxwell.

Ingredients:
2 cups/ 8.8oz/ 250g Plain Gluten Free Flour or a mixture of Rice, Oat and Buckwheat Flours
1 teaspoon/ 0.17oz/ 5g Xanthan Gum or Guar Gum
2/3 cup/ 5.2 oz/ 150g Caster Sugar
¼ teaspoon/ 0.07oz/ 2g Salt
1 Tablespoon/ 0.49oz/ 14g Baking Powder
2 teaspoons/ 0.42oz/ 12g Bicarbonate of Soda
3½ Tablespoons/ 1.6fl.oz/ 50ml Coconut Oil, melted
1 1/3 cups/ 10.1fl.oz/ 300 ml Plant-Based Milk or Water
1 Tablespoon/ 0.5fl.oz/ 15ml Apple Cider Vinegar or Lemon Juice
1 Tablespoon/ 0.5fl.oz/ 15ml Vanilla Extract

Pre-heat the oven to 350 °F/ 180 °C (160°C fan)/ Gas Mark 4
Grease, flour (with gluten free flour) and line with parchment paper, two 6 inch/ 15cm sandwich tins or spring form pans. (This can be done in one 9 inch/ 23cm pan but the baking times will be longer.)
Whisk together the plain flour, xanthan gum, sugar, salt, baking powder and bicarbonate of soda to ensure there are no clumps and the ingredients are well combined. Melt the coconut oil before adding it to the flour mixture and stir briefly. Add the plant-based milk, cider and vanilla and mix thoroughly to combine.
Divide the batter evenly between the sandwich tins. Smooth the top of the batter ensuring there is a slight depression in the centre of each pan. This will help to have a level cake after baking. Place the cakes in the centre of the preheated oven and bake for 30 to 35 minutes or until the cake springs back at a touch and a toothpick inserted in the centre of the cake comes out clean.
Let the cakes cool for 5 minutes in their tins before removing them to cool completely on a cooling rack.
Serve with fresh fruit and jam and a good dusting of icing sugar on the top of the cake, or follow the American Buttercream icing recipe in the R&D chapter subbing in appropriate butter and milk alternatives.

Makes 1 cake or 8 slices.

This cake lacks common allergens of wheat, gluten, milk, eggs and soya.

Contribution By: Sara Robinson

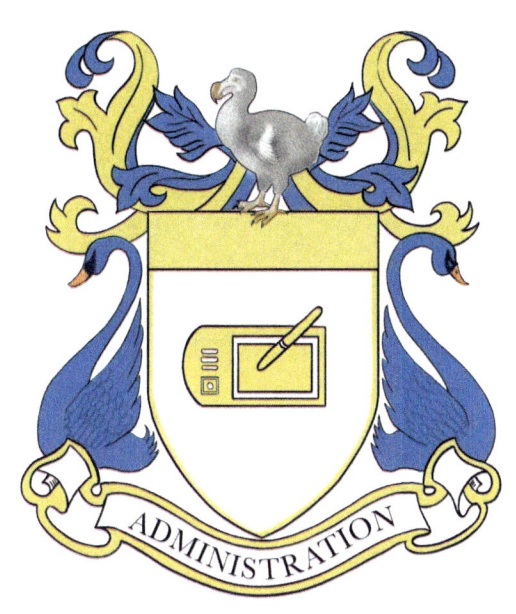

Chapter Seven:
The Administration Department or What Really Keeps St. Mary's Going: Cakes, Biscuits, Tarts and Afternoon Tea

Where would we be without our admin staff? They are the beating heart of St. Mary's and they perform the magic that keeps us running and, more importantly, ensure that we are paid! They also keep the rest of us going with a kind word, a cup of tea, a biscuit or a swift kick in the … Well you get the picture.
Between the Admin Staff and the great St. Mary's tea break …
We know what keeps everyone here going!

Recipes:

Mrs. Partridge's Afternoon Tea	152 to 155
Victoria Sponge, Tea Sandwiches, Blini Pancakes, Lemon Posset, Never-Fail Scones	
Whipped Shortbread	157
Millionaire's Shortbread and **Flavoured Shortbread**	158
Jam Tarts with Matthew	159
Knock! Knock! Guess Again Biscuits	159
Chocolate Chip Cookies	160
Oatmeal Chocolate Chip Cookies, Triple Chocolate Chip Cookies	
Crazy Brownies For the Professor	163
Oat Biscuits for Dr Dowson	164
Dr Stone's Rich Hot Cocoa Prescription	165
Quick Hot Cocoa, Spiced Hot Cocoa Biscuits	
More Tea Time Treats	166 to 167
Mad Madeleines, Tea Loaf, Spiced Lemon Ginger Biscuits	
Chocolate Cake	168 to 169
Pour L'Amour du Chocolat, Easy as Cake, Not Exactly 'Healthy' Cocoa Cake, Incredible Chocolate Orange	
Drizzle Cake	171
Lemon, Ginger and Chocolate Cakes	
Mars Bar Squares and **Peanut Butter Squares**	172
Bath Buns	174
TaDa Doughnuts and **TaDa Doughnut Pudding**	175
New High Energy Biscuits	177
Mrs Shaw's Chocolate Biscuits	178
Bourbon Biscuits for Good Boys and Girls	
Chocolate Forked Biscuits For Those Difficult Days	

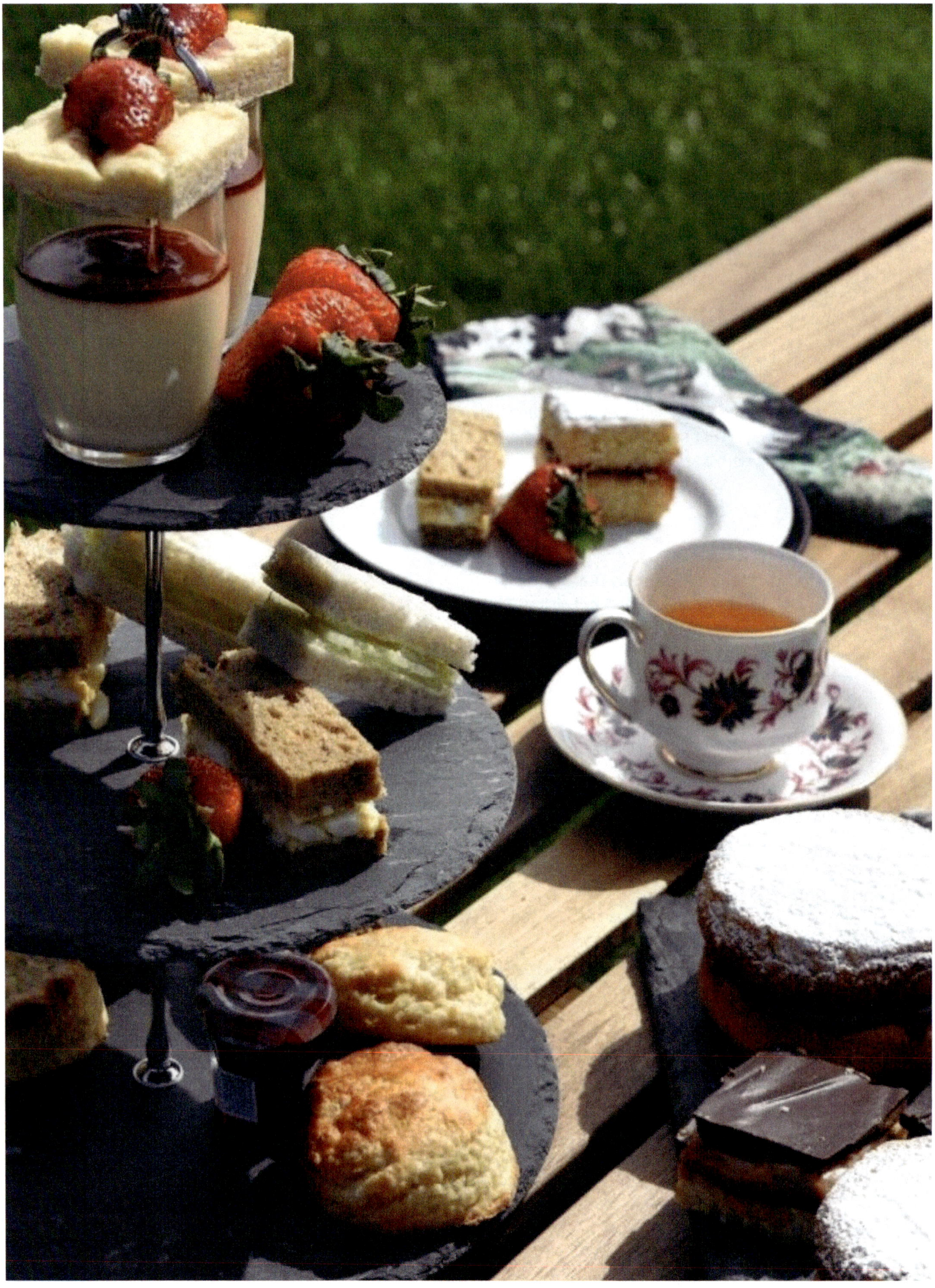

Mrs Partridge's Afternoon Tea

Tea first made an appearance in England in the 1660s but it wasn't until the 1840s that the practice of Afternoon Tea began to take hold. It is attributed to Anna, the seventh Duchess of Bedford, who would have a small meal at about four o'clock to tide her over until the fashionably late dinner at eight o'clock. This light meal in the afternoon is what became the popular practice of Afternoon Tea. Traditional afternoon tea consists of dainty sandwiches, scones, cakes and pastries.

Victoria Sponge

Ingredients:

¾ cup/ 6oz/ 175g Butter, softened
3/4 cup plus 2 Tablespoons/ 6oz/ 175g Caster Sugar
¼ teaspoon/ 0.04fl.oz/ 1ml Vanilla Extract
3 Eggs well beaten
7/8 cup/ 6oz/ 175g Self Raising Flour
To finish:
3 Tablespoons/ 1.5fl.oz/ 52ml Raspberry Conserve
Caster Sugar, for dusting

Grease and base line 2 tins with parchment paper. Sandwich tins or round cake tins should measure 18cm/7inch each.

Preheat the oven to 350°F/ 180°C (160°C fan)/Gas Mark 4.

In a mixing bowl, cream together the butter, sugar and vanilla extract until pale, smooth and fluffy. Gradually add in the eggs a little at a time, beating well after each addition. If the mixture curdles, add a spoonful of the flour. Using a large, metal spoon, fold in the flour.

Divide the mixture between the tins, levelling the surfaces, then make a slight dip in the centre of each cake – this ensures a final cake that has an even rise. Bake in the centre of the oven for about 25 minutes, until the cakes are risen, golden and springy to the touch. A cake tester, if inserted, should also come out clean.

Remove from the oven and leave to cool in the tins for five minutes before turning out onto a wire rack to cool. If you do not want the top of your cake to be marked by the cooling rack, first turn the cake out into a clean and dry tea towel, remove the lining paper then carefully turn them base side down onto the wire rack so that the surface of the cake faces up.

Once cooled, spread the conserve evenly over one of the sponges. Place the other sponge on top and press down lightly to join the two. Dust the cake with sugar and serve.

(Adapted from WI)   Contribution By: Beckie Parsons

Mrs. Partridge's Afternoon Tea

Tea Sandwiches

Ingredients:
Sandwich filling of choice
4 to 8 slices of your favourite bread
Butter (or vegan alternative)

There are a plethora of options for tea sandwiches, but they all start the same. Use your favourite bread and put a very light layer of butter on the inside side of the bread slices. This will act as a barrier between the filling and the bread, ensuring there are no soggy sandwiches. Spread your favourite filling, close the bread slices into a sandwich and gently cut off the crusts of the bread. Then, slicing length-ways, create 3 to 4 finger sandwiches or triangles. Repeat as necessary to complete filling choices.

Sandwich Fillings:

Cucumber, thinly sliced with skins on and Cream Cheese

Sliced Deli Ham and Pickle (relish) or Picalilli

Sliced Deli Ham and Mustard * Roast Beef and Horseradish
Cheddar Cheese and Picalilli * Coronation Chicken
Egg Mayo and Watercress * Tuna Mayo and Cucumber

Thinly Sliced Strawberries, Mint leaves and Cream Cheese

Vegan options:

Tomato and Hummus

Roasted Red Pepper and Guacamole

Blini Pancakes

Ingredients:
1 cup/ 3.5oz/ 100g Plain Flour
1 Egg, separated
2/3 cup/ 5fl.oz/ 150ml Milk
1 ¾ Tablespoons/ 0.88oz/ 25g Butter, melted
Pinch of Salt
Neutral Oil, for cooking

Whisk together the flour and salt. Add in the egg yolk and half the milk, mixing well. Slowly add in the remaining milk, and butter. At this point the mixture should be a smooth, pancake-like batter. In a separate bowl, whisk the egg whites to stiff peaks and gently fold this into the mixture. Preheat a frying pan or griddle and lightly grease the cooking area. Working with just a few at a time, drop spoonfuls onto the cooking surface. These small pancakes will take about two minutes per side to cook but watch them to make sure they do not burn. These can be served warm or cold.

Blini's are amazing little pancakes that can be served with a wide variety of toppings, such as: Smoked Salmon with Cream Cheese and Dill, Grilled Banana with Chocolate, Strawberry with Mint, or Roasted Red Peppers and Chives

Contribution By: Sara Robinson and Afton Cochran

Mrs. Partridge's Afternoon Tea

Lemon Posset

Ingredients
1 ¾ cup/ 14fl.oz/ 417ml Double Cream
¾ cup/ 5.3oz/ 150g Caster Sugar
2 Lemons, zested and juiced

In a thick based saucepan, place the sugar and cream over a low heat. Stir the mixture slowly and constantly until the sugar has completely dissolved. Slowly bring the cream mixture to a boil and turn down the heat to a simmer for 3 minutes.
Remove the cream mixture from the heat and whisk in the lemon juice and zest. Leave the mixture to cool for 5 to 6 minutes. At this point it should be starting to thicken and be about the consistency of custard.
To remove the zest pieces and any impurities pass the mixture through a sieve or pour directly into individual serving dishes. Place posset in the fridge and leave to cool.
Serve with raspberries and a little whipped cream or as is.

Serves 4 to 6

Contribution By: Sara Robinson

Never Fail Scones

Ingredients:
5 Tablespoons/ 3oz/ 70g Butter
1 cup plus 2 Tablespoons/ 9.5oz/ 270g Plain Flour
1/3 cup/ 2.1oz/ 60g Granulated Sugar
2 teaspoons Baking Powder
a Pinch of Salt
1 Egg
EITHER ½ cup/ 3.5oz/ 100g Creme Fraiche OR ¼ cup/2.1oz/ 60g Mascarpone plus 1/3 cup/1.4oz/ 40g Plain Yoghurt
1 Tablespoon/0.7fl.oz/20mls of Milk

Rub butter into plain flour, and then stir in granulated sugar, baking powder and salt. In another bowl beat the egg and add and in EITHER creme fraiche OR mascarpone and plain yoghurt. Add 20mls of milk and beat until less lumpy (smooth is optimistic). Tip the wet ingredients into the dry and mix well. Tip the mixture onto a lightly floured board and knead. You might not think it will combine all the dry ingredients in but kneading it will do it. Divide the mix into eight and shape those into flattened rounds of about 7 to 8cm across.
Put a sheet of baking paper on a big-enough tray, don't let the scones touch each other. Brush the tops with milk.
Bake for 15 to 20 minutes at 425°F/220°C/ Gas Mark 7
After the scones have cooled, split and add the filling of choice; clotted cream and jam or marmalade is delicious.

Contribution By: Caroline Price

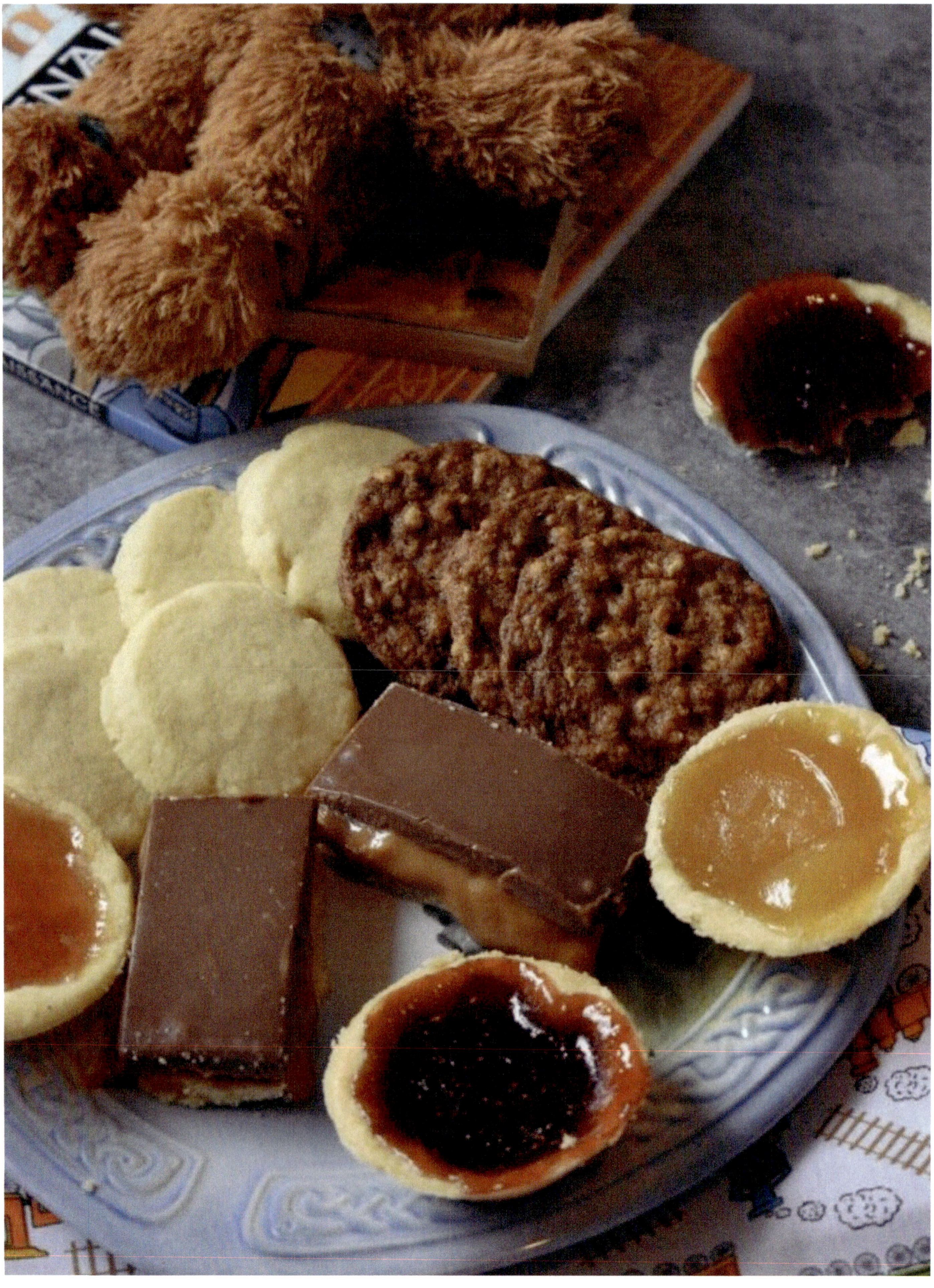

WHIPPED SHORTBREAD

Major Ian Guthrie has never been one for cooking and used to let Mr Markham have all the fun in cooking in the early days, before Mrs. Mack arrived at St. Mary's. We are all a lot safer because of her timely intervention.
When Guthrie was missing his beloved Caledonian landscape, he had us make these amazing biscuits. They are a little different from traditional shortbread and will melt in your mouth.

Ingredients:
- 2 cups/ 16oz/ 450g Salted Butter
- ¾ cup/ 2.6oz/ 75g Icing/Powdered/Confectioners' Sugar
- ¼ cup/ 1.1oz/ 32g Cornflour/ Corn Starch
- 3 ½ cups/ 18oz/ 500g Plain/ All Purpose Flour (you may need a little extra)

This recipe works best when is it done in a stand mixer because the key to the success of this recipe is making sure the butter is well whipped. The recipe can be done with a hand mixer, but it will take longer to get the same results. The recipe will not have the same effect if it is mixed by hand.

Whip the butter in your stand mixer until it is light and fluffy, scraping down the sides occasionally. The kitchen usually whips ours for half an hour. On a low speed, mix in the remaining ingredients until thoroughly blended. You may need to add more flour, depending on how wet it seems. It should bind together but still be crumbly. Chill. You can then roll the dough into balls and press down using a cookie press dipped in icing sugar. Bake at 325°F/ 160°C (140°C fan)/Gas Mark 3 for 15-20 min.

Do not allow the cookies to go golden brown. Cool and enjoy.

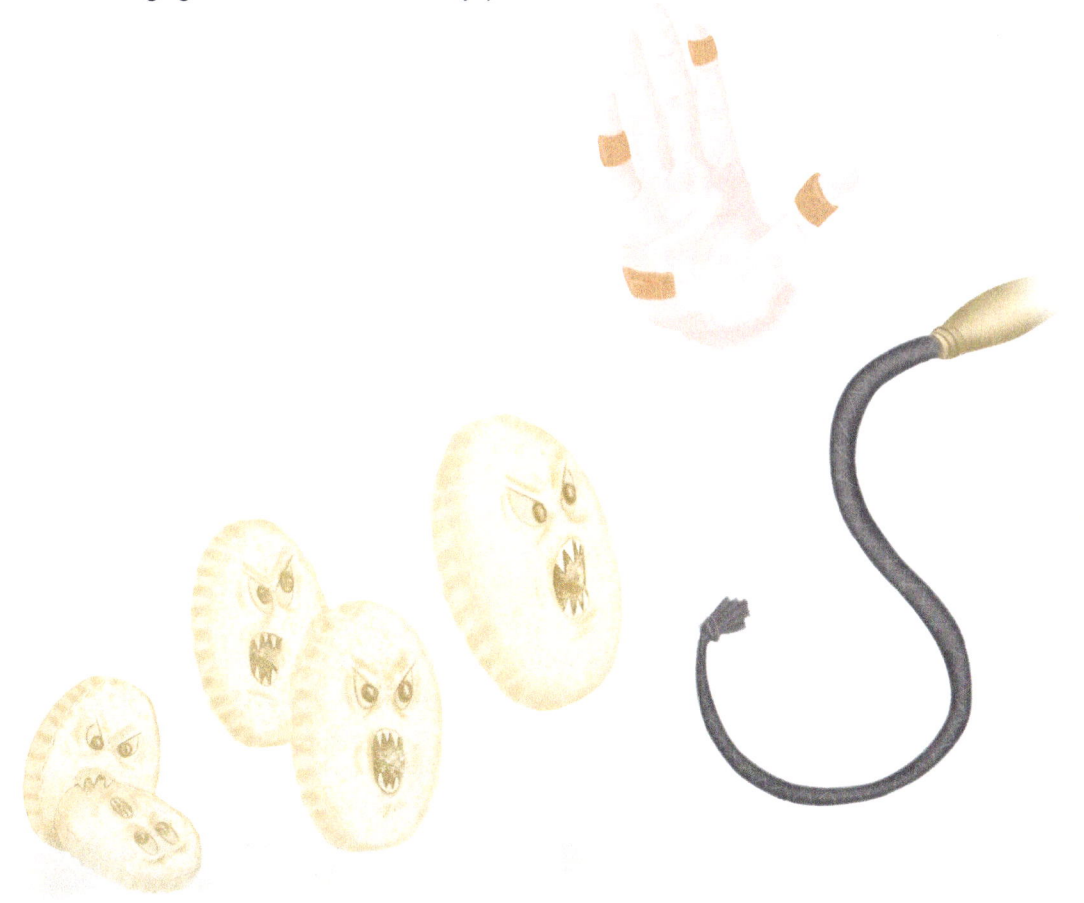

Contribution By: Afton Cochran   Photo By: Sara Robinson

Millionaires' Shortbread

For something a little fancier, might we suggest these amazing additions to the Whipped Shortbread?

Ingredients:
1 recipe of Whipped Shortbread
1 cup/ 7oz/ 200g Light Brown Sugar
3/4 cup plus 2 Tablespoons/ 7oz/ 200g Butter
14 oz/ 397g Sweetened Condensed Milk

Or, you can be lazy and just use:
2 tins of Condensed Milk Caramel

1 1/2 cups/ 8.8oz/ 250g Dark Chocolate, chips, galettes, or chopped chocolate
1/2 cup/ 4.2fl.oz/ 125 ml Double/ Heavy Cream

Grease and line (with baking parchment) a 22.5x32.5cm/ 9x13 inch pan. Make sure you leave excess on two sides to allow you to lift it out of the pan more easily. Make the shortbread as per previous page. Press evenly into the pan. Dock the dough well. Bake at 325°F/ 160°C (140°C fan)/ Gas Mark 3 or until golden brown. Allow to cool.
If making the caramel, melt the butter and brown sugar on a very low heat until all the butter is melted and the brown sugar is completely dissolved. Turn up the heat and slowly pour in the condensed milk, stirring constantly. Bring to the boil and boil for 2-3 minutes. Do not let it stick to the pan. Pour over cooled crust. Let cool and then chill. If you like, you can sprinkle the layer with some flaked sea salt, or even some smoked sea salt!
Or: open the two cans and pour it on the cooled crust. This won't set as well as making it yourself. Chill.
For the ganache, place chocolate in a heat-safe bowl. Place the cream in a microwave-safe jug. Heat your cream at 30 second intervals until it's almost boiling, don't let it scald. Pour the hot cream over the chocolate and let it sit for a few minutes. Then stir well until the chocolate is all melted and the cream is well incorporated. Pour on the top of the caramel layer and let cool. When cool, chill so the whole thing firms up. Carefully lift the shortbread from the pan using the parchment flaps and place on a cutting board. Carefully remove the parchment and cut into even squares using a hot knife.

Contribution By: Afton Cochran

Flavoured Whipped Shortbread

Ingredients:
1 recipe of Whipped Shortbread
1 to 2 measured flavouring ideas

Make the whipped shortbread as directed. Add the chosen flavourings to the mixture after the initial flour and cornflour are just mixed into the dough. Combine the flavourings and dough well and then shape and bake as directed.

Added Flavouring Ideas:

½ cup/ 2.6oz/ 75g Mini Chocolate Chips
½ cup/ 0.38oz/ 11g Honeycomb Candy
½ cup/ 1.7oz/ 50g Dried Sweetened Cranberries
½ cup/ 0.5oz/ 15g Candy Coated Chocolate Drops
½ cup/ 5.2oz/ 150g Nuts of Choice, chopped

1 Tablespoon/ 0.1oz/ 3g Dried Lavender
1 Tablespoon/ 0.2oz/ 6g Orange Zest
1 Tablespoon/ 0.2oz/ 6g Lemon Zest
1 teaspoon/ 0.07oz/ 2g Cinnamon
1 teaspoon/ 0.07oz/ 2g Mixed Spice (recipe in R&D)
2 teaspoons/ 0.1oz/ 3g Expresso Powder
2 teaspoons/ 0.07oz/ 2g Rosemary
2 teaspoons/ 0.07oz/ 2g Thyme Leaves

You could also make the Incredible Chocolate Orange recipe on page 179 to dip the shortbread in all the lovely chocolate!

Contribution By: Sara Robinson

Jam Tarts with Matthew

Did we mention that Mrs Mack is a genius in the kitchen? Using what she has on hand these quick jam tarts are fun to make with kids of all ages.
Just make sure a grown-up does the work with anything hot!

Ingredients:
1 Recipe Whipped Shortbread
Jam of choice
Extra Plain Flour for rolling out dough

Follow Whipped Shortbread recipe up to baking instructions. Use about 1 to 2 tablespoons' or about the size of a walnut's worth of dough. You can either squish the dough into 3-inch/ 7.5cm egg tart pans or roll it out before placing it in the pans. Trim the edges and fill with 1 to 2 tablespoons of jam. Bake at 325°F/ 160°C (140°C fan)/ Gas Mark 3 for 20 to 25 min. Allow the tart to completely cool before removing from the tin and enjoying.

Knock! Knock! Guess Again Biscuits

David Sands is not necessarily a long-time member of the admin. team, but he is always there with a knock knock joke when you need it. Okay, not sure anyone needs a knock knock joke, but these tasty biscuits will keep you guessing and are perfect with a cup of tea.

Ingredients:
1 cup/ 8oz/ 227g Butter
1 cup/ 7oz/ 200g Sugar
1 cup/ 7.1oz/ 220g Muscovado Sugar
2 Eggs
2 cups/ 9oz/ 250g Plain Flour
1/2 teaspoon Baking Powder
1 teaspoon Bicarbonate of Soda
1/2 teaspoon Salt
2 cups/ 11oz/ 312g Oatmeal
2 cups/ 2oz/ 58g Puffed Rice Cereal
1 cup/ 2.5oz/ 71g Desiccated Coconut

Cream together butter, sugars and eggs. Sift together flour, baking powder, bicarbonate of soda and salt and add slowly to the creamed butter mixture. Add oats, cereal and coconut to the bowl. At this point the mixture will be extremely stiff to incorporate so mixing with your hands is acceptable. Roll the mixture into balls the size of walnuts. Place on ungreased cookie sheet and flatten with fork. Bake at 350°F/ 180°C/ Gas Mark 4 about 10 to 15 minutes. he biscuits will have a lightly toasted brown colour.

Makes about 3 dozen biscuits.

Contribution By: Sara Robinson

CHOCOLATE CHIP COOKIES

Our Mrs Enderby doesn't allow any food inside the wardrobe department. It is for a good reason with all of the delicate fabrics that they house. Little projects make their way to the dining room from time to time. Just be careful, chocolate can get everywhere!

Oatmeal Chocolate Chip Cookies

Ingredients:
1 cup/ 7.9oz/ 225g Plain Flour
1/3 cup/ 1.7oz/ 50g Porridge Oats
1 teaspoon/ 0.2oz/ 6g Cinnamon
1 teaspoon/ 0.2oz/ 6g Baking Powder
½ teaspoon/ 0.14oz/ 4g Bicarbonate of Soda
½ teaspoon/ 0.14oz/ 4g Salt
1/3 cup/ 2.6oz/ 75g Raisins
¾ cup/ 3.5oz/ 100g Chocolate Chips
½ cup/ 3.5oz/ 100g Caster Sugar
½ cup/ 3.8oz/ 110g Muscovado Sugar
1/3 cup/ 2.82fl.oz/ 80ml Dark Brewed Black Tea
¼ cup/ 2.1oz/ 60g Vegetable Oil

In a small bowl, place raisins in the warm tea to soften. In a separate bowl, weigh or measure out plain flour, oats, spices, baking powder, bicarbonate of soda and salt and add the chocolate chips. Mix well to combine. Do not drain the raisins before adding them to the mix. Combine with the caster sugar, brown sugar and oil. Combine the wet and dry ingredients until well mixed.
Chill the dough for at least 2 hours. Portion the dough using a standard ice cream scoop and place balls onto a tray and into the freezer for 30 to 40 minutes. This will keep the cookies from spreading too much.
Preheat oven to 350°F/180°C (170°C fan)/ Gas Mark 4

Place cookies onto a baking sheet with 1 ½ inches/4cm around each ball. Bake cookies for 10 to 12 minutes. Let cool for 5 to 10 minutes and enjoy!
Makes 8 to 10 large cookies.

Triple Chocolate Chip Cookies

Ingredients:
1 cup/ 7.9oz/ 225g Plain Flour
½ cup/ 2.1oz/ 60g Cocoa Powder
1 teaspoon/ 0.2oz/ 6g Baking Powder
½ teaspoon/ 0.14oz/ 4g Bicarbonate of Soda
½ teaspoon/ 0.14oz/ 4g Salt
¾ cup/ 3.5oz/ 100g Milk Chocolate Chips
¾ cup/ 3.5oz/ 100g Dark or White Chocolate Chips
½ cup/ 3.5oz/ 100g Caster Sugar
½ cup/ 3.8oz/ 110g Muscovado Sugar
1/3 cup/ 2.82fl.oz/ 80ml Dark Brewed Black Tea
¼ cup/ 2.1oz/ 60g Vegetable Oil

In a large bowl weigh or measure out plain flour, cocoa powder, baking powder, bicarbonate of soda and salt together and add the chocolate chips. Mix well to combine.
Combine the brewed tea, caster sugar, brown sugar and oil. Combine the wet and dry ingredients until well mixed.
Chill dough for as least 2 hours. Portion the dough using a standard ice cream scoop and place balls onto a tray and into the freezer for 30 to 40 minutes. This will keep the cookies from spreading too much.
Preheat oven to 350°F/180°C (170°C fan)/ Gas Mark 4

Place cookies onto a baking sheet with 1 ½ inches around each ball. Bake cookies for 10 to 12 minutes. Let cool for 5 to 10 minutes and enjoy!
Makes 8 to 10 large cookies.

(Adapted from Food 52.)   Photo and Contribution By: Sara Robinson

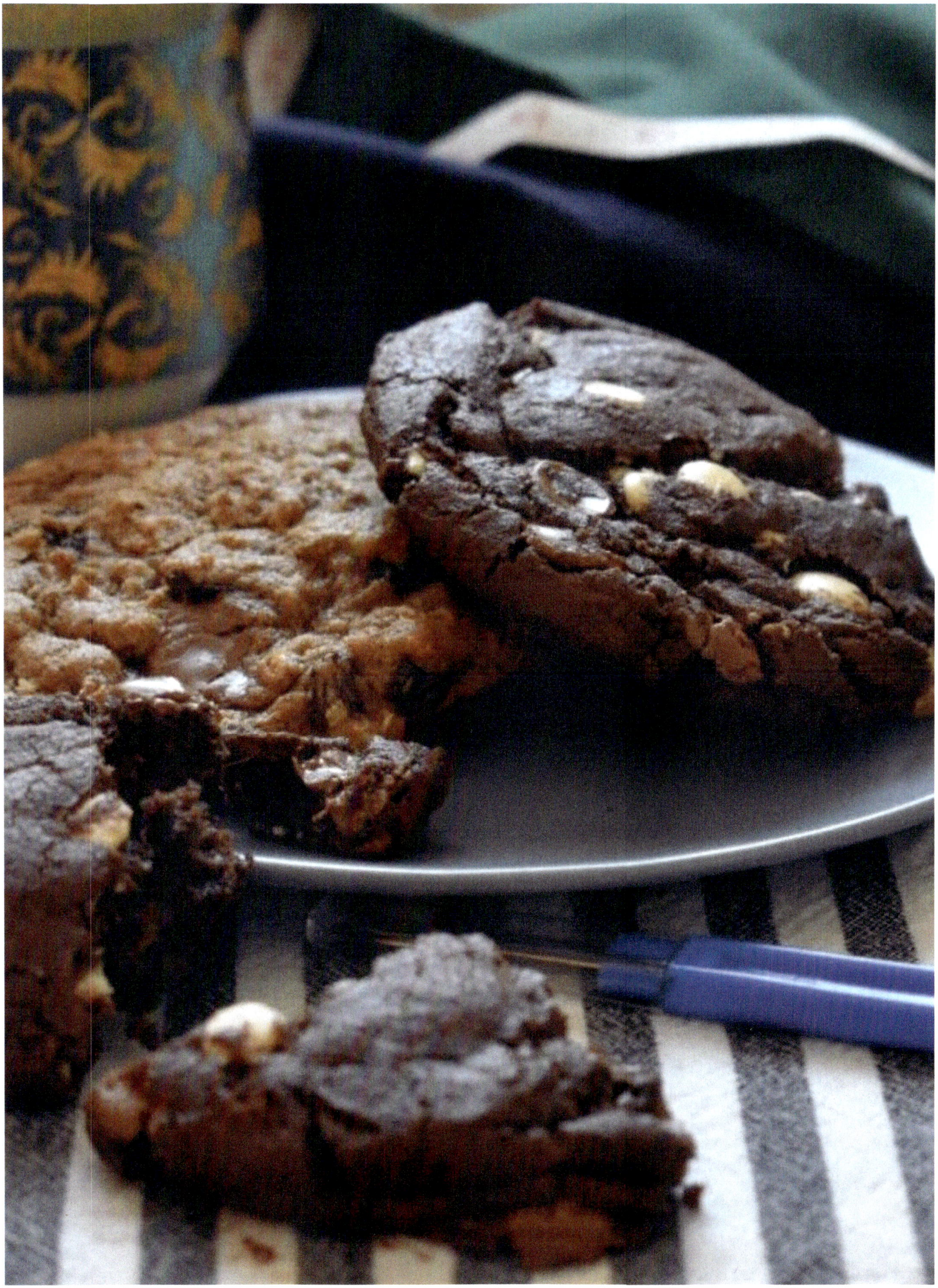

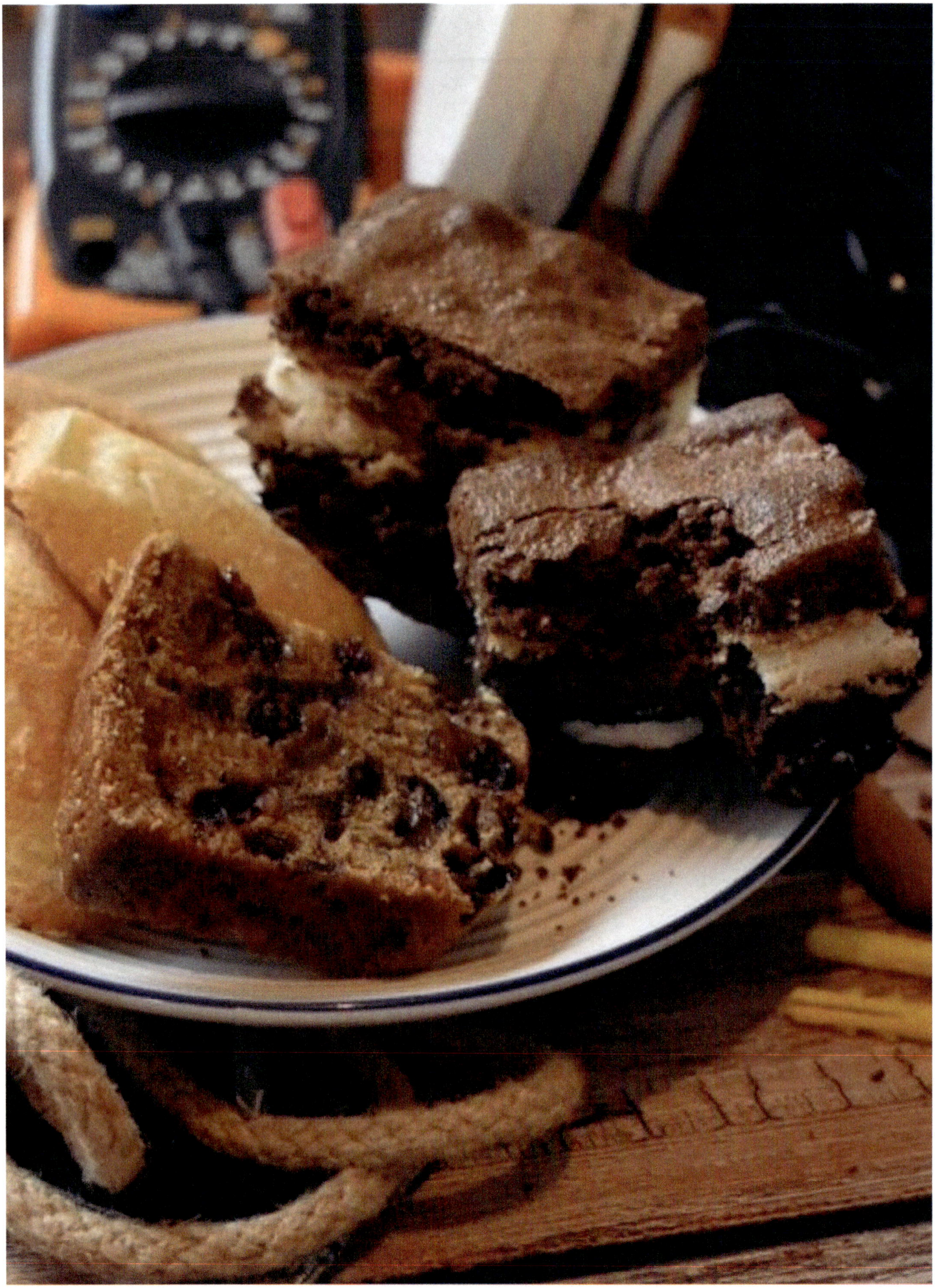

Crazy Brownies For the Professor

These were developed by Miss Lingoss for Professor Rapson for a very specific purpose, to be easy, changeable and so good to eat. Because the stuffing in the middle of the brownies and an be changed to keep them interesting and they never get old.
We love them because, well, they are amazingly chocolatey!

Ingredients
3 Eggs
1 ½ cups/ 10.5oz/ 300g Caster Sugar
¾ cup/ 5.3oz/ 150g Light Brown Sugar
2/3 cups/ 5.25oz/ 150g Butter, melted
1 ½ cups/ 7.9oz/ 225g Plain Flour
1 cup/ 3.5oz/ 100g Cocoa Powder
1 cup/ 6oz/ 150g 70% Dark Chocolate, melted
2/3 cup/ 5fl.oz/ 150ml Whole Milk
*And whichever Biscuit/ Chocolate bar you choose to go in the middle

Use a lined 8 inch/ 20cm square brownie tin.
Preheat the oven to 350°F/180°C (160°C fan)/Gas Mark 4
Whisk the eggs and sugar together then stir in the melted butter. Add the flour and cocoa powder, followed by the melted chocolate. Finally add the milk, mixing well. You should now have a smooth batter. Pour half of the mixture into the lined tin and smooth the top. Now add your biscuits or chocolate bars and cover them completely with the second half of the batter.

Bake for about 40 minutes. Cool and then slice!

The recipe can be made as just normal brownies but 18 Oreos, 3 Kitkats cut into pieces, 4 Crunchies smashed, 4 Snickers, all the Reeses Peanut Butter Cups, and 5 Twix bars are all favourites of the kitchen staff for stuffing into the brownies!

Contribution By: Sara Pickering

Oat Biscuits For Dr Dowson

Not to be outdone, Dr Dowson has his own tasty biscuits as well!

Ingredients:
½ cup/ 3oz/ 75g Self Raising Flour
½ cup/ 3oz/ 75g Oats
6 Tablespoons/ 3oz/ 75g Caster Sugar
5 Tablespoons/ 3oz/ 75g Butter or Margarine
1 Tablespoon/ 0.5fl.oz/ 15ml Golden Syrup
1 teaspoon/ 0.16fl.oz/ 5ml Milk
½ teaspoon/ 0.03oz/ 1g Bicarbonate of Soda

Preheat the oven to 350°F/ 180°C (160°C fan)/Gas Mark 4

Mix together the flour, oats and sugar. In a small pan over a low heat, melt together the margarine and sugar. Dissolve the bicarbonate of soda in the milk and add to the dry ingredients. Add the margarine and syrup then mix well. Make into small balls, place onto greased or lined trays and press down tops slightly. Bake for 7 to 10 mins. Cool for 2 mins on the tray then remove to a cooling rack.

Makes 15 to 18 cookies.

Photo by: Sara Robinson   Contribution By: Beckie Parsons

Hot Cocoa
Add Boiling Water
Stir Well
Add Marshmallows
Enjoy

Dr Stone's Hot Cocoa Prescription

Life in the medical field is never easy, so it is best to be prepared for anything. Hot Cocoa can soothe even the most temperamental historians and give them some grounding to start rebuilding life after a tough assignment.
According to many historians and some security staff, cookies help at these times too.

Quick Hot Cocoa

Ingredients:
2 Tablespoons/ 0.5oz/ 15g Unsweetened Cocoa Powder
1 Tablespoon/ 0.5oz/ 17g Granulated Sugar
Pinch of Salt
2 Tablespoons/ 0.5oz/ 15g Non-Fat Dry Milk
1 Tablespoon/ 0.3oz/ 10g Milk Chocolate Grated or Mini Chips
18/ 0.017oz/ 0.5g Mini Marshmallows

This mix can be saved for emergencies in individual bags. Empty contents of the bag into a large mug, add boiling water to about half of the mug. Stir the contents until a chocolatey paste is formed. Fill the rest of the mug with boiling water and stir well. Add desired toppings. Enjoy!

Individual bags make for a great gift too!

Makes 1 individual serving

Excellent Toppings for Hot Cocoa: Marshmallows, Whipping Cream, Sprinkles, Crushed Honeycomb or Hard Candies, Chocolate Shavings or something fiery from the bottom drawer.

Spiced Hot Cocoa Biscuits

Ingredients:
Topping:
1/3 cup/ 2.3oz / 68g Caster Sugar
½ teaspoon/ 0.1oz / 3g Cinnamon
1 teaspoon/ 0.2oz/ 6g Unsweetened Cocoa Powder

Cookies:
½ cup/ 4fl.oz / 119ml Vegetable Oil
1 cup/ 7oz/ 200g Caster Sugar
¼ cup/ 2.11oz / 60ml Golden Syrup or Maple Syrup
3 Tablespoons/ 1.52fl.oz/ 45ml Water
1 teaspoon/ 0.16fl.oz/ 5ml Vanilla Extract
1 2/3 cups/ 7.5oz/ 213g Plain Flour
½ cup/ 1.3oz/ 50g Unsweetened Cocoa Powder
1 teaspoon Bicarbonate of Soda
¼ teaspoon/ 0.07oz/ 3g Salt
½ teaspoon/ 0.03oz/ 1g Cinnamon
¼ teaspoon/ 0.01oz/ less than 1g Fine Ground Black Pepper (optional)

Preheat oven to 350°F/180°C (160°C fan)/Gas Mark 4. Line two baking sheets with parchment paper, or silicone mats. For the topping, mix the sugar, cinnamon and cocoa powder together in a shallow bowl, set aside.
In a medium mixing bowl mix together oil, sugar, syrup, water and vanilla.
Sift in the remaining ingredients and mix well into the wet ingredients. The dough should be glossy and pliable.
Measure the dough into walnut-sized balls, or about 20g each. Roll the balls to coat entirely with the sugar topping mixture. Place the balls onto the parchment paper lined baking sheets at least 2 inches apart.
Bake for 10-12 minutes, they should spread and crack on the top. Remove from the oven and let cool for 5 minutes before transferring the cookies to a cooling rack to cool completely.

Makes about 2 dozen cookies

Contribution and Photo By: Sara Robinson

More Tea Time Treats

Our Miss Lee is a force of nature! She is also an amazing cook, and if Maxwell would ever stop harassing her she might, just might, bring some of those treats into the office. Here are a few of Miss Lee's favourites and are Benjamin approved!

Of course, if she started bringing treats in then she would never get anything else done!

She would never have time to help in wardrobe or

keep that unruly lot in R&D under control.

And who would bring up the mail?

Mad Madeleines

Ingredients:
½ cup/ 3.9oz/ 113g Butter, melted
½ cup plus 1 Tablespoon/ 3.9oz/ 113g Granulated Sugar
1 teaspoon/ 0.2fl.oz/ 6ml Vanilla Extract
3 Eggs
1 cup/ 4.5g/ 130g Plain Flour
½ teaspoon/ 0.1oz/ 3g Baking Powder
½ teaspoon/ 0.1oz/ 3g Salt
1 Lemon, zested (optional)

Melt butter and allow to cool while making the batter.
Whisk flour, baking powder and salt together. In a separate bowl, whisk together the eggs and sugar until the batter is glossy and has tripled in volume. Whisk in the vanilla.
Slowly add the flour into the egg mixture, use a rubber spatula to fold it in so that the eggs' volume is not lost.
Try not to over mix. Add the lemon zest at this time as well.
Gradually add the cooled butter into the mixture, folding it into the batter in the same way as the flour.
Cover the mixture and refrigerate for at least 30 minutes, but preferably for several hours.
The batter should be slightly firm to the touch.
Generously butter and flour two Madeleine pans, or a 24-hole mini muffin tray.
Drop a generous teaspoon into each mould, leaving the batter
mounded in the centre.
Preheat oven to 375°F/ 190°C/ Gas Mark 5. Bake for 7 to 9 minutes,
until the edges are golden and the middle springs back when touched.
Rap tin/pan sharply on the counter to release and cool on a wire rack.

We have been told that they do keep well,
but be prepared, they will disappear quickly!

Contribution By: Sara McKenna

Tea Loaf

Ingredients:
¾ cup/ 6oz/ 170g Dark Brown Sugar
1 ¼ cups/ ½ pint/ 284ml Black Tea
2 cups/ 14oz/ 395g Dried Fruit of Choice (cranberries, raisins, golden sultanas, or cherries)
1 Egg
1 teaspoon/ 0.17oz/ 5g or more Mixed Spice
1 7/8 cups/ 8 oz/ 228g Self-Raising Flour

Line a small loaf tin or 8 inch/ 20cm square pan with parchment paper and a little butter or oil. Dissolve dark brown sugar into black tea. The kitchen loves using Earl Grey, but most tea works. Pour the dried fruit of choice into the sweet tea and leave to soak for at least an hour. After that time, add to the bowl one beaten egg, a good dollop of mixed spice and self-raising flour then mix well. Pour the mixture into the prepared pan.
Lining the tin is VITAL as there's no fat in the loaf.
Bake at 330°F/ 170°C/ Gas Mark 3 for 40 mins to an hour, or until a skewer comes out clean.
Slather with butter or eat just as it is.

Contribution By: Caroline Price

Spiced Lemon and Ginger Biscuits

Ingredients:
Cookies:
¾ cup/ 6.1oz/ 175g Unsalted Butter, softened
½ cup/ 2.9oz/ 85g Muscovado Sugar
1 ½ teaspoon Ground Ginger
¾ teaspoon Ground Cinnamon
Up to 1/4 teaspoon Ground Black Pepper (optional)
1 Lemon, zested and juiced (3 to 4 teaspoons)
1 ½ cups/ 7.9oz/ 225g Plain Flour
About a 1-inch piece/ 1.8oz/ 50g Stem Ginger, finely chopped

Topping:
½ cup/ 3.5oz/ 100g Caster Sugar
½ teaspoon/ 0.1oz/ 3g Ground Ginger
½ teaspoon/ 0.1oz/ 3g Lemon Zest

Preheat oven to 350°F/ 180°C/ Gas Mark 4. Line two baking sheets with parchment paper, or silicone mats.
For the topping, mix the sugar, ground ginger and lemon zest together in a shallow bowl, set aside.
In a medium mixing bowl, cream together the butter and sugar with a spoon or handheld mixer.
Sift the remaining ingredients together and mix well into the butter and sugar. The dough can be a little tough to get together, you may need to mix it with your hands.
Measure the dough into walnut-sized balls, or about 20g. Roll the balls to coat entirely with the sugar topping mixture. Place the balls onto the parchment paper lined baking sheets at least 2 inches/ 5cm apart. Using the flat of your hand smash each ball to about a 2-inch/ 5cm disk.
Bake for 10 to 12 minutes, they should not spread much. Remove from the oven and let cool for 5 to 10 minutes before transferring the cookies to a cooling rack to cool completely.
Makes about 2 dozen cookies

(Adapted from BBC Good Food)   Contribution By: Gina Burnside

Pour L'Amour du Chocolat

So many chocolate cakes... so little time

Ingredients:
¾ cup/ 3.1oz/ 90g Plain Flour
1 cup/ 4.9oz/ 140g Dark Chocolate, chopped (minimum 70% Cocoa Solids)
2/3 cup/ 4.9oz/ 140g Caster Sugar, plus extra for the tin
¼ cup/ 2.4oz/ 70g Butter, plus about 2 Tablespoons/ 0.8 oz/ 25g for the tin
4 Eggs
1 Tablespoon/ 0.5fl.oz/ 15 ml Water
A deep, 7 inch/ 20cm round tin

Preheat the oven to 350°F/ 180°C/ Gas Mark 4. Put 2 Tablespoons/ 25g butter in the tin then place in the hot oven to melt. Meanwhile, in a bowl set over a pan of simmering water, melt together the remaining butter, chocolate and water. Once melted, set aside to cool.
Separate the eggs and stir the yolks into the cooled chocolate mixture. Add the flour to the chocolate mixture, stirring well to combine and then add the sugar.
In an impeccably clean bowl, whisk the egg whites until stiff. Fold the egg whites into the chocolate mixture using a metal spoon - first folding in about a quarter of the beaten whites to loosen the chocolate mixture then folding in the remaining egg whites.
Now, working quickly but carefully, remove the tin from the oven and swirl the melted butter around the tin to coat the base and sides. Scatter sugar onto the base and sides of the tin to coat it, then pour the cake mixture into the tin. Bake for 40 to 50 minutes, until a skewer poked into the cake comes out clean.
Cool in the tin for several minutes before turning out to cool completely. Good served with crème Chantilly or crème fraîche - the tartness of the latter counters the sweetness of the cake very well.

Contribution By: Beckie Parsons

Easy as Cake

Who doesn't have time to make a delicious chocolate cake when it is this simple!

Ingredients:
1 2/3 cups / 7.5oz/ 235g Plain Flour
1 ½ cups/ 12oz/ 357g Caster Sugar
2/3 cup/ 2.4oz/ 65g Cocoa Powder
1 ½ teaspoons/ 0.25oz/ 7g Bicarbonate of Soda
1 teaspoon/ 0.1oz/ 3g Salt
1 ½ cups/ 11.9fl.oz/ 354ml Milk or Plant Based Alternative
¼ cup/ 3.5oz/ 100g Butter, melted or neutral oil
2 Eggs (optional)
1 tsp/ 0.25oz/ 7g Instant Coffee or Espresso Granules

Prepare a 20 cm/ 8-inch pan well-greased and lined with parchment paper. This cake batter is a very thin liquid, so we do not recommend using a loose bottom pan.

This is a very easy batter to mix by putting all ingredients into a food processor or blender and mixing well. Pour into the prepared tin.

Bake at 350°F/180°C/ Gas Mark 4 for 50 to 60 minutes until a skewer comes out clean. The cake should have risen a lot and spring back gently when you press it. The top may crack but frosting will cover it.
Cool in tin for 5 minutes then finish cooling on a rack.
Ice with regular chocolate icing/frosting

It bakes well in a regular muffin tin, well lined, for approximately 18 to 20mins.

To make it gluten free: Replace the plain flour with GF flour, reduce cocoa to 1/2 cup, use 1 tsp baking soda and 1/2 tsp baking powder to give it more structure. Let it sit in the tin for 10 minutes before baking.

Contribution By: Catherine Cruickshank

Not Exactly 'Healthy' Cocoa Cake

Alright, so we probably shouldn't call this healthy, but it does have almonds and pears in it and did we mention it's chocolate cake?!

Ingredients:
For the pears:
4 Pears, peeled, cored and quartered
2.8 Tablespoons/ 1.4oz/ 40g Butter
2 Tablespoons/ 0.98oz/ 28g Soft Brown Sugar
1 Orange, zested

For the Cake Mixture:
1 cup/ 3.5oz/100g Ground Almonds
½ cup plus 2 Tablespoons/ 3.5oz/ 100g Self-Raising Flour
¼ cup/ 0.88oz/ 25g Cocoa Powder
2/3 cup/ 5.2oz/ 150g Butter
¾ cup/ 5.2oz/ 150g Caster Sugar
2 Large Eggs
A Splash of Milk or Dairy Free Alternative

A greased and lined 7 inch/ 20cm round cake tin.
Preheat the oven to 375°F/ 190°C (170°C fan)/ Gas Mark 5
Start by preparing the pears. Heat the butter in a pan large enough to hold all the pear quarters in a single layer. Add the sugar and zest and stir to melt the sugar and combine the ingredients. Add the pears then cook over a medium heat, turning frequently, until the pears are caramelized and tender but still holding their shape – this depends on the ripeness of the pears, expect it to take 5 to 10 minutes. Once tender, set aside in the pan while you make the cake.
Cream together the fat and sugar, then blend in the eggs one at a time, adding a spoonful of the flour if the mixture begins to curdle. Fold in the flour, ground almonds and cocoa until well combined, adding a splash of milk at the end to make a dropping consistency.
Spoon the cake mixture into the tin, top with the pears, arranged artfully, then drizzle over any of the juices remaining in the pan. Bake for about 45 minutes, until the cake is well risen and firm to the touch. Cool in the tin.

Contribution By: Beckie Parsons

Incredible Chocolate Orange

What could be better then chocolate you can serve four different ways!

Ingredients:
1 cup/ 8.8oz/250g Dark Chocolate, chopped
1 Orange, zested
1 Tablespoon/ 0.5oz/ 15g Butter
2/3 cup/ 5fl.oz/ 150ml Double/Heavy Cream

Place all ingredients in a glass bowl and either melt them over a double boiler, or very carefully in the microwave. Gently stir the mixture occasionally as it is melting. Be sure not to overheat it in the microwave and cause it to seize.
It can be put into a dish and served immediately as a fondue, with fruit, cakes and other treats to dip into it.
It can be poured into chocolate moulds and set to cool overnight for an amazing gift.
It can be set to cool overnight and then formed into balls that can be dusted with cocoa powder for truffles and a different treat.
Best yet, it can be poured over chocolate cake as a topping!

Contribution By: Sara McKenna

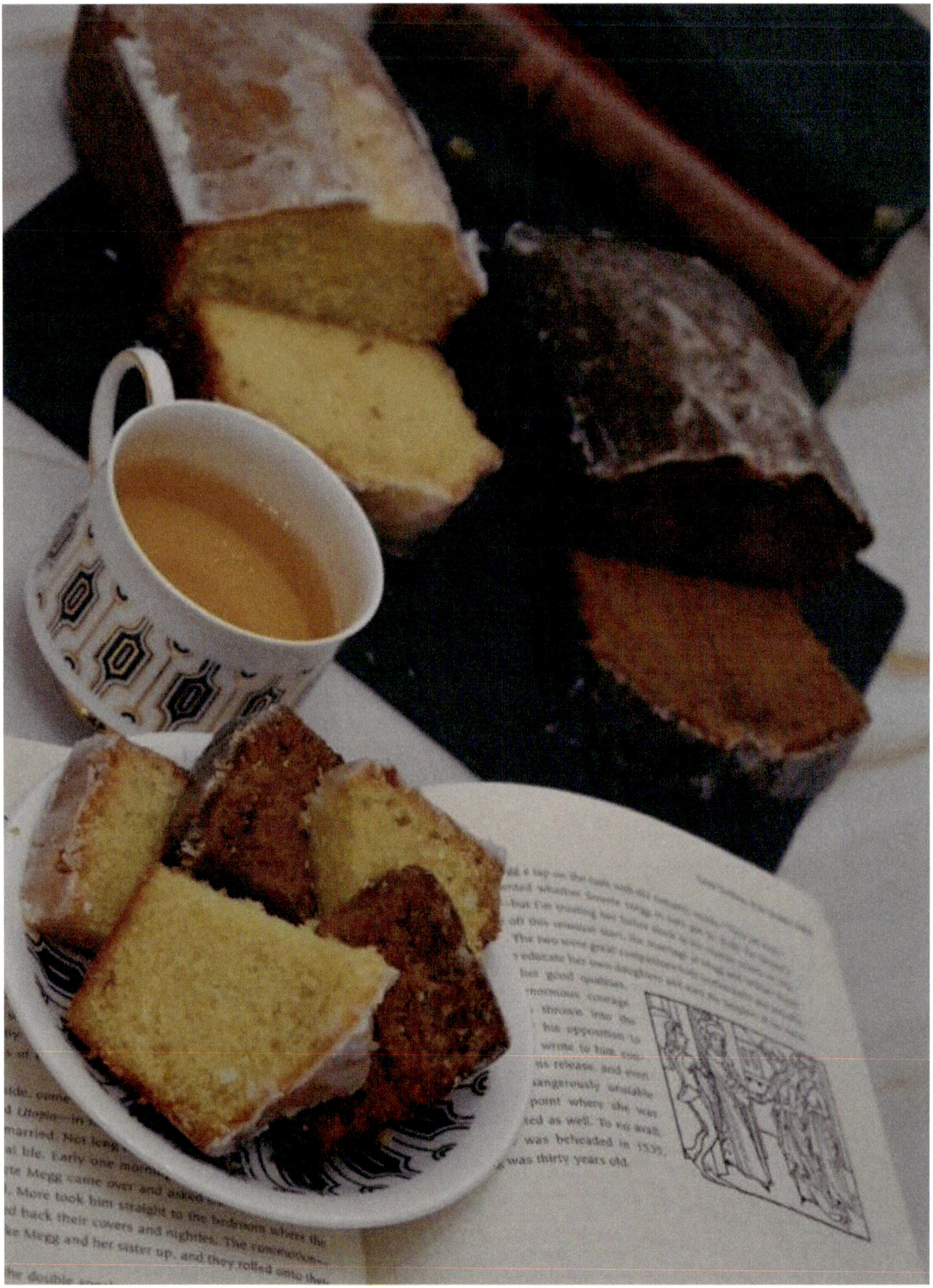

was beheaded in 1535,
was thirty years old.

Drizzle Cake

Our Miss North was missing the big city coffee shops with their trendy drizzle cakes. So, in true St. Mary's fashion she rolled up her sleeves and made her own. Let us just say, they are perfect!

Lemon Cake

Ingredients
Cake:
1 Lemon, zested
¾ cup/ 6oz/ 170g Butter, softened
¾ cup/ 6oz/ 170g Caster Sugar
3 Eggs
1 1/3 cups/ 6oz/ 170g Self-Raising Flour
Topping:
Juice from the zested lemon above, about 2 Tablespoons/ 1fl.oz/ 30ml
½ cup/ 3oz/ 85g Caster or Icing Sugar

Ginger Cake

Ingredients
Cake:
¾ cup/ 6oz/ 170g Butter, softened
¾ cup/ 6oz/ 170g Muscovado Sugar
2 Tablespoons Treacle or Molasses
3 Eggs
1 1/3 cups/ 6oz/ 170g Self-Raising Flour
1/2 teaspoon/ 0.1oz/ 3g Ground Cinnamon
1 teaspoon / 0.2oz/ 6g Ground Ginger
Pinch of Allspice
Topping:
2 Tablespoons Brewed Black Tea of Choice
½ cup/ 3oz/ 85g Caster or Icing Sugar

Chocolate Cake

Ingredients
Cake:
¾ cup/ 6oz/ 170g Butter, softened
¾ cup/ 6oz/ 170g Caster Sugar
3 Eggs
1 cup/ 5oz/ 150g Self-Raising Flour
¼ cup/ 1.1oz/ 30g Cocoa Powder
1/2 teaspoon/ 0.1oz/ 3g Instant Coffee Granules
¼ cup/ 2oz/ 50g Chocolate Chips (optional)
Topping:
2 Tablespoons Milk
½ cup/ 3oz/ 85g Caster or Icing Sugar

Preheat Oven to 325°F/170°C Fan Assisted Oven/Gas Mark 3

Cream together the softened butter and sugar. Mix in treacle/ zest/ milk and eggs. Mix in the dry ingredients self-raising flour and spices until just combined.

Grease and line a bread tin measuring 9x5x2.5 inches/ 23x13x6 cm or a one-pound loaf size. Put cake mixture into prepared tin.

Bake for approx. 35 to 45 mins

Take out of oven and spread the topping over while still warm. Cool in the tin then cut into slices.

Freezes well.

Contribution By: Clare Rice and Sara Robinson   Photo By: Sara Robinson

Mars Bar Squares

This is a perfect St Mary's recipe because, whilst it looks easy, it is also complicated. This is because: A UK Mars bar is a US Milky Way. A US Mars bar has almonds and has no UK equivalent. A UK Milky Way is called a Three Musketeers in the US, and there is no UK Three Musketeers.

There, clear as chocolate.

Ingredients:
4 Bars of 51g each or 4 bars of 1.84oz each of Mars Bars roughly chopped
1/3 cup/2.6oz/ 75g Butter
3 Tablespoons/ 1.5fl.oz/ 44 ml Golden Syrup
7 ¾ cups/ 7.9oz/ 225g Crispy Rice Cereal
1 ¼ cups/ 7oz/ 200g Milk Chocolate Chips

Grease and line with parchment a 9 x 9 inch/ 23 x 23cm pan.
Melt the chopped Mars bars, syrup, and butter over a very low heat, or in a double boiler. Stir occasionally until completely melted and combined. Combine mixture with the crispy rice cereal until all the cereal is coated. Press evenly in the lined pan and let cool. Melt the chocolate and spread over the top of the cooled bars. Let the chocolate set and then cut into squares.

Any extra Mars bars can be used to decorate the top of the squares or try white chocolate instead of milk chocolate. Try not to eat the whole pan yourself.

Photo and Contribution By: Afton Cochran

Peanut Butter Squares

Peanut Butter isn't the big deal in Britain that it is in the United States. There are still many that enjoy it and it has grown in popularity since being introduced after WWII.

Ingredients:
½ cup/ 6oz/ 170g Golden Syrup
½ cup/ 3.8oz/ 110g Muscovado Sugar
½ cup / 4.2oz/ 120g Smooth Peanut Butter (This will work with most nut or seed butters.)
3 cups / 2.6oz/ 75g Crispy Rice Cereal

Prepare a 9 x 9 inch/ 23x23cm square pan that is well greased. Add the golden syrup and brown sugar to a saucepan and over a low heat bring the mixture up to temperature where it is bubbling around the edges. Add the peanut butter (or other seed or nut butter) and mix well until all are warm and well combined. Pour into a large bowl over the crispy rice cereal and mix well until it is well coated. Press into the prepared well-greased pan.

When cooled cut into squares AND make sure to share!

Contribution By: Sara Robinson

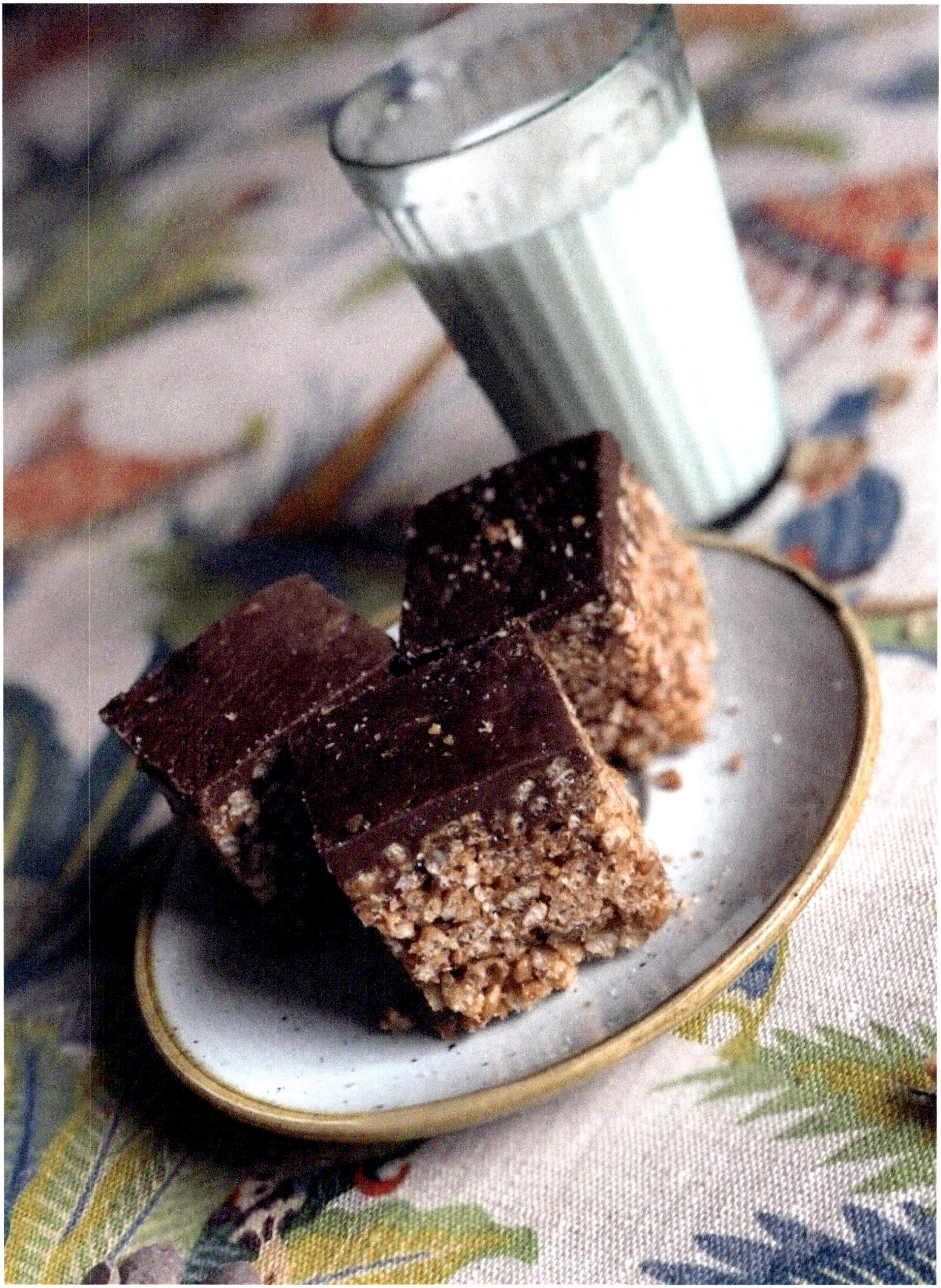

Bath Buns

In the lovely Georgian city of Bath, that is situated in the south-west of England, there is the story of the Bath Bun. There is some debate over which is the more authentic bun for the city; the Sally Lunn Bun or the Bath Bun. The Sally Lunn Bun is thought to predate the Bath Bun, so many believe it to be the more authentic of the two, having been brought to Bath by a French Huguenot refugee in 1680 (Solange Luyon). The Sally Lunn Bun is more of a brioche type bun, and much less of the 'cakey' sweet consistency of a Bath Bun. The Sally Lunn Bun is often found sporting caraway seeds and the like and so could be adapted to be savoury or sweet as required. Both Buns continue to be sold in Bath, but this is a recipe for the sweeter, 'cakey' Bath Bun.

Ingredients:
Buns:
1 cup/ 8fl.oz/ 250g Whole Milk
1 teaspoon/ 0.3oz/ 10g Quick-Action Dried Yeast
5 ¼ cups/ 22.9oz/ 650g Strong White Flour, plus a little more for kneading
2 ½ Tablespoons/ 1oz/ 30g Caster Sugar
1 teaspoon/ 0.1oz/ 5g Salt
1 cup/ 9.7oz/ 275g Unsalted Butter, softened
¼ cup/ 1.7oz/ 50g Sultanas
1 Egg, beaten

Syrup Glaze:
3 Tablespoons/ 1.4oz/ 40g Caster Sugar
4 teaspoons/ 0.7oz/ 20g Water
4 White Sugar Cubes

Warm the milk so that it is warm to the touch but not boiling and then whisk in the yeast. Let the mixture stand for 10 minutes or so - it should be nice and frothy. In a separate bowl, measure in the flour and salt and then work the butter in with your fingers until it resembles a fine crumb. Add the milk mixture and mix into a dough. Let the dough rest for about 20 minutes. Then knead the dough by hand on a floured board for about 15 minutes or with a stand mixer for about 8 minutes. Cover and leave in a warm place to double in size.
Tip the dough back out onto a lightly floured board, squishing the dough flat. Spread the sultanas evenly across the dough and fold to incorporate them. Divide the dough into 12 pieces. (Some bakers place a sugar lump in the bottom of each bun, but this is optional). Shape each bun by pulling and stretching the top until the surface is taut and smooth. Place on a silicone sheet or baking paper lined tray and allow to double in size again.
Preheat the oven to 350°F/ 180°C/ Gas Mark 4. Gently paint each bun with the beaten egg wash. Bake for 20 to 25 minutes, or until the underside of the bun sounds hollow when tapped.
While they are baking, make the syrup glaze. First dissolve the caster sugar in hot water and crush the sugar cubes into little lumps. Paint the hot well-cooked bun with the syrup glaze and sprinkle with the crushed sugar cubes.
These can be eaten most deliciously split and spread with clotted cream and your favourite jam.

(Adapted from thehappyfoodie.co.uk)   Contribution By: Jacqui Ryder

TaDa doughnuts

Make sure your chosen opponent is able and willing for the challenge!
These bite-sized doughnuts always disappear fast!

Ingredients
1 ¼ cups/ 6.2oz/ 176g Plain Flour
2 teaspoons/ 0.35oz/ 10g Baking Powder
½ teaspoon/ 0.07oz/ 2g Bicarbonate of Soda
¼ teaspoons/ 0.07oz/ 2g Salt
½ cup/ 4.05fl.oz/ 120 ml Buttermilk
¼ cup/ 1.7oz/ 50g Caster Sugar
3 Tablespoons/ 1.48oz/ 42g Butter, melted
3 ½ cups/ 28fl.oz/ 828ml Vegetable Oil, or other neutral oil for frying

For Coating
1/3 cup/ 2.32oz/ 66g Caster Sugar or Icing Sugar
1 teaspoon/ 0.07oz/ 2g Ground Cinnamon

In a medium mixing bowl, whisk together flour, sugar, baking powder, bicarbonate of soda and salt.
In a separate bowl, whisk together the buttermilk and melted butter. Pour the buttermilk mixture into the flour mixture and mix just until well combined. Be careful, it is easy to over-work the mixture! In a separate bowl mix together the cinnamon and sugar and set aside.
Pour about 1/2-inch/1.5cm oil into a large frying pan, cast iron skillet or heavy well-balanced pot. Heat oil over medium heat to 350°F/180°C. Do not leave the oil pan unattended while it is hot!
Roll dough into 1 tablespoon balls or about roughly the size of a walnut. Once the oil has reached temperature, fry only a few of the dough balls at a time. Over crowding the pan will lower the temperature of the oil making the balls not fry well and soak up oil!
Fry until just golden brown, flipping once to get that lovely colour all over.
Carefully remove with a spider strainer and drain onto a paper towel lined sheet pan.
While the dough balls are still warm, toss them in the sugar and cinnamon to coat well.
Repeat this process with the remaining dough.

(Adapted from Cooking Classy.)   Contribution By: Sara Robinson

TaDa Doughnut Pudding

Ever wonder what to do with left over doughnuts? HAHA! HAHA!
I know, but it does happen from time to time. This is an amazing treat!

Ingredients:
3 to 4 Grocery Store Style Stale Doughnuts
¾ cup/ 5.9 fl.oz/ 177ml Whole Milk or Cream
2 Eggs
Pinch Ground Nutmeg
Pinch Ground Cinnamon
Butter, for greasing the mugs
Unlike most bread puddings this one probably doesn't need any sugar but feel free to add up to
3 Tablespoons/ 1.4 oz/ 40g Caster Sugar.

Preheat oven to 350°F/ 180°C/ Gas Mark 4
Mix the eggs, milk, and spices in a medium sized bowl. Slice doughnuts into bite-sized pieces. We used raspberry jam filled doughnuts that were sugar coated. Place the doughnuts in the egg mixture and mix to coat well. Grease 2 large mugs or ramekins with butter. Divide the mixture between the two cups making sure that it does not go all the way to the rim. Place the cups on a baking tray before putting them in the oven. Bake for 35 to 40 minutes until well puffed and a skewer stuck in the middle will come out clean. Serve with custard, ice cream, or just enjoy as is!

Serves 2

Contribution By: Gina Burnside and Sara Robinson

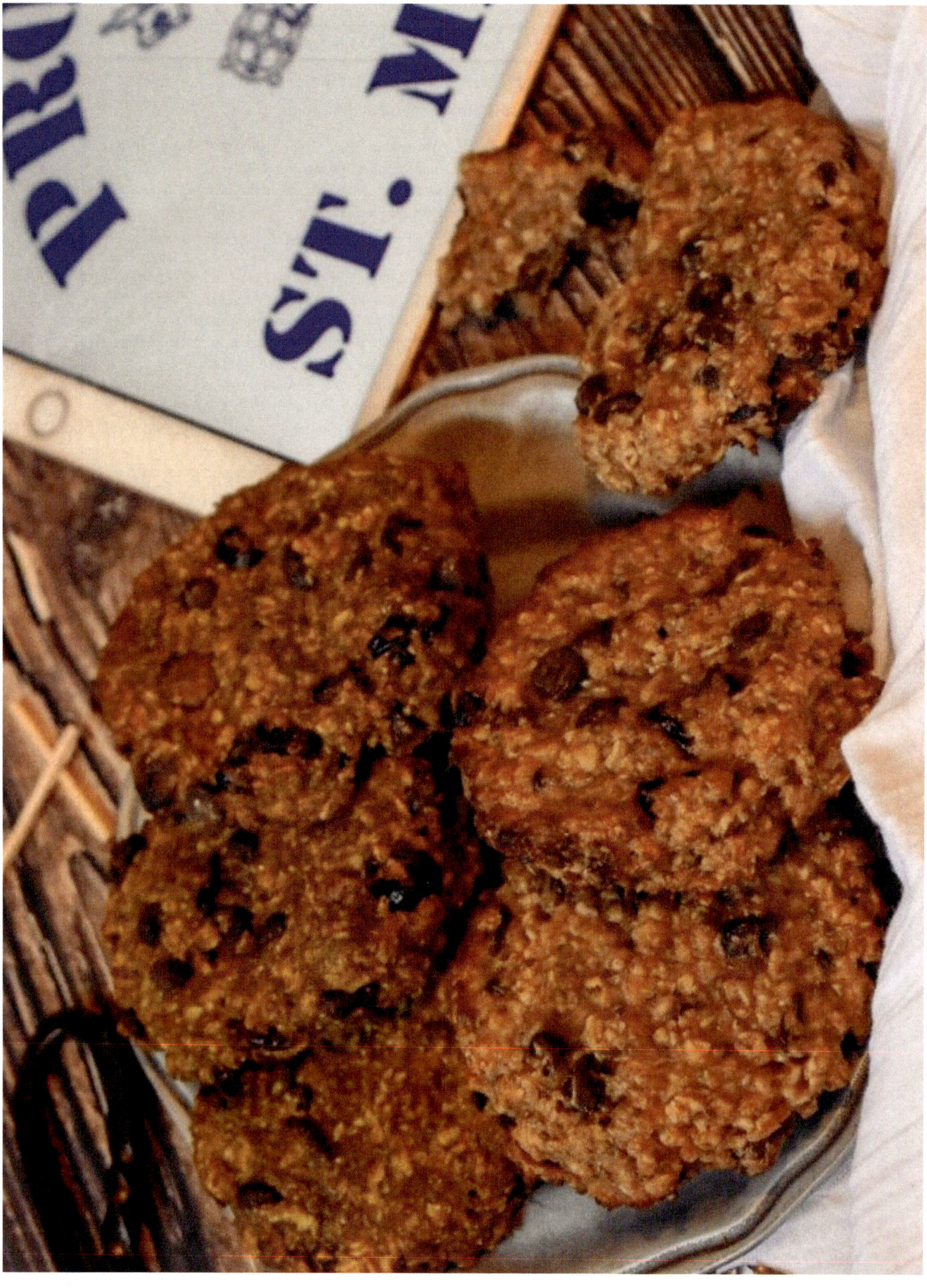

New High Energy Biscuits

After years of complaints from historians and the security section, we have been striving to create the perfect high energy biscuit. The taste is greatly improved and it is still guaranteed to keep you going through the jump.

Peanut Butter High Energy Biscuits

Ingredients:
2 cups/ 5.6oz/ 230g Quick or Porridge Oats
¾ teaspoon/ 0.15oz/ 5g Salt
1 Tablespoon/ 1.7oz/ 6g Almond Meal
2 Tablespoons/ 0.9oz/ 27g Chia Seeds
¼ cup/ 1.2oz/ 35g Whole Grain Flour
1 teaspoon/ 0.1oz/ 3g Cinnamon
¾ cup/ 7.1oz/ 200g Banana, mashed
2 Eggs
1 cup/ 5.9oz/ 170g Smooth Peanut Butter
¼ cup/ 2.6oz/ 75g Golden Syrup or Honey
½ cup/ 2.6oz/ 75g Mixed Dried Fruit
½ cup/ 2.6oz/ 75g Dried Cranberries
¾ cup/ 5.2 oz/ 150g Chocolate Chips

Preheat Oven to 350°F/ 180°C/ Gas Mark 4. Line 2 cookie sheets with parchment paper.

Combine oats, salt, chia seeds, flour, spices and bran/meal/germ in a large mixing bowl.

Add mashed banana/pumpkin, eggs, peanut or pumpkin seed butter and honey. Mix to combine, this will be a very stiff batter.

Add dried fruit and chocolate chips. Mix until it is well combined.

Use an ice cream scoop or ¼ cup to drop cookies onto the prepared sheets.

Using damp fingers, slightly flatten the scoops to desired thickness. The cookies will not spread in the oven

Bake for 15 to 18 minutes or until the edges are slightly brown.

Allow to cool fully on the cookie sheets. Enjoy!

Nut Free High Energy Biscuits

Ingredients:
2 cups/ 5.6oz/ 230g GF Quick or Porridge Oats
¾ teaspoon/ 0.15oz / 5g Salt
1 Tablespoon/ 1.7oz/ 6g GF Oat Bran
2 Tablespoons/ 0.9oz/ 27g Chia Seeds
¼ cup/ 1.2oz/35g Buckwheat Flour
1 teaspoon/ 0.1oz/ 3g Mixed Spice or Pumpkin Pie Spice
¾ cup/ 7.1 oz/ 200g Pumpkin, mashed
2 Eggs or Egg substitute
1 cup/ 5.9oz/ 170g Smooth Pumpkin Seed Butter or Sunflower Seed Butter
¼ cup/ 2.6oz/ 75g Maple Syrup or Honey
½ cup/ 2.6oz/ 75g Dried Raisins
½ cup/ 2.6oz/ 75g Dried Cranberries
¾ cup/ 5.2oz/ 150g Chocolate Chips

Makes 10 to 12 biscuits.

Biscuits will stay fresh at room temperature for about a week.

Contribution and Photo By: Sara Robinson

Mrs Shaw's Chocolate Biscuits

Mrs. Shaw is one of the nicest and most patient of people. She would have to be, working with Peterson every day! Supplying him with chocolate biscuits is almost a full time job. We think her biscuits should be world famous!

Bourbon Biscuits for Good Boys and Girls

Ingredients:
½ cup/ 3.8oz/ 110g Light Muscovado Sugar
½ cup/ 3.8oz/ 110g Salted Butter, Softened
1 cup/ 3.8oz/ 110g Plain Flour
½ cup/ 1.5oz/ 45g Dark Cocoa

Pinch of Instant Coffee Granules
1 teaspoon Bicarbonate of Soda.
¼ teaspoon Salt
2 Tablespoons/ 1.4oz/ 40g Golden Syrup

Cream the butter and sugar until light and fluffy, then add the golden syrup and mix until well combined.
Sieve all dry ingredients together and add to the above mix to make a smooth dough. Roll out to about 4-5mm thick between cling film and chill until firm.
Preheat the oven to 325°F/ 170°C/ Gas Mark 3.
Cut into equal sizes. Bake on lined baking sheets for 10 minutes - leaving space to allow for spreading.
Remove from the oven and sprinkle with granulated sugar, pressing the sugar in slightly. Cool for 15 minutes on the tray, then transfer to a wire rack. Cool completely before spreading with ganache and sandwiching together.

Bourbon Biscuit Ganache

Ingredients:
1 cup/ 7oz/ 200g Icing Sugar
7 Tablespoons/ 3.5oz/ 100g Salted Butter
5 teaspoons/ 0.88oz/ 25g Dark Cocoa
2 Tablespoons/ 0.42oz/ 12g Instant Coffee Granules
2 Tablespoons/ 1oz/ 30ml Boiling Water
1 teaspoon/ 0.15oz/ 4g Vanilla Paste

Dissolve the coffee granules into the boiling water. Use a hand mixer to beat the butter and sugar until fluffy. Add cocoa, vanilla and coffee. Beat well.
Spread on a biscuit and gently sandwich with a second biscuit. Repeat with the remaining cookies.

Salted Butter is important for the taste of the Bourbon biscuits!   Contribution By: Sara McKenna

Chocolate Forked Biscuits For Those Difficult Days

Ingredients:
7 Tablespoons/ 3.5oz/ 100g Butter, softened
1 2/3 Tablespoons/ 0.88oz/ 25g Caster Sugar
3 ½ Tablespoons/ 0.88oz/ 25g Ground Almonds
1 cup/ 4.2oz/ 120g Self-Raising Flour
2 Tablespoons/ 0.5oz/ 15g Cocoa Powder
1 teaspoon/ 0.07oz/ 2g Instant Coffee Granules (optional)

Pre-heat your oven to 350°F/ 180°C/ Gas Mark 4
Grease and line 2 baking trays.
Add the butter and sugar to a bowl and beat together until smooth.
Add in the flour and mix well, then add in the cocoa powder, ground almonds and coffee granules and beat until it forms a stiff dough.
Form the dough into balls, about the size of a walnut and place well apart on the trays.
Dip a fork in boiling water and use this to flatten the biscuits.
Bake in the oven for 15 to 20 minutes until browned then leave on the tray to cool.

Contribution By: Anne Brown

Chapter Eight:
Drinks Afterhours
At
The Blue Swan
(And a few for the hours in the middle of the day!)

Recipes:

A Few for After Hours — 180
  Can You Do the Dodo?, Is That a Woolly Mammoth on the Trolley?, Dr. B's Beloved Bentley, Rocket Fuel, Swan Attack, What the Hell?, The Rose of Windsor, Where's Pinky?, Eternal Youth, The Stuart Queen

More From the Bar — 181
  Sneaky Peterson, Thor's Chicken, The Flash, Jump Start, Hope for the Best Margarita,
  We Really Need A Holiday Martini, Red, White or Rosé Wine

A Few More from the Bar — 182
  Bashford's Stick Blender, Moon Over Stonehenge, Technical Breakfast Shot,
  The Chocolate Association, Bloody Bollocking Hell, The Nine Day Queen, Two Beer Mats and Half a Lime

Historical Drinks — 183
  Water, Lemonade

More From the Bar, Because We Are Not Alcoholics — 184
  Shirley Temple, Roy Rogers, Bashford Brakes, Almost Instant Lemonade, Blushing Sykes,
  Refreshing Knots, Hot Chocolate Milano, Winter Warmer

Drinks From the Bar When We Have a Jump the Next Day — 185
  Hair of the Dog That Bit You, The Yeti's Milk, Orange you Glad to See Me?, Bombs Away!,
  Sock it to me!, The Black Point/ Rock Your Universe

Fresh Raspberry Kir — 185
Elderflower Cordial — 186
Raspberry Lemonade Cordial — 186
Rhubarb Cordial — 186

A Few For After Hours in the Bar

*The wonderful people in the bar have seen us at our best and at our worst.
They have seen it all and still the good stuff keeps flowing...*

Can You Do the DoDo?

3fl.oz/ 90ml Gin
1fl.oz/ 30ml White Crème de Menthe
1fl.oz/ 30ml Lemon Juice
Shake in cocktail shaker over ice then strain

Dr Bairstow's Beloved Bentley

1fl.oz/ 30ml Apple Brandy
1fl.oz/ 30ml Dubonnet
Stir over ice then strain

The Swan Attack

3fl.oz/ 90ml Dry Gin
3fl.oz/ 90ml Dry Vermouth
Dash Angostura Bitters
Dash Lemon Juice
Shake over ice and strain

The Rose of Windsor

3fl.oz/ 90ml Dry Gin
2fl.oz/ 60ml Dubonnet
1fl.oz/ 30ml Campari
Stir over ice and strain

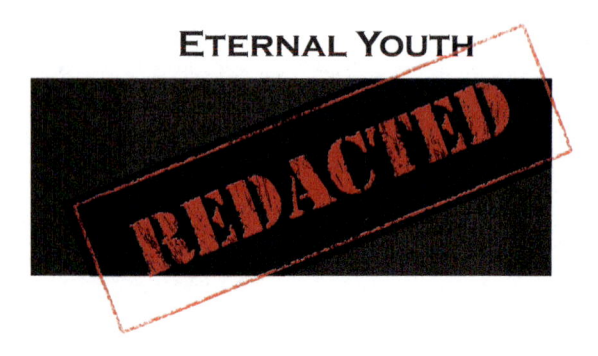

Eternal Youth

REDACTED

Is That a Woolly Mammoth on the Trolley?

1fl.oz/ 30ml Tequila
1fl.oz/ 30ml Peach Schnapps
1fl.oz/ 30ml Coconut Rum
1fl.oz/ 30ml White Rum
1fl.oz/ 30ml Lime Cordial
Shake in cocktail shaker over ice then strain

Rocket Fuel

REDACTED

What The Hell?

1fl.oz/ 30ml Dry Gin
1fl.oz/ 30ml Apricot Brandy
1fl.oz/ 30ml Dry Vermouth
Dash of Lemon Juice
Stir over ice then strain

Where's Pinky?

2fl.oz/ 60ml Rye Whiskey
1fl.oz/ 30 Lemon Juice
4 dashes Grenadine
1 teaspoon Sugar
Shake over ice and strain

The Stuart Queen

2fl.oz/ 60ml Crème de Cacao
2fl.oz/ 60ml Dry Gin
2fl.oz/ 60ml Sweetened Fresh Cream
Shake over ice and strain

All Contributed By: Ann Hughes

More From the Bar

Sneaky Peterson

1fl.oz/ 30ml Coffee Liqueur
1fl.oz/ 30ml Rye Whiskey
4fl.oz/ 120ml Whole Milk
Shake in cocktail shaker over ice then strain

Thor's Chicken

REDACTED

The Flash

REDACTED

Jump Start

1 1/2fl.oz/ 45ml Amaretto
1 1/2fl.oz/ 45ml Cinnamon Schnaps
Pour together. Enjoy.

Contribution By: Afton Cochran and Sara Robinson

Hope For the Best Margarita

Ingredients:
3oz/ 88.72 ml White or Reposado Tequila
1oz/ 30ml Cointreau
Lime sliced for garnish
Coarse Salt, for rimming the glass
Ice

At least 2 hours before serving, zest and juice limes. Let the zest steep in the lime juice, then strain before using. This step can be skipped, but it is worth the extra time.
Rub edge of rocks glass with lime wedge, then dip into a bowl of coarse sea salt. Add ice to a cocktail shaker. Add tequila, lime juice and Cointreau. Shake thoroughly. Fill glass halfway with ice, add the lime slices, then more ice. Strain the margarita into the glass and prepare to become the life of the party.

Contribution By: Merry Schepers

We Really Need a Holiday Martini

Ingredients:
2fl.oz/ 60ml Vanilla Vodka
½fl.oz/ 15ml Lime Juice
1fl.oz/ 30ml Coconut Cream
1fl.oz/ 30ml Pineapple Juice
1fl.oz/ 30ml Double Cream
Digestive Biscuit Crumbs

Rim a cocktail glass with the digestive biscuit crumbs.
Fill a martini shaker with ice and put all the other ingredients in it. Shake thoroughly and strain into the prepared cocktail glass. Garnish with a wheel of lime or a lime twist.

Contribution By: Cheryl Harper

Red, White or Rosé Wine

Ingredients:
1 Glass, Wine Glass or Jam Jar
1 Wine Bottle of choice
1 Wine Bottle opener

Open wine bottle with opener. Poor wine into the glass, or drink directly from the bottle depending on how your day went.

Contribution By: Afton Cochran and Sara Robinson

A Few More From the Bar

Bashford's Stick Blender
It's a Hair-raising Experience

Ingredients:
1 Orange Wedge
Cinnamon Sugar for rimming the glass
2oz/ 60ml Fireball Whiskey
Splash Grenadine
4oz/ 120 ml Ginger Ale
Ice
Cinnamon Stick, for garnish

Wet the rim of a rocks glass with the wedge of orange. Roll the wetted rim in the cinnamon sugar. Fill the glass with ice. In a cocktail shaker, add the fireball and grenadine. Add ice and shake well. Strain into the rocks glass, add the ginger ale, stir, and garnish with the cinnamon stick.

Contribution By: Afton Cochran

Moon Over Stonehenge

0.5fl.oz/ 15ml Lemon Juice
0.5fl.oz/ 15ml Creme de Violette liqueur
2fl.oz/ 59ml Gin (works best with a botanical gin, but dry gin will work if preferred)
Shake and strain into a chilled coupe glass. Garnish with lemon wheel or wedge.

Contribution By: Cheryl Harper

The Chocolate Association

13.5fl.oz/ 400ml Cocktail Shaker
6.7fl.oz/ 200ml Cold Espresso or Strong Coffee
2.1fl.oz/ 65ml Vodka
1.35fl.oz/ 40ml Coffee Liqueur
1.35fl.oz/ 40ml Chocolate Liqueur
1.35fl.oz/ 40ml Cointreau (optional)
Pop in a couple of ice cubes and then shake vigorously, strain and serve.

Contribution By: David Sprakes

The Nine Day Queen

1 Dash Angostura Bitters
0.5fl.oz/ 15ml Cognac
0.5fl.oz/ 15ml Benedictine Liquor
1.5fl.oz/ 44ml Vodka
Stir with ice and strain into a chilled coupe glass. Garnish with twist of lemon peel.

Contribution By: Cheryl Harper

Technical Breakfast Shot

1fl.oz/ 30ml Irish Whiskey
0.5fl.oz/ 15ml Butterscotch Liqueur
Glass of Orange Juice
1 slice of bacon
Pour the Irish whiskey and the butterscotch liqueur into a shot glass. Pour orange juice into a lowball glass and a lay a piece of bacon across the top of the glass. Shoot the shot, chase it with OJ and take a bite of bacon.

Contribution By: Cheryl Harper

Bloody Bollocking Hell

1/4 cup/ 2fl.oz/ 59ml Tomato Juice
3 Tablespoons/ 1.5oz/ 44ml Vodka
1 teaspoon/ 0.16fl.oz/ 5ml Worcestershire Sauce
1/2 teaspoon Horseradish, freshly grated
3 dashes Hot Sauce
1 pinch of Salt
1 dash of Ground Black Pepper
1 cup of Ice Cubes
1/4 teaspoon Lemon Juice
1 Celery Stalk (optional)
1 slice of Lemon (optional)
Shake over ice to combine then garnish with lemon and a celery stalk if using.

Contribution By: Ann Hughes

Two Beer Mats and Half a Lime

HEALTH & SAFETY REDACTED

Historical Drinks
Historians will talk about everything

Medieval Water

One of the biggest misunderstandings about the past is that everyone drank beer or wine and no one drank water because it was not safe to drink.
This, as they say in the biz, is a myth, as in it did not happen.
There is plenty of evidence even before the medieval period, with health and medical texts explaining the benefits of drinking water from a good source, such as in 7th century Byzantine. Fifteenth century letters have been found that instruct a son to cook the water from nearby rivers before drinking it because they were known to be dirty. There are also ledgers in later period Scotland that outline paying a servant to fetch water for the table.
So, people in the past were smart and
understood that water could be dirty and not safe to drink.
This knowledge does not diminish the fact they boiled water to drink,
and they actually drank water.

Lemonade

The word lemonade has been around since 1663 referring to a sweetened lemon juice diluted with water. Recipes have changed somewhat through the years:

XIV. Lemonade water at a cheap rate.
Dissolve half 2 pound of sugar in a quart of water; rasp over it the yellow part of one, two, or three lemons, as you, like, and mix a few drops of essential oil of sulphur in the liquor.
Then cut three or four slices of lemon in the bowl, when you put the liquor in it.
Secrets Concerning Arts and Trades, 1795

How to make Lemonade (Orangeade)
Peel the rind of one lemon very thinly without any of the white pith, and put the rind into a jug; pare off all the white pith from three lemons so as to lay the pulp quite bare, cut them into slices, take out all the seeds, or, as they are more generally termed, the pips, as their bitterness would render the drink unpalatable; add one ounce of sugar, or honey, pour a quart of boiling water to these, cover up the jug, and allow the lemonade to stand and steep until quite cold; it may then be given to the patient. This is a cooling beverage, and may be safely given in cases of fever.
Charles Esme Francatelli, A Plain Cookery Book for the Working Classes, 1861

987. LEMONADE
Two pounds of castor sugar, one ounce of citric acid, the grated rind of three oranges, three tumblerfuls of cold water. Let it stand three or four days, stirring occasionally.
Then strain, bottle, and cork tight.
May Byron, The British Home Cookery Book, 1914

The biggest change though is that Lemonade currently in the UK, pretty much universally refers to a carbonated beverage that is lemon or lemon and lime flavoured.

More From the Bar, Because We Are Not Alcoholics

The Doll

½fl.oz/ 15ml Grenadine
¼fl.oz/ 7ml Lime Juice
5fl.oz/ 150ml Ginger Ale
Mix juice and ale together, add ice cubes and garnish with Maraschino Cherries

Contribution By: Afton Cochran

Bashford Brakes

1fl.oz/ 30ml Carrot Juice
5fl.oz/ 150ml Ginger Ale or Ginger Beer
Mix juice and ale together, add ice cubes and garnish with carrot stick or celery stick.

Contribution By: Sara Robinson

Blushing Sykes

0.5fl.oz/ 15ml Grenadine
8fl.oz/ 250ml Lemonade
8fl.oz/ 250ml Iced Tea
Wedge of Lemon
Combine tea, lemonade and grenadine. Serve over ice and garnish with lemon wedge.

Contribution By: Sara Robinson

Hot Chocolate Milano

1 Tablespoon/ 0.3oz/ 8g Cocoa Powder
1 teaspoon/ 0.1oz/ 3g Plain Flour
1 to 2 Tablespoons/ 0.4 to 0.8oz/ 12 to 25g Sugar
½ cup/ 4.2fl.oz/ 120ml Water
½ cup/ 4.2fl.oz/ 120ml Milk
Whisk all the dry ingredients together in a heavy based saucepan.
Make a paste with a little of the liquid, then gradually whisk in the rest, stirring well so it's lump free. Heat gently while whisking until it reaches your preferred consistency - about 5 minutes or so. Italian hot chocolates are thick. The Milano can be thinned with more milk, but who would want to!

Contribution By: Sara McKenna

The Cowboy

6fl.oz/ 177ml Cola
½fl.oz/ 15ml Grenadine
Mix all ingredients together, add ice cubes and garnish with Maraschino Cherries

Contribution By: Afton Cochran

Almost Instant Lemonade

2 Tablespoons/ 1fl.oz/ 30ml Lemon Juice
½ Tablespoon/ 0.2fl.oz/ 7ml Lime Juice
2 Tablespoons/ 0.88oz/ 25g Caster Sugar
2 cups/ 16fl.oz/ 473ml Soda Water
Mix the juices and sugar till the sugar dissolves. Add soda water and ice cubes. Enjoy!

Contribution By: Sara McKenna

Refreshing Knots

0.5fl.oz/ 15ml Balsamic Vinegar or to taste
8fl.oz/ 250ml Lemon Lime Soda
Frozen Berries
Combine balsamic and soda. Serve over ice and garnish with frozen berries.

Contribution By: Sara Robinson

Winter Warmer

1 ½ Cinnamon Sticks
¼ tsp Black Peppercorns
2 or 3/ ¼ tsp Whole Cloves
Pinch of Nutmeg, ground
2 cups/ 16fl.oz/ 475ml Apple Juice
¼ tbsp Orange Zest
Combine spices and juice in a saucepan and cook over medium-high heat. Simmer for 15 to 20 minutes. Pour through a fine mesh sieve to strain. Allow to cool slightly before serving.

Contribution By: Sara Robinson

Drinks from the Bar When We Have a Jump the Next Day

Hair of the Dog That Bit You

REDACTED

Orange You Glad To See Me?

3.75fl.oz/ 110ml Fresh Orange Juice
2.25fl.oz/ 67ml Grapefruit or Lemon Sparkling Water
Pour the fresh orange juice and grapefruit/lemon sparkling water into a tall glass.
Stir gently and then pour into champagne flutes.

Contribution By: Sara Robinson

Sock it to Me!

2fl.oz/ 60ml Cranberry Juice
0.5fl.oz/ 15ml Lemon or Lime Juice
1fl.oz/ 30ml Orange Juice
2fl.oz/ 60 Ginger Ale or Sparkling Water
In a tall glass, gently stir everything together.
Garnish: lemon and orange slices

Contribution By: Sara Robinson

The Yeti's Milk

1/2 cup/ 5fl.oz/ 150g Yoghurt, plain and a very thick consistency
1/3 cup/ 2 1/2fl.oz/ 75ml Milk
2 Tablespoons/ 1fl.oz/ 30ml Maple Syrup
1 teaspoon/ 0.16fl.oz/ 5ml Vanilla Extract
Place all ingredients in a tall glass and stir vigorously, pour into a fresh glass, garnish with a little fresh grated nutmeg and serve.

Contribution By: Sara Robinson

Bombs Away!

8.4fl.oz Lemon Lime Soda or Sparkling Water
1fl.oz/ 30ml Grenadine
1fl.oz/ 30ml Lime or Lemon Juice
2 Strawberries, to garnish
Mix all together in a tall glass. Pour over ice and garnish with strawberries.

Contribution By: Sara Robinson

The Black Point or Rock your Universe

REDACTED

Fresh Raspberry Kir

Non-Alcoholic

Ingredients
3oz/ 85g Raspberries
1 teaspoon/ 0.16fl.oz/ 5ml Lemon Juice
Sparkling Apple Juice.

Purée raspberries and lemon juice in a blender. Strain through a fine sieve. Add about 2 Tablespoons/ 1fl.oz/ 30ml to a tall glass and then top up the glass with about 8fl.oz/ 237ml of sparkling apple juice. Add ice cubes, fresh raspberries and maybe some mint leaves to garnish.
(Add a little sugar if the raspberries are overly tart.)

Contribution By: Sara McKenna

ELDERFLOWER CORDIAL

Non-Alcoholic

Ingredients:
88oz/ 2 ½kg Granulated Sugar
2 Lemons
20 fresh Elderflower Heads, stalks trimmed, and well cleaned
2.9oz/ 85g Citric Acid
1.5 litres Water

Put the water and sugar in a large heavy-based saucepan and bring gradually to the boil, stirring occasionally. Use a vegetable peeler to remove the peel from the lemons. Slice the pared lemons into rounds. Put the lemons, peel and elderflowers into a large bowl and then pour the syrup over the flowers and lemon and stir in the citric acid. Stir until well combined. Cover and put aside for 24 hours. Strain through a tea-towel in a colander to remove all the bits. Squish the bits to get all the lemon juice etc out. Pour into sterilised bottles. Will keep for about 2 months in the fridge and can also be frozen

Contribution By: Sara McKenna

RASPBERRY LEMONADE CORDIAL

Non-Alcoholic

Ingredients:
Juice and Zest of 4 Lemons and 1 Lime
7oz/ 200g Raspberries
4.7oz/ 135g Caster Sugar
12.6fl.oz/ 375 ml Water

Zest your lemons and lime before juicing them. Add all to a small saucepan. Add in your raspberries, sugar and water. Over low heat stir until the mixture is heated through and the sugar has dissolved. You should not boil the mixture at any point. Pass the mixture through a sieve. Let the mixture cool completely and bottle. The cordial will keep in the fridge for a couple of weeks.

Contribution By: Afton Cochran

RHUBARB CORDIAL

Non-Alcoholic

Ingredients:
1lb/ 453g Rhubarb, washed and cut into 2-inch chunks
2 cups/ 14.1oz/ 400g Caster Sugar
2 to 3 Tablespoons/ 1 to 1.5fl.oz/ 30 to 45ml Honey
4 cups/ 32fl.oz/ 946ml Water
1 small piece of Cinnamon Stick or
    1 teaspoon/ 0.14oz/ 4g Ground Cinnamon
1 Vanilla Pod sliced lengthways or
    1 teaspoon/ 0.16fl.oz/ 5ml Vanilla Paste
A small splash of Lemon Juice (optional)

Put everything in a large heavy based pan and bring to the boil. Stir occasionally. Reduce heat and simmer for 15 minutes until it has slightly thickened, and all the sugar crystals have dissolved. Cool for 5 to 10 minutes. Strain and then bottle in sterilised bottles. Lovely and refreshing when diluted with soda water. Keep it in the fridge and use within 1 month.

For a clearer cordial use the cinnamon stick and vanilla bean and have care not to squeeze the cooked rhubarb too much. Either way it is delicious!

Contribution By: Sara McKenna

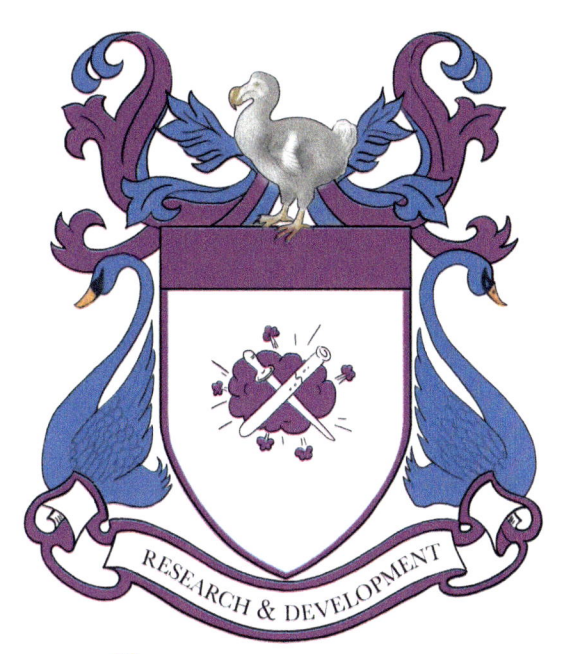

Chapter Nine:
R&D Department
or What To Do If You Don't Have All The Ingredients
Please Remember That All Of This Is Experimental And We Take No Responsibility For The Consequences

Recipes:

Vanilla Extract and **Candied Citrus Peel**	188
Cake Flour and **Self Raising Flour**	188 to 189
Caster Sugar and **Golden Syrup**	189
Icing Sugar and **Buttercream** and **Icing**	190 to 191
Salted Caramel	191
Quick and Easy Breads and what you can make from them	192 to 193

Dinner Rolls, Iced Fingers, Chelsea Buns, Cinnamon Rolls, Pesto Whirls and Gorgeous Bread

Spice Mixes — 194 to 197

Pumpkin Pie Spice, Apple Pie Spice, Mixed Spice, Soup Spice, Italian Seasoning, Creole Spice, Cajun Spice, Sazon Spice, Caribbean Curry Seasoning, Markham's Season All, Onion Seasoning, Poultry Seasoning, Mild Curry Powder, Mexican Spice Blends, Better Than Spice

Vegetable Bouillon Powder	197
Oven Dried Tomatoes	198
Sauces	198 to 200

Worcestershire Sauce, Stone Ground Mustard, Brown Sauce, Piccalilli, Mushroom Ketchup

Jam Sugar	201
Jams and Chutney	201 to 202

Red Chilli Jam, Vanilla Rhubarb Jam, Marmalade, Lemon Curd, Apple and Cranberry Chutney

Pesto Sauce and **Cornflour Slurry**	203
Italian Sausage and **Sour Cream**	203
Cabbage Bomb	204

Vanilla Extract

Extracts such as Vanilla Extract are expensive to buy and vary in quality. This is quick, easy and so much cheaper then buying it. Plus, there are so many different flavours that can be used!

Ingredients:
4 Whole Vanilla Pods
1 cup/ 8oz/ 237ml Hard Alcohol such as Vodka, Rum, Bourbon, or Whiskey
1 cup/ 8oz/ 237ml Bottle with a good fitting stopper or lid.

Carefully use a sharp knife to split the vanilla bean lengthways. You may also need to cut the pods in half depending on the size of your jar. Place the vanilla pod pieces into the jar and pour the spirits over the pods. Place the lid on the bottle and let sit in a cool dry place out of direct sunlight for 6 to 8 weeks. To help the flavour disperse, give the bottle a gentle shake a few times a week. Extracts will last years if stored correctly.

Other Extract Flavouring Ideas
½ cup Coffee Beans, ½ cup Blanched Almonds, Zest from 2 Lemons, Zest from 1 Orange, ½ cup Fresh Coconut, 4 Cinnamon Sticks and so much more!

Contribution By: Sara Robinson

Candied Citrus Peel

Ingredients:
4 Large Unwaxed Oranges or 2 Grapefruit, or 2 Oranges and 2 Lemons
1 ¼ cups/ 10.1fl.oz/ 300ml Water or as needed to cover the peel
1 ½ cups/ 10.5oz/ 300g Caster Sugar or as needed in ratio to water

Cut the fruit into wedges, then scoop out the flesh leaving about less than ¼ inch or about 5mm thickness of peel and pith. Cut each wedge into thin strips. Put the peel in a small pan and cover with cold water. Bring to the boil then simmer for 10 mins, this takes a lot of the bitterness out of the treat. Drain, return to the pan and re-cover with fresh water. Bring to the boil, then simmer for 20 mins. Set a sieve over a bowl and drain the peel, reserving the cooking water. Add 100g sugar to each 100ml water you have. Pour into a pan and gently heat, stirring to dissolve the sugar. Add the peel and simmer for an additional 20 mins until the peel is translucent and soft. Be careful to keep the temperature low as you are not aiming to make caramel. Leave the peel to cool in the syrup, then remove with a slotted spoon and arrange in one layer on a wire rack set over a baking sheet. Put in the oven at the lowest setting for 30 mins to dry. Toss with caster sugar to coat a few pieces at a time.
Store in an airtight container out of direct sunlight for up to 2 months.

Contribution By: Sara Robinson

Cake Flour or Soft Flour

Cake Flour is a low protein flour, 8% or less, that is used in the creation of cakes and baked goods. Mostly you should be able to substitute in Plain Flour, but if that is not an option please follow this recipe.

In Metric and Imperial, it is:
3.7oz/ 105g Plain Flour
0.7oz/ 20g Cornflour

For cups it is a little different:
Measure 1 cup of Plain Flour. Then remove 2 Tablespoons of flour from that cup and replace them with 2 Tablespoons of Cornflour so that the filling of the cup is never exceeded.

Use for every 1 cup/ 4.4oz/ 125g of cake flour in your favorite recipe.

Contribution By: Sara Robinson

Self Raising Flour

We understand that not everyone has access to Self-Raising Flour and some countries put salt in it! Very despicable!

Ingredients:
2 teaspoons/ 0.34 oz/ 9.8g of Baking Powder
1 cup/ 7.6oz/ 220g Plain Flour

Mix enough for a recipe or store in an airtight jar away from direct sunlight. Use in recipes calling for self-raising flour. If you have self raising flour but it's a bit elderly and you are unsure if the raising agent is still active then add 1/4 to 1/2 tsp of baking powder per 100g flour to the recipe.

Contribution By: Sara Robinson

Caster Sugar

Not every white granulated sugar has such fine sugar crystals as Caster Sugar. With a little luck it is easy to make your own!

Ingredients:
White Granulated Sugar

Add 1 cup of white granulated sugar to a blender jar, and close the lid
Pulse the blender 5 or 6 times but not enough to make it turn to powder
Wait for the dust to settle in the blending jar
Open the jar and measure or weigh the sugar for your recipe, or store in a airtight container away from direct sunlight.

Contribution By: Sara Robinson

Golden Syrup

Golden Syrup has so many uses! We put it on pancakes, waffles, toast, porridge and use it in recipes, just to name a few!

Ingredients:
First:
½ cup/ 4oz/ 115g Caster Sugar
¼ cup/ 2fl.oz/ 60ml Water
Second:
2 ¼ cup/ 18oz/ 507g Caster Sugar
1 ½ cup/ 10.5fl.oz/ 300ml Boiling Water
1 Tablespoon Lemon Juice or 1 Thick Slice of Lemon, pipped

This is something that must always be attended while cooking! In a medium to large size saucepan heat the 115g caster sugar with the 60ml water over a medium to low heat until all the sugar has dissolved. Bring the temperature up slightly to a simmer to form a nice caramel with a beautiful golden colour, usually 8 to 10 minutes. Add the remaining sugar and slowly add the remaining water and lemon juice/slice. The sugar will clump a little but whisk the mixture and continue heating to dissolve the lumps.
On medium low heat, simmer the mixture for about 15 to 20 minutes. You are looking for a rich amber colour and a thicker consistency. Remove from the heat, remove the lemon slice and allow to cool completely in the pan. The syrup will continue to thicken as the mixture cools. When cool, pour into a well-sealing jar and store at room temperature away from direct sunlight for up to 3 months. Note: If the mixture is too thick, gently heat it again dissolving a little water into the mixture. If the mixture is too thin, gently heat it and dissolving in a little additional sugar.

(Adapted from Bigger Bolder Baking)   Contribution By: Sara Robinson

Icing Sugar

Ingredients:
2 ½ cups/ 17.6oz/ 500g Granulated Sugar
1 teaspoon/ 0.08oz/ 2.3g Cornflour/ Corn Starch

Pulse the blender a few times long enough to turn the sugar into powder. Wait for the dust to settle in the blending jar. Open the jar and measure or weigh the sugar for your recipe, or store in a airtight container away from direct sunlight.

Contribution By: Sara Robinson

Italian Buttercream

Ingredients:
1 cup/ 8oz/ 227g Granulated Sugar
½ cup/ 4oz/ 114g Water
Pinch of Salt
4 Large/ 132g Egg Whites
1 ½ cups/ 12oz/ 340g Butter at room temperature
1 tsp/ 5ml Vanilla Extract or other flavoured extract

This is easiest done with a stand mixer but can be done working in a team with a hand whisk. It is also a good idea to have all ingredients measured and waiting before you start putting everything together.

On the hob, mix the water and sugar in a saucepan with a lid and bring to a boil over medium heat. Keep boiling with the lid on for 2 to 3 minutes to ensure that all the sugar has been dissolved, as this will give the frosting a creamier consistency. Remove the lid and continue cooking until the syrup reaches 240°F/ 115°C. Whip the egg whites to soft peaks, adding the salt to the whites. Slowly start pouring the sugar solution into the whipped egg whites. This is much easier to do in a stand mixer with a steady trickle of syrup into the whipping egg whites on low speed. Continue whipping the eggs and sugar mixture until it reaches stiff peaks. Cool the mixture in the refrigerator for 15 minutes. After the mixture is cooled bring it back out and add the butter and vanilla. Whip it for as long as needed, it really will come together and be a lovely smooth frosting. Store in the fridge in an air-tight container and bring back to room temperature before icing a cake.
Makes 4 cups of buttercream.

Contribution By: Sara Robinson

Swiss Meringue Buttercream

Ingredients:
4/ 4oz/ 114g Fresh Egg Whites
1 cup/ 8oz/ 227g Sugar
1 ½ cups/ 12oz/ 340g Butter, unsalted
1 teaspoon/ 5ml Vanilla Extract or other flavour of extract
¼ teaspoon Salt

In a medium saucepan fill with about 2 inches/ 5cm of water and bring to a simmer. Place egg whites and sugar into the bowl and place the bowl over the simmering water. The bowl should not touch the water. Whisk mixture to combine and continue whisking every 30 seconds or so to distribute the heat evenly. If you don't whisk you could scramble the eggs, which is gross and you will have to start again. Once the mixture reaches 110°F/ 43°C or the sugar has dissolved so that you can no longer feel any granules in between your fingers, it is done. Be careful, the mixture will be hot. Move the mixture to a stand mixer with the whisk attachment. Whisk on high until you reach stiff glossy peaks of meringue. Cool quickly in the refrigerator for 10 to 15 minutes. Bring the cooled mixture back out and begin whipping again adding extract, salt and small chunks of butter slowly to the mixture. Continue whipping until the buttercream is fluffy and creamy. Makes 4 cups of buttercream.

Contribution By: Sara Robinson

Easy Icing

Ingredients:
2 cups/ 8oz/ 227g Icing Sugar
Pinch of Salt
2 Tablespoons/ 1oz/ 30g Butter, unsalted and melted
1 teaspoon/ 0.16fl.oz/ 5ml Vanilla Extract
2 to 3 Tablespoons/ 1 to 1.5fl.oz/ 30 to 45ml Whole Milk or Cream

Whisk together the icing ingredients. Add milk a little at a time so as to make a thick but spreadable icing. Continue whisking until well combined and smooth.
This is perfect for iced buns, Chelsea buns and cinnamon rolls.

Contribution By: Sara Robinson

American Buttercream

Ingredients:
1 cup/ 8oz/ 227g Shortening, at room temperature
1 cup/ 8oz/ 227g Butter, at room temperature
2 teaspoons Vanilla Extract or other flavour of extract
6 cups plus 3 Tablespoons/ 32oz/ 907g Icing Sugar
2 Tablespoons/ 1fl.oz/ 30ml Milk or Water
¼ teaspoon Salt

Beat together the butter and shortening until smooth and well combined. Gradually add in the sugar and salt, beating well so as not to create lumps. Keep beating until it is white and fluffy in texture. If the mixture is becoming too stiff slowly add in the milk a little at a time. Beat until perfectly smooth. Store in an air-tight container in the fridge but remember to bring it to room temperature before beginning to ice a cake.
Makes 6 cups of buttercream.

Contribution By: Sara Robinson

Golden Dreams

HEALTH & SAFETY REDACTED

Salted Caramel

Ingredients:
2 Tablespoons/ 1oz/ 30g Butter
½ cup/ 3.7oz/ 105g Dark Brown Sugar
¼ cup/ 2fl.oz/ 60ml Double Cream
¼ teaspoon/ 0.07oz/ 2g Sea Salt or to taste
½ teaspoon/ 0.07oz/ 2g Vanilla Paste or
1 teaspoon/ 0.07oz/ 2g Vanilla Extract

Whisk everything except the vanilla and salt in a heavy based saucepan and heat gently over low heat until the butter melts. Slowly increase the heat until the mixture comes to a boil. When it hits boiling point, reduce the heat and simmer for 5 minutes, whisking occasionally to ensure there are no hot spots that might burn. Remove from the heat and mix in your vanilla, and then allow to cool for a couple of minutes. The mixture will be extremely hot! Be careful, this can cause extreme burns if you get it on your skin. Add your salt, remember that the salt taste will increase as the mixture cools.

This is phenomenal when you whisk double cream to stiff peaks and stir into the caramel, once it has slightly cooled. Other ideas are to pour over a cake, swirl through brownies, swirl through cream for ice cream, there are so many more options!

Contribution By: Sara McKenna

Bread

Bread is one of the fundamental foods that has nourished the rich and the poor for a millennia or longer. Bread is also a very versatile food being able to be transformed into so many different sweet and savoury foods.

Incredibly Quick Bread

Ingredients:

1 ½ cups/ 12fl.oz/ 355ml Warm Water
2 Tablespoons/ 0.88oz/ 25g Granulated Sugar
2 sachets of Instant Yeast (4 ½ teaspoons/ 0.5oz/ 14g)
2 Tablespoons/ 0.9oz/ 28g Butter, softened
1 teaspoon/ 0.17oz/ 5g Sea Salt
4 cups/ 16.9oz/ 480g Plain Flour

In a small bowl add water, sugar and yeast. Stir the contents lightly and allow to sit for 5 minutes or until the mixture is frothy.

While the yeast is activating, measure butter, salt and half of the flour into a large bowl.

This recipe works well in a stand mixer with a dough hook or as a good workout with muscle power. Mix the yeast mixture with the contents of the bowl. Then slowly start adding the flour until the dough is well combined and slightly sticky. Knead on medium speed for a further five minutes.

Cover the bowl, there is no need to transfer to another, with oiled film and leave to rise for 20 minutes.

Contribution By: Sara McKenna

Breads can use an 'egg wash' (1 well beaten egg with a splash milk or water), whole milk, melted butter or a very light dusting of flour as a 'wash' or coating on the outside, applied just before baking to make a gorgeous crust!

Easy Basic Bread

Ingredients:

2 ½ cups/ 12.7oz/ 360g Strong Flour
½ cup/ 2.1oz/ 60g Plain Flour or Wholemeal Flour
2 Tablespoons/ 1 oz/ 30g Butter, softened
¾ Tablespoon/ 0.3oz/ 10g Sugar
¾ teaspoon/ 0.17oz/ 5g Salt
2 1/4 teaspoons/ 0.24oz/ 7g Dry Yeast
½ cup/ 4.5fl.oz/ 133ml Warm Water
½ cup 4.5fl.oz/ 133ml Warm Milk

In a large bowl whisk flour, sugar, salt and yeast together. Add butter, warm water and warm milk to the flour mixture and mix well. Using a mixer with a dough hook continue, to mix for 5 to 10 minutes allowing gluten to form for a better bread texture. By hand you can continue to mix in the bowl with your hands or better still, transfer the dough to a lightly floured surface and continue to knead for 10 to 15 minutes. Place the dough in a well-oiled bowl and allow to double in size. This will depend on the temperature of your kitchen but 35 minutes to an 1 hour as a general rule. This time allows a lot of flavour to be produced in the bread dough. Punch the dough down kneading it a few times on your lightly floured surface and shape the dough to desired final product.

Both of these bread recipes can be shaped into dinner rolls, iced fingers, cinnamon rolls, Chelsea buns, hamburger buns, finger rolls, batons, or loaves of gorgeous bread.

Contribution By: Sara Robinson

Dinner Rolls

Grease a 9inch/ 228mm square dish with melted butter.
Punch down the dough and divide into 15 to 20 equal pieces. Gently form into balls and place in the dish. They should be snug, but not tight. Brush with a little melted butter, and sprinkle with good sea salt. Cover, let rise for a further 20 minutes for Quick and 35 minutes for Basic or until doubled in size. Preheat your oven to 400°F/ 200°C/ Gas Mark 6. Bake for 15 to 20 minutes till golden. Brush with plenty of melted butter for a really lovely tear apart dinner roll.

Iced Fingers

Grease a 9inch/ 228mm square dish with melted butter. Cut dough into 8 to 16 equal pieces and form finger shapes. Brush lightly with butter with a tiny bit of vanilla mixed in. Cover and let rise for 20 minutes for Quick and 35 minutes for Basic or until it has doubled in size. Preheat your oven to 400°F/ 200°C/ Gas Mark 6. Bake for 15 to 20 minutes till golden. Allow to cool and ice.

Chelsea Bun

Butter a 9inch/ 228mm dish. After the first rise, gently roll out your dough to about ¼ inch/ 5mm and brush with butter. Sprinkle with light brown sugar, some sultanas, orange peel, mixed spice/ apple pie spice and cinnamon. Take care not to overload the roll. Roll up from the widest edge and roll toward you until all of the filling is in the roll and the end is tucked under the roll. Cut into 16 equal pieces or about 1 inch/ 26mm wide. Put in the buttered dish snuggly but not tightly. Cover and rise for 20 minutes for Quick and 35 minutes for Basic or until it has doubled in size.
Preheat your oven to 400°F/ 200°C/ Gas Mark 6. Bake for 15 to 20 minutes till golden. While still hot, brush well with melted apricot jam. Allow to cool and drizzle with a runny icing with a splash of orange essence.

Cinnamon Rolls

Butter a 9inch/ 228mm dish. After the first rise, gently roll out your dough to about ¼ inch/ 5mm and brush with butter. Sprinkle with dark brown sugar, some sultanas, chopped walnuts or pecans and cinnamon. Take care not to overload the roll. Roll up from the widest edge and roll toward you until all of the filling is in the roll and the end is tucked under the roll. Cut into 16 equal pieces or about 1 inch/ 26mm wide. Put in the buttered dish snuggly but not tightly. Cover and rise for 20 minutes for Quick and 35 minutes for Basic or until it has doubled in size.
Preheat your oven to 400°F/ 200°C/ Gas Mark 6. Bake for 15 to 20 minutes till golden. While still warm, drizzle with vanilla or caramel icing. Allow to cool and enjoy.

Pesto Swirls

Oil a 9inch/ 228mm dish. After the first rise, gently roll out your dough to about ¼ inch/5mm and brush with pesto sauce. Sprinkle with fine grated Parmesan cheese and chopped pine nuts. Take care not to overload the roll. Roll up from the widest edge and roll toward you until all of the filling is in the roll and the end is tucked under the roll. Cut into 16 equal pieces or about 1 inch/ 26mm wide. Put in the buttered dish snuggly but not tightly. Cover and let rise for 20 minutes for Quick and 35 minutes for Basic or until it has doubled in size. Sprinkle a little additional cheese across the top of the buns.
Preheat your oven to 400°F/ 200°C/ Gas Mark 6. Bake for 15 to 20 minutes till golden. Allow to cool and enjoy.

Gorgeous Bread Loaf

Oil a loaf tin with melted butter or other neutral oil.
Punch down the dough and roll into a smooth shape before placing it in the prepared tin. The dough should be snug, but not tight. Brush with a little melted butter. Cover, let rise for a further 20 minutes for Quick and 35 minutes for Basic or until it has doubled in size. Gently paint the top of the loaf with a little added butter or a well beaten egg. Preheat your oven to 400°F/ 200°C/ Gas Mark 6. Bake for 25 to 35 minutes till golden. Well baked bread should give a hollow sound when tapped from the bottom. Cool completely before slicing.

Bread can be shaped into so many things!

Contribution By: Sara McKenna and Sara Robinson

Pumpkin Pie Spice

Ingredients:
3 ½ Tablespoons/ 1.5oz/ 43g Ground Cinnamon
2 teaspoons/ 0.14oz/ 4g Ground Ginger
1 ½ teaspoons/ 0.1oz/ 3g Ground Nutmeg
1 teaspoon/0.07oz/ 2g Ground Allspice
1 teaspoon/0.07oz/ 2g Ground Cloves

Mix all together and store for up to 6 months in an airtight container away from direct sunlight.

The spice is delicious in so many sweet treats!

Contribution By: Sara Robinson

Apple Pie Spice

Ingredients:
4 ½ Tablespoons/ 2oz/ 57g Ground Cinnamon
1 ½ teaspoons/ 0.1oz/ 3g Ground Nutmeg
½ teaspoon/0.03oz/ 1g Ground Allspice
1 ½ teaspoons/0.1oz/ 3g Ground Ginger
1 ½ teaspoons/0.07oz/ 2g Ground Cardamom

Mix all together and store for up to 6 months in an airtight container away from direct sunlight.

The spice is lush in so many sweet treats!

Contribution By: Sara Robinson

Mixed Spice

Ingredients:
1 ½ Tablespoons/ 0.3oz/ 6g Ground Cinnamon
2 teaspoons/0.14oz/ 4g Ground Allspice
2 teaspoons/ 0.14oz/ 4g Ground Nutmeg
1 teaspoon/0.07oz/ 2g Ground Cloves
1 teaspoon/ 0.07oz/ 2g Ground Ginger
1 teaspoon/ 0.07oz/ 2g Ground Coriander
3/4 teaspoon/0.03oz/ 1g Ground Mace

Mix all together and store for up to 6 months in an airtight container away from direct sunlight.

The spice is yummy in so many sweet treats!

Contribution By: Sara Robinson

Soup Spice

Ingredients:
1 Tablespoon/ 0.29oz/ 8g Ground Cumin
1 Tablespoon/ 0.21oz/ 6g Ground Coriander
½ Tablespoon/ 0.1oz / 3g Ground Ginger

Mix all together and store for up to 6 months in an airtight container away from direct sunlight.

The spice is so tasty in savoury soups!

Contribution By: Caroline Price

Italian Seasoning

Ingredients:
2 Tablespoons/ 0.14oz/ 4g Dried Basil
2 Tablespoons/ 0.14oz/ 4g Dried Oregano
1 Tablespoon/ 0.1oz/ 3g Dried Rosemary
2 Tablespoons/ 0.07oz/ 2g Dried Parsley
1 Tablespoon/ 0.1oz/ 3g Dried Thyme
1 ½ teaspoons/ 0.14oz/ 4g Garlic Powder
1 ½ teaspoons/ 0.14oz/ 4g Onion Powder

Mix all together and store for up to 6 months in an airtight container away from direct sunlight.

The seasoning is delicious in soups and stews, your favourite pasta dish, in scrambled eggs and as a seasoning on chips/fries, or as a seasoning on fish.

Contribution By: Sara Robinson

Creole Spice

Ingredients:
1 Tablespoon/ 0.07/ 2g Thyme
2 teaspoons/ 0.1oz/ 3g Dried Basil
2 teaspoons/ 0.4oz/ 12g Salt
1 Tablespoon/ 0.7oz/ 20g Onion Granules
1 teaspoon/ 0.21oz/ 6g Smoked Paprika
1 Tablespoon/ 0.17oz/ 5g Dried Oregano
2 teaspoons/ 0.17oz/ 5g Ground Black Pepper
2 Tablespoons/ 1.4oz/ 40g Garlic Granules
2 Tablespoon/ 1oz/ 30g Sweet Paprika
1 Tablespoon/ 0.35oz/ 10g Cayenne (hot) or Mild Chilli Powder

Grind all ingredients together in a blender jar and store for up to 6 months in an airtight container away from direct sunlight. This spice mix is a flavour bomb! Use it in gumbo, jambalaya, soups and stews, eggs, salad vinaigrette, as a meat rub, shrimp and fish dishes, grilled chops, in burgers, on popcorn, sprinkled on roasted potatoes or on rice or roasted vegetables.

Contribution By: Merry Schepers

Cajun Seasoning

Ingredients:
1 ½ Tablespoons/ 0.38oz/ 11g Paprika
2 teaspoons/ 0.4oz/ 12g Salt, or to taste
2 teaspoons/ 0.17oz/ 5g Garlic Powder
2 teaspoons/ 0.17oz/ 5g Onion Powder
1 teaspoon/ 0.02oz/ 0.6g Oregano, dried
1 teaspoon/ 0.03oz/ 1g Thyme dried
1 teaspoon/ 0.07oz/ 2g Black Pepper
1 teaspoon/ 0.07oz/ 2g Cayenne Pepper, or to taste

Mix all ingredients together and store for up to 6 months in an airtight container away from direct sunlight.

The seasoning is delicious in soups and stews, your favourite pasta dish, in scrambled eggs and as a seasoning on chips/fries, or as a seasoning on fish.

Contribution By: Sara Robinson

Sazon Seasoning

Ingredients:
1 Tablespoon/ 0.17oz/ 5g Ground Coriander
1 Tablespoon/ 0.21oz/ 6g Ground Cumin
1 Tablespoons/ 0.21oz/ 6g Ground Annatto or Paprika
½ Tablespoon/ 0.1oz/ 3g Ground Turmeric
1 Tablespoon/ 0.21oz/ 6g Garlic Granules
1 ¼ Tablespoons/ 0.81oz/ 23g Salt
2 teaspoons/ 0.07oz/ 2g Dried Oregano
1 teaspoon/ 0.07oz/ 2g White Pepper
½ teaspoon/ 0.03oz/ 1g Cayenne Pepper (optional)

Mix all together and store for up to 6 months in an airtight container away from direct sunlight.

The seasoning is delicious in soups and stews, your favourite Cuban or Caribbean dish, in scrambled eggs and as a seasoning on chips/fries, or as a seasoning on fish, chicken or pork.

Contribution By: Sara Robinson

Caribbean Curry Seasoning

Ingredients:
3 Tablespoons/ 0.63oz/ 18g Ground Turmeric
1 Tablespoon/ 0.21oz/ 6g Ground Cumin
¾ Tablespoon/ 0.14oz/ 4g Ground Coriander
2½ teaspoons/ 0.31oz/ 9g Ground Fenugreek
2 teaspoons/ 0.14oz/ 4g Allspice
2 teaspoons/ 0.14oz/ 4g Ground Ginger
½ teaspoon/ 0.03oz/ 1g Ground Nutmeg
¼ teaspoon/ 0.01oz/ 0.3g Ground Cinnamon
¼ teaspoon/ 0.01oz/ 0.3g Ground Cloves
½ teaspoon/ 0.03oz/ 1g Garlic Granules
1 teaspoon/ 0.03oz/ 1g Dried Thyme
2 teaspoons/ 0.14oz/ 4g Ground Mustard
1½ teaspoons/ 0.1oz/ 3g Ground White Pepper
½ teaspoon/ 0.03oz/ 1g Cayenne Pepper

Mix all together and store for up to 6 months in an airtight container away from direct sunlight.

The seasoning is delicious in soups and stews, your favourite Caribbean dish, in scrambled eggs and as a seasoning on chips/fries, or as a seasoning on fish, chicken or goat.

Contribution By: Sara Robinson

Markham's Steak Rub or Season All

Ever wonder how Markham makes some of the worst glop taste amazing? Well this might be some of his secret to success. A little pinch here or there can take the ordinary to extraordinary!

Ingredients:
2 Tablespoons/ 0.5oz/ 14g Fresh Ground Black Pepper
2 Tablespoons/ 0.49oz/ 14g Garlic Powder
2 Tablespoons/ 1.2oz/ 36g Kosher Salt
2 Tablespoons/ 0.5oz/ 14g Sweet or Spanish Paprika
1 Tablespoon/ 0.25oz/ 7g Onion Powder
1 Tablespoon/ 0.1oz/ 3g Dried Dill Weed
1 Tablespoon/ 0.1oz/ 3g Dried Pepper Flakes (Aleppo or Ancho) or ½ Tablespoon of Hot Pepper Flakes

Mix all ingredients together in a bowl. Store in an airtight container away from direct sun light. It is great on egg, potatoes, meats and fish.

It also is perfect to keep in a little tin in your pocket while you are on assignment. You know … to add to a bubbling pot … preferably when no one is looking.

Contribution By: Merry Schepers

Onion Seasoning

Ingredients:
2 teaspoons/ 0.28oz/ 8g Parsley
2 Tablespoons/ 0.98oz/ 28g Celery Salt
2 Tablespoons/ 0.49oz/ 14g Garlic Powder
3 Tablespoons/ 0.74oz/ 21g Onion Powder

Mix all together and store for up to 6 months in an airtight container away from direct sunlight.
The seasoning is delicious in mashed potatoes, across toasted bread as garlic toast, as a seasoning on chips/fries, or as a seasoning on steaks or fish.

Contribution By: Sara Robinson

Poultry Seasoning

Ingredients:
1 ½ Tablespoons/ 0.24oz/ 7g Ground Sage
1 Tablespoon/ 0.17oz/ 5g Ground Thyme
1 teaspoon/ 0.03oz/ 1g Ground Marjoram
2 teaspoons/ 0.07oz/ 2g Ground Rosemary
¼ teaspoon/ pinch Ground Nutmeg
½ teaspoon/ 0.03oz/ 1g Ground Bay Leaf
½ teaspoon/ 0.03oz/ 1g White Pepper
½ teaspoon/ 0.03oz/ 1g Black Pepper

Mix all together and store for up to 6 months in an airtight container away from direct sunlight. Works well in soups and stews, stir fry, fried chicken and so much more!

Contribution By: Sara Robinson

Mild Curry Powder

Ingredients:
4 Tablespoons/ 0.84oz/ 24g Ground Coriander Seeds
2 Tablespoons/ 0.98oz/ 28g Ground Cumin Seeds
1 ½ Tablespoons/ 0.49oz/ 14g Ground Turmeric
1 ½ teaspoons/ 0.1oz/ 3g Ground Dry Ginger
1 teaspoon/ 0.07oz/ 2g Ground Dry Mustard
2 teaspoons/ 0.28oz/ 8g Fenugreek Powder
1 teaspoon/ 0.07oz/ 2g Ground Black Pepper
1 teaspoon/ 0.07oz/ 2g Ground Cinnamon
½ teaspoon/ 0.03oz/ 1g Ground Cloves
¼ teaspoon/ 0.03oz/ 1g Allspice
½ teaspoon/ 0.02oz/ 1g Ground Cardamom
¼ teaspoon/ 0.02oz/ 1g Cayenne Pepper (optional)

Mix all together and store for up to 6 months in an airtight container away from direct sunlight.

The seasoning is delicious in soups and stews, your favourite Indian dish, in scrambled eggs and as a seasoning on chips/fries, or as a seasoning on fish or chicken.

Contribution By: Sara Robinson

Mexican Spice Mixes

US Style Chilli Powder

Ingredients:
2 teaspoons/ 0.31oz/ 9g Crushed Chilli Flakes
2 teaspoons/ 0.38oz/ 11g Ground Cumin
2 teaspoons/ 0.1oz/ 3g Oregano
2 teaspoons/ 0.35oz/ 10g Garlic Granules
2 teaspoons/ 0.35oz/ 10g Onion Granules
1 teaspoon/ 0.21oz/ 6g Ground Allspice
1/8 teaspoon/ 0.03oz/ 1g Ground Cloves
2 Tablespoons/ 1.2oz/ 35g Paprika
¼ teaspoon/ 0.03oz/ 1g Cayenne Pepper

Fajita Seasoning

Ingredients:
* 4 Tablespoons/ 1.4oz/ 40g US Style Chilli Powder
* 1 Tablespoon/ 0.4oz/ 12g Ground Black Pepper
* 1 Tablespoon/ 0.5oz/ 15g Garlic Granules
* 2 Tablespoons/ 0.7oz/ 20g Ground Cinnamon
* 1 Tablespoon/ 0.28oz/ 8g Ginger

Taco Seasoning

Ingredients:
2 Tablespoons/ 0.24g/ 7g Basil
1 Tablespoon/ 0.56oz/ 16g Onion Granules
1 Tablespoon/ 0.56oz/ 16g Garlic Granules
1 Tablespoon/ 0.07oz/ 2g Oregano
1 teaspoon/ 0.017oz/ 0.5g Thyme
2 Tablespoons/ 0.74oz/ 21g Ground Cumin
7 Tablespoons/ 2.2oz/ 64g US Style Chilli Powder
½ teaspoon/ 0.03oz/ 1g Ground White Pepper
3 Tablespoons/ 1.1oz/ 32g Sweet Paprika
2 teaspoons/ 0.21oz/ 6g Ground Cinnamon
2 Tablespoons/ 0.95oz/ 27g Salt

* 2 Tablespoons/ 0.7oz/ 20g Smoked Paprika
* 1 Tablespoon/ 0.5oz/ 15g Onion Granules
* 1 Tablespoon/ 0.07oz/ 2g Oregano
* 2 Tablespoons/ 1.9oz/ 55g Salt
* ½ Tablespoon/ 0.17oz/ 5g Cayenne Pepper

Grind all ingredients together in a blender jar and store for up to 6 months in an airtight container away from direct sunlight.

Contribution By: Sara Robinson

Better Than S£% Spice

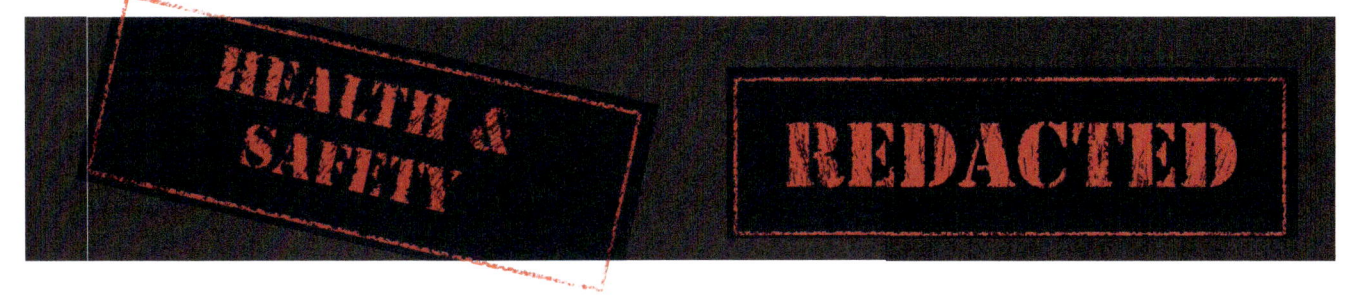

HEALTH & SAFETY REDACTED

Vegetable Bouillon Powder

This gorgeous mixture can be used in a pinch for Chicken or Vegetable Bouillon, and has none of the icky extras store bought bouillon has!

Ingredients:
2 cups/ 3.1oz/ 90g Nutritional Yeast
¼ cup/ 2.5oz/ 72g Salt
¼ cup/ 1oz/ 30g Garlic Granules
¼ cup/ 1oz/ 30g Onion Granules
3 Tablespoons/ 0.31oz/ 9g Dried Basil
3 Tablespoons/ 0.31oz/ 9g Dried Oregano
2 Tablespoons/ 0.24oz/ 7g Dried Rosemary
2 Tablespoons/ 0.1oz/ 3g Dried Parsley
1 Tablespoon/ 0.24oz/ 7g Black Pepper
1 Tablespoon/ 0.1oz/ 3g Dried Thyme
1 Dried Bay Leaf

Place all ingredients into a blender and pulse until it is very finely ground. Place the combined ingredients into an airtight container. Store away from direct sunlight.
To make broth:
use 1 tablespoon of powder mixed well into 1 cup/ 8oz hot water

Contribution By: Sara Robinson

Flaming Swan

HEALTH & SAFETY

REDACTED

Oven Dried Tomatoes

These little nuggets are pure gold! Tasty and take ordinary things to new heights. Use them in pasta, salads and even eat them plain as a snack.

Ingredients
8.8oz/ 250g Ripe Plum or Cherry Tomatoes
½ teaspoon/ 0.07oz/ 2g Sea Salt
A little olive oil for greasing the pan.

Preheat oven to 470 °F/240 °C (220 °C fan)/ gas mark 9
Cut the tomatoes in half lengthways by cutting through the stem end. Lightly oil a small roasting pan or rimmed cookie sheet. Place tomatoes cut side down and season with salt and roast for 15 minutes. Reduce the heat to 300 °F/ 150 °C (fan 130 °C)/ Gas Mark 2. Continue roasting the tomatoes for an additional 60 to 90 minutes depending on the size of the fruit. Tomatoes will shrink to about half their starting size but still be spongy in the middle.
Cool completely and store in an airtight container in the refrigerator for up to a week.

Contribution By: Sara Robinson

Worcestershire Sauce

Nothing beats homemade! Hands down this is the best sauce you have ever eaten!

Ingredients
2 Tablespoons/ 1fl.oz/ 30 ml Neutral Oil,
    with a high smoke point
4 Tablespoons/ 2.1oz/ 60g Mustard Seed
2 teaspoons/ 0.35oz/ 10g Whole Peppercorn
1 Stick Cinnamon,
    or ½ teaspoon/ 0.1oz/ 3g Ground Cinnamon
1 teaspoon/ 0.17oz/ 5g Whole Clove,
    or 1/2 teaspoon/ 0.1oz/ 3g Ground Cloves
½ teaspoon/ 0.1oz/ 3g Curry Powder
4 Dried Chillies (your choice of Scoville units (heat))
1" of Fresh Ginger, peeled, and coarsely chopped
5 Green Cardamom Pods, crushed,
    or 1 teaspoon/ 0.17oz/ 5g of Ground Cardamom
2 cups/ 16fl.oz/ 500ml Malt Vinegar
3 Tablespoons/ 1.58oz/ 45mg Sea Salt
8 Anchovy Fillets,
    or 2 Tablespoons/ 1oz/ 30g Anchovy Paste
2 Tablespoons/ 1fl.oz/ 30ml Fish Sauce
½ cup/ 4.2fl.oz/ 125ml Soy Sauce
3 Cloves Garlic, crushed
¼ cup/ 2.3oz/ 60g Tamarind Paste
½ cup/ 4.9oz/ 140g Treacle or Blackstrap Molasses
1 Large Onion, peeled and coarsely chopped
½ cup/ 4oz/ 113g Sugar

Heat oil in a large, non-reactive (stainless steel or enamelled) stock pot. When oil shimmers, add dried chillies and toast for 1 minute. Remove from heat and add the dry spices (not the salt) to the chillies and oil. Stir till fragrant.
Add all other ingredients except the sugar. Bring to a rolling boil then reduce the heat and simmer for 10 minutes.
Cook sugar in a skillet over a medium-high heat, stirring constantly until it becomes dark amber and the consistency of syrup. Add caramelized sugar to the vinegar mixture, stirring well to incorporate. Cook sauce at a simmer for an additional 10 minutes.
Transfer the entire contents of the pan into a large glass jar and cover with a tight lid.
Refrigerate, covered, for 1 month. Strain through a sieve to remove solids. Pour liquid off into bottles with well-fitted lids. Refrigerate and use.

Optional: Take the solids from the sieve and blend into a paste and put into a container with a tight lid. Use the paste as a rub or to thicken sauces! The flavour will be very concentrated, so experiment with quantities.

Contribution By: Merry Schepers

Stone Ground Mustard

- Cold water for hot mustard, warm water for mild mustard
- Vinegar sets flavour and preserves the mustard
- Mustard will keep in the refrigerator for 6 months to one year
- Always add water first, wait 10-15 minutes, then add the vinegar. They are two separate chemical reactions. Ducking and covering is an optional step if Professor Rapson is involved
- Wait a minimum of 24 hours between mixing the mustard and using it, which allows the flavours to set and reduces bitterness

Ingredients:
3 Tablespoons/ 0.88oz/ 25g Mustard Seeds, white or brown or a mixture of the two
¼ cup/ 0.88oz/ 25g Powdered Mustard Flour, such as Colman's
¼ cup/ 1.9fl.oz/ 59ml Water
1 teaspoon/ 0.14oz/ 4g Salt
1 ½ Tablespoon/ 0.74fl.oz/ 22ml Vinegar, apple cider, malt or white wine

1. Grind the mustard seeds in a spice grinder or a mortar and pestle till it is a mix of powder and coarse pieces. Pour into a small bowl and add the powdered mustard flour, stir to incorporate.
2. Pour the water into the mustard and stir with a spoon to mix. Let stand for 10 to 15 minutes.
3. Stir in the salt, then add the vinegar and mix. The mixture may seem loose at this point, but it will firm up during its rest in the refrigerator. Put the mixture in a jar with a tight lid and refrigerate for 24 hours. This allows the bitterness of the mustard seeds to dissipate and for the flavours to develop and set.

Variations on the theme:
- Replace the water with an equal amount of ale or stout.
- Add a small quantity of minced herbs – such as mint, tarragon, chives, garlic.
- Add finely ground nut flour, as the early Romans did, almond, hazelnut or pine nuts are good.
- Add fruit juice as a partial substitute for water.
- Make a Dijon style mustard by using white wine vinegar and stirring in 1 teaspoon/ 4g mayonnaise.

Contribution By: Merry Schepers

Brown Sauce

Ingredients:
3 Ripe Plums, peeled, pitted and coarsely chopped
5 Medium Apples, cored, peeled and coarsely chopped
1/3 cup/ 2oz/ 58g Pitted Dates, minced
2 tins or tubes/ 12oz/ 340g Tomato Puree/ Paste
2 Medium Onions, coarsely chopped
1 Large Orange, zested and juiced
2 Cloves Garlic, minced
10fl.oz/ 300ml Tamarind Concentrate
¾ cup plus 2 Tablespoons/ 6 ¾fl.oz/ 200ml Malt Vinegar
¾ cup plus 2 Tablespoons/ 6 ¾fl.oz/ 200ml Apple Cider Vinegar
4 Tablespoons/ 2fl.oz/ 60ml Treacle or Molasses
3 Tablespoons/ 1.5oz/ 45g Brown Sugar
¼ teaspoon/ 0.01oz/ 0.3g Ground Black Pepper
1 teaspoon/ 0.07oz/ 2g Ground Dry Mustard
¾ teaspoon/ 0.07oz/ 2g Ground Allspice
½ teaspoon/ 0.03oz/ 1g Ground Ginger
2 teaspoons/ 0.56oz/ 16g Sea Salt
½ teaspoon/ 0.03oz/ 1g Ground Cardamom
½ teaspoon/ 0.03oz/ 1g Ground Cinnamon
½ teaspoon/ 0.03oz/ 1g Cayenne Pepper or Aleppo (milder) Chilli Powder

Put all ingredients into a large saucepan, stockpot, or Dutch oven (non-reactive material) and stir to incorporate them all. Bring to a boil, then reduce heat to medium and cook for one hour, stirring occasionally. Reduce heat if necessary to keep from scorching.

Blend in a stand blender or with a stick blender until completely smooth.

Bottle into sterile jars and apply sterile, hot lids. If you are not familiar with sterile bottling/canning practices, place bottles in refrigerator instead of on the shelf.

Let sauce mature 4 to 6 weeks before using.
Refrigerate after opening.

Contribution By: Merry Schepers

Piccalilli

Mr. Dieter is one of our favourite engineers. He is the nicest guy, and always able to give us a hand in keeping the kitchen equipment going. We love Mr. Dieter but his love of all things mustard is not his most enduring quality. This of course includes the English Piccalilli. Piccalilli is amazingly versatile because it can be used as a pickle, a dip and as a sandwich spread.

Ingredients:
4.4 pounds/ 2kg of any or all or a mix of the following:
Cauliflower Florets
Courgette (Zucchini)
Green beans
Onion
Carrot
Fennel Bulb
Celeriac Root

Rock Salt
1.14L / 39 fl.oz Pickling Vinegar
1 1/4 cups/ 10.5oz/ 300g Brown Sugar or to taste
2 Tablespoons/ 0.45oz/ 13g Mustard Seeds
1 Bay Leaf
3 Tablespoons/ 1oz/ 29g Turmeric
Thumb size piece of Ginger, peeled and julienned or minced
4 Garlic Cloves, minced
Cornflour Slurry, amount will vary depending on thickness

Wash, peel and dice a combination of the above vegetables, or any that you prefer. Put them into a large bowl and liberally sprinkle over with the rock salt. Stir well to ensure that it's all coated in the salt. Cover and leave for 24 hours. After a few hours the vegetables will have produced a lot of liquid, this will need to be drained so the vegetables don't become soggy. After 24 hours, pour your vegetables into a large colander, drain well, then rinse well in cold water so any residual salt is rinsed away. Leave to drain while you prepare the vinegar.

In a large stock pot or pan, add your vinegar, spices, ginger, garlic and bay leaf. Bring to the boil. Add the drained vegetables and brown sugar. Boil for 20-30 minutes. Taste. If it needs more brown sugar, then add it now. When you're satisfied with how it tastes, slowly add your cornflour slurry. Add it in intervals so it doesn't get too thick too quickly. You may need more. Just add it until you like how thick it is. It needs to be quite thick because you need to be able to spread it on bread. Fill sterilised jars and seal. It is tasty if eaten straight away or you can leave the mixture for 2 to 3 weeks so the flavour intensifies.

Makes about 3L (3.17 quarts).

Contribution By: Afton Cochran

Mushroom Ketchup

Ingredients:
5 lbs Mushrooms of choice, not poisonous, obviously.
    For dried porcini or wild mushrooms, see note.
5 ½ Tablespoons/ 2.8oz/ 80g Kosher Salt
1 Tablespoon/ 0.28oz/ 8g Black Pepper
5 Cloves Garlic, minced
6 Sprigs of Fresh Thyme
3 Bay Leaves
1 Tablespoon/ 0.21oz/ 6g Allspice Berries or
    2 teaspoons/ 0.14oz/ 4g Ground Allspice
2 Tablespoons/ 0.5oz/ 15g Fresh Ginger, chopped
12 Whole Cloves
2 Tablespoons/ 1fl.oz/ 30ml Worcestershire sauce,
    Soy Sauce (v), or Tamari (for gf)
1 cup/ 8fl.oz/ 250ml Cider Vinegar
Pinch of Freshly Grated Nutmeg
Pinch of Mace (optional)

In a dry pan over a medium heat, toast your peppercorns, allspice, and cloves. Crush using a mortar and pestle and set aside. Roughly chop up your mushrooms or pulse in batches in a food processor. Place all your ingredients in the stock pot. Cover with enough water (and your porcini liquid) to make it slushy, but not overly wet. This will depend on the type of mushrooms you use. It could be anywhere from 500ml to a litre. Cover and bring to a boil. Boil for 5-10 minutes. Turn off the heat and leave for 12-24 hours. Strain through cheesecloth into a clean stock pot. Bring to the boil again and reduce to desired consistency. Let cool and then strain 2-3 more times through a cheesecloth lined wire strainer to remove all mushroom particles and sediment. Pour into sterilised jars and leave for 2 weeks to mature.

The yield will vary due to amount of liquid used and level of reduction you desire.

Note: if you want to use dried mushrooms, rehydrate and prepare them according to the package. If using porcini, use 100g and rehydrate with 1L of boiling water. Let it sit for 1/2 an hour and remove with a slotted spoon. Strain the liquid through a cheesecloth and set aside.

Contribution By: Afton Cochran

Jam Sugar

Making your own jams may be a delight but not having it gel is unsightly!
Save the jam! We need it for our crumpets!

Ingredients:
1 cup/ 7oz/ 200g Granulated Sugar
Slightly more than 2/3 teaspoon/ 0.0017oz/ 0.05g Powdered Pectin

Whisk together and use in your favourite jam recipes, or store in an airtight container out of direct sunlight until needed.

Contribution By: Sara Robinson

Red Chilli Jam

Ingredients:
½ cup/ 2.25oz/ 65g Red Chillies, diced or a mixture, choose your favourite
1 Medium Onion, diced
2 Cloves Garlic or 2 teaspoons Chopped Garlic
½ cup/ 4.39oz/ 125ml Water
2 cups/ 7oz/ 400g Granulated or Jam Sugar
1 Lime, zested and juiced
¼ cup/ 1.6oz/ 50ml Malt Vinegar

Finely chop all the ingredients and place in a large heavy pan. Bring the mixture to a boil for about 5 minutes and then simmer for around 30 minutes.
After about 20 to 25 minutes start testing the mixture. To test, use a cool plate or saucer and pop a teaspoon of the mixture in the middle of the plate. The mixture should start to set immediately on the cool plate. If it doesn't, continue simmering the mixture and try again. If the mixture gets a bit stubborn, bring it back to a boil stirring constantly and keep testing.
The end product should give a thick sticky consistency.

Contribution By: Sara McKenna

Vanilla Rhubarb Jam

Ingredients:
2 ½ pounds/ 40oz/ 1.134kg of Rhubarb Stalks, washed trimmed and sliced into large pieces
½ cup/ 4fl.oz/ 64g Water
7 cups/ 112oz/ 1.4 kg Granulated Sugar
2 Tablespoons/ 1.04 fl.oz/ 29g Lemon Juice
Seeds from 1 large Vanilla Bean
5 Tablespoons/ 2.5oz/ 71g Powdered Pectin

The night before you are to make the jam, or at least 2 hours before, place the cleaned and sliced rhubarb in a large pot with 2 cups of sugar and mix it well to coat all the rhubarb with sugar. Cover and refrigerate so that the fruit will macerate or form a lovely liquid.

Remove the rhubarb from the refrigerator in the morning, adding the water. Bring this mixture to a boil and quickly remove from the heat, line a sieve with cheesecloth and allow the rhubarb to drain all its juices into a large bowl. Be careful not to squeeze the mixture too vigorously as it may make the jam cloudy. At this point you will start to see the beautiful rosy colour of the juice.
Mix the remaining 5 cups of sugar and pectin in a large bowl. Slice the vanilla pod with a sharp knife down the middle to make two long halves. Put the rhubarb juice and vanilla pod halves into a clean large pot, adding sugar, pectin and lemon juice. Bring the mixture to a boil while stirring almost constantly. Once the mixture has reached a full rolling boil it must keep this temperature for 3 minutes. Stir the mixture and skim any foam from the top of the mixture into a small bowl.
Take the jam off the heat and skim any remaining foam from the top of the mixture. Remove the vanilla pod. Fill sterilised jars to within ¼ inch of the top. If you are preserving using the water bath method, then wipe the rim of the jar to remove any spilled jam and screw the lids on without over spinning them. Process in boiling water for 10 minutes to preserve and seal the jars. If you are not preserving, then let the jars cool before capping them and refrigerate.
Makes about 4 medium sized jars. (4 cups/ 32fl.oz/ 946ml)

Rhubarb Leaves are poisonous and should not be eaten.

Contribution By: Sara Robinson

Marmalade

Ingredients:
2.2lb/ 1kg Oranges, Seville variety is preferred
2 Small Lemons, juiced
9 cups/ 72fl.oz/ 2.1L water
9 cups/ 4lb/ 1.8kg Sugar

Cut the oranges in half and squeeze out all the juice. Scoop out all the pips from the orange peels and tie into a small piece of muslin, or into a cloth bag. Slice the peel into small chunks or strips and place a in preserving pan together with the orange and lemon juice and water. Add the package of pips. Simmer gently for 1 to 1 ½ hours or until the peels are very soft and the liquid has reduced by half. Remove the bag of pips and carefully squeeze all the beautiful juice back into the pot. Add the sugar and heat, stirring until the sugar has completely dissolved. Bring to the boil and boil rapidly for 12 to 15 minutes or until the setting point is reached.
Leave to cool slightly, then put into warm sterilised jars and cover the tops with waxed discs. When completely cooled, cover with cellophane or lids, label and store in a cool place.

Contribution By: Caroline Price

Lemon Curd

Ingredients:
4 Lemons, unwaxed, zest and juice
4 Eggs
½ cup/ 3oz/ 110g Butter, unsalted
2 ¼ cups/ 16oz/ 450g Caster Sugar

Grate the zest finely and juice the lemons. Put the sugar, zest, juice and butter in a large bowl set on top of a pan of barely simmering water. Stir with a wooden spoon until the butter and sugar have melted and all is combined. Lightly whisk the eggs into the lemon/butter mix. Stir until the mix is thick and coats the back of a spoon. Pour into sterilised jars, cover and seal. Keep in the fridge for up to one week.

Contribution By: Sara McKenna

Apple and Cranberry Chutney

Ingredients:
12oz/ 340g Whole Cranberries, fresh or frozen
3 cups/ 16oz/ 453g Apples, chopped (about 2 large apples)
2 Oranges
½ cup/ 0.9oz/ 26g Onion, finely diced
1½ cups/ 12fl.oz/ 355ml Water
2 teaspoons/ 0.14oz/ 4g Fresh Ginger, grated
4inches/ 10cm Cinnamon Sticks, broken into big pieces
2 Whole Star Anise
½ teaspoon/ 0.07oz/ 2g Ground Nutmeg
½ teaspoon/ 0.07oz/ 2g Ground Allspice
½ teaspoon/ 0.07oz/ 2g Ground Cloves
½ cup/ 3.8oz/ 110g Brown Sugar, firmly packed
¼ cup/ 1oz/ 30g Crystallized Ginger, finely chopped
½ cup/ 2.3oz/ 65g Dried Cranberries, roughly chopped
½ cup/ 2.3oz/ 65g Golden Raisins, roughly chopped
½ cup/ 3oz/ 85g Dried Pineapple, roughly chopped
½ cup/ 2oz/ 58g Walnuts, chopped (optional)

Working over a bowl to catch all the juice, finely zest the oranges. Using a sharp knife, peel the oranges, removing all the bitter white pith, cut in between the membranes to release the sections, squeeze the juice from the membranes into the bowl. Tear the orange sections into 1-inch pieces. Place the cranberries, apples, orange zest, juice and pieces, onion, fresh ginger and water in a large saucepan and cook over a medium-low heat stirring occasionally, until the cranberries start to pop. Turn the heat down to low. Add all the spices, brown sugar, candied ginger, dried cranberries, raisins and dried pineapple. Let it simmer gently, stirring occasionally until it starts to thicken, about 20 minutes or so.
Add the walnuts and continue to simmer for about 10 minutes or until the apples are soft and you like the texture. It will thicken up a bit as it cools, add a bit of warm water if it's too thick for you.
Serve hot or cold. Refrigerate the leftovers for up two weeks or cool completely, divide up and freeze.

Contribution By: Constantia Mead

Pesto Sauce

Ingredients:
½ cup/ 0.35oz/ 10g Fresh Basil Leaves
½ cup/ 0.5oz/ 15g Fresh Spinach Leaves
3 Cloves Garlic, peeled and smashed
¼ cup/ 1.19oz/ 34g Pine Nuts, toasted
1/3 cup/ 1.16oz/ 33g Parmesan Cheese, finely grated
Salt and Pepper, to taste
5 Tablespoons/ 2.5fl.oz/ 75ml Olive Oil

To toast the pine nuts, place them in a dry frying pan over medium heat. Stir the nuts often to prevent burning. Remove from the heat when the nuts are fragrant and a toasted golden colour. Place on a plate or directly into the food processor to cool slightly.

To make pesto you will need a food processor, or a mortar and pestle. Place all ingredients, except the oil, into the bowl provided in your chosen way to make the sauce. Grind the ingredients together until a paste starts to form. Start slowly mixing in the oil one spoonful at a time. Continue mixing until the contents are well combined and the oil has emulsified. Use straight away or store in an air-tight container in the refrigerator for about a week.

Contribution By: Sara Robinson

Cornflour/Corn-starch Slurry

Ratios are important in making a cornflour slurry. If you are just starting out, then it's wisest to use the 1:2 ratio: one part cornflour to two parts cold water, stock, or wine to add to a simmering soup or sauce. Do not use warm liquids to make a slurry. For example: to thicken 237ml (1 cup) of sauce to make it medium-thick
Use:
1 Tablespoon/ 0.3oz/ 9g Cornflour
2 Tablespoons/ 1fl.oz/ 30ml Cold Water
In a bowl or jug add the cornflour and water, and quickly mix well until the cornflour is completely dissolved. Slowly add some of the slurry to whatever concoction is simmering. Don't add it all at once, or you may end up with a sludgy mess. Stir continuously whilst it does its work. Remember, you control how thick it gets.
When you feel confident, you can decrease the liquid so the ratio is 1:1

Contribution By: Afton Cochran

Italian Sausage

Ingredients:
2 pounds/ 907g Lean Pork, ground
1 Tablespoon/ 0.2oz/ 6g Fennel Seeds, coarsely ground
2 Bay Leaves, finely ground
1 Tablespoon/ 0.07oz/ 2g Dried Parsley
3 to 5 Cloves Garlic, crushed and minced
1/8 to ¼ teaspoon/ 0.01oz/ 0.3g Red Pepper Flakes
1 teaspoon/ 0.2oz/ 6g Salt
¼ teaspoon/ 0.01oz/ 0.3g Ground Pepper
4 Tablespoons/ 2fl.oz/ 60ml Water

Mix all the ingredients together thoroughly. Cover and rest the mixture for one hour. Work the mixture more to make sure everything is completely and evenly combined. You can mix the sausage by hand or in a stand mixer. Do not skip the resting time it is important.

Once evenly combined, the sausage is ready to portion for use in a recipe, fry for eating or can be frozen to use in the future. If you are brave, it can be stuffed into sausage casings.

Contribution By: Constantina Mead

Sour Cream

Ingredients:
1 cup/ 8oz/ 240ml Double Cream
about 1 Tablespoon/ 0.5fl.oz/ 15ml Lemon Juice.
Pour the juice into the cream and set aside for a couple of minutes to start the curdling process,
then whisk briskly until it is the thickness you like.

Contribution By: Sara McKenna

Cabbage Bombs
The Smell Will Linger

We left this one to the end. These are amazingly diverse; tasty meal, a weapon against any enemy, and maker of noxious vapers to get a quiet night in the pod...
Or maybe
everyone could use a little fresh air!

Ingredients:
1 White or Green Cabbage
2 Tablespoons/ 1fl.oz/ 30ml Vegetable Oil
6oz/ 175g Streaky Bacon, cut into lardons
½ Medium Onion, finely diced
1 Large Slice of Onion
½ cup/ 4fl.oz/ 120ml BBQ Sauce + 4 Tablespoons/ 2fl.oz/ 60ml for basting
1 Tablespoon/ 0.5fl.oz/ 15ml Neutral Oil
13oz/375g Streaky Bacon Rashers/ Slices
BBQ Sauce for serving

Wash the cabbage, and remove any brown or damaged outer leaves. Heat the oven to 330°F/ 170°C (150°C fan)/Gas Mark 3. Carefully cut the core out of the cabbage (seriously, we do not want sick bay coming after us for this one) and remove enough of the middle of the cabbage to fit the filling. You want the diameter of the hole to be the size of the slice of onion. In a frying pan over a medium heat, add the oil. Add the minced onion and gently fry until the onion is soft and translucent. Remove and set aside. Add the 1 tablespoon of oil and the bacon lardons and fry until beginning to crisp. Drain any excess oil out of the pan and add the onion back in along with the BBQ sauce. Heat through. Spoon the bacon and BBQ sauce mixture into the cavity of the cabbage. Cover the hole with the thick slice of onion. Wrap the slices of streaky bacon evenly around the outside of the cabbage. If you fancy and have extra bacon, you can make a lattice work around the cabbage. If you are like most of R&D, slap it on and hope it does not fall off. Wrap the cabbage tightly in foil, place on a baking sheet and roast for 1½ to 2 hours or until the cabbage is soft, the bacon well cooked on the outside and the filling is piping hot.
~~Throw at unsuspecting attackers.~~
Cut into wedges and serve with mashed potatoes and lots of extra BBQ sauce.

Serves 4

Photo and Contribution By: Afton Cochran

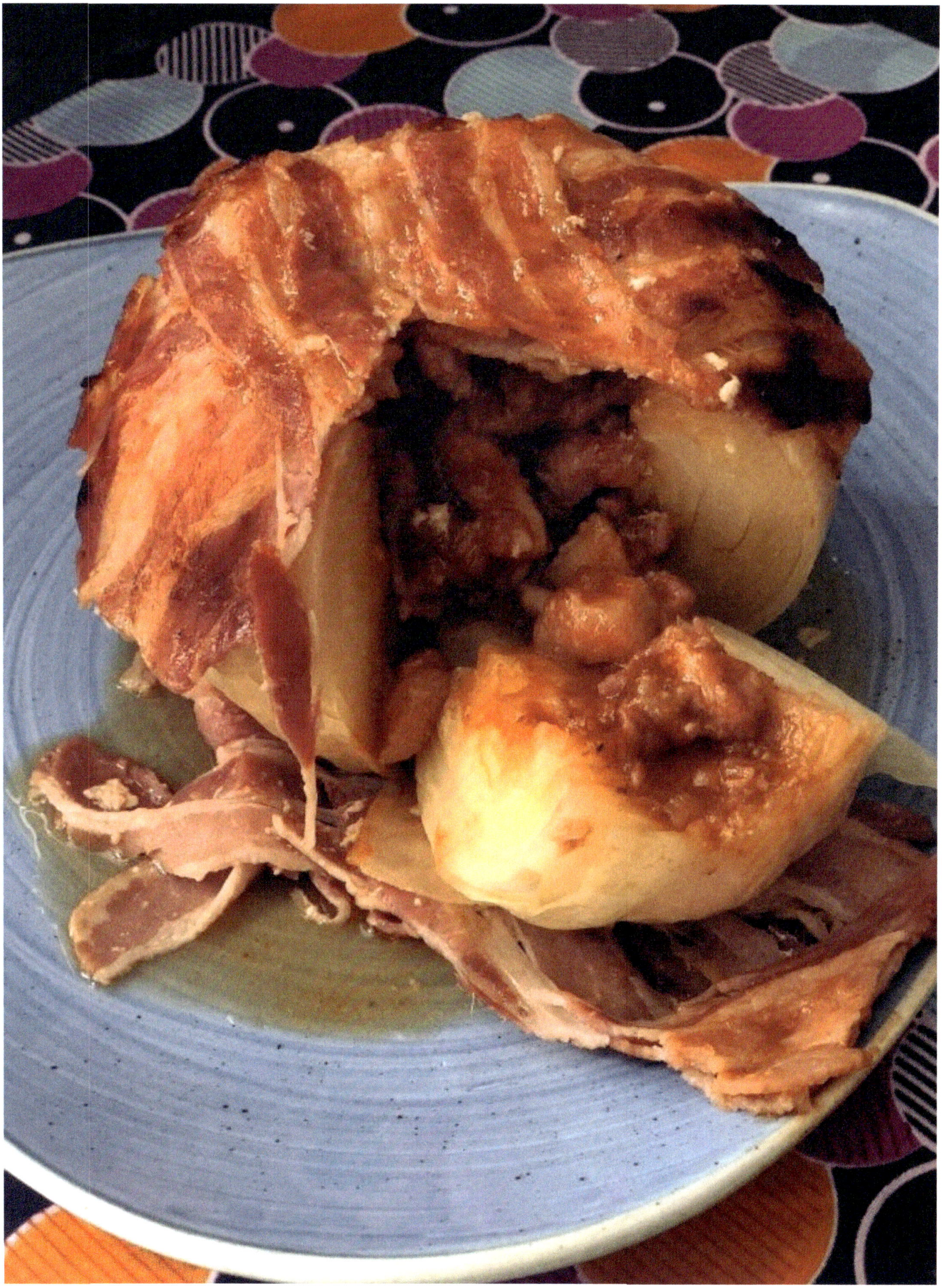

THIS BOOK IS DEDICATED TO:

This book is dedicated to Jodi Taylor who opened up a whole new world and invited us to join her in the Chronicles of St. Mary's Books. In this book we hope that our love of history, cooking and Jodi Taylor's amazing books are felt with each turn of the page. The pages of the Chronicles of St. Mary's books are filled with adventure, camaraderie and true friendship. We hope that this book will add another layer to the stories and maybe, just maybe bring us all a little closer together. We have had an amazing time compiling this and hope that you will enjoy it as much as we have. We wait with baited breath for Jodi's next book to be released.

We would like to take a moment to remember Mort Reading. Mort was a founding member of VSM and a long time member of the Kitchen Department. She, like so many members of St. Mary's, were taken too soon.

All of us would like to dedicate this book to our Mothers, Grandmothers, Fathers and Grandfathers as well as all the wonderful people who taught us to cook and to honour family traditions. For many of us there are just too many individuals to name and we hope that all of you receive our heartfelt 'thank you.' We have learned that the kitchen is the heart of the home and where warmth, adventure and love were given out in equal measure together with nourishing foods, tasty treats and the occasional nugget of wisdom. This book is one way that we honour all of those who came before us and make sure that there is a record for those who come after us.

As always, it has been an honour and a privilege.

Special Thank You To Everyone that Made This Book Possible:

Jodi Taylor and Hazel Cushion:
    Well, that should really be self evident!

Our Executive Chefs: Sara Robinson, Afton Cochran, Merry Schepers, Sara McKenna, Barb Ruddle

Rachel Garstang Penman for all the beautiful artwork.

Our Photographers:
    Sara Robinson, Afton Cochran, Merry Schepers, Hannah Holt

Welcome, Essentials, Terms, Names, Equipment and Measurements:
    Sara Robinson and Sara McKenna

Stories and Histories:
    Sara Robinson, Afton Cochran, Merry Schepers, Sara McKenna

Cover and Cover Art
    Hazel Cushion

Our Publicity Team:
    Sara McKenna, Afton Cochran, Sara Robinson, Merry Schepers, Barb Ruddle

Our Proof Readers:
    Jacqui Ryder, Carol Robinson, Becky Parsons, Afton Cochran

Our Recipe Testers:
    Caroline Price, Gina Burnside, Afton Cochran, Sara Robinson, Sara McKenna

Our Editing, Layout and Production Engineer or General Computer Monkey:
    Sara Robinson

All contributions are credited with the individual recipes.
Our sincerest apologies if we have missed or mislabelled anything.

Many thanks to everyone for this cookbook, for giving us some direction and a safe harbour from all the chaos of 2020.

Special thanks to all of those wild and crazy people in the Virtual St. Mary's Facebook Group. Your upbeat and supportive manner, along with a few shenanigans, has been the glue that brought us together and a light in our lives as we all stumble forward.

We really couldn't have done this without all of you!

INDEX:

Apple
- Roman Pork and Apple Stew — 29
- Spiced Apple Muffins — 59

Avocado
- Guacamole — 127

Baking Pans and Tins Guide — 12

Bannock
- Sunflower — 25

Bean
- Caribbean Rice and Beans — 37
- White Bean and Orzo Soup — 66
- Sausage and Bean Casserole — 85
- Bean and Onion Salad — 128
- Vegan Burrito — 132
- Bean and Lentil Stew — 142

Beef
- Roman Burger — 28
- Shooters Sandwich — 53
- Cowboy Stew — 54
- Swiss Beef — 72
- Sausage Pasta — 73
- Beef Stroganoff — 81
- Rib of Beef — 89
- Bobotie — 103
- Carbonnade Flamande — 110
- Borscht — 118
- Peppercorn-Pthast — 120
- Goulash — 121
- Pastel de Choclo — 123

Biscuits
- Shortbread — 157
- Millionaires' Shortbread — 158
- Flavoured Shortbread — 158
- Jam Tarts — 159
- Guess Again — 159
- Oatmeal Cookies — 160
- Triple Chocolate Chip — 160
- Oat Biscuits — 163
- Hot Cocoa Biscuits — 165
- Madeleines — 166
- Lemon Ginger Biscuit — 167
- High Energy Biscuits — 177
- Bourbon Biscuits — 178
- Forked Biscuits — 178

Breads/Rolls and Baked
- Ancient Loaf — 22
- Bread Sauce — 35
- Crumpets — 39
- Toast — 56
- Muffins — 59
- Pancakes — 60
- Potato Scones — 57
- Brioche Rolls — 68
- Cheese Puffs — 68
- Polenta Muffins — 69
- Sweet Potato Scones — 69
- Onion Cheese Scones — 70
- Yorkshire Puddings — 92
- Turkish Pizza — 101
- Bath Buns — 174
- Doughnuts — 175
- Incredibly Quick Bread — 192
- Easy Basic bread — 192

Broth
- Brown Stock/Bone Broth — 66
- Vegetable Stock — 146

Brownies — 163

Buttercream; See Icing

Cabbage Bomb — 204

Cakes
- Seed Cake — 40
- Victoria Sponge — 41
- Honey Cake — 44
- Pear and Ginger Skillet Cake — 44
- Pineapple Upside Down Cake — 46
- Tarta De Santiago — 47
- GF Vanilla Cake — 150
- Victoria Sponge — 151
- Madeleines — 166
- Chocolate Cake — 168
- Easy as Cake — 168
- Cocoa Cake — 169
- Drizzle Cake — 171

Candy
- Chocolate Orange — 169
- Citrus Peel — 188
- Salted Caramel — 191

Carrot
- Carrot Fritters — 42

Cheese
- Mac and Cheese — 30-31
- Ember Day Tart — 32
- Cheese Toasty — 52
- Shooter Sandwich — 53
- Cheese Puff — 68
- Sw. Potato Cheddar Scones — 69
- Cheese and Onion Scone — 70
- Nidi di Rondine — 87
- Croque Monsieur — 112
- Tartiflette — 114
- Leek and Cheese Pie — 134
- Saag Paneer — 139

Chicken
- Another Chicken — 27
- Chicken and Noodle Soup — 67
- Chorizo Orzotto — 72
- Chicken and Rice Dish — 73
- Chicken and Vegetable Pie — 78
- Roast Chicken — 90
- Cashew Chicken — 97

Index:

Mafe/ Peanut Stew	104	
Pollo alla Cacciatore	109	
Chicken Mushroom Fricassee	114	
Pastel de Choclo	123	
Canja	128	

Chocolate
- Millionaires' Shortbread — 160
- Chocolate Chip Cookies — 160
- Crazy Brownies — 163
- Quick Hot Cocoa — 165
- Hot Cocoa Biscuits — 165
- Chocolate Cake — 168
- Easy as Cake — 168
- Cocoa Cake — 169
- Chocolate Orange — 169
- Chocolate Drizzle Cake — 171
- Mars Bar Squares — 164
- High Energy Biscuits — 177
- Bourbon Biscuits — 178
- Forked Biscuits — 178

Conversion and Measurements Guide — 15
Cookies: See Biscuits
Cooking Terms — 6-7
Corn: See Sweet Corn
Cornmeal: See Polenta

Cous Cous
- Tabbouleh — 102

Cutting Boards — 9

Drinks, Alcoholic
- After Hours — 180
- More From Bar — 181
- A Few More — 182

Drinks, Non-Alcoholic
- Quick Hot Cocoa — 165
- Historic Drinks — 183
- We Are Not Alcoholics — 184
- Jump Next Day — 185
- Fresh Raspberry Kir — 185
- Elderflower Cordial — 186
- Raspberry Lemonade — 186
- Rhubarb Cordial — 186

Eggs
- Scrambled Eggs — 56
- Shakshuka — 106
- Lost Eggs — 120
- Pastel de Choclo — 123

Equipment Guide — 6-12

Fish/Prawns
- Cullen Skink — 63
- Fish Pie — 76
- Po' Boy Sandwich — 71
- Salt and Pepper Prawns — 99
- Greek Fish Stew — 108
- Mediterranean Cod — 109
- Caesars Tossed Greens — 141

Flour
- Cake Flour — 188
- Self Raising Flour — 189

Food Names — 4-5
Frosting; See Icing

Goat
- Jamaican Goat Curry — 37

Ham
- Succotash — 26
- Pea Soup — 34
- Lentil and Ham Soup — 62

Icing
- Icing Sugar — 190
- Italian Buttercream — 190
- Swiss Buttercream — 190
- Easy Icing — 191
- American Buttercream — 191

Jam
- Jam Sugar — 201
- Red Chilli Jam — 201
- Vanilla Rhubarb Jam — 201
- Marmalade — 202
- Lemon Curd — 202

Ketchup
- Lemon Ketchup — 50
- Mushroom Ketchup — 200

Knives Guide — 8

Lamb
- Roman Burger — 28
- Jamaican Goat Curry — 37
- Spicy Lamb Meatballs — 82
- Lancashire Hotpot — 84
- Roast Leg of Lamb — 90
- Turkish Pizza — 101

Lentil
- Ham and Lentil Soup — 62
- Mud Soup — 62
- Sri Lankan Dhal — 96
- Mujadara — 133
- Sweet and Sour Lentils — 134
- Lentil and Vegetable Pie — 137
- Bean and Lentil Stew — 142
- Lentil and Mango Dahl — 145
- Vegetarian Shepherd's Pie — 146

Loaf
- Cable Street Loaf — 49
- Tea Loaf — 167
- Drizzle Cake — 171

Measurements Guide — 15
Mixing Bowl Guide — 11

INDEX:

Muffins
- Banana Muffins — 59
- Apple Spice Muffins — 59
- Polenta Muffins — 69

Noodles: See Pasta

Nuts
- Paganens/ Nut Soup — 23
- Mafe/ Peanut Stew — 104
- Peanut Butter Squares — 172
- High Energy Biscuits — 177

Oats
- Porridge — 56
- Overnight Porridge — 58
- Banana Muffins — 59
- Oatmeal Cookies — 160
- Oat Biscuits — 163
- High Energy Biscuits — 177

Orzo
- White Bean and Orzo Soup — 66
- Chorizo Orzotto — 72
- Lemon Orzo — 140

Pancake
- Hoe Cakes — 38
- English Pancake — 60
- Drop Scone — 60
- American Pancake — 60
- Blini Pancake — 154

Pasta
- Mac and Cheese — 30-31
- Tortellini Sausage Soup — 64
- White Bean and Orzo Soup — 66
- Chicken and Noodles — 67
- Sausage Pasta — 73
- Beef Stroganoff — 81
- Spicy Lamb Meatballs — 82
- Nidi di Rondine — 87
- Curry Udon — 99
- Vegetarian Lasagne — 145

Pastry/Pie
- A Tart For Ember Day — 32
- Fish Pie — 76
- Chicken and Vegetable Pie — 78
- Big Murdoch Pie — 85
- Onion Tarte Tatin — 115
- Vegetarian Wellington — 131
- Leek and Cheese Pie — 134
- Lentil and Vegetable Pie — 137
- Jam Tarts — 159

Polenta
- Sunflower Bannock — 25
- Hoe Cakes — 38

Pork
- Roman Burgers — 28
- Roman Pork and Apple Stew — 29
- Bacon — 56
- Sausages — 57
- Bacon Butty — 57
- Tortellini Sausage Soup — 64
- Borscht — 118
- Goulash — 121
- Pork Carnitas — 125
- Cabbage Bomb — 204

Potato
- Potato Scone — 57
- Creamy Vegetable Soup — 63
- Cullen Skink — 63
- Leek and Potato Soup — 67
- Sweet Potato Scone — 69
- Fish Pie — 76
- Lancashire Hotpot — 83
- Roast Potatoes — 92
- Bombay Aloo — 96
- Mafe/ Peanut Stew — 104
- Carbonnade Flamande — 110
- Tartiflette — 114
- Best Wurst — 116
- Syracuse Salt Potatoes — 140
- Vegetarian Shepherd's Pie — 146
- Oven Chips — 147
- Jacket Potatoes — 147

Pots and Pans Guide — 10

Rice
- Caribbean Rice and Beans — 37
- Chicken and Rice Dish — 73
- Damn Casserole — 75
- Beef Stroganoff — 81
- Sri Lankan Dhal — 96
- Cashew Chicken — 97
- Jollof Rice — 102
- Geelrys — 103
- Canja — 128
- Sweet and Sour Cauliflower — 131
- Vegan Burrito — 132
- Mujadara — 133
- Mushroom Risotto — 144

Rolls: see Breads

Salad
- Greek Village Salad — 108
- Bean and Onion Salad — 128
- Tossed Cauliflower — 136
- The Great Salad — 147

Sandwich
- Grilled Cheese — 52
- Cheese Toasty — 52
- Shooters Sandwich — 53
- Bacon Butty — 57
- Sandwich ideas — 70
- Po' Boy Sandwich — 71
- Croque Monsieur — 112
- Tea Sandwiches — 154

Index:

Sauces
- Lemon Ketchup — 50
- Mustard Vinaigrette — 136
- Caesars Dressing — 141
- Worcestershire Sauce — 198
- Ground Mustard — 199
- Brown Sauce — 198
- Piccalilli — 200
- Mushroom Ketchup — 200
- Apple Cranberry Chutney — 202
- Pesto Sauce — 203

Sausage
- Sausages — 57
- Tortellini Sausage Soup — 64
- Chorizo Orzotto — 72
- Sausage Pasta — 73
- Big Murdoch Pie — 85
- Sausage and Bean — 85
- Nidi Di Rondine — 86
- Toad in the Hole — 88
- Best Wurst — 116
- Italian Sausage — 203

Scone
- Drop Scone — 60
- Sweet Potato Scone — 69
- Cheese and Onion Scone — 70
- Never Fail Scone — 155

Seeds
- Sunflower Bannock — 25
- Seed Cake — 40
- Tossed Cauliflower — 136

Shortbread
- Shortbread — 157
- Millionaires' Shortbread — 158
- Flavoured Shortbread — 158
- Jam Tarts — 159

Soup/ Stew
- Paganens/Nut Soup — 25
- Pea Soup — 34
- Cowboy Stew — 54
- Nettle Soup — 54
- Ham and Lentil Soup — 62
- Mud Soup — 62
- Creamy Vegetable Soup — 63
- Cullen Skink — 63
- Tortellini Sausage Soup — 64
- Mushroom Stew — 65
- White Bean and Orzo Soup — 66
- Brown Stock/ Bone Broth — 66
- Cool as a Cucumber Soup — 67
- Leek and Potato Soup — 67
- Chicken and Noodle Soup — 67
- Mafe/ Peanut Stew — 104
- Greek Fish Stew — 108
- Onion Soup — 112
- Borscht — 118
- Vegan Mexican Stew — 142
- Roasted Vegetable Soup — 144

Spice Mixes — 194-197
Stock: see Broth
Store Cupboard Essentials — 3

Sweet Corn
- Succotash — 26
- Thai Corn Fritters — 94
- Pastel de Choclo — 123
- Vegetarian Shepherd's Pie — 146

Tea
- How to Make — 17-20
- Cable Tea Loaf — 49
- Oatmeal Cookies — 160
- Triple Chocolate Cookie — 160
- Tea Loaf — 167

Temperature Guide — 16
Terms — 6-7
Tortellini
- Tortellini Sausage Soup — 64

Utensils Guide — 13

Vanilla Extract — 186
Vegetable Bouillon Powder — 197
Welcome — 2

Gluten Free:

Chapter 2: Tea
- 18-20- Tea is usually gluten free but read the package ingredients to be sure.

Chapter 3: History:
- 25- Algonquin Sunflower Bannock is gluten free.
- 25- Algonquin Nut Soup is gluten free.
- 26- Succotash is gluten free.
- 27- Roman Honey Chicken is gluten free if using appropriate fish sauce.
- 28- Roman Burgers are gluten free if using appropriate fish sauce and GF bun or pitta.
- 29- Roman Pork and Apple Stew is gluten free if using appropriate fish sauce.
- 32- Onion Tart can be made gluten free by substituting buckwheat flour in the crust plus adding ½ teaspoon/2g Xanthan gum.
- 34- Pea soup is gluten free.
- 37- Jamaican Goat Curry and rice is gluten free when using appropriate stocks and Boullion powder.
- 38- Hoe cakes work well by subbing out plain flour with gluten free flour.
- 39- Crumpets do not work with gluten free flour.
- 46- Pineapple Upside Down Cake is gluten free when using the appropriate ingredients list.
- 47- Tarta de Santiago is gluten free.
- 50- Lemon Ketchup is gluten free.
- 52- Cheese Toasties are gluten free when using gluten free bread.
- 53- Shooters sandwich can be gluten free by using appropriate bread.
- 54- Cowboy Stew and Nettle Soup are gluten free by omitting the Pearl Barley.

Chapter 4: Kitchen:
- 56- Porridge and Cooked Breakfast are gluten free if using the appropriate oats and toast.
- 57- Bacon Butty is gluten free when using appropriate rolls.
- 59- Muffins can be gluten free.
- 62-67- All soups are gluten free when using appropriate stocks, GF tortellini, GForzo, GF pasta/noodles, and appropriate sausages.
- 68- Cheese Puffs are very good when using GF Plain Flour with ½ teaspoons Xanthan Gum and 2 teaspoons GF Baking Powder for the flour in the recipe.
- 69- Polenta Muffins work well to replace the plain flour with GF flour.
- 73- Sausage Pasta is gluten free when using GF sausage and GF Pasta.
- 75- Damn Casserole is gluten free.
- 81- Beef Stroganoff is gluten free when using Tamari and Worcestershire Sauce and serving on GF Pasta or Rice.
- 82- Lamb Meatballs is gluten free when served on gluten free pasta.
- 89-90 Sunday Roast is gluten free.
- 92- Roasted Potatoes and Roasted Carrots are gluten free.

Chapter 5: Security:
- 94- Thai Corn Fritters are gluten free when using GF Baking Powder.
- 96- Sri Lankan Dhal and Bombay Aloo are gluten free.
- 97- Cashew Chicken can be made gluten free by using tamari sauce instead of soy sauce.
- 99- Salt and Pepper Prawns are gluten free when using Rice Flour.
- 102- Jollof Rice is gluten free when using appropriate Bouillon Powder.
- 103- Geelrys is gluten free.
- 104- Mafe is gluten free when using appropriate fish sauce.
- 106- Shakshuka is gluten free.
- 108- Fish Stew and Salad are gluten free.
- 109- Pollo alla Cacciatore and Baked Cod are gluten free
- 110- Carbonnade Flamande is gluten free when using appropriate beer and stock.
- 112- Onion soup and croque monsieur are gluten free when using appropriate bread and stocks.
- 114- Tartiflette is gluten free.
- 118- Borscht is gluten free.
- 121- Goulash is gluten free.
- 123- Pastel De Choclo is gluten free.
- 125- Pork Carnitas are gluten free.
- 127- Guacamole is gluten free.
- 128– This soup and salad are gluten free.

Chapter 6: Medical:
- 131- Sweet and Sour is gluten free when using GF tamari.
- 134- Sweet and Sour Lentils is gluten free when using tamari.
- 136- Tossed Cauliflower is gluten free.
- 139- Saag is gluten free.
- 140- Syracuse Potatoes is gluten free.
- 141- Caesars Greens can be gluten free when using GF bread.
- 144- Roasted Vegetables are gluten free when using appropriate stocks.

Gluten Free:

147-149- St Marys Salad, Oven Chips, Jacket Potatoes and steamed vegetables are all gluten free.

150- Vanilla cake is gluten free.

Chapter 7: Admin:

155– Lemon Posset is gluten free.

165- Hot Cocoa is gluten free when using appropriate ingredients.

165- Cocoa Biscuits work well as gluten free subbing out the plain flour for gluten free flour plus ½ teaspoon Xanthan Gum.

169- Chocolate orange is gluten free.

172- Mars bars are not gluten free.

172- Peanut butter squares are gluten free.

177- Nut free high energy biscuits are gluten free.

Chapter 8: The Blue Swan:

Most of the drink s are gluten free but please read on your individual products to be sure.

Chapter 9: R&D:

194-197- With the exception of the Bouillon Powder all spice mixes are gluten free.

198-203- Most of the sauces, jams and preserves are gluten free but check individual products to be sure.

203- Sausage and Sour Cream are gluten free.

204- Cabbage bombs are gluten free if using an appropriate BBQ sauce.

This is meant only as a guide.

Common Gluten Free Flours are:
Plain Mixed Gluten Free Flour   *   Rice*   Buckwheat
Teff   *   Potato Starch   *   Cornflour*   Cornmeal
Oats and Oat Flour must be marked as gluten free
Amaranth Flour   *   Sorghum Flour   *   Arrowroot Flour
Almond Flour   *   Chickpea Flour   *   Coconut Flour
Tapioca Flour   *   Cassava Flour

To get the correct mouth feel on most baked goods you need to use a combination of several flours plus a little extra help from a gum or sweet rice flour. Generally the help needed for gluten free flours will come from Xanthan Gum or Guar Gum. These gums make the dough more elastic and airy for a superior baked good.

Please use common sense and read all ingredients on products used.
It is your health and only you can protect it!
Please, also listen to your doctor on what you should be eating.

Why is This Charity So Important?
We wanted to share this from Afton:

28 October 1999, is a day I will never forget. It is the day everything changed for my family.

It is the day that my 14-month-old daughter, Samantha Victoria Backham (known as Sammie) was diagnosed with a cancerous brain tumour. The next few months were hell on earth. She and I travelled from home to go to the hospital in Oxford, England that had a paediatric neurosurgical unit, where she had 2 brain surgeries (the tumour removal took over 8 hours), recovery, and then travelling again to the children's hospital in Bristol, England that was doing the paediatric clinical trial that Sammie would be undergoing.

Our whole world was in upheaval, not to mention the trauma our family, which included a very precocious 3 year old, who had no comprehension of why her sister was in hospital and her mummy not at home with her. The procedures that Sammie was experiencing were horrible and traumatic for her, and all of us, especially me, who could only sit by and watch and hold her. I did a lot of crying. It was just Sammie and I in the hospital for months. The one constant was the amazing cancer charity that supported us. The charity provided a "home from home" so I didn't have to sleep in the hospital, but have a quiet space to sleep, wash clothing, prepare food, or just sit and watch telly. They not only provided this for me, but my husband at the time and daughter when they were able to visit us. The charity's support didn't end there. They also provided a place for my parents and sister to stay when they flew in from the US to be of support to us.

Later, when Sammie was on her second protocol of chemotherapy, and was able to have treatment from our home hospital in Reading, England, this charity provided me with a social worker, who helped us get all the paperwork together to get her disability benefits, and her statement of special educational need started so she could go to school when she was better. Sammie is now 23 years old, and despite the disabilities she has due to the damage from the tumour, she is a happy (and often sassy) young woman. We are forever indebted to the charity for all the support they gave us. Sales from this cookbook will all go to this wonderful charity who helped us all those years ago.

Thank you for your support.

-Afton Cochran, Autumn 2021.

ALL PROFITS FROM

THIS BOOK

WILL BE

DONATED TO

CHARITY

ONE LAST THING:

All of these recipes have been published in good faith and results may vary. All food should be stored appropriately to prolong shelf life and to prevent food born bacteria. All meat should be adequately cooked to prevent food born illness. Cool, cover and store foods well to prevent food born illness. We do not advise leaving food out for hours.

It is not advisable for pregnant women or small children to eat uncooked or under-cooked eggs, soft cheeses, or deli meats.

Most of all, listen to your doctor on what you should and should not be eating!

Any claim to actual people in this book is purely accidental,

and your cyborg overlords will have a few words with us later.

Printed in Great Britain
by Amazon